FOREIGN FIGHTERS IN UKRAINE

Foreign Fighters in Ukraine is the first comprehensive academic study taking an in-depth look at foreigners who have chosen to fight in the conflict in Ukraine.

While there has been considerable focus in policy, security and academic circles on the threat from returning jihadists – so-called returnee foreign terrorist fighters – the same danger from right-wing, but not essentially terrorist, extremists and others has been largely overlooked. As Westerners rushed to join the nascent Caliphate in Syria/Iraq, others simultaneously traveled to another foreign war on what many would call Europe's doorstep: the Russo-Ukrainian war. This book unmasks this largely unknown group of fighters as the author dives into the fighters' ideological and social backgrounds, their motivations for joining the conflict, their travails on the way there and their battle record in Eastern Ukraine. To a large extent based on interviews with the fighters themselves, it is a study on how and why men risk their lives while fighting a foreign war – and attract the attention of security services at home upon their return. Particularly, given the Russian invasion of Ukraine in February 2022 and the growing interest in far-right violence worldwide, the book evaluates whether these returnees constitute another security threat to the West.

This volume will be of interest to all those researching small wars, terrorism, peace and conflict studies and right-wing extremism.

Kacper Rękawek is a Postdoctoral Fellow at the Center for Research on Extremism (C-Rex), University of Oslo, Norway, and a Researcher at the Counter Extremism Project (CEP).

Routledge Studies in Fascism and the Far Right
Series editor: Nigel Copsey

Teesside University, UK and Graham Macklin, Center for Research on Extremism (C-REX), University of Oslo, Norway

This book series focuses upon national, transnational and global manifestations of fascist, far right and right-wing politics primarily within a historical context but also drawing on insights and approaches from other disciplinary perspectives. Its scope also includes anti-fascism, radical-right populism, extreme-right violence and terrorism, cultural manifestations of the far right and points of convergence and exchange with the mainstream and traditional right.

Titles include:

Histories of Fascism and Anti-Fascism in Australia
Edited by Evan Smith, Jayne Persian and Vashti Jane Fox

Foreign Fighters in Ukraine
The Brown–Red Cocktail
Kacper Rękawek

The Nazi Party and the German Communities Abroad
The Latin American Case
João Fábio Bertonha and Rafael Athaides

Nazi Occultism
Between the SS and Esotericism
Stéphane François

The Rise of the Radical Right in the Global South
Edited by Rosana Pinheiro-Machado and Tatiana Vargas-Maia

Global Identitarianism
Edited by José Pedro Zúquete and Riccardo Marchi

For more information about this series, please visit: www.routledge.com/Routledge-Studies-in-Fascism-and-the-Far-Right/book-series/FFR

FOREIGN FIGHTERS IN UKRAINE

The Brown–Red Cocktail

Kacper Rękawek

Routledge
Taylor & Francis Group

LONDON AND NEW YORK

Cover image: © Getty Images

First published 2023
by Routledge
4 Park Square, Milton Park, Abingdon, Oxon OX14 4RN

and by Routledge
605 Third Avenue, New York, NY 10158

*Routledge is an imprint of the Taylor & Francis Group,
an informa business*

© 2023 Kacper Rękawek

British Library Cataloguing-in-Publication Data
A catalogue record for this book is available from the British Library

Library of Congress Cataloging-in-Publication Data
Names: Rękawek, Kacper, author.
Title: Foreign fighters in Ukraine : the brown-red cocktail /
Kacper Rękawek.
Description: Abingdon, Oxon ; New York : Routledge, 2023. |
Series: Routledge studies in fascism and the far right |
Includes bibliographical references and index.
Identifiers: LCCN 2022037678 (print) | LCCN 2022037679 (ebook) |
ISBN 9781032030807 (hardback) | ISBN 9781032043982 (paperback) |
ISBN 9781003192992 (ebook)
Subjects: LCSH: Ukraine Conflict, 2014---Participation, Foreign. |
Military service, Voluntary--Ukraine. | Soldiers--Ukraine--Interviews. |
Soldiers--Ukraine--Attitudes. | Right-wing extremists--Travel--
Ukraine. | Left-wing extremists--Travel--Ukraine | Noncitizens--
Ukraine--Attitudes. | Insurgency--Ukraine. | Ukraine--Politics and
government--21st century. | Ukraine--Foreign relations--21st century.
Classification: LCC DK508.852 .R453 2023 (print) |
LCC DK508.852 (ebook) | DDC 947.7086--dc23/eng/20220816
LC record available at https://lccn.loc.gov/2022037678
LC ebook record available at https://lccn.loc.gov/2022037679

ISBN: 978-1-032-03080-7 (hbk)
ISBN: 978-1-032-04398-2 (pbk)
ISBN: 978-1-003-19299-2 (ebk)

DOI: 10.4324/9781003192992

Typeset in Bembo
by KnowledgeWorks Global Ltd.

CONTENTS

ACKNOWLEDGMENTS

As this book is being finished in June 2022 in Oslo, it might seem like something rushed to capitalize on the gory reality of Russian (re-)invasion of Ukraine on February 24, 2022. Moreover, it focuses on foreigners who became involved in the fighting, and this comes against the backdrop of a torrent of news about Ukraine's "foreign" or "international" legion, which at some point was said to have had up to 40,000 prospective members. In short, it might look like a highly opportunistic move by a scholar or expert seeking attention and appreciation. Of course, this is partly right. Don't we all, academics, think tankers and the like, seek these? At the same time, however, this is not rushed or deployed so that the book can jump onto the bandwagon of Russia's (re-)invasion of Ukraine.

In fact, this book has a very long back story which is full of inspirational people who need to be thanked here. It would not have been even dreamt of had it not been for the fact that on a hot summer day in 2014, *Russia Today* (yes, this TV channel) decided to run a segment on French foreign fighters in Donetsk. I admit, I watched it live. That event started off the whole journey which, to some extent, culminates in this book.

Secondly, a big thank you to Jan Raudszus, a great colleague from Germany whom all readers should follow on twitter, who once told me that I should stop writing reports, articles and the like and simply write a book about these foreign fighters in Ukraine. Well, here it is, Jan. I hope you like it.

Thirdly, and regardless of Jan's encouragement, this would have never happened had it not been for a string of people at PISM, the Polish Institute of International Affairs. Upon seeing this *Russia Today* segment I came to my line manager, Marcin Terlikowski, and asked if I could spend some time researching these individuals. Marcin quickly gave a resounding yes and the first paper on the issue, quoted in this monograph, came to life. Arkadiusz Legieć, then an intern at PISM, now a full research fellow there, was of tremendous help while performing data collection. With the paper ready I took it upstairs – to research office director, Jaroslaw Cwiek-Karpowicz, and the then PISM director, Marcin Zaborowski, to ask for their blessing. They graciously gave one and the rest is history. In the meantime, I got Olgierd Syczewski to hold the camera at the filming of my first promo video ever, which was fun.

This paper led to my organizing a conference on the issue in Moldova of all places (its results were later turned into an edited volume by IOS Press), which was sponsored by NATO Emerging Threats Division. Jadwiga Winiarska was indispensable in organizing and running it, whereas Anna Szostak and Aleksander Szalanski looked after the admin side of things in Warsaw. The conference in Chisinau was a tremendous affair during which people studying foreign fighters in Syria met those who looked at the issue on both sides of the Russo-Ukraine war. It was at this moment that I realized that this topic was not niche and that it belonged to what would be dubbed "Eastern Studies" in my native Poland. Here was a community of like-minded researchers who were interested in issues close to my heart. In short, to all who trekked to Chisinau, a big thank you.

In the meantime, I literally took the show on the road and presented my research findings at a few places. Here, I would like to thank all the individuals who read my abstracts, approved them and gave me a platform to speak on the issue publicly. It was all the get togethers of the Society for Terrorism Research or European Expert Network on Terrorism Issues, and other gigs around the planet, really, which enabled me to sharpen the message and tailor it so I could present it to different audiences. This was also done in writing, so a big thank you to all who published my research on the subject prior to this book being written. Through such smaller publications I was able to proverbially keep the flame burning.

To be fair, I lived with the topic of this book and took it with me wherever I went. After 2016 and the conference in Chisinau, it took a backseat but it never left me. The conflict got colder or cooler, no new fighters were coming so it looked like the case was closed. Nonetheless, my bosses and colleagues at GLOBSEC in Slovakia kindly gave me time to respond to inquiries about former fighters, dare I say – returnees, who were resurfacing in their home countries between 2016 and 2019. Through such engagements I kept the topic close to my heart and never forgot about it.

Interestingly, it had not been the 2022 Russian (re-)invasion of Ukraine which pushed the issue of foreign fighters in Ukraine back into the spotlight but the 2019 events of Christchurch, New Zealand. The perpetrator of these attacks was at first said, wrongly, to have been a foreign fighter in Ukraine and the attack's high profile ensured that the world was again interested. Nonetheless, I still felt unsure whether it made sense to write a book on the topic. As it later turned out, some people felt otherwise. Here I must mention the Counter Extremism Project (CEP) and in particular Hans Jakob Schindler, a true friend and a believer in my work. Hans and the CEP have always been interested in the topic, regardless of the Christchurch link, and brough me on as an affiliated researcher, providing two grants for papers on foreign fighters in Ukraine that we published and I cite later in the book.[1] I was then finally able to focus just on the issue of the foreign fighters in Ukraine and this is when, between 2019 and 2021, this book was largely prepared and written. I need to mention the CEP's David Ibsen and Lara Pham, who were more than supportive in the process, read and commented on all I prepared and were always keen, alongside Hans, to develop a 360 degree outlook on extremism and ways of countering it at their organization. Without their and the organization's generous support (a shout out to Robert, Darlene, Marco, Joshua and Alexander is also in order here) this book would have never been completed. Thank you for all this, it has been a pleasure. I look forward to working with you all on future projects.

As this book was being finalized I again moved to, this time the Center for Research on Extremism (C-Rex) at the University of Oslo, one of the world's leading outfits researching such topics. I have been here for almost a year now and I must say I completely understand why it was – and is! – regarded as such a terrific place. Here one is surrounded with colleagues working on similar issues and is exposed to their ideas and findings. Moreover, C-Rex maintains and expands a network of allies, contacts and friends who have been coming in to be with us as visiting fellows. All of this happens in an atmosphere of utmost collegiality and support. This is also a place where I am now looking at the next stage of my foreign fighters/volunteers in Ukraine fascination – their post-conflict lives. Stay tuned.

The subsequent pages would not have been written without a large and influential group – my interviewees. Some were happy to be quoted, others asked for anonymity, but all gave their time and were patient and gratuitous with my inquiries. I learnt so much from them and I am grateful to all. I also need to thank people who know Ukraine way better than me, and whose works are also quoted throughout the subsequent chapters. Thank you for your work and for bringing the country and the war to the attention of the wider public. You are doing an immense service to us all.

A big thank you to Graham Macklin, an editor of this series, and to Routledge. It goes without saying that they had to like what I was writing on the fighters for it to appear in print.

Finally, a big thank you to, in chronological order, Ryszard Machnikowski from the University of Lodz, who supervised my MA thesis, and Richard English from Queen's University Belfast, who supervised my PhD thesis, later turned into another Routledge book. You have both been there for me for years and for that I am extremely grateful. Ryszard set me off on the academic/think tank track. Richard convinced me not only to get out there and speak to different audiences, but also to find topics I can claim as my own and master these while never letting go of the academic rigor. I tried my best to do so with this book, but all mistakes and omissions are, of course, all mine. It is my sincere hope that our paths will cross again in the future.

Książka nie powstałaby bez najbliższych. Bez ich cierpliwości, wsparcia, zrozumienia. Im ją dedykuję. Dziękuję Wam za wszystko.

Note

1 Part of the CEP's publication by me, *Looks can be deceiving: Extremism meets paramilitarism in Central and Eastern Europe*, June 2021, available at https://www.counterextremism. com/sites/default/files/2021-06/CEP%20Report_Looks%20Can%20Be%20Deceiving_ Extremism%20Meets%20Paramilitarism%20in%20CEE_June%202021_1.pdf are reproduced in the "Central-Eastern European" chapter of this monograph. Likewise, my work on *Career Break or New Career? Extremist Foreign Fighters in Ukraine* Monday, published by the CEP (May 4, 2020), available at https://www.counterextremism. com/sites/default/files/CEP%20Report_Career%20Break%20or%20a%20New%20 Career_Extremist%20Foreign%20Fighters%20in%20Ukraine_April%202020.pdf, has been incorporated in multiple sections.

1

INTRODUCTION

The Western European Foreign Fighter Secret Society

The Westerners fighting in the Russo-Ukrainian war were first encountered by the author in news reports from Donetsk from the summer of 2014.[1] At first, they seemed like an oddity, an alien element in a widely misunderstood war happening in the Eastern Europe. It quickly became apparent, however, that these individuals were in fact foreign fighters. Consequently, the author, one of the few interested in the topic from 2014 onwards, worked in an on and off fashion on the issue.[2] While doing so, not only did the author read and collect sources on the foreign fighters in Ukraine but also initiated and continued conversations over different social media platforms with some of the fighters from either side of the conflict. Finally, between January 2020 and June 2021, thanks to a grant from the Counter Extremism Project, he was able to devote more time to the research and turn its results into a major report,[3] a series of videos[4] and, finally, this research monograph.[5]

The author's interest in the foreign fighters in Ukraine coincided, as it later turned out, with a growing focus on the threat of extreme right-wing violence and terrorism in the broader West. This became evident after March 2019 and the now infamous Christchurch attacks in New Zealand, where 51 people died.[6] The attacker, at first suspected of "train[ing] with other right-wing violent extremists" in Ukraine, looked like "the first example of an act of terrorism committed by a white supremacist foreign fighter."[7] Consequently, and throughout the next year, different top European decision-makers admitted that the threat of right wing terrorism had reached an unprecedented level. First, the executive director of Europol's EU law enforcement agency stated that "a wave of [extreme] right-wing violent incidents [...] also reached Europe," and the German Federal Interior Minister followed up shortly afterwards with a statement which described "right-wing extremism [... as] the biggest threat to security in Germany."[8] Such

DOI: 10.4324/9781003192992-1

opinions followed influential voices from the U.S., which warned that the world's extreme right-wingers organized into an Al-Qaeda style network and, following the terrorist organization's example, established its Afghan-like "laboratory and training ground" in Ukraine.[9]

In short, such a reading of the situation regards the threat from the extreme right to the West as fueled by the conflict in Ukraine and an extremist mobilization of foreigners who flocked to join the war. As this research monograph will demonstrate, not all parts of this analysis withstand scrutiny. It is true that at least 17,000 foreign fighters, but not all of them extreme right-wingers, fought in the war in Ukraine.[10] The majority of them, however, had been Russians whose ability physically to threaten the West with terrorism is limited, to say the least. Moreover, as the author found out in his interviews, even the most right-wing Westerners present on the front lines, who in total numbered around 700,[11] were adamant they could not "start a war here" (the West) as they were too "weak."[12] Simultaneously, however, the conflict gave them a chance to train and test themselves while literally under fire – a skill which many would not have obtained while living in the West. This helped undermine the reputation of their host units, especially on the Ukrainian side of the conflict, as they then stood accused of turning into extremist "laboratories." As will be shown, these hosts often came to regret their willingness to accept foreign fighters and had no intention of turning their organizations into a right-wing terrorist international, akin to Al-Qaeda.

At the same time, some of the Westerners present in Ukraine constituted, in the eyes of a journalist embedded with a far-right Western foreign fighter unit, a "Western foreign fighter society." Its young members "will want another war."[13] The "society" was allegedly said to cut across the divides of the Ukrainian conflict as recruiters, like former foreign fighters from the Yugoslav wars of the 1990s,[14] working e.g. for Ukraine provided military references to foreign fighters associated with the other side.[15] The interviewed far-right fighters themselves corroborated this account and confirmed acquaintanceship with each other, including their supposed enemies from before the war.[16] Some of the fighters later resurfaced in other conflicts (e.g. in Syria and Iraq, but also in Libya, Somalia and the Central African Republic as private military contractors).[17]

Consequently, one could argue that the above-mentioned society, and not a "laboratory" or a "training ground" exists. Moreover, this entity has the markings of a "secret society" i.e. "a persisting pattern of relationships which directly or indirectly links the participants in related secret activities,"[18] based upon "reciprocal confidence of its members."[19] It is in fact an order formed to protect a secret which is socialized amongst its members.[20] Outsiders might learn of the society's existence but are not privy to its content – in the current case: contacts, travel routes, safe houses, resources of the foreign fighters, etc.[21] These are only available to the members of the above-mentioned order, who see themselves as an elite or aristocracy (the "free men" in the words of one such fighter) and look down on the non-initiated.[22]

As the author was able to discover, and this book will demonstrate in subsequent chapters, members of the secret society often have, as they would call it, "nationalist," "conservative" or "right wing" views. Closer scrutiny, however, would often but not always place these Western self-confessed nationalists, conservatives or right-wingers on the radical if not far-right of the political spectrum. They are thus "anti-system," "hostile to liberal democracy" and opposing "the postwar liberal democratic consensus."[23] This finding to a degree chimes in with the worries of different officials focused on the threat of violence from the right wing extremists to the West. It does not, however, automatically mean that any foreign fighter who ventured to the conflict in Eastern Ukraine should be considered a potential right-wing terrorist. In addition to this, nor does it mean that such fighters had all been right wingers in the first place. This is becoming evident in 2022, with up to 30 veterans of the People's Defense Units (Yekîneyên Parastina Gel, YPG) in Syria, veterans of the civil war in Syria, already engaged in the Russo-Ukrainian war.[24] These had hardly been right wing individuals but seem to develop their own foreign fighter "secret society," which sees its members deploy to different conflicts around the world. In this sense, such fighters resemble Daymon, de Roy van Zuijdewijn and Malet's "career foreign fighters," who in the latter years predominantly came from the Islamist milieu.[25]

As is evident from the research on foreign volunteers and fighters in different and earlier wars,[26] these often mobilize along the lines of the above-mentioned "secret society" – clandestinely, on a need to know basis, available only to the initiated and trusted. In this sense, this reality in the Russo-Ukrainian war is not new. However, this society not only cuts across the front line but also across the ideological divides. No longer is it the case of Islamist or leftist or right-wing volunteers mobilizing for a given side. Instead, it is a situation in which "nationalists [were present] on both sides" of the conflict but this did not stop them from, at times, literally shooting at one another.[27] Moreover, the war also featured individuals coming from the broader leftist milieu, mostly on the "separatist" side, but, such as the above-mentioned YPG veterans, also in the Ukrainian ranks.

To confuse the situation further, some fighters present in Ukraine from 2014 onwards, especially in the relatively high-profile French foreign fighter contingent, espoused a truly national-Bolshevik, a brown-red, combination of views;[28] brown for their nationalism and red for their communistic influences and fascinations. Individuals with views mixing nationalism/fascism and far-left ideologies have existed for around a century in countries such as Germany[29] and later even Soviet Russia.[30] Moreover, they are also common features of extremist scenes in countries such as the U.S. as recently as 2021.[31] Initially, the term encompassed commitment to "class struggle and total nationalization of means of production with extreme state chauvinism."[32] Later on, it also featured on the fringes of the likes of the French far-right milieu, which was to produce this country's foreign fighters for the Russo-Ukrainian war.[33] This anti-Western, anti-elite and pro-Russian (formerly pro-Soviet Union) and/or pro-China socio-political trend seemingly mixed the proverbial fire and water but its adherents made their mark as foreign fighters in Ukraine. For this reason, the subtitle of this monograph is the "brown-red cocktail." The cocktail from the subtitle does not simply refer to the national-Bolshevik fighters who, albeit influential and recognized, had been the minority of all the foreigners in the ranks of the Ukrainian volunteer battalions or the "separatist" militias. It is also to encompass the purely brown, nationalist/fascist or neo-Nazi, fighters from their ranks or the purely "red" ones, especially from the "separatist" side. They all, the brown, the brown-red and the red, form the ingredients of the above-mentioned cocktail.

Literature Review

This monograph is informed by different scholarly literatures. It discusses how extremists, mainly but not exclusively "brown" (fascist) individuals, are mobilized for violent activities outside their places of origin and domicile. Consequently, it adds to the body of knowledge on how and for what the far right mobilizes.[34] Taking a look at a peculiar and relatively rare activity, foreign fighting, it demonstrates how this option could be attractive to Western extremists or radicals who feel socio-politically constrained at home. In short, they travel abroad to do things they would not dream of doing in their country of origin.[35]

Moreover, the monograph also focuses on the transnational angle of the brown-red cocktail – it discusses the connectivity of the fighters before their departure for Ukraine, their backgrounds and how many of them attempted to form some sort of "international brigades" while out "there." It also discusses the role of gatekeepers who operate transnationally while bringing people to the front lines. Thus, it adds to the growing body of literature on the transnationality of the far right.[36]

The monograph, however, not only discusses or adds to literature focusing on the far right or violent right-wing extremism. The author is of the opinion that it possesses a certain cross-over status as it focuses on foreign fighting, a phenomenon which throughout the last decade has been mostly associated with Islamism or jihadism. Thus, it will engage with the works from the field of jihadism studies which map history and composition of jihadi foreign fighter waves and the motivations of individual fighters.[37] In 2010, Thomas Hegghammer, influential terrorism studies scholar and one of the pioneers of the research on foreign fighters, assessed that foreign fighting was an understudied phenomenon.[38] Throughout the next decade or so, however, the issue of foreign fighters, defined by David Malet as "non-citizens of conflict states who join insurgencies during civil conflict,"[39] has captivated academics and experts from a range of disciplinary backgrounds such as political science, criminology, sociology, psychology, etc.[40] It must be noted, however, that this attention was almost solely concentrated on the so-called foreign terrorist fighters who joined the Islamic State of Iraq and Syria (ISIS) in Syria and Iraq.[41] Sociological studies on given sets (e.g. Belgian, French or females) of such fighters who traveled to join ISIS in Syria and Iraq dominated the field.[42] Alongside analyses on "who" the fighters were, or what motivated them,[43] literature assessing the "fall-out" from their

joining of a terrorist organization (and e.g. staging terrorist attacks upon returning home) quickly developed.[44] It was later to question the scale of the threat
from the returnee foreign fighters as relatively few of them either became "career
fighters" who would engage in terrorism in their countries of origin.[45]

While the number of studies of foreign terrorist fighters mushroomed, the
fates of individual foreign fighters from Ukraine also received some attention,[46]
widely disproportionately in some cases.[47] Consequently, their stories helped
reduce the pro-Ukraine fighters to extreme nationalists or outright neo-Nazis.[48]
At the same time, often no less far-right fighters from the pro-"separatist" side
were getting a bit more preferential treatment which in certain cases stressed e.g.
their alleged leftist or brown-red ideological orientation.[49] However, the media
attention would soon shift to other topics and even the author's interviewees
from amongst the fighters seemed not to mind this state of affairs.[50] It might have
actually suited them as they, it could be argued, wanted anonymity or wished to
get over their often not-so-successful deployments to Eastern Ukraine.

This growing lack of interest from the media was also mirrored amongst
other potential producers of secondary sources on the fighters. At times, the
current author seemed like one of the very few researchers who actually stayed
on the topic after the 2014–2015 period.[51] Consequently, Murauskaite was not
wrong when she claimed in her policy report devoted to foreign fighters in
Ukraine that the current author's 2017 edited collection[52] "has been the only
academic study thus far to consider the issue of foreign fighters in Ukraine."[53]
Jayakumar in his study of the anti-ISIS foreign fighters in Syria mentioned only
five other sources which focused on such fighters not in ISIS ranks.[54] Hardly
any of these sources, with the exception of Koch,[55] feature a discussion on far-
right anti-ISIS fighters, acknowledge (rare) studies of earlier right-wing foreign
fighter mobilizations or briefly touch upon such a mobilization for the war in
Ukraine.[56] Thus, this research monograph will plug an important theoretical,
empirical and market gap.[57]

It will take a look at the foreign fighters on both sides in the war in Ukraine,
and not only the "separatists" who in this scenario would be regarded as Malet's
"insurgents." The fact that some joined the "governmental" side, i.e. Ukrainian,
did not turn them into professional soldiers as the fighters flocked to the ranks
of the so-called "volunteer battalions," which were only later integrated into
the ranks of the military or the national guard.[58] Upon this transformation, the
foreign fighters of yesterday (who were assisted by Ukraine and Russia respectively)[59] effectively turned into foreign volunteers, i.e. non-local members of a
given country's military forces. For some of them, the transformation in question
spelt the end of their Ukrainian deployment as e.g. the later formation would not
allow foreigners to join its ranks. Nonetheless, foreign fighters had been present
on the seemingly "insurgent" (effectively non-local, external, i.e. pro-Russian,
"separatists") but also on the non-"insurgent" side (Ukrainian). None, however,
had been members of David Malet's "transnational insurgencies,"[60] which attract
such fighters in the first place. For this reason, the current research monograph

will adopt a broader definition of foreign fighters, i.e. Moore and Tumelty's "non-indigenous, non-territorialised combatants who, motivated by religion, kinship, and/or ideology rather than pecuniary reward, enter a conflict to participate in hostilities."[61]

The key issue of the above-mentioned definition is not only the "non-indigenous" (i.e. foreign) character of such fighters but also their motivation. As was shown by Malet's classic work on foreign fighters, this motivation has historically and recently been assured by recruiters who would convincingly "frame" the conflict and, thus, convince the wannabe recruits that their (real or imaginary) "group" (social, religious, political, ethnic, etc.) is under threat.[62] Consequently, only the outside intervention of well-meaning foreigners, effectively displaying what Moore called "fictive kinship" – based on bonds and relations,[63] is able to save the day or a given insurgency. As will be demonstrated, however, both sides of the conflict did relatively little to attract transnationally minded individuals to their cause as they hardly prioritized this issue. In such conditions, for wannabe recruits and later fighters the "fictive kinship" had truly to develop along fictional lines with so many fighters later projecting their own, invented, argued or rehearsed socio-political motivations onto a foreign war. It is true, however, that many of the people who made it to Ukraine to fight in the war had been, in line with Malet's findings, political activists but operating outside the political mainstream.[64] In effect, they constituted the brown-red cocktail which is the title of this monograph. Some of the most highly rated research on foreign fighters indicates that their existence as transnational combatants is strictly and solely tied to a given conflict and they literally either win or disappear, i.e. return home and attempt to regain their previous lives. The exception to this rule, as was stated by Malet after surveying numerous "transnational insurgencies," were the jihadists, who had no home to return to as their states would act against them upon their resurfacing at home.[65] Interestingly, the non-insurgent foreign fighters, the protagonists of this monograph, seem to have more in common with the jihadists as some of them constitute what the author will refer to as the Western Foreign Fighter Secret Society – a "band of brothers" type of entity which looks for future conflicts to join. This has already been evident in 2022 when some of the veterans of the 2014 stage of the war decided to rejoin the fighting in Ukraine, this time, however, not as foreign fighters but rather as volunteers while effectively joining the Ukrainian military.[66]

The fact that they are keen to return to the conflict zones or seek new ones in the future could indicate that, in the light of events such as the Christchurch attack and its alleged and spurious connection to Ukraine, host countries of the foreign fighters could be faced with a serious security threat from the returnees. That was definitely the case with the fighters who deployed to fight in Syria but has not been the case with their equivalents who fought in Ukraine.[67] This is not to suggest that all safely and quietly returned home but, so far,[68] to the best of the current author's knowledge, none has engaged in terrorist violence at home. This finding further validates Malet and Hayes' theory on returnees not constituting an "indefinite threat" to their country of origin as most of "their" violence happens within 6–12 months of returning home.[69] Thus, the brown-red cocktail looks like a socio-political oddity and its members could be trouble-makers but may not be one's security nightmare in the mid- to long term.

Methodology

The book is based on qualitative research which saw the author not only collect original data but also work with primary and secondary sources. The research focused on the members of the Western foreign fighter secret society, i.e. Western individuals who joined either side of the war in Ukraine between April 2014 and July 2020 (the latest, largely holding ceasefire which to a large extent broke down in March 2021)[70] of whom many, if not the majority, would be recruited from the far-right milieu.

The author agrees with Blee and Latif that there is now availability of data which allows for a "comparative interdisciplinary research that can elucidate how the agenda and strategies adopted by the far right are shaped through interaction with global networks."[71] This data can increasingly be found online as the members of the far-right milieu, and in this case – "nationalist" or extremist foreign fighters in Ukraine/the so-called brown-red cocktail – leave a sometimes heavy digital footprint behind them. Some of the footprint's contents might be of little value to researchers but it presents insights into real-time actions of given individuals, their thoughts, feelings or, more broadly, a spread of a given ideology and how networked it is in the West.

The digital data's inaccuracies, subjectivities and outright bias constituted a challenge to the current author, who attempted to mitigate these via building up a set of complementary and, to some extent, competing set of sources on the foreign fighters in Ukraine. These included primary and secondary sources such as media reports, especially written by the correspondents or freelance journalists present on the scene, social media content produced by such observers and other participants, semi-structured interviews with intermediaries, i.e. journalists embedded with foreign fighter units, humanitarian activists, government officials and international observers. What is more, the digital footprint accumulated on the social media accounts of the fighters also presents researchers with a possibility to reach out to them and even interview them at these platforms. Thus, the author derived a multi-start and multi-national heterogenous snowball sample of interviewees from the ranks of the secret society's members. To mitigate bias in the author's sample of interviewees, it was deliberately purposive in nature as the author especially sought out nationals of different countries, self-confessed "nationalists" or far-rightists. In essence, this led to a production of a heterogenous sample of interviewees who kindly gave their time and participated in semi-structured interviews with the author. The interviews focused on how they joined the society, why they did so, how they coped on the front lines and what had happened to them since they had left Ukraine.[72] Some were conducted during their time in Eastern Ukraine, others when a given fighter returned home. The interviews planned for 2020 were meant to include those conducted not over digital platforms or the phone but also during in-person meetings. Unfortunately, due to the Covid-19 pandemic, some of these plans did not come to fruition.

The author reached the interviewees either directly, e.g. through their social media profiles after picking up reports on them from secondary sources,[73] or through intermediaries, effectively gatekeepers such as journalists who interviewed the fighters in the field.[74] Generally, the author found the fighters forthcoming and open to research, more than media, inquiries. In some cases, their enthusiasm for a conversation visibly reduced after learning that the author worked for the Counter Extremism Project – with the word "extremism" irking them; or in the earlier period, for Globsec – an NGO that, in their view, "must be taking Soros' money," or for the Polish Institute of International Affairs, PISM, a governmental think tank which by default was seen as hostile to anti-systemic "nationalists" who flocked to either side of the war in Ukraine. While upfront about his affiliations, the author did not engage with such comments and attempted not to counter these with denials or, which would be even worse, corrections. He refrained from ridiculing such inaccurate opinions and suspended judgment while asking the fighters for their opinions and views. These, as the book will show, were at times anti-democratic, anti-Semitic, anti-feminist and homophobic.

Critics could argue that by interviewing the fighters and subsequently publishing articles quoting them, and finally, this research monograph, the author effectively gave his interviewees a platform to air their views in a setting which up to that point had been beyond their reach. It is also true that the abovementioned views also often disabled the author's attempts to "build commonality" with his research subjects.[75] What helped, however, was an assertive approach in which the author would be open about his affiliations and views on subjects discussed. The fighters might not have liked all of the author's answers to their probing questions (e.g. what is your political standpoint? Is this or that party "far right" in your view? Are you a "fan" of this or that political leader? What do you think of XYZ social issue? Have you done your military service? etc.) but generally respected his stances and were civil in responding to questions which seemed controversial to them (e.g. what if Ukraine joins the EU? – to a fighter of a nationalist Azov Battalion or what if Ukraine wins this war? – to a member of a "separatist"[76] militia, etc.). In short, the author attempted to understand the fighters by not endorsing or sharing their beliefs while treating them in conversations like he would others and steered clear of, if there was any, racist or homophobic behavior or comments.[77]

At the same time, the author is of an opinion that it is precisely the fact that showcasing the fighters' views and actions that allows the academic, experts, policy-makers and the broader public understand what motivates non-jihadi

Westerners to go fight in a foreign war. Moreover, it is also a chance for us all to assess the extent to which such individuals pose a security threat to their home or host countries in the West. After all, they often constitute the proverbial "tip of the spear" as far as meting out violence on behalf of the far right is concerned. They, however, conduct this violence while at war and abroad, and, as will be shown, in many cases seem to settle back home without actually attempting to turn their countries into e.g. "a French Donbass."[78] Interviewing such individuals – members of the Western foreign fighter secret society – demystifies them and, in line with Dobratz and Waldner's recommendations, allows for a better "understand[ing of] the meanings [... they] attribute to their actions."[79]

More approaches to fighters were ultimately successful than not and led to insightful semi-structured interviews conducted over the phone, WhatsApp, signal, telegram or Facebook Messenger. The author respected the fighters' limitations in those conversations – they sought anonymity, refrained from detailing their exploits on the front lines as they feared this could put them in harm's way from a legal standpoint, some refused to discuss numbers of other foreigners in their units. They did, however, provide a great deal of information as to why they joined the war in Ukraine and how they got there, and were keen to comment on what they encountered on or near the front lines. In all, this, plus data gleaned from other sources, allowed the author to produce a multi-national picture of foreign fighters in the war in Ukraine.

The gathered data has been analyzed via the means of thematic analysis so that the author was able to provide evidence in support of emerging themes in the "national" chapters.[80] These chapters focus on a given contingent of fighters from one country or a set of countries present on either side of the conflict. Each depicts the fighters via the mixed means of:[81]

- a movement focus study, i.e. how people are mobilized for or by the far-right, in this case for the war in Ukraine within a specific unit or with specific individuals as one's "brothers in arms'"
- a context focus study, i.e. "how far-right networks at the regional, national, and global levels affect the strength and direction of specific right-wing efforts," in this case: recruitment of foreign fighters for the war in Ukraine. The given "national" chapter will focus on the strength of the network and its transnational (or lack of) connectivity, which would be key as far as sending people abroad is concerned. The chapters will also assess the extent to which going "there" was more a result of push or pull factors, an important distinction developed by scholars studying the jihadist foreign fighters (see below for literature review). As will be demonstrated, the foreign far-right fighters in Ukraine were mostly motivated by pull factors, e.g. their colleague(s) arriving in Ukraine first and then encouraging others to follow suit. Nonetheless, push factors such as a desire to escape prosecution at home for relatively petty acts of crime, the inability to cope with pressures of

family and professional life, disgust with political developments in the country of origin etc., also motivated some of the fighters;

- an ideology focused study, i.e. one which looks into beliefs, ideas and rhetoric of the networks, scenes or milieus which produced the fighters and the fighters themselves. As will be shown, the fighters would often refer to themselves as "nationalists" and their political convictions would be shallow or of memetic depth and quality. Nonetheless, after arriving at the front, they gladly associated themselves with like-minded units and colleagues and continued to spread far-right ideology in their interviews, relatively widely given to the international media and e.g. the author, or on their social media platforms. Moreover, they also reinterpreted local conditions so that these would suit the macro-level operating ideologies they followed, e.g. for the far-right Swedes in the Azov Battalion/Regiment saw the enemy, separatists, as an emanation of not only Russian but also "Asian," un-European "invasion" threatening "white" and "traditional" Europe; alternatively, the co-foreign led "Rusicz" group, while pan-Slavic in nature, managed effectively to remove Ukrainians, against whom it fought, from the world of Slavdom;

- a members focused study, i.e. one which discusses the individual members, in this case: foreign fighters on either side of the conflict. Who were they, what were their backgrounds, what, apart from the activities of the above-mentioned networks and colleagues present at the front, ultimately motivated them to fight in a foreign war? How did they make the trip and how (dis)satisfied they were with what they witnessed at the front and in the rear? Did they feel appreciated, welcome, or more like public relations tools deployed in front of the journalists with the hope of pulling more of their nationals into the ranks of a given side in the conflict?

- a leaders focused study, i.e. one which studies individuals who promote discourses, narrative, recruit others for the war effort, construct and frame identity of the group. In fact, in line with social categorization theory, they are instrumental to the process of the fighters closing in its ranks, or maximizing similarities amongst themselves, and differentiating themselves from the non-initiated outsiders.[82] Simultaneously, they are also facilitators who ensure a fighter "make[s] the connection from their local circumstances to become involved in a transnational mobilization."[83]

Book's Outline

The above-mentioned "national" chapters, covering different brown-red cocktail amongst foreign fighters in Ukraine, are the core of this book. These are, however, preceded by three introductory chapters on: the conflict in Ukraine; hosts of the foreign fighters in Ukraine; and ideological background on the far-right and its attitude towards foreign fighting, especially in the light of the conflict in Ukraine.

The first of these uses the author's 30-plus semi structured interviews with the war's participants, international observers, government officials, academics and experts in an attempt to deconstruct some of the Ukraine war's most potent myths, namely – its perception as a civil war between Kyiv's government and the "Russian" Eastern regions of the country. In fact, the war began with Russia's annexation of Crimea and later importation of the conflict into the east of Ukraine via the means of oligarchic/state-supported Russian intervention with both Russian military and genuine Russian foreign fighters present on the front lines. This internationalization of an alleged civil internal conflict radically altered its international perception and subsequently paved the way for an environment which seemingly welcomed the arrival of a "NATO's foreign legion" or "the Donbass International Brigades" onto the battlefields.[84]

The second of the three chapters studies the hosts of these alleged legions or brigades. These, in fact, arrived on the battlefield as appendices to existing Ukrainian or "separatist" units, or actually functioned as lone-standing forces on either side of the conflict. Only a few of the Ukrainian so-called volunteer battalions, however, accepted such recruits, and the situation was not entirely different on the pro-"separatist" side. As will be shown, the foreign fighters were often distrusted and only deployed as fundraising tools in propaganda videos and articles. The chapter will paint a mixed picture of the foreign fighter reality on the front lines as it had been the Ukrainian side which seemed to have made more of the expertise of some of "its" guests, whereas "separatists" were not always successful in tapping their skills.

These skills, however, as the third of the three chapters will show, were meant to have been honed for years, if not decades amongst Europe's far right, which sought literally to fight its battles, lost in 1945 in Europe, outside of the continent. This chapter will discuss the perhaps most potent of such projections – that of Jean Francois Thiriart and his theory of an "outside lung." His approach would see the extreme right-wingers deploy to a foreign war, train, get the necessary experience so that they would return back home, ready for a conflict akin to a European civil war with the continent's "patriots" triumphing over the pro-American, pro-liberal order.[85] To some extent, the war in Ukraine could be regarded as such a "lung." The next chapters will demonstrate the extent to which this had indeed been the case for the European far-right radicals, of whom some traveled to Ukraine to join units on both sides of the war.

These chapters, six thematic analyses of the "national" or "regional" (encompassing sets of countries) contingents of the foreign fighters on either side of the war in Ukraine, follow the three introductory ones and focus on:

1. France: the "French" chapter will discuss the pro-separatist mobilization of the elements of France's far-right, and the role played in the process by facilitators or trailblazers, i.e. people who, after a set of often quasi-farcical predicaments, arrived relatively early in the conflict zone and attempted

to set up international units fighting for the separatists. The story of their largely failed attempts at "transnational" mobilization, construction of "Donbass International Brigades," is largely a "French" story. Motivated by their anti-Americanism, and convinced of the fact that the war was in fact another example of U.S. imperialism at play, and an attempt to further weaken Russia, the only, in their view, serious force capable of opposing America, they set up their "Continental Unity" unit and wished to stop the allegedly pro-American Ukraine from regaining its territory. Interestingly, the above-mentioned unit still exists but includes individuals who arrived in Donetsk much later and are adamant in their anti-far-right political outlook. Interestingly, some far-right French, and veterans of the Balkan wars from the 1990s, also fought on the other side of the war, and famously acted as recruiters for the far-right Azov Battalion/Regiment. As it later turned out, this did not stop them from socializing with their compatriots who featured in the ranks of the "separatists," and e.g. provide them with glowing references for future private military contractor/mercenary work. Such cases offer evidence of an actual split in the French far-right milieu, demonstrate that continuity in "career" foreign fighting, a relative rarity for the jihadists, could be the case in the extreme right circles.[86]

2. Sweden: the "Swedish" chapter will discuss the pro-Ukraine mobilization of the elements of the Swedish far-right and, just like in the French case, discuss the role of facilitators/trailblazers who because of personal push factors arrived early on the scene. Moreover, it will also showcase a complete reversal of the Swedish far-right milieu away from a pro-Ukraine position towards an unashamedly pro-Russian one with the Nordic Resistance Movement, a leading transnational and not only Swedish group, aligning itself with the Russian Imperial Movement, an entity which spawned a paramilitary unit fighting on the side of the "separatists" in the war in Ukraine. Interestingly, this volte face did not undermine the commitment of the Swedish far-right contingent, mostly in the ranks of the Azov Battalion/Regiment, whose members are still present on the front lines. They did, however, face ostracism from their previous comrades upon returning home, and allegedly a media campaign equaling their exploits to those of the Swedish foreign terrorist fighters in the ranks of ISIS.

3. The Balkans: the "Balkan" chapter will discuss the either pro-Ukraine or pro-separatist mobilizations amongst the far-right scenes in different post-Yugoslav countries, namely in Serbia (pro-"separatist" mobilization) and Croatia (pro-Ukraine mobilization), with smaller groups or contingents of fighters from Bosnia and Herzegovina or Montenegro. Some of the fighters had previous experience from the Balkan Wars of the 1990s and, to some extent, their respective mobilizations for Ukraine or the separatists could be seen as not only another instance of "career" foreign fighting, but also an attempt to settle scores with old former Yugoslav rivals.

The Serbian mobilization is led, again, by recruiters or trailblazers, in this case – individuals actually working in Russia before the war, bringing their comrades into the war, also with the help of some other (French) foreign fighters. Subsequently, their contingent, or more accurately – a community as the Serbs constituted one of the most significant foreign fighter contingents in the war in Ukraine, split because of personal rivalries and accusations of defrauding the contingent's far from impressive financial means. Its activities and members came to light due to a string of judicial proceedings in Serbia which brought the fighters to justice as it most probably wanted to curry favor with the EU. The Croat mobilization was smaller but, again, brought into the light activities of facilitators/recruiters, some with experience of serving in the ranks of the French Foreign Legion, either Croats or residents of Croatia.

4. Western Europe: the "Western European" chapter will discuss either pro-Ukraine or pro-separatist mobilizations amongst far-right scenes in different Western countries, e.g. Germany, UK, Spain, Italy, Switzerland, the Netherlands, Denmark, Finland or Norway. The national contingents originating from these scenes were more low key than these of France and Sweden, respectively, and did not feature trailblazers or key facilitators/recruiters in their ranks. Nonetheless, mere presence of the fighters from the above-mentioned countries testifies to the fact that some far-right individuals indeed heard the call to join one of the conflict's warring sides. Moreover, in many cases the national contingents were more evenly split than the French (predominantly pro-separatist) as fighters from one country featured on both sides in more equal numbers. Interestingly, some had not been of far-right backgrounds, e.g. the Spanish contingent, mostly pro-separatist, came from the extreme left, but its members had no problem sharing trenches with extreme right-wingers, who also came to oppose "American imperialism."[87]

5. Central and Eastern Europe: in the words of a Western far-right foreign fighter, his Central-Eastern European (CEE) colleagues "still go on territorial disputes—it is different in the West" where right-wing extremists almost seamlessly are able to unite against their capitalist, globalist or liberal protagonists.[88] This surprisingly shrewd opinion from a pro-"separatist" combatant helps understand the seeming reluctance of far-rightists from EU countries neighboring Ukraine (Poland, Slovakia, Hungary, Romania but also the Czech Republic, Estonia, Latvia and Lithuania) to join the war there. On one side, their extreme nationalisms disable any attempt to join pro-Ukraine radical right units, spawning propaganda and imagery hailing past Ukrainian, and thus – anti-Polish/Hungarian/Slovak etc., heroes and leaders. On the other, their often anti-Russian approach prevents them from joining with their ideological brethren on the "separatist" side. This simplified macro analysis, however, only partially explains the seeming underrepresentation of the neighboring far-right individuals in the conflict zones. Some have indeed traveled to Eastern Ukraine and laid down their lives in

a conflict which should have hardly concerned them.[89] The Czech and the Slovak contingents, whose members fought on the side of the "separatists" and many of whom are still living in Donetsk, clearly stand out in this respect, and their discussion will occupy the most prominent part of the chapter. At the same time, a look into an alleged, phantom pro-separatist Hungarian presence, an attempt by a pan-Slavic Polish organization to align itself with the "separatists," and individual cases of Baltic (Estonian, Latvian or Lithuanian) fighters who joined the conflict, will also be featured.

6. Russia: a monograph on the conflict's foreign fighters must feature a chapter devoted to Russians, as was shown, the biggest of the "national" contingents. This chapter will discuss the Russian volunteer mobilization for the war in general, and its far-right component in particular. It will bring to brought to light the little known fact that the Russian extreme right-wingers fought on both sides as many actively ended up as political refugees in Ukraine before the war. These subsequently opted to fight against the Putin regime, which they saw as authoritarian and intent on pulverizing the Russian far-right scene with repressive measures. Interestingly, some of the Russian far-right individuals, who had not relocated to Ukraine before the war, either of conviction or because of the state's blackmail also enlisted in the war, this time on the side of the "separatists." This little-known split in the far-right scene of a state directly involved in the war provides a fascinating context to the Western mobilizations for the conflict, and a case study in how a belligerent deniably mobilizes its own citizens to join a seemingly foreign war.

The introductory chapters and the thematic analyses will be followed by a concluding chapter which sets out the findings of this study. Moreover, the monograph also includes a post-script chapter, written in the spring of 2022, which focuses on the developments in 2022 when Russia effectively (re-)invaded Ukraine. In turn, this led to the creation of the so-called International Legion by the Ukrainian government, an elusive formation which was open to foreign volunteers. Volunteers and not foreign fighters as these were joining a clearly defined and set out state structure and not some "volunteer battalion." Some of its members were veterans of the 2014 war, and some had been members of the brown-red cocktail. Thus, the author deemed it necessary to not only bring the story up to date but to also to showcase how the 2014 phenomenon of foreign fighters might have metastasized and continued into the third decade of the twenty-first century. In addition to this, the 2022 mobilization of the volunteers offers an interesting comparison with that of foreign fighters from eight years before. It is almost exclusively focusing on only one of the conflict's sides, it involves more individuals, it is performed openly and not clandestinely and is less brown-red in nature and composition.

Conclusion

This monograph is the first in-depth comprehensive study of the foreign fighters and volunteers in Ukraine. It focuses on the brown-red, far right/far left, radicals who flocked to Ukraine or the "separatist" republics but situates them among the broader mass of individuals who found themselves there in 2014 and later. Its contents are informed by multi-year research projects conducted by the author at or with the help of different institutions and/or organizations. It was also preceded by a string of publications on the topic from the author which date back to the spring of 2015. Conversations with the fighters inform and feature in its chapters, especially those focusing on the national or regional case studies of foreign fighter contingents on the front lines.

The monograph's adds to different literatures which focus on far right mobilization, far right violence but also foreign fighters, especially from the ranks of different jihadi organizations. It also contributes to the growing literature on the so-called returnees, mostly from the ranks of ISIS, and the extent to which they could constitute a threat to their countries of origin.[90] As the conflict in Ukraine "froze,"[91] the Western foreign fighters quickly realized "there was nothing left to do [t]here."[92] This prompted returns home or further foreign travel, at times to other conflict zones, either as foreign fighters or, for example, as private military contractors. Interestingly, some then returned to Ukraine as the conflict flared up with ferocious intensity in 2022. Such a turn of events proves the author's thesis that there exists a Western foreign fighter secret society which (re-)mobilizes itself for different conflicts around the world. As this monograph will demonstrate, the society is likely to endure beyond 2022 and the Russian (re-)invasion of Ukraine, and the brown-red cocktail is likely to resurface in another war, either in Europe or in its immediate proximity. Its ingredients, members of the above-mentioned society, will thus resemble not so much the ISIS returnees but the post-Vietnam American veterans who rejuvenated and militarized the American far right from the 1970s onwards.[93]

Notes

1 Kacper Rekawek, *Career Break or a New Career? Extremist Foreign Fighters in Ukraine* (Berlin: Counter Extremism Project, 2020), 8, https://www.counterextremism. com/sites/default/files/CEP%20Report_Career%20Break%20or%20a%20New%20 Career_Extremist%20Foreign%20Fighters%20in%20Ukraine_April%202020.pdf, accessed: February 9, 2021.

2 Kacper Rekawek, "It Ain't Over 'til It's Over: Extreme Right-Wing Foreign Fighters in Ukraine" (Counter Extremism Project, September 23, 2019, https://www. counterextremism.com/blog/%E2%80%9Cit-ain%E2%80%99t-over-%E2%80% 98til-it%E2%80%99s-over%E2%80%9D-extreme-right-wing-foreign-fighters-ukraine, accessed: February 9, 2021 for a rundown of the author's publications on the issue and the coverage they received. See also https://twitter.com/Kacper Rekawek/status/1030766261024772096?s=09 for the author's tweet of August 18, 2018 in which he lists his frustrations with others only recently discovering the topic, accessed: February 9, 2021.

3 Rekawek, *Career Break*.
4 See https://www.youtube.com/watch?v=yfhpKepqfQg, accessed: February 9, 2021.
5 This monograph was refined during the author's first year at Center for Research on Extremism (C-Rex) at the University of Oslo, which he joined in the summer of 2021 as a post-doctoral fellow.
6 *Royal Commission of Inquiry into the Terrorist Attack on Christchurch Mosques on 15 March 2019*, "Report of the Royal Commission of Inquiry into the terrorist attack on Christchurch masjidain on 15 March 2019," (November 2020), https://christchur-chattack.royalcommission.nz/the-report/, accessed: February 9, 2021.
7 See https://twitter.com/ColinPClarke/status/1109140921118015488 for Colin Clarke's, a renowned terrorism expert, twitter status of March 22, 2019, accessed: February 9, 2021.
8 Kacper Rekawek, Alexander Ritzmann, and Hans Jakob Schindler, *Violent Right-Wing Extremism and Terrorism – Transnational Connectivity, Definitions, Incidents, Structures and Countermeasures* (Berlin: Counter Extremism Project, November 2020), 7, https://www.counterextremism.com/sites/default/files/CEP%20Study_Violent%20Right-Wing%20Extremism%20and%20Terrorism_Nov%202020.pdf, accessed: February 9, 2021.
9 Max Rose and Ali H. Soufan, "We Once Fought Jihadists. Now We Battle White Suprem-acists," *The New York Times*, February 11, 2020, https://www.nytimes.com/2020/02/11/opinion/politics/white-supremacist-terrorism.html, accessed: February 10, 2021.
10 The Soufan Center, *White Supremacy Extremism: The Transnational Rise of the Vio-lent White Supremacist Movement* (New York: The Soufan Center, 2019), 29, https://thesoufancenter.org/wp-content/uploads/2019/09/Report-by-The-Soufan-Center-White-Supremacy-Extremism-The-Transnational-Rise-of-The-Violent-White-Supremacist-Movement.pdf, accessed: February 10, 2021 for Arkadiusz Legieć's data on numbers of such fighters. Legieć worked with the author on the first attempt at estimating the phenomenon's scale. See n 1 in Kacper Rekawek, "Neither 'NATO's Foreign Legion' Nor the 'Donbass International Brigades': (Where Are All the) Foreign Fighters in Ukraine?," *PISM Policy Paper*, no. 6(108) (March 2015), https://www.pism.pl/files/?id_plik=19434, accessed: February 10, 2021.
11 See ibid. n 9, 29.
12 See ibid. n 5, 25.
13 See ibid. n 5, 15.
14 See https://www.youtube.com/channel/UC-y9nsRc_QbKhsrDrtTEZCg for a You-Tube channel of Gaston Besson, French recruiter for the Ukrainian Azov Battalion/Regiment.
15 Author's interviews and online exchanges with an anonymous journalist embedded with the foreign fighters on the pro-"separatist" side in 2015 and 2016.
16 Rekawek, "Neither 'NATO's Foreign Legion' Nor the 'Donbass International Brigades'," n 5, 12, 15–16.
17 Rekawek, "It Ain't Over 'til It's Over."
18 Bonnie H. Erickson, "Secret Societies and Social Structure," *Social Forces* 60, no. 1 (1981): 189.
19 Georg Simmel, "The Sociology of Secrecy and of Secret Societies," *American Journal of Sociology* 11, no. 4 (1906): 471.
20 Ibid. 477.
21 Erickson, 189–199.
22 Frédéric Lynn, *Les Hommes Libres* (Paris: Editions bios, 2017).
23 Cas Mudde, *The Far Right Today* (Cambridge: Polity Press, 2019), 7.
24 See https://twitter.com/guicorneau/status/1516161853700939784?s=20&t=7N3ir8 RfHKziv1O2vlItrA, accessed: May 6, 2022, a tweet from April 18, 2022 by Guillaume Corenau, a Canadian researcher, studying Western veterans from Syria who then fought in Ukraine.

25 Chelsea Daymon, Jeanine de Roy van Zuijdewijn, and David Malet, *Career Foreign Fighters: Expertise Transmission Across Insurgencies* (Resolve Research Report, April 2020), https://www.resolvenet.org/system/files/2020-04/RSVE_CareerForeignFighters_ April2020%20%281%29.pdf, accessed: February 11, 2021.

26 Nir Arieli, *From Byron to bin Laden: A History of Foreign War Volunteers* (Cambridge, MA: Harvard University Press, 2018); Thomas Hegghammer, "The Rise of Muslim Foreign Fighters: Islam and the Globalization of Jihad," *International Security* 35, no. 3 (2010); David Malet, *Foreign Fighters: Transnational Identities in Foreign Conflicts* (Oxford: Oxford University Press, 2013).

27 Rekawek, "Neither 'NATO's Foreign Legion' Nor the 'Donbass International Brigades'," n 5, 12.

28 Erik van Ree, "The concept of 'national bolshevism': an interpretative essay," *Journal of Political Ideologies* 6, no. 3 (2001): 289–307.

29 Klemens von Klemperer, "Towards a Fourth Reich? The History of National Bolshevism in Germany. The Review of Politics," *The Review of Politics* 13, no. 2 (1951) 191–210, doi:10.1017/S0034670500047422.

30 Charles Clover, *Black Wind, White Snow. The Rise of Russia's New Nationalism* (London: Yale University Press, 2016), Kindle.

31 Mark Greenblatt and Lauren Knapp, "Extremist Heimbach to Relaunch Hate Group, Says He Supports Violence," *Newsy*, July 20, 2021, https://www.newsy.com/stories/ extremist-heimbach-to-relaunch-hate-group-supports-violence-3/, accessed: May 6, 2022.

32 van Ree, 289.

33 More on this phenomenon in Frace – see the French chapter of this monograph.

34 For a concise primer on the issue see Pietro Castelli Gattinara and Iris Beau Segers, "What explains far-right mobilization?," *C-Rex Compendium*, September 7, 2020, https://www.sv.uio.no/c-rex/english/groups/compendium/what-explains-far-right-mobilization.html, accessed: May 9, 2022.

35 See e.g. for how Western extremists practice violence at "home": Michael Scott Kimmel, *Healing from hate: How young men get into – and out of – violent extremism* (Berkeley, USA: University of California Press, 2018); Jacob Ravndal, "Explaining right-wing terrorism and violence in western Europe: Grievances, opportunities and polarisation," *European Journal of Political Research* 57, no. 4 (2017): 845–866; Jacob Ravndal, "Right-wing terrorism and militancy in the Nordic countries: A comparative case study," *Terrorism and Political Violence* 30, no. 5 (2018) 772–792; Megan Sweeneyand Arie Perliger, "Explaining the spontaneous nature of far-right violence in the United States," *Perspectives on Terrorism* 12, no. 6 (2018): 52–71.

36 Rekawek, Ritzmann, and Schindler. For studies focusing on different aspects of the far right's transnationality see e.g. Lars E. Berntzen, *Liberal Roots of Far Right Activism: The Anti-Islamic Movement in the 21st Century* (Abingdon, Routledge, 2020); Manuela Caiani and Patricia Kröll, "The transnationalization of the extreme right and the use of the Internet," *International Journal of Comparative and Applied Criminal Justice* 39, no. 4 (2015): 331–351; Caterina Froio and Bharath Ganesh, "The transnationalisation of far right discourse on Twitter: Issues and actors that cross borders in western European democracies," *European Societies* 21, no. 4 (2019): 513–539; Graham Macklin, "Transnational networking on the far right: The case of Britain and Germany," *West European Politics* 36, no. 1 (2013): 176–198; Michael Minkenberg, "Between Party and Movement: Conceptual and Empirical Considerations of the Radical Right's Organizational Boundaries and Mobilization Processes," *European Societies* 21, no. 4 (2019): 463–486, Jens Rydgren, "Immigration sceptics, xenophobes or racists? Radical right-wing voting in six West European countries," *European Journal of Political Research* 47, no. 6 (2008): 737–765.

37 See e.g. Maxime Bérubé and Benoit Dupont, "Mujahideen Mobilization: Examining the Evolution of the Global Jihadist Movement's Communicative Action Repertoire," *Studies in Conflict & Terrorism* 42, nos. 1–2 (2019): 5–24; Carola García-Calvo,

There is no life without jihad and no jihad without hijrah': the jihadist mobilisation of women in Spain, 2014-16 (Real Institute Elcano, April 2017), https://www.realinstitutoelcano.org/en/analyses/there-is-no-life-without-jihad-and-no-jihad-without-hijrah-the-jihadist-mobilisation-of-women-in-spain-2014-16/; Hegghammer, "The Rise of Muslim Foreign Fighters." 53–94; Olivier Roy, *Jihad and death: the global appeal of Islamic State*, (London: Hurst Publishers, 2017).

38 Hegghammer, "The Rise of Muslim Foreign Fighters," 53.

39 Malet, *Foreign Fighters*, 9.

40 JSTOR lists 3240 items of "academic content" (i.e. journal articles, book chapters or research reports) which feature the term "foreign fighters." Accessed: 30 November 2020.

41 The author found the following works on foreign terrorist fighters most useful while writing this chapter: Edwin Bakker and Roel de Bont, "Belgian and Dutch Jihadist Foreign Fighters (2012–2015): Characteristics, Motivations, and Roles in the War in Syria and Iraq," *Small Wars & Insurgencies* 27, no. 5 (2016): 837–857, DOI: 10.1080/09592318.2016.1209806; Alessandro Boncio, "The Islamic State's Crisis and Returning Foreign Fighters: The Case of Italy," *ISPI Working Paper*, November 3, 2017, https://www.ispionline.it/en/pubblicazione/islamic-states-crisis-and-returning-foreign-fighters-case-italy-18545; Linus Gustafsson and Magnus Ranstorp, "Swedish Foreign Fighters in Syria and Iraq: An Analysis of open-source intelligence and statistical data," *CATS*, (2017), http://fhs.diva-portal.org/smash/get/diva2:1110355/FULLTEXT01.pdf; Marc Hecker, "137 Shades of Terrorism: French Jihadists Before the Courts," *IFRI* (April 2018), https://www.ifri.org/sites/default/files/atoms/files/hecker_137_shades_of_terrorism_2018.pdf; Pieter van Ostaeyen and Guy van Vlierden, "Citizenship and Ancestry of Belgian Foreign Fighters," *ICCT Policy Brief* (May 2018), https://icct.nl/app/uploads/2018/06/ICCT-Van-Ostaeyen-Van-Vlierden-Belgian-Foreign-Fighters-June2018.pdf; Carola García-Calvo and Fernando Reinares, "Patterns of Involvement among Individuals Arrested for Islamic State-related Terrorist Activities in Spain, 2013-2016," *Perspectives on Terrorism* 10, no. 6, (2016), http://www.terrorismanalysts.com/pt/index.php/pot/article/view/562/html, all accessed: February 11, 2021; Johannes Saal, *The Dark Social Capital of Religious Radicals: Jihadi Networks and Mobilization in Germany, Austria and Switzerland, 1998-2018* (Berlin: Springer, 2021); and Aaron Y. Zelin, *Your Sons Are at Your Service: Tunisia's Missionaries of Jihad* (New York: Columbia University Press, 2020).

42 Kacper Rekawek et al., *Who Are the European Jihadis?* (Bratislava: Globsec, 2018), 34, nn 10 and 15, https://www.globsec.org/wp-content/uploads/2018/09/GLOBSEC_WhoAreTheEuropeanJihadis.pdf, for a brief bibliography on the Western jihadist foreign fighters.

43 Lorne L. Dawson, "A Comparative Analysis of the Data on Western Foreign Fighters in Syria and Iraq: Who Went and Why?," (ICCT Research Paper, February 2021), https://icct.nl/app/uploads/2021/02/Dawson-Comparative-Analysis-FINAL-1.pdf, accessed: February 9, 2021 for the most recent and comprehensive, encompassing 34 academic articles and reports, review of the available data on the issue.

44 See e.g. Thomas Hegghammer, "Should I Stay or Should I Go? Explaining Variation in Western Jihadists' Choice between Domestic and Foreign Fighting," *American Political Science Review* 107, no. 1 (February 2013): 1–15; and David Malet, "The European Experience with Foreign Fighters and Returnees," in Thomas Renard and Rik Coolsaet, eds., "Returnees: Who are they, why are they (not) coming back and how should we deal with them?" *Egmont Paper* 101 (February 2018): 6–19, https://www.egmontinstitute.be/content/uploads/2018/02/egmont.papers.101_online_v1-3.pdf?-type=pdf for a survey of sources on the "fall out."

45 Malet, "The European Experience with Foreign Fighters and Returnees," 15; David Malet and Rachel Hayes, "Foreign Fighter Returnees: An Indefinite Threat?,"

Terrorism and Political Violence, DOI: 10.1080/09546553.2018.1497987; Daymon, de Roy van Zuijdewijn, and Malet, *Career Foreign Fighters.*

46 Patrick Jackson, "Ukraine war pulls in foreign fighters," *BBC News*, August 31, 2014, https://www.bbc.com/news/world-europe-28951324, accessed: February 3, 2021; Pierre Sautreuil, "Des paras français dans le Donbass," *Le Monde*, August 26, 2014, https://www.lemonde.fr/europe/article/2014/08/26/des-paras-francais-dans-le-donbass_4476646_3214.html, accessed: February 3, 2021; Shaun Walker, "We are preventing a third world war: the foreigners fighting with Ukrainian rebels," *The Guardian*, September 24, 2015, https://www.theguardian.com/world/2015/sep/24/ukraine-conflict-donbass-russia-rebels-foreigners-fighting, accessed: February 3, 2021; Marcin Wyrwał, "Najemnik. W drodze do Walhalli," *Onet.pl*, January 19, 2020, https://wiadomosci.onet.pl/tylko-w-onecie/rafael-lusvarghi-historia-najemnika-z-brazylii/wsxdzc3, accessed: February 3, 2021.

47 Dina Newman, "Ukraine conflict: 'White power' warrior from Sweden," *BBC News*, July 16, 2014, https://www.bbc.com/news/world-europe-28329329, accessed: February 3, 2021.

48 *Hate Speech International*, "Ukraine's far-right forces," February 3, 2015, https://www.hate-speech.org/ukraines-far-right-forces/, accessed: January 20, 2021.

49 Patricia Ortega Dolz, "We fought together, communists and Nazis alike, for the liberation of Russia," *El Pais*, February 27, 2015, http://elpais.com/elpais/2015/02/27/inenglish/1425051026_915897.html, accessed: February 3, 2021 or Walker, "We are preventing a third world war."

50 Author's WhatsApp interview with a Swedish fighter from the Azov/Battalion regiment, January 28 2020, where he agreed that even while some of the foreign fighters had been present in all of the "big battles" of the war, they "hardly made a difference" as there were too few of them. Moreover, he also stressed that "war is a private issue" of any individual present on the front lines. In some cases, however, the fighters' stories would be picked up at different, deemed newsworthy, turns of their lives. See Wyrwał, "Najemnik," or Christopher Miller, "From Brazilian Poster Boy For Ukraine's Separatists To 'Man Of God'," *RadioFreeEurope, RadioLiberty*, May 3, 2018, https://www.rferl.org/a/ukraine-russia-from-brazilian-separatist-poster-boy-to-man-of-god/29206373.html, accessed: February 3, 2021 for their articles on Rafael Lusvarghi, one of the most iconic foreign fighters from the war, whose life trajectory will be presented in more detail in later chapters.

51 See Rekawek, "Neither 'NATO's Foreign Legion' Nor the 'Donbass International Brigades'" in n 9 for the author's first major publication on the issue, from early 2015 and see this volume generally for the most recent.

52 Kacper Rekawek, ed, *Not Only Syria? The Phenomenon of Foreign Fighters in a Comparative Perspective* (The Hague: IOS Press, 2017).

53 Egle E. Murauskaite, *Foreign Fighters in Ukraine: Assessing Potential Risks* (Vilnius: Vilnius Institute for policy analysis, 2020), https://vilniusinstitute.lt/wp-content/uploads/2020/02/foreign-fighters-in-ukrain-assessing-potential-risks.pdf.

54 Shashi Jayakumar, *Transnational Volunteers Against ISIS* (London: ICSR, 2019), 9, https://icsr.info/wp-content/uploads/2019/08/ICSR-Report-Transnational-Volunteers-Against-ISIS.pdf for the information on the other (five) available sources.

55 Ariel Koch, "The Non-Jihadi Foreign Fighters: Western Right-Wing and Left-Wing Extremists in Syria," *Terrorism and Political Violence* (2019), DOI: 10.1080/09546553.2019.1581614.

56 Kyle Burke, *Revolutionaries for the Right: Anticommunist Internationalism and Paramilitary Warfar-e in the Cold War* (NC: University of North Carolina Press, 2018); Christopher Othen, *Franco's International Brigades: Foreign Volunteers and Fascist Dictators in the Spanish Civil War* (London: Reportage Press, 2010).

57 A parallel gap on the far left foreign fighters has been filled by e.g. David Malet, "Workers of the world, unite! Communist foreign fighters 1917–91," *European Review of History: Revue européenne d'histoire* 27, nos. 1–2 (2020): 33–53.

58 Rosaria Puglisi, "Heroes or Villains? Volunteer Battalions in Post-Maidan Ukraine," *IAI Working Papers* 15/8 (March 2015), http://www.iai.it/sites/default/files/iaiwp1508.pdf, accessed: February 8, 2021.

59 Research on effectiveness on the fighters demonstrates that they need some state support, e.g. from a belligerent state or a country bordering the one involved in war, to effectively deploy to a foreign war and later recruit other foreigners for the same war effort. See David Malet, "Foreign Fighter Mobilization and Persistence in a Global Context," *Terrorism and Political Violence* 27, no. 3 (2015): 461. The Russia-Ukraine war proves this point both in 2014 and in 2022 – it is especially telling in the latter case which would not have happened with Moscow's tacit approval of transfers of foreign fighters through its territory to the "separatist" republics. As will be shown, however, this approval was not always working well and some fighters encountered serious surprises, e.g. arrests, while in Russia.

60 Malet, *Foreign Fighters*.

61 C. Moore and P. Tumelty, "Foreign Fighters and the Case of Chechnya: A Critical Assessment," *Studies in Conflict & Terrorism* 31, no. 5 (May 2008) 412. The above-mentioned definition is also broader than that of Hegghammer, which stressed that foreign fighters join an insurgency and not a recognized military organization, lack kinship to factions involved in war and are unpaid. As discussed above, the Ukrainian case does not meet this criteria. See Hegghammer, "The Rise of Muslim Foreign Fighters," 58. It also must be noted here that Malet, the world's most renowned scholarly authority on foreign fighters, acknowledges that one should not expect the fighters to go through the war unpaid, or at least with some expenses covered. See Malet, "Foreign Fighter Mobilization," 462.

62 See Malet, *Foreign Fighters*.

63 Cerwyn Moore, "Foreign Bodies: Transnational Activism, the Insurgency in the North Caucasus and 'Beyond'," *Terrorism and Political Violence* 27, no. 3, (2015): 396–398.

64 Ibid.

65 Malet, *Foreign Fighters*, 455–457.

66 See e.g. Azov's Mikael Skillt, who re-joined the war on March 8, 2022. He was showcased on one of Azov's social media channels: https://www.facebook.com/intermarium.today/posts/116646670955277, accessed: March 25, 2022.

67 The author is conducting a multiyear research project at the Center for the Study of Extremism, C-Rex, University of Oslo, Norway, which is a study of the afterlives of the foreign fighters from the war in Ukraine.

68 Rekawek, "It Ain't Over 'til It's Over" for examples of their militant or paramilitary post-war activity.

69 David Malet and Rachel Hayes, "Foreign Fighter Returnees: An Indefinite Threat?," *Terrorism and Political Violence*, DOI: 10.1080/09546553.2018.1497987.

70 Pavel Felgenhauer, "Russia Escalates Its Proxy War in Eastern Ukraine," *Eurasia Daily Monitor* 18, no. 41 (11 March 2021), https://jamestown.org/program/russia-escalates-its-proxy-war-in-eastern-ukraine/, accessed: March 31, 2021.

71 Kathleen Blee and Mehr Latif, "Sociological Survey of the Far- Right," in Stephen D. Ashe, Joel Busher, Graham Macklin, and Aaron Winter, *Researching the Far Right. Theory, Method and Practice* (London: Routledge, 2020), 46, 53.

72 The author communicated with 23 of the foreign fighters who fought in Ukraine before February 24, 2022 – the Russian (re-)invasion of Ukraine. Some of the exchanges he participated in, however, had not been truly semi-structured or structured interview but more conversations on different social media platforms, conducted on background. These were rapid, often conducted in many instalments. The interviewed or contacted fighters represent a minority of all Westerners present on the front lines. Since, however, they represent different nationalities and are of different ideological backgrounds, this subset constitutes a unique

snapshot of the foreign fighter reality in Ukraine, and forms, in the author's view, an important contribution to our understanding of the phenomenon of foreign fighting.

73 As of May 2022, at least two foreign (former) members of the Azov Battalion/ Regiment maintain active twitter accounts. Many more are present and active on Facebook or Telegram. The same can be said about the foreign fighters from the pro-"separatist" side. The quintessential foreign fighter pro-"separatist" unit, Continental Unity, also maintains a Facebook page.

74 Kacper Rekawek, "Conducting Field Research on Terrorism in Northern Ireland," in Adam Dolnik, ed., *Conducting Terrorism Field Research: A Guide* (Abingdon: Routledge, 2013) for more on the issue of gatekeepers in field research.

75 André Gingrichm and Marcus Banks, *Neo-Nationalism in Europe and Beyond: Perspectives from Social Anthropology* (Oxford: Berghahn Books, 2006), 24.

76 The author will continue to use the word "separatist" in quotation marks throughout this book. As will be shown in the introductory chapter on the war in Ukraine, the leaders of these "separatists," and many of their foot soldiers, had in fact been assembled, trained and supported if not directly sent by the Russian Federation to Eastern Ukraine. Many had, in fact, been Russians with little or no previous connection to Ukraine. This effectively means that the war in Eastern Ukraine is in fact a Russo-Ukraine war and not a civil war in which restive regions seek separation from the yoke of the central government in Kyiv.

77 Martyn Hammersley, "Ethnography: Problems and Prospects," *Ethnography and Education* 1, no. 1 (2006): 3–14.

78 See the chapter on the French fighters.

79 Betty A. Dobratz and Lisa K. Waldner, "Interviewing Members of the White Power Movement in the United States. Reflections on Research Strategies and challenges of Right-Wing Extremists," in: Stephen D. Ashe, Joel Busher, Graham Macklin, and Aaron Winter, *Researching the Far Right. Theory, Method and Practice* (London: Routledge, 2020), 221.

80 Chad R. Lochmiller, "Conducting a thematic analysis with qualitative data," *The Qualitative Report* 26, no. 6) 26(6), 2021: 2029:2044.

81 Blee and Latif, "Sociological Survey of the Far-Right," 46.

82 Pasko Kisic Merino, Tereza Capelos, and Catarina Kinnvall, "Getting Inside 'the Head' of the Far-Right. Psychological Responses to the Socio-Political Context," in Stephen D. Ashe, Joel Busher, Graham Macklin, and Aaron Winter, *Researching the Far Right. Theory, Method and Practice* (London: Routledge, 2020), 77–78.

83 Timothy Holman, "'Gonna Get Myself Connected': The Role of Facilitation in Foreign Fighter Mobilizations," *Perspectives on Terrorism* 10, no. 2 (2016), http://www.terrorismanalysts.com/pt/index.php/pot/article/view/497/html, accessed: February 9, 2021.

84 Rekawek, "Neither 'NATO's Foreign Legion' Nor the 'Donbass International Brigades'" in n 9.

85 Anton Shekhovtsov, *Russia and the Western Far-Right: Tango Noir* (Abingdon: Routledge, 2017) for a discussion of Thiriart's ideas and vision. Alexander Jacob's "Introduction" to Thiriart's re-issued magnum opus *An Empire of 400 Million* (London: Arktos, 2021) is also useful in this respect.

86 Daymon, de Roy van Zuijdewijn, and Malet, "Career Foreign Fighters."

87 Ortega Dolz, "We fought together." 1.

88 Rekawek, "Neither 'NATO's Foreign Legion' Nor the 'Donbass International Brigades'" n 5, 16.

89 Tomas Forro, "Naši chlapci v Donbase. Babie leto u československých separatistov," *Dennik N*, December 1, 2016, https://dennikn.sk/622947/nasi-chlapci-v-donbase-babie-leto-u-ceskoslovenskych-separatistov/, accessed: September 27, 2022.

90 Malet, "The European Experience with Foreign Fighters and Returnees."
91 See e.g. Gulliver Cragg, "Ceasefire in Ukraine's Donbas region: Peace or frozen conflict?," *France 24*, October 23, 2020, https://www.france24.com/en/tv-shows/focus/20201023-ceasefire-in-ukraine-s-donbas-region-peace-or-frozen-conflict, accessed: September 27, 2022.
92 Rekawek, "Neither 'NATO's Foreign Legion' Nor the 'Donbass International Brigades'" n 5, 24
93 Kathleen Belew, *Bring the War Home The White Power Movement and Paramilitary America* (London: Harvard University Press, 2018).

2

CONFLICT

Myth and Reality in the War in Ukraine

Introduction

Before introducing different national contingents of the brown-red cocktail, one must first take stock of the conflict in Ukraine which was the foreign fighters' excuse to travel eastward. As will be shown, there is already a vast literature on different aspects of the war in Ukraine and, due to the limited space, this chapter will not attempt to offer alternative explanations nor compete with scholars whose work will be cited later. Given the complexity of the conflict and its relative anonymity for Western and/or English-speaking audiences, and the expert/scholarly community focusing on counter-terrorism/or prevention/countering of violent extremism, who remain at the core of the book's audience, the author decided that this chapter would be of most use if it focused on the conflict's causes and factors which led to its eruption and escalation. It remains his opinion that studying the foreign fighters without some appreciation and understating of the conflict they decided to join would be counterproductive. Studying such fighters without the context in which they operate provides us with few additions to the already existing knowledge and oftentimes, at best, yet another sociological and statistically oriented study which would fail to explain what actually made such people "go to war" in the first place. The next three chapters will thus contextualize this going to war by focusing first on the conflict itself, then on the hosts of those fighters who arrived in Eastern Ukraine (on either side of the war) and, finally, on the ideological, transnational backgrounds of the fighters present on the Ukrainian front lines. As will be shown, the last of the three will outline the case for calling such fighters a brown-red cocktail but the chapter below will also include sections pertaining to that issue, especially in relation to war being framed by either side as a struggle against the "imperialist" West or fascist "banderites" by the so-called "separatists" and their backers.

DOI: 10.4324/9781003192992-2

The War

At the time of this writing, the war in Eastern Ukraine has been going on for more than eight years. It has already been called a "forgotten"[1] or a "frozen" conflict.[2] Simultaneously, however, it took eight ceasefires (with the latest of July 27, 2020)[3] for the conflict to dramatically deescalate in the 2020–2021 period with e.g. "only" 129 civilians fatalities and injuries in 2020, compared e.g. to 486 in 2017.[4] In total, more than 13,000 people lost their lives in the war, a further 30,000 plus have been wounded, and more than 1.5 million have been internally displaced as a result.[5] Although dwarfed by the civil war in Syria in terms of casualties and the conflict's internationalization, the war in Ukraine has been the latest reminder that Europe, up until 2020 and the renewed Nagorno-Karabakh war, was never free of armed conflict. All of this, however, was soon eclipsed by the February 24, 2022 Russian invasion or in fact, re-invasion (after that of 2014 "hybrid" invasion, which is discussed below) of Ukraine.[6] By March 24, 2022 approximately 2,600 new civilian casualties were recorded,[7] with invading Russian troops also suffering "significant" losses.[8]

In 2019, a respected German think tank, SWP – the German Institute for International and Security Affairs, published a research paper in which the conflict in Ukraine was summarized in the following manner: "[i]n 2014, in response to the Ukrainian 'Euromaidan,' Russia annexed Crimea and provoked a war in eastern Ukraine."[9] This statement by no means exhausts the complexity of the conflict but introduces the three key terms which need to be defined while attempting to provide a background to the conflict which attracted the brown-red cocktail, namely: Euromaidan, Crimea, Eastern Ukraine (Donbas). These are all interconnected and appear in a linear fashion in the story of the conflict, and will be discussed below.

Euromaidan was a series of protests in Kyiv's Maidan Nezalezhnosti (Independence Square) against the Ukrainian government's decision not to sign an association agreement with the European Union. The protests began on November 21, 2013 and continued until late February 2014, when President Viktor Yanukovych fled the country, and resulted in more than 100 deaths and 2,000 injuries, mostly on the side of the anti-government protestors.[10] The protests were followed by "a military occupation [of Crimea] that [was] staged as a non-occupation," i.e. the arrival of anonymous troops bearing no insignia, in Crimea, in Southern Ukraine. These were "polite and yet frightening," and, despite being widely recognized as belonging to the Russian army, were also "different from the Russian army."[11] In a creeping manner, they occupied the peninsula and paved the way for its annexation by the Russian Federation, officially affirmed by a hastily organized "referendum" on March 16, 2014 (organized without the consent of Ukraine) and the signing of "a treaty on accession of the Republic of Crimea and Sebastopol to the Russian Federation" a mere two days later.[12] Next, the action shifted away from Kyiv or Crimea to Donbas, or Donets Basin, a region in Eastern Ukraine and Western Russia, where the "Russian spring," i.e. pro-Russian protests began.[13]

As these failed to copy the success of the Crimea's "polite people" (without their actual involvement), Russia militarized the situation by backing them with its special forces and the veterans of the so-called Crimean "self-defense" forces, such as a unit led by a former Russian military intelligence (GRU) operative Igor Girkin, which marched into Ukraine's Eastern city of Slovyansk on April 12, 2014.[14] The region's "separatists" then organized referenda in the parts of the Donetsk and Luhansk *oblasti* (provinces) of Eastern Ukraine they controlled and declared the establishment of two "People's Republics" – the Donetsk People's Republic (DNR) and the Luhansk People's Republic (LNR). In the meantime, Ukraine declared an "anti-terrorist operation" and effectively counterattacked to restore its territorial integrity.[15] Throughout the summer, its offensive almost cut off the "Republics" from the border with Russia, which would spell their swift collapse, but they were then saved by a direct Russian military intervention.[16] Early 2015 brought another bout of fighting but, since then, "both sides have barely moved an inch over the 'Contact Line,'" which cuts the Ukrainian Donbas into two.[17] While the war was raging, in September 2014 and February 2015 respectively, the so-called Minsk Agreements were negotiated. These stipulated an immediate ceasefire, to be monitored by the Organisation for Security and Co-operation in Europe, the effective reintegration of the DNR and the LNR into a decentralized Ukraine, "local elections in the contested areas, under Ukrainian control and international observation; the withdrawal of illegal armed units from Ukrainian territory etc."[18] These effectively became null and void after Russia (re-)invaded Ukraine on February 24, 2022. Despite new rounds of peace talks, held in Belarus and in Turkey, no new blueprint for peace has so far been produced and agreed by both sides.[19]

Root Causes of the Conflict

The linear narrative presented above provides a snapshot of the conflict's history but does not explain its roots nor explanations for the conflict's eruption and escalation. Andrew Wilson neatly catalogued the most popular ones and simultaneously rightly concluded that these fail fully to account for the origins of the war. In his view, the popular explanations include: the termination of balance between competing parts of Ukraine, i.e. the Ukrainian-speaking West (Galicia) and the Russian-speaking East (Donbas), which resulted in a backlash from the Russophone east against the pro-Western west, Donbas' growing alienation from Western and Central Ukraine after the 2004 Orange Revolution,[20] alleged state collapse in the aftermath of the Euromaidan protests allowing Russia to penetrate Ukraine more effectively, revolt of the regions threatened by economic marginalization (as a result of not joining the Russian-led Eurasian Economic Community) or outright Russian aggression. In his view, Donbas was alienated from Kyiv and that allowed for a "baseline for a local civil conflict" but not for an "all-out war," which was instigated by the alliance of the local elites and Russia. Moscow effectively created "a separatist movement from weak and patchy 'grassroots' material." This movement and rebellion had in fact been "a triple failure," which could not win on its own against Ukraine in the spring of 2014 and had to be assisted by the first Russian detachment led by the above-mentioned Girkin, who "reshuffled all the cards on the table [...] to set the flywheel [of war] into motion,"[21] but then still could not win over the alleg-edly pro-Russian cities of Kharkiv[22] and Odessa[23] to its cause, effectively ter-minating chances of the so-called Novorossiya (a statelet encompassing a much wider stretch of Eastern Ukraine than the" People's Republics") being estab-lished in Eastern Ukraine,[24] and finally had to be saved by a direct Russian mili-tary intervention in the summer of 2014, which helped the "People's Republics" to consolidate somewhat.[25]

While refuting some of the popular explanations for the war's outbreak, Wilson especially pierced through the argument on perennial imbalance or out-right division of Ukraine, which was meant, at some point, to lead to the separa-tion of its restive east (or south east). As Rabinovych and Shelest rightly pointed out, Ukraine, due to the fact that parts of its territory belonged to a string of competing and different states in the past, is not a homogenous country "in terms of ethnic composition, national and regional identities, language identities and practices, religious affiliation, beliefs and practices, and foreign policy attitudes." Regardless of its internal divisions, they noted, exacerbated by the 2004 con-troversial presidential election which pitted the "pro-Western," and associated with Western Ukraine, Viktor Yuschenko versus the "pro-Moscow," and from Donbas in Eastern Ukraine, Viktor Yanukovych, Ukraine had been a centralized state.[26] Some of the author's interviewees came back to the above-mentioned electoral battle and the ensuing 2004 Orange Revolution as a pivotal moment in the country's history – or a moment which allowed "both elites [allegedly pro-Western and pro-Russian] to carefully construct electoral lines from which they profited."[27] These lines were visible on Ukraine's electoral maps with the "orange," pro-West, pro-democracy, Western and Central part of the country facing the "blue," pro-Russia, authoritarian, post-Soviet south and the eastern part of Ukraine.[28] This reading of the situation stressed that the "informal divi-sion"[29] or polarization should not be taken for granted. It had been allegedly arti-ficially created or enabled by Ukrainian elites of different shades, supported by the ever-present and flexible in developing their alliances country's oligarchs,[30] so that they could augment their political and economic stranglehold over the country. Interestingly, this polarized arrangement was supposedly not even upset by the capturing of the presidency by Viktor Yanukovych, the highly controver-sial loser of the 2004 election, firmly on the "eastern" side. This balance or, in reality, division of spoils had only been turned upside down when a new pres-idential oligarchy, the so-called *simja* (family) came into being and rivaled the existing nexuses of economic and political control in the country. It instituted and ran a bottom-up system of centralized corruption, or a kleptocracy, akin if not rivaling that of the Mubarak family in Egypt.[31] Surprisingly, this kleptoc-racy, run by an individual with criminal past and widely seen as a representative of Ukraine's east, attempted a truly Nixonian manoeuvre when Yanukovych came tantalizingly close to signing an association agreement with the European Union, allegedly a ploy to curry favor with the country's Western voters before the 2015 presidential election.[32]

As the inevitability of the regional clash argument is clearly insufficient to explain the post-2014 events in Ukraine, Wilson focused his "civil conflict" but not civil war explanation on Eastern Ukraine, and the conflict drivers that had been present there before 2014. He rightly dismissed any claims that the Euromaidan's logical if not obvious conclusion was an eruption of a "civil war"/ Russian intervention in Ukraine. In fact, Ukraine had seen other mass protests in its history, including the above-mentioned Orange Revolution, but these did not result in an armed conflict, nor an annexation of one of its provinces by Ukraine's eastern neighbor, Russia. In reality, had it not been for the governmental escalation of violence against the protestors in Kyiv's Independence Square on November 30, 2013, when the riot police brutally assaulted a small protest by Ukrainian students, the Euromaidan might have never evolved into an iconic sit in, which helped to oust the then government of Ukraine.[33] It took the protestors almost three months to accomplish this and, during that time, Russia, initially intent on drawing Ukraine into its Eurasian Economic Union and opposed to Kyiv's association agreement with the European Union,[34] must have planned for Crimea's annexation which was executed and then "legalized" in an abovementioned "referendum" and "a treaty of accession" in less than 30 days after President Yanukovych's departure from Ukraine. As the Crimean operation was taking place immediately after the triumph of Euromaidan, so was the so-called "Russian spring," a series of "anti-Maidan" protests held in the Russophone cities of Eastern Ukraine. These, as it later turned out, were spearheaded by locals attempting to overthrow the kleptocratic order prevailing in Ukraine in general, and in its eastern part, a bastion of President Yanukovych, in particular, and included representatives of a weak "separatist" movement functioning in Donbas. Moreover, these protests quickly, less than four weeks after annexation of Crimea, escalated into an armed struggle, instigated and coordinated by individuals who literally marched into Eastern Ukraine via its porous border from Russia, such as the above-mentioned Igor Girkin.[35] In short, the speed with which the conflict was first ignited and then broadened suggests a high degree of external assistance and planning, independent of Euromaidan success.

Donbas: The Decline of the "Wild West"

The annexation of Crimea saw very little violence as Ukraine, politically healing from the clashes which led to Yanukovych's departure, found itself unable to oppose the invaders – especially given the state of its underfunded armed forces, no match for its opponents who maintained a naval base in Crimea after Ukraine's independence, and used it as a conduit for its invading units.[36] The swiftness of the operation might have convinced Moscow that Ukraine was so weak that it would be worthwhile to gamble for more of its territory or, if things were to go well, to bank on its actual collapse and a secession of its Russophone parts. As was demonstrated, however, the regional divisions and a cause for separatism had been too weak to break Ukraine but strong enough to destabilize Donbas permanently. While admitting this, one must also remember that the war in Donbas had not been preordained by the annexation of Crimea or the Euromaidan. The region was restive but an extra push was needed to engulf it into a conflict resembling a civil war. The appliance of the push, instigated by the likes of Girkin and his men, was solely's Russia choice. Nonetheless, the fact that Moscow might have even hoped for a success of its broadening of the battlefield beyond Crimea necessitates a brief focus on Donbas, which, as will be shown, was an odd one out type of a region in Ukraine where pro-Russian, or more accurately, pro-Soviet, sentiment was indeed well represented.

The area which later became known as Donbas was in the early modern period a part of the so-called "wild fields," i.e. a steppe settled by the Zaporozhian Cossacks, technically subjects of the Polish-Lithuanian Commonwealth.[37] In the eighteenth century, the region became a part of Russia and constituted the so-called and short-lived New Russia Governorate, or Novorossiya Governorate – a name to which the region's separatists will attempt to return to in 2014. As it had newly discovered vast quantities of coal, it quickly boomed economically and also drew in criminals and chancers.[38] Moreover, it also attracted outcasts or rejects (such as the "dekulakized" (from dekulakization – repression aimed at allegedly rich peasants in the USSR between 1929 and 1932) peasants, Jews after another bout of antisemitism in the Soviet Union,[39] the Ukrainian nationalists after the military defeat of the Ukrainian Insurgent Army (UPA) in the late 1940s/early 1950s, or convicts released from the Soviet gulag as a result of the 1953 amnesty)[40] who would all settle there while looking for a fresh start.[41] Donbas' "wild West" status and the fact that it had been USSR's "most important hub of heavy industry" before the discovery of gas and oil in Siberia meant there was plenty of work there. This state of affairs provided a modicum of security for above-mentioned and often free-spirited individuals in the highly repressive USSR.[42] As a result, the region saw the birth of one of the first cases of sociopolitical dissidence or outright attempts to establish independent trade unions in the history of USSR.[43] Donbas, as it turned out, was restless and in this sense, became "the most Ukrainian" of all of Ukraine's regions, effectively still a part of the Cossack "wild fields."[44] It developed a culture which fetishized industry on one hand[45] and embraced a mix of "looking after one's own," and "winner takes all" mentality on the other. Add to that the fact that up to a fifth of a population had an experience of Soviet prisons, and the relative weakness of its middle class or intelligentsia,[46] and an unfair and distorted picture of a region beyond the pale or "moronic," in the eyes of the rest of Ukraine, emerges.[47]

At the same time, as Hiroaki Kuromiya, the world's leading authority on the history of Donbas, would stress, the region often defied expectations and its complexity was said to have dumbfounded seasoned political operators such as

Lev Trotsky.[48] It overwhelmingly (80 percent) voted for Ukrainian independence in the 1991 referendum but found itself at odds with a country largely led by pro-Western elites, which in 1996 decided on a restructurization of the Donbas' industry. This latter act resulted in closure or privatization of mines which often amounted to nothing more than a handover of a given industrial complex to local chieftains connected to the underworld. This was performed, as the Ukrainian government was to claim, under pressure from the World Bank, which only fanned the flames of a Soviet nostalgia in the region and augmented its suspicion towards Western and Central Ukrainian elites (referred to in a derogatory fashion as fascists or "Banderites," i.e. supporters of the pre-World War II Ukrainian nationalist leader, Stepan Bandera) and their Western European and/or American alleged or real backers.[49] Consequently, as late as 2013, 57 percent of the inhabitants of the Ukrainian Donbas regretted the fall of the Soviet Union.[50] They also emotionally reacted to the so-called "Leninopad" (Lenin-fall), i.e. decommunization process which started in the aftermath of the Euromaidan and e.g. saw a removal of about half of approximately 2,500 statues of Lenin from Ukraine.[51]

The "Banderite" or "fascist" sloganeering effectively pitting Eastern versus Western Ukraine became a crude way of political polarization and a chance for a more successful territorialization of the Donbas, post-Soviet or pro-Russian (as Russia was seen as a successor of the now fondly remembered USSR) vote.[52] This was especially evident in the aftermath of the 2004 Orange Revolution, which allegedly pitted the pro-Western parts of Ukraine against it pro-Russian east. This division was further exploited by the "political technologists" and the Ukrainian elite to cement their popularity in "their" respective parts of the country. In Donbas, such an approach allowed the local bigwigs, often with criminal connections, including the *simja*, i.e. "family" of the 2010–2014 Ukrainian President, Viktor Yanukovych who hailed from Donbas, to divert the voters' attention away from their shortcomings such as corruption, incompetence or nepotism.[53] Moreover, Yanukovych's government might have furthered this territorialization by simultaneous attempts to "promote" (through the ample provision of prime time slots in *simja*-friendly media) the nationalist and technically oppositional *Svoboda* (Freedom) party, which ideally played the role of a "Banderite" bogeyman to the inhabitants of Donbass.[54]

After 2014, the post-Maidan Ukrainian government was also referred to as "Banderite" by the Russian media, who attempted to mobilize the Russians along the lines known from the 1941–1945 struggle with Nazi Germany. In this scenario, Russia and its Donbas/New Russian/Donetsk or Luhansk supporters were once again, just like the USSR did almost 70 years ago, facing proponents of fascism, including alleged ideological (grand)children of Bandera's Organization of Ukrainian Nationalists (OUN-B), who were now running the government in Kyiv.[55] Deployment of such a "emotionally and historically loaded" construct allowed Russia, in the eyes of some observers, to prolong the fiction of its official non-involvement as it had been the individuals and not the neighboring state, revolted by the "fascist" trappings of the new Ukraine government, who successfully rebelled against the "Banderite" yoke.[56] Such individuals in May 2014 broke into the Great Patriotic War's Museum in Donetsk to get their hands on the World War II guns displayed there as they hoped to use these in their fight against "fascists."[57] These were allegedly coming to "get you" to Donbas and force the once flourishing region back into the fold of a weak, ungovernable Ukraine – a contrast with the more fondly remembered Soviet Union.[58] Interestingly, Russia returned to the "Banderite" sloganeering during its 2022 (re-)invasion. This time, however, it did away with the local trappings and instead of calling Ukraine by the name of its nationalist figure, it resorted to an outright "Nazi" slur. In this sense, Russia had to "de-Nazify" Ukraine, which was run by "nationalists" who threatened both Russia and the "People's Republics" which emerged after 2014.[59] Initially, it seemed that any hostilities would be concentrated around the territories of the "republics," as Russia recognized them on February 21, 2022, a mere three days before the (re-)invasion, and then sent troops into their territories as alleged "peacekeepers."[60] This could have suggested an intention not to attack Ukraine from three different directions, as had been the case on February 24, 2022, but fight a localized war for winning over the totality of the Donetsk and Luhansk original provinces for the "People's Republics" and achieving a quick and relatively easy victory. Events, however, moved quickly from there, as was evident during the now infamous live televised meeting of the Security Council of Russia with its members claiming that Ukraine had conducted "genocide" against Russians living in the country or preparing its own nuclear program which could constitute a grave threat to Russia.[61] Such wildly inaccurate claims laid the ground for a full-scale war, not just an attempt to enlarge the "People's Republics."

As much as the "Banderite" argument and slogan proved popular in Donbas after 2004, the case for outright separation of the "People's Republics" from Ukraine remained weak (with almost 70 percent of its inhabitants professing a regional, "Donbas," but not automatically Russian identity in 2004).[62] Its proponents were grouped in "small, non-influential and disparate groups with diverse ideological and cultural orientations, including Cossacks, paratroopers (*desantniki*), Orthodox activists, neo-Nazi-neo-pagans, and supporters of neo-fascist publicist Aleksandr Dugin."[63] One such group was called, conveniently, as it later turned out, the "Donetsk Republic." Founded in 2005, its leaders, including the "first prime minister" of the future DNR, took part in summer camps in Russia during which they were allegedly "taught methods of espionage, sabotage and guerrilla tactics."[64] These came in handy around a decade later when activists of this seemingly obscure group were at the forefront of anti-Maidan protests and the so-called "Russian spring" of 2014 in Eastern Ukraine.[65] At the outset of these protests, only approximately 30 percent of the region's inhabitants backed outright separation from Ukraine and more than 50 percent remained in favor of "Ukrainian options," i.e. preservation of the status quo or decentralization. Simultaneously, however, between 40 and 60 percent of the inhabitants were fearful of either Western Ukrainians, the government in Kyiv or "European and American politicians."[66]

Such real or imaginary grievances added to the strong feeling of economic insecurity in the region. In 2013, Donbas was inhabited by about 15 percent of the Ukrainian population and more than 100 coal mines still operated there – a marked decline from the mid-1990s, when this number stood at approximately 250.[67] The region, styling itself on an economic and industrial powerhouse which allegedly worked while "lazy Kyiv protested,"[68] accounted for approximately only 8 percent of Ukraine's GDP.[69] Simultaneously, Donbas, a fiefdom of Yanukovych's *simja* and the bedrock of his Party of Regions, turned into the epicenter of Ukrainian kleptocracy, where in order to think of any social advancement and promotion, one had to join the dominant political clan which controlled 274 of 304 seats in the regional parliaments of Donetsk and Luhansk.[70]

The reality of an outlier and misunderstood region which found itself in an economic decline[71] was confused by a clash of its competing regional, Ukrainian, post-Soviet or pro-Russian/separatist identities, and was politically dominated by a cabal beholden to the country's president, produced a powerful feeling of discontent which was then successfully channeled, in the words of Oksana Mikheieva, "against the Maidan, its values, mythical 'Banderites'."[72] Moreover, it also swept away the dominant local elites, who were replaced by individuals without chance of advancement and promotion opportunities by Yanukovych's kleptocracy, i.e. "minor crime bosses" and "third-rank officials," including "militia [police] officials" and allegedly had "much to gain from a radical upheaval of this kind"[73] as their loyalty had previously been not to the center (Kyiv) but to the local oligarchs or the *simja*.[74] They would not, however, have attempted this without encouragement and assistance from Russia.

Russia: Philosophy and Interests

At this point, one must ask why Russia, apart from the above-mentioned desire to see Ukraine in the Eurasian Economic Union and not associated with the EU, would even bother destabilizing a neighboring country and, in an unprecedented move as far as the twenty-first century is concerned, annexed a part of its territory. Michel Eltchaninoff, who attempted to deconstruct the ideological backbone of Vladimir Putin, the Russian President, provided an answer while studying the writings of relatively unknown, but appreciated at the Kremlin, Russian twentieth century philosophers, especially Ivan Ilyin. Ilyin wrote about a "national dictatorship" which would emerge from the collapse of the Soviet Union, led by a "guide." The guide would rule a country which was akin to "an organism," different from its "imperialist neighbors" who are intent on dismembering it by seizing the likes of Ukraine, the Baltic States, the Caucasus or Central Asia. The preferred method for this dismemberment consisted, in Ilyin's eyes, of "hypocritical championing of values such as 'freedom'."[75]

It is not hard to imagine that Putin could also have seen himself in the role of the guide, and his colleagues from the KGB as his loyal praetorian guard,[76] and the Ukrainian Euromaidan as another "hypocritical" attack on his country. This reading of the international situation locked Russia in a permanent siege mentality in which the Western reaction towards annexation of Crimea is the next step in "policy of containment," dating back to the eighteenth century, which sought to "isolate Russia [… and] to prevent it from occupying the place it rightfully deserved."[77] This line of thinking was clearly on display during the Orange Revolution: for Putin, nothing more but another "attempt to isolate the Russian Federation" by a de facto Western annexation of Ukraine and separating it from Russia who, in his view, was a compliant participant in international politics and had "no intention of annexing anybody."[78] This happened against the backdrop of Putin's statements on the two countries sharing common roots, cultural space, history, tradition, mentality etc.,[79] and e.g. "Russian university textbooks […] routinely [questioned] the territorial integrity of Ukraine," and Russian politicians visited Crimea and openly spoke of its integration with Russia.[80] At the same time, Putin's Russia also stressed the importance of the *Russkij mir* (Russian world) in practice – Moscow's obligation to "look after the Russians who live in other states, even if they do not hold Russian citizenship," which was meant to please the internal (especially the nationalist and/or pious Orthodox Russians) and external (Russian communities in the former Soviet republics) audiences.[81] In its broadest reading, such an approach allowed Russia to claim that anyone speaking Russian was automatically Russian, including, allegedly, 15 million Ukrainians who used this language on a daily basis.[82] This number enabled Russia effectively to construct a narrative on the need to protect its "citizens" and the alleged Ukrainian state's immaturity and its artificial character. The non-agency of Ukraine, as far as international politics is concerned, was easier to construct as Russia, as Bērziņš described it, saw it and Belarus "as [being] part of itself."[83]

In such conditions, the Kremlin had little problem in depicting the post-Euromaidan Kyiv government as junta involved in an "anti-constitutional coup,"[84] which sent "neo-Nazi gangs" ("Banderites") to quash "the Russian spring," a peaceful protest which only turned violent with the Ukrainian invasion of the Eastern territories opposed by the "freedom fighters."[85] At the same time, this alleged junta was nothing more than an understudy of the West, intent on "geopolitical expansion" at the cost of Russia.[86] Given this "aggression," Moscow decided to act so that it would "preserve its regional interests," including basing of the Russian Black Sea fleet in Crimea, and sending a vivid message to the West that Ukraine constitutes "a real red line and it should remain in the Russian sphere of influence."[87] At the same time, this was also a useful decoy from Russia's vast socio-political domestic challenges which were eating away President Putin's popularity throughout 2013.[88] Moreover, the Ukrainian armed forces were underfunded, incompetently led by ministers who were in fact Russian nationals (such as Pavel Lebediev, who led the ministry between 2012 and 2014 and later fled to Russia),[89] and penetrated by the Russian security ser-vices, which only seemed to suggest that any aggressive actions by Russia would pay off.[90] These actions took the form of a "hybrid war."

Hybrid War

As Rácz noted in 2015, hybrid war combines elements of diplomatic, economic, information and political methods of war waging with open warfare but also "concealed, non-open use of force, such as paramilitary and civilian insurgent units," attacks on the adversary's critical infrastructure, including via the reli-ance of special forces deployed in large numbers.[91] Originally, the term was coined in the 1990s to described half regular warfare waged by non-state actors. Its appropriation by the Russian military doctrine broadened its optics and intro-duced many of the diplomatic or economic measures which would be beyond the capabilities of non-state actors such as insurgents.[92]

Rácz divided Russia's ideal hybrid war into three phases, i.e.

1. preparatory (no violence is conducted, concentrates on infiltration of the state administration, economy and the armed forces of the adversary; establishment of "friendly" voices in the adversary country, e.g. NGOs, media; induction of dissatisfaction with the central government in the adversary country while supporting local separatist movements – also via bribery and recruitment of the local chieftains, such as oligarchs or criminals, to Russia's cause);
2. attack (escalation of the above-mentioned tensions by organization of anti-government clashes and demonstrations in the adversary country; introduc-tion of special military forces to "deliver the first sabotage attacks, cap-ture the first administrative buildings in the targeted regions (with the active or passive support of corrupt local officials and police), in coopera-tion with local criminal groups"; launching of a disinformation campaign in the adversary country; positioning of the armed forces on the border of the attacked country – to provide cover for the saboteurs and weaken the central government's attempt to resist the Russian pressure; disablement of the central government's authority in the restive region by occupation of the administrative buildings and the critical infrastructure; disorientation of the international public opinion via disinformation operations; establishment of an "alternative political power" center); and;
3. stabilization (organization of a "referendum" confirming the region's seces-sion from the adversary country).[93]

Such a scenario for an ideal hybrid war would see Russia, a stronger force and an aggressor, taking on features and qualities of the insurgents, a weaker side in the conflict, but also allowing for a modicum of deniability as Moscow attempted not to claim the "polite people" of Crimea nor the "separatists" of Donbas as its own.[94] This linear plan for rolling out a conflict in stages, however, was interrupted by "a well-known military history lesson" in which the Ukrainian army was able to crush the abetted "rebels," who were only saved by a direct military intervention which transformed the hybrid into "a conventional, albeit limited interstate war."[95] This intervention was, just like during the Crimean operation,[96] predictably denied by Russia.[97] All of this happened against the backdrop of arrivals of Russian nationals in the ranks of the "separatists," i.e. undercover active members of the Russian security services like the Russian Federal Security Service (FSB) or GRU, sometimes with some Donbas pedigree, or even a Ukrainian passport, "ideologically mobilized Russian nationalists," and veterans of the wars in Afghanistan, Chechnya and Georgia, mobilized via the conscription offices of the Russian military in Russia proper. Their influx effectively meant a coup within a coup as they pushed aside the pro-"separatist" locals who played leading roles in the largely failed events of the "Russian spring." By August 2014, however, this Russification was again put on the back burner as more local leaders were coming to the force, including Alexander Zakharchenko, who became the prime minister of the DNR in August 2014. He might have received his post in order for Moscow to cover up for the influx of the regular Russian troops in August, whose presence in Donbas he later acknowledged.[98]

Hybrid Postmodernity

While invading Ukraine, be it in a hybrid or more conventional manner, Russia broke the following international agreements: the Budapest Memorandum, which had it as one of the guarantors of Ukraine's independence and sovereignty, and its borders; the bilateral Treaty of Friendship, Cooperation and Partnership between the Russian Federation and Ukraine from 1997 in which it affirmed "the inviolability of their existing borders;" and the 2003 agreement between the Russian Federation and Ukraine on the Russian-Ukrainian border.[99] While attempting to limit the damage arising from these deeds, Moscow waged a proactive disinformation campaign aimed not only at Russian-speaking but also external, i.e. non-Russian and non-Russian-speaking, audiences in the West. The campaign had a postmodern tinge to it as it developed into an amorphous construct cutting across ideological and political divides. It would attempt to please different, at times contradictory, constituencies, such as the European far right with tales of Euromaidan protestors as stooges of the EU and the European far left. with portrayals of Ukraine as an agent of American imperialism.[100] In practice, this meant that, just as President Yanukovych was briefing his Western interlocutors on the alleged fascist and anti-Semitic character of the Euromaidan,[101] the Russian television would speak of "gay Europe," which allegedly encroached upon Ukraine.[102] The competing narratives helped Moscow mobilize a wide variety of individuals to support the "People's Republics," including "imperial monarchists, ethnic nationalists, international communists, saints, tsars and Bolshevik leaders"[103] or "fun-house mirror of contemporary Russia. Bearded Cossacks in parade dress, tattooed skinhead

bodybuilders, bearded philosophers, camouflage-wearing, beer-bellied mercenaries, priests in cassocks, Chechens."[104]

By default, this postmodernity was later consequently extended onto the
"People's Republics" which became an "amalgam" of Soviet communism, and
nostalgia for it, and Russian nationalism and these both seemed to co-exist under
their roofs.[105] Marlene Laruelle also noted that the original Novorossiya, an
entity which was meant to precede the "People's Republics," combined not two
but three ideological paradigms, i.e. post-Soviet (red), Tsarist nostalgia mixed
with ultraconservative orthodoxy (white), revolutionary, anti-systemic fascism
(brown).[106] All of these played a role in the original "Russian spring," which
saw Novorossiya as a chance for the whole of Russia to be reborn – cleansed of
Western influences, oligarchs, "spiritual and moral decadence," and back to its
Eurasian identity. Such a reading of the events in Eastern Ukraine was even too
much for Novorossiya's alleged backers in Moscow who, after initial enthusiasm for the project with President Putin mentioning Novorossiya in his speech
in April 2014, seemed content with exporting some of its above-mentioned
"fun-house" to Donbas but were not keen on empowering it enough so that
Novorossiya's success would later turn against the Kremlin.[107] Here the success of
the Russian hybrid postmodernity was brought to an abrupt end by its instigator.
The "People's Republics," postmodern or not, however, persevered.

Outcome: the "People's Republics"

The two "People's Republics" which emerged out of the conflict do not comprise the whole of the Ukrainian Donbas and only a third of the original Donetsk
and Luhansk *oblasti* (provinces). They include Donbas' most built up and densely
populated areas and its "industrial assets" but are still inhabited, due to an unprecedented population displacement and a brain drain, by less than three million people, i.e. less than half of the provinces' pre-2014 population.[108] They constitute
nothing more than a rump of the original Novorossiya, which in the spring of 2014
was meant to encompass the whole of the south and the east of Ukraine.[109] In this
sense, the DNR and the LNR effectively are downgrades as far as the initial plan, if
there had been any, was concerned and "are almost fully dependent on Russia." As
Nikolaus von Twickel argues in his work, they effectively are "puppet states" and
their aim, as articulated by their leaders, is to join Russia rather than become independent, which only strengthens Moscow's hegemonial hand in these territories.
What is more, Moscow is said to be subsidizing both with around €1 billion a year.
Surprisingly, this does not mean that Russia enjoys full control in the DNR and/
or the LNR, as its local chieftains continue their infighting and Russian "curators"
of different separatist factions clash with each other in Moscow.[110] Evidence of that
might be, for example, the recent surprise announcement by Margarita Simonyan,
editor of *Russia Today* – while visiting Donetsk, for "Mother Russia, [to] take
Donbas home!"[111] This call, as expected, fell on deaf ears as other "curators,"
such as the Russian security services and the Kremlin itself, display no interest in

following up on such proposals. Instead, they seem to be content with the trend of tightening control over the "People's Republics," e.g. via a coup in the LNR in November 2017 and perhaps even a "convenient" assassination (whose authors remain unknown) of the DNR leader in August 2018.[112] Both cases saw the emergence of leaders less independent and more pliable to Russia.[113]

The reality of the two "People's Republics" is grim, to say the least[114]: they are unrecognized by Moscow (only South Ossetia, another pro-Russian and widely unrecognized statelet,[115] recognized the "People's Republics"), their citizens do not enjoy rule of law, no viable opposition is functioning there, elections are rigged, and any dissent is violently repressed.[116] The Republics conduct their trade via the above-mentioned South Ossetia to avoid sanctions, but many of their inhabitants, mostly the elderly, still cross the line of contact, demarcating these from Ukraine, so they can register on the Kyiv government held side to collect their Ukrainian pensions.[117]

Interestingly, the Russian non-recognition does not prevent Moscow from claiming the "People's Republics" are "quasi states" whose inhabitants rebelled against e.g. Ukraine proper denying them a right to their language (Russian). This stops short of an outright official endorsement of the rebellion and the subsequent "separation" as the international law does not recognize such an act without the endorsement of the mother state (Ukraine). Consequently, and in line with the Minsk Agreements, Russia effectively prefers the two "People's Republics" to be integrated back into Ukraine as de facto autonomous provinces beyond Kyiv's control, and potentially, ever-present spoilers which could e.g. frustrate attempts at further integration with the West.[118] Theoretically, Ukrainian President Volodymyr Zelenskyi, elected in 2019, was said to have been more amenable to implementing the above-mentioned agreements in this respect but effectively backtracked after vehement opposition from the veteran/victims of the war lobby. Such an outcome might also, paradoxically, as some argue, suit Russia as no movement on the issue deepens the chasm in the Ukrainian society and continues to perplex and tie down the resources of the country's decision-makers.[119] Effectively, contact between Kyiv and the "People's Republics" is seen as beyond the pale for the former as it would be seen as granting them recognition and legitimacy and, as von Twickel writes, is limited to the Minsk Trilateral Contact Group, "which meets under OSCE mediation once every two weeks in the Belarusian capital," with Ukraine represented there not by a government representatives but by "emissaries" appointed by the president.[120] What is more, the relationship suffers from the 2017 Ukrainian "blockade" of the "republics" and the subsequent "nationalizations" of the enterprises still functioning on the other side of the contact line by the DNR and the LNR, respectively.[121]

Despite the fact that the "People's Republics" are now a semi-permanent feature of the political landscape, even if in unrecognized status, and a successful takeover of Crimea, the outcome of the war so far is hardly an outright Russian victory. Moscow managed to "push a lot of the Ukrainian population against" itself, failed, so far, to see Kyiv "reintegrate" the "Republics" into its territory, and saw a spectacular collapse of the Novorossiya project. Moreover, Ukraine did finally sign the association agreement with the EU. At the same, the DNR and the LNR remain a "thorn" in Kyiv's side, which will prevent Ukraine from joining the EU and/or NATO.[122]

Conclusion

The Russian decision effectively to re-invade Ukraine in late February 2022 brought home to many the reality of the fact that, since 2014, a major war has been taking place in Eastern Europe. It might have been, as this chapter has demonstrated, hybrid in nature but nonetheless it was a full-scale state versus state conflict and not a civil war in Ukraine. However, while limited to Donbas, an odd one out type of a region in Ukraine, with a contested and an unhappy relationship with the country's center and its Western part, the war seemed to have been a localized affair, of little interest to Western observers. The fact that some of its inhabitants either had connections to Russia or came from Russia in the first place, and thus, spoke Russian, might have comforted many that the case for "separatism" in Ukraine had always been real. As this chapter has showed, however, such a claim is relatively ungrounded as the events of 2014 were not a "Russian spring" conducted in a bottom-up manner against a hated regime residing in far-away Kyiv. In fact, the local "separatists" had been weak, and the upheaval was, to a large degree, on top of the anti-Euromaidan feeling in the region, a revolt against the socio-political order of Donbas. This part of Ukraine had ironically been dominated by a pro-Russian kleptocratic organization of the then Ukrainian President, Viktor Yanukovych, who hails from the region. Add to that the direct Russian prodding and intervention by first, "volunteers," special services and forces and, finally, the country's military, and one is faced with a perfect storm which was to produce a larger statelet to be called Novorossiya. This was to function as a large thorn in Ukraine's side, effectively rendering it economically unfeasible. Ukrainian resistance, however, limited the Russian gains to just parts of the two provinces of Donetsk and Luhansk. At the same time, Ukraine was unable to win back control over the totality of its territory and both sides effectively froze the conflict from the 2015–16 period.

Notes

1 *BBC News*, "Ukraine: Avdiivka, the front line of Europe's 'forgotten war'," January 31, 2017, https://www.bbc.com/news/av/world-europe-38818543, accessed: February 23, 2021.
2 Kenneth S. Yalowitz, Denis Corboy, and William Courtney, "Hitting the Pause Button: The 'Frozen Conflict' Dilemma in Ukraine," *Wilson Center Publication*, accessed: February 23, 2021.
3 Olha Polishchuk and Franklin Holcomb, "Breaking the pattern: the relative success of the latest ceasefire agreement in Ukraine," *ACLED*, November 24, 2020, https://acleddata.com/2020/11/24/breaking-the-pattern-the-relative-success-of-the-latest-ceasefire-agreement-in-ukraine/, accessed: February 23, 2021.

4 Organization for Security and Co-operation in Europe Special Monitoring Mission to Ukraine, *2020 Trends and Observations*, January 28, 2021, https://www.osce.org/special-monitoring-mission-to-ukraine/476809, accessed: February 23, 2021 for above-mentioned data.

5 RFE/RL, "Death Toll Up to 13,000 in Ukraine Conflict, Says UN Rights Office," *Radio Free Europe/Radio Liberty*, February 26, 2019, https://www.rferl.org/a/death-toll-up-to-13-000-in-ukraine-conflict-says-un-rights-office/29791647.html, accessed: February 23, 2021.

6 See https://edition.cnn.com/europe/live-news/ukraine-russia-news-02-24-22-intl/index.html, accessed: April 12, 2022, for the updates from *CNN* on the conflict's first day.

7 *United Nations Human Rights Office of the High Commissioner*, "Ukraine: civilian casualty update 24 March 2022," https://www.ohchr.org/en/news/2022/03/ukraine-civilian-casualty-update-24-march-2022, accessed: April 12, 2022.

8 *BBC News*, "Ukraine War: Kremlin spokesman Peskov admits 'significant' Russian losses," April 8, 2022, https://www.bbc.com/news/world-europe-61033173, accessed: April 12, 2022.

9 Sabine Fischer, *The Donbas Conflict: Opposing Interests and Narratives, Difficult Peace Process* (Berlin: SWP, April 2019), 5, https://www.swp-berlin.org/fileadmin/contents/products/research_papers/2019RP05_fhs.pdf, accessed: February 23, 2021.

10 For more on the Maidan or Euromaidan protests see Michał Kacewicz, *Sotnie Wolności. Ukraina od Majdanu do Donbasu* (Warszawa: Ringier Axel Springer Polska), 204.

11 Katri Pynnöniemi, "The Metanarratives of Russian Strategic Deception," in Katri Pynnöniemi and András Rácz, eds., *Fog of Falsehood: Russian Strategy of Deception and the Conflict in Ukraine* (The Finnish Institute of International Affairs Report 45, 2016) 94–95, https://www.fiia.fi/wp-content/uploads/2017/01/fiiareport45_fogoffalsehood.pdf?fbclid=IwAR2KBIqIsseqsE0tPHD39W7xYlr85dZaiyymWFGKvmYl3oAZG TuJPtjEORo, accessed: February 25, 2021.

12 Anatolij V. Pronin, "A treaty on accession of the Republic of Crimea and Sebastopol to the Russian Federation. Unofficial English translation with little commentary," (March 2014, self-published), https://www.academia.edu/6481091/A_treaty_on_accession_of_the_Republic_of_Crimea_and_Sebastopol_to_the_Russian_Federation_Unofficial_English_translation_with_little_commentary, accessed: March 2, 2021.

13 Paweł Pieniążek, "Strange war. Russian-Ukrainian Conflict in the Donbas," Speech at the Yale University, December 9, 2015 (Pieniążek, an author focusing on the Donbas and the newly emerged "People's Republics," whose work is cited throughout this chapter, kindly sent the text of the speech to the author).

14 For more on Girkin and his reign of terror in Slovyansk see Chris Miller, "The Executioners of Slovyansk," *Radio Free Europe/Radio Liberty*, July 23, 2020, https://www.rferl.org/a/the-executioners-of-slovyansk/30743132.html, accessed: March 2, 2021.

15 Nikolaus von Twickel, *The State of the Donbass: A study of eastern Ukraine's separatist-held areas* (Brussels: CEPS, 2019), 5, https://3dcftas.eu/publications/the-state-of-the-donbass-a-study-of-eastern-ua-separatist-held-areas, accessed: February 23, 2021.

16 Lucian Kim, "The Battle of Ilovaisk: Details of a Massacre Inside Rebel-Held Eastern Ukraine," *Newsweek*, November 4, 2014, https://www.newsweek.com/2014/11/14/battle-ilovaisk-details-massacre-inside-rebel-held-eastern-ukraine-282003.html, accessed: March 2, 2021.

17 Nikolaus von Twickel, "The State of Play in the Donbass," *The Moscow Times*, March 11, 2019, https://www.themoscowtimes.com/2019/03/11/the-state-of-play-in-the-donbass-a64764, accessed: March 2, 2021.

18 Fischer, *The Donbas Conflict*, 12.

19 *Reuters*, "Russia will not pause military operation in Ukraine for peace talks," April 11, 2022, https://www.reuters.com/world/europe/russia-will-not-pause-military-operation-ukraine-peace-talks-2022-04-11/, accessed: April 12, 2022.

20 The Orange Revolution was a political crisis, featuring a string of protests centred in Kyiv, in the aftermath of the 2004 rigged presidential election. It pitted Viktor Yuschenko, former prime minister and head of the central bank, popular in Western Ukraine, seen as a pro-Western moderniser and Viktor Yanukovych, of Donbas and widely seen as a pro-Russian candidate. The former eventually triumphed after a repeated run-off vote. Author's interviewees often remarked that since then many outsiders began to perceive Ukraine as a country divided along political, ideological and linguistic lines in which an allegedly pro-democratic, pro-Western and Ukrainian-speaking West was always competing for primacy with the autocratic, backward, criminal and pro-Russian and Russian-speaking East. This viewpoint was especially augmented by production of maps in which regions favouring Yuschenko would be coloured in orange, and Yanukovych in blue – the colours of their respective movements but also a striking visual contrast which allowed some authors to ponder whether "partition" of Ukraine would solve its problems. See, e.g.: Ethan S, "Could partition solve Ukraine's problems?," *openDemocracy*, February 19, 2010, https://www.opendemocracy.net/en/odr/could-partition-solve-ukraines-problems/, accessed: February 18, 2021. For an authoritative study of the Orange Revolution see: Andrew Wilson, *Ukraine's Orange Revolution* (London: Yale University Press, 2005).

21 Lucian Kim, "Should Putin fear the man who 'pulled the trigger of war' in Ukraine?" *Reuters*, November 25, 2014, https://www.reuters.com/article/idUS368525725520141125, accessed: February 18, 2021.

22 Natalia Shapovalova, Balázs Jarábik, "How Eastern Ukraine Is Adapting and Surviving: The Case of Kharkiv," *Carnegie Europe Paper*, 12 September 2018, https://carnegieeurope.eu/2018/09/12/how-eastern-ukraine-is-adapting-and-surviving-case-of-kharkiv-pub-77216, accessed: February 18, 2021.

23 See: David Frum, "The Ukrainian City That Refuses to Implode," *The Atlantic*, 19 May 2014, https://www.theatlantic.com/international/archive/2014/05/odessa-the-ukrainian-city-that-refuses-to-implode/371121/, accessed: February 21, 2021.

24 Initially, the separatist movement was energized by the idea of re-establishment of Novorossiya or the New Russia which was a north of the Black Sea province of the tsarist Russia. This concept assumed a swathe of support for separatism and then joining with Russia in wide parts of Eastern Ukraine. See Thomas de Waal and Nikolaus von Twickel, *Beyond Frozen Conflict. Scenarios for the Separatist. Disputes of Eastern Europe* (Brussels: CEPS, 2020), 104–105.

25 Andrew Wilson, "The Donbas in 2014: Explaining Civil Conflict Perhaps, but not Civil War," *Europe-Asia Studies* 68, no. 4 (2016): 631–633. Girkin himself confirms this in a series of interviews after he had been ordered back to Moscow by a close aide of Vladimir Putin, and an alleged "curator" of Moscow's involvement in the war in Ukraine, Vladislav Surkov. See https://twitter.com/den_kazansky/status/1353964594914537472?s=20, tweet by Deniz Kazansky of January 26, 2021, one of Ukraine's most astute commentators on the war, originally from Donbas, where he linked Girkin's latest interview, accessed: February 18, 2021.

26 Maryna Rabinovych and Hanna Shelest, "Introduction: Regional Diversity, Decentralization, and Conflict in and around Ukraine," in Maryna Rabinovych and Hanna Shelest, eds., *Decentralization, Regional Diversity, and Conflict. The Case of Ukraine* (London: Palgrave Macmillan, 2020), 3.

27 Author's WhatsApp exchange with Pavel Klymenko, formerly of FARE network, December 15, 2020.

28 Ethan S. Burger, "Could partition solve Ukraine's problems?," *openDemocracy*, February 19, 2010, https://www.opendemocracy.net/en/odr/could-partition-solve-ukraines-problems/, accessed: February 18, 2021.

29 Author's signal exchange with Piotr Pogorzelski, a Polish journalist who has been focusing on Ukraine for more than 20 years, December 16, 2020.

30 David Dalton, "How did the Ukrainian oligarchy keep going after Euromaidan?," *vox ukraine*, February 6, 2021, https://voxukraine.org/en/how-did-the-ukrainian-oligarchy-keep-going-after-euromaidan/?s=09, accessed: February 23, 2021.

31 Zbigniew Parafianowicz and Michał Potocki, *Wilki Żyją Ponad Prawem. Jak Janukowycz Przegrał Ukrainę* (Wołowiec: Czarne, 2015), 1547, Kindle.

32 Karolina Baca-Pogorzelska and Michał Potocki, *Czarne Złoto: Wojny o węgiel z Donbasu* (Wołowiec: Czarne, 2020) for more on Yanukovych's rationale for negotiating with the European Union.

33 Zbigniew Parafianowicz and Michał Potocki, *Wilki Żyją Ponad Prawem. Jak Janukowycz Przegrał Ukrainę* (Wołowiec: Czarne, 2015), 3064, Kindle. The book's chap. 4 ("Bandido: Why the System Collapsed So Quickly") provides a fascinating account of how the decision was made to introduce brutal police repression against the protestors.

34 Such an agreement would effectively terminate some of the illicit business and transnational/cross-border (Russo-Ukraine) which were profitable to e.g. members of the Russian elite. Consequently, they, i.e. Russian oligarchs, were pressurising Kremlin to oppose such developments not only on the grounds of geopolitics but also business. Author's phone interview with Kacper Wańczyk, PhD student at Kozminski University, Poland and a former diplomat at the Ukraine desk within the Polish ministry of foreign affairs, December 16, 2020.

35 Paweł Pieniążek, "Strange war."

36 Author's phone interview with Anna Maria Dyner, Polish Institute of International Affairs (PISM) expert on Russia's military, December 15, 2021.

37 Władysław Andrzej Serczyk, *Na dalekiej Ukrainie: dzieje Kozaczyzny do 1648 roku* (Kraków: Wydawnictwo Literackie, 1984) for more on the "wild fields."

38 Paweł Pieniążek, "Kuromiya o Donbasie: Dziki Wschód oferuje wolność," *Krytyka Polityczna*, August 20, 2015, https://krytykapolityczna.pl/swiat/kuromiya-o-donbasie-dziki-wschod-oferuje-wolnosc-rozmowa/, accessed: February 25, 2021.

39 Ibid.

40 Baca-Pogorzelska and Potocki, *Czarne Złoto*, 20.

41 Grzegorz Motyka, *Ukraińska partyzantka 1942–1960. Działalność Organizacji Ukraińskich Nacjonalistów i Ukraińskiej Powstańczej Armii* (Warszawa: Rytm, 2006), for a comprehensive study of the UPA's history.

42 Grzegorz Szymanik and Julia Wizowska, *Po Północy w Doniecku* (Warszawa: Agora, 2016), 240, Kindle.

43 Paweł Pieniążek, Kuromiya o Donbasie: Dziki Wschód oferuje wolność, *Krytyka Polityczna*, August 20, 2015, https://krytykapolityczna.pl/swiat/kuromiya-o-donbasie-dziki-wschod-oferuje-wolnosc-rozmowa/, accessed: February 25, 2021.

44 Baca-Pogorzelska and Potocki, *Czarne Złoto*, 15.

45 Szymanik and Wizowska, *Po Północy w Doniecku*, 291.

46 Hiroaki Kuromiya, *Freedom and Terror in the Donbas: A Ukrainian-Russian Borderland, 1870s–1990s* (Cambridge: Cambridge University Press, 1998), 116, quoted in Wilson, *Ukraine's Orange Revolution*, 637.

47 Baca-Pogorzelska and Potocki, *Czarne Złoto*, 22.

48 Paweł Pieniążek, "Kuromiya o Donbasie: Dziki Wschód oferuje wolność," *Krytyka Polityczna*, August 20, 2015, https://krytykapolityczna.pl/swiat/kuromiya-o-donbasie-dziki-wschod-oferuje-wolnosc-rozmowa/, accessed: February 25, 2021.

49 Baca-Pogorzelska and Potocki, *Czarne Złoto*, 22.

50 Wilson, *Ukraine's Orange Revolution*, 638.

51 For more on Leninopad see Neils Ackermann and Sebastien Gobert, *Looking for Lenin* (London: FUEL, 2017).

52 Stepan Bandera, one of the key leaders of Ukrainian nationalists before World War II, was associated with Western Ukraine, where his OUN-B, Organization of Ukrainian Nationalists-Bandera, attempted to establish a pro-German independent Ukraine in the Summer of 1941. This failed attempt, and unsuccessful political and military

OUN-B forays into Eastern Ukraine during and after World War II, augmented the organization's unpopularity in parts of Ukraine originally less associated with the country's nationalism (i.e. Central or Eastern parts). The Soviet Union and the Russian or Eastern Ukrainian "political technologists" of the late twentieth and early twenty-first centuries built up on this legacy while further smearing the already controversial image of Bandera, his organization and Western Ukraine in general in the eyes of the Central and Eastern Ukrainians. This state of affairs allowed the remnants of OUN-B and other Ukrainian nationalists consequently to develop a defensive mechanism in which any critique aimed at their dealings with Nazi Germany before or after 1941 as either Soviet and subsequently Russian propaganda. See Grzegorz Rossoliński-Liebe, *Stepan Bandera: the Life and Afterlife of a Ukrainian Nationalist: Fascism, Genocide and Cult* (Stuttgart: ibidem-Verlag/ibidem Press, 2014) for a biography of Bandera and a discussion of the above-mentioned points.

53 Wilson, *Ukraine's Orange Revolution*, 639–40.
54 Anton Shekhovtsov, "From electoral success to revolutionary failure," *Eurozine*, March 5, 2014, https://www.eurozine.com/from-electoral-success-to-revolutionary-failure/, accessed: February 25, 2021.
55 "The Boris Nemtsov Report in English, in full length: 'Putin. The War,' about the Involvement of Russia in the Eastern Ukraine conflict and the Crimea," *European Union Foreign Affairs* Journal, Special Edition (May 2015), https://archive.org/stream/B-001-004-132/EUFAJ-Special-NemtsovReport-150521_djvu.txt, accessed: February 25, 2021.
56 Pynnöniemi, "The Metanarratives," 72.
57 Peter Pomerantsev, *Nothing is True and Everything is Possible* (London: Faber and Faber, 2015), 1604, Kindle.
58 Author's phone interview with Agnieszka Lichnerowicz, Poland's Radio Tok Fm reporter, former correspondent in Ukraine, including Donbas, December 17, 2020.
59 Rachel Treisman, "Putin's claim of fighting against Ukraine 'neo-Nazis' distorts history, scholars say," *NPR*, March 1, 2022, https://www.npr.org/2022/03/01/1083677765/putin-denazify-ukraine-russia-history, accessed: April 12, 2022.
60 "Russia recognizes independence of Ukraine separatist regions," *Deutsche Welle*, February 21, 2022, https://www.dw.com/en/russia-recognizes-independence-of-ukraine-separatist-regions/a-60861963, accessed: April 13, 2022.
61 Mark Galeotti, "The Personal Politics of Putin's Security Council Meeting," February 22, 2022, https://www.themoscowtimes.com/2022/02/22/the-personal-politics-of-putins-security-council-meeting-a76522, accessed: April 13, 2022.
62 Wilson, *Ukraine's Orange Revolution*, 638.
63 Nikolay Mitrokhin, "Infiltration, Instruction, Invasion: Russia's War in the Donbass," *Journal of Soviet and Post-Soviet Politicsa and Society* 1, no. 1 (2015): 219, 222, https://spps-jspps.autorenbetreuung.de/files/07-mitrokhin.pdf, accessed: February 22, 2021. This publication is a translated, expanded and revised version of an article previously published in Russian: "Grubye liudi," Grani.ru, August 27, 2014; and in German: "Infiltration, Instruktion, Invasion. Russlands Krieg in der Ukraine," *Osteuropano* 8 (2014): 3–16.
64 Anton Shekhovtsov, "The 'Ukraine crisis' is a long-planned operation," *Anton Shekhovtsov's Blog*, August 29, 2014, http://anton-shekhovtsov.blogspot.com/2014/08/the-ukraine-crisis-is-long-planned.html, accessed: February 25, 2021.
65 Paweł Pieniążek, *Pozdrowienia z Noworosji* (Warszawa: Krytyka Polityczna, 2015) for more on the "Russian spring."
66 Wilson, *Ukraine's Orange Revolution*, 642–643.
67 See von Twickel, *The State of the Donbass*, 17.
68 Szymanik and Wizowska, *Po Północy w Doniecku*, 322.
69 Fischer, *The Donbas Conflict*, 7.
70 Konstantin Skorkin, *A Counter-Elite Takes Power: The New Leaders of the Donbas*, Carnegie, February 16, 2018, https://carnegie.ru/commentary/75549, accessed: February 22, 2021.

71 Marci Shore, *Ukraińska noc: Rewolucja jako doświadczenie* (Warszawa: Krytyka Polityczna, 2017), 2334 on how "mainstream" Ukraine used to look down on Donbas with whom it was hard to have an "intellectual conversation."

72 Wilson, *Ukraine's Orange Revolution*, 642.

73 Mitrokhin, "Infiltration, Instruction, Invasion," 222.

74 Author's WhatsApp exchange with with a Ukrainian political analyst who wished to remain anonymous, December 16, 2020.

75 Michel Eltchaninoff, *Inside the Mind of Vladimir Putin* (London: Hurst, 2018), 639–657, Kindle.

76 Catherin Belton, *Putin's People: How the KGB Took Back Russia and Then Took On the West* (New York: Farrar, Straus and Giroux, 2020) for more on how this guard came to life and perceived itself after the fall of the Soviet Union.

77 Eltchaninoff, *Inside the Mind of Vladimir Putin*, 894.

78 Ibid. 1714.

79 Ibid. 1697, 1705, 1732.

80 Anton Shekhovtsov, "The 'Ukraine crisis' is a long-planned operation," *Anton Shekhovtsov's Blog*, August 29, 2014, http://anton-shekhovtsov.blogspot.com/2014/08/the-ukraine-crisis-is-long-planned.html, accessed: February 25, 2021.

81 Eltchaninoff, *Inside the Mind of Vladimir Putin*, 1823, 1844.

82 According to Anton Moiseienko, research fellow at RUSI, this is a highly inaccurate reading of the situation as Russian-speaking parts of Ukraine, e.g. Kyiv, are often in no way "pro-Russian" nor its inhabitants feel any special connection to Russia. In his view, linguistic lines never really neatly translated into political divides as e.g. many of Ukrainian nationalists, including leading members of the Azov movement, come from the allegedly Russophone East of the country. Author's interview with Moiseienko, December 22, 2020.

83 Jānis Bērziņš, "Russia's New Generation Warfare in Ukraine: Implications for Latvian Defense Policy," *Policy Paper*, no. 2 (April 2014), National Defence Academy of Latvia Center for Security and Strategic Research, p. 1.

84 Pynnöniemi, "The Metanarratives," 82.

85 Lucian Kim, "Should Putin fear the man who 'pulled the trigger of war' in Ukraine?," *Reuters*, November 25, 2014, https://www.reuters.com/article/idUS368525725520141125, accessed: March 1, 2021.

86 Pynnöniemi, "The Metanarratives," 84–85.

87 Bērziņš, "Russia's New Generation Warfare in Ukraine," 3.

88 Author's phone interview with Ola Cichowlas, AFP correspondent in Moscow, December 23, 2020. For more details on the issue of president Putin's ratings see "The Boris Nemtsov Report in English," 6.

89 Author's phone interview with Piotr Andrusieczko, a *Gazeta Wyborcza* and *Outriders* correspondent in Kyiv, December 14, 2020.

90 Roger N. McDermott, *Brothers Disunited: Russia's Use of Military Power in Ukraine* (Fort Leavenworth: FMSO Monographs, 2015), 5, https://www.act.nato.int/images/stories/events/2015/sfpdpe/sfpdpe15_rr01.pdf, accessed: March 1, 2021.

91 András Rácz, "Russia's Hybrid War in Ukraine Breaking the Enemy's Ability to Resist," The Finnish Institute of International Affairs (FIIA), FIIA Report 43, (2015), 27, 36, https://www.fiia.fi/wp-content/uploads/2017/01/fiiareport43.pdf.

92 Ibid. 43.

93 Ibid. 59, 63, 67.

94 Mitrokhin also divides the war in Eastern Ukraine into 3 phases but focuses more on who played the key roles on the ground, i.e. in phase 1 (April 2014) – "special forces (spetsnaz) troops and secret service officials supported criminals from the Donbass region and Russian nationalists who had traveled in from Russia with the aim of seizing power in several cities in the Donbass region"; phase 2 (from mid-May 2014) – "huge numbers of former fighters from the wars in Afghanistan and Chechnya and politicized

supporters of Russian neo-imperialist organizations recruited by conscription officers in Russia streamed into Ukraine." This was followed by arrival of the regular army in the second week of August, and phase 3. Their task was to force a ceasefire, enshrined in the Minsk Protocol. See Mitrokhin, "Infiltration, Instruction, Invasion," 222.

 95 Ibid. 68.
 96 "The Boris Nemtsov Report in English," 11.
 97 See von Twickel, *The State of the Donbass*, 7; McDermott, *Brothers Disunited*, 28.
 98 Mitrokhin, "Infiltration, Instruction, Invasion, 223–245. See also the above quoted "Nemtsov Report," p. 24 for testimonies of Russian who fought in Ukraine.
 99 See n 53, 14.
100 Pomerantsev, *Nothing is True and Everything is Possible*, 3310, 3244–51.
101 See chap. 3 in this volume for more on the issue of right-wing extremism in the ranks of the Euromaidan participants, and subsequently, Ukrainian volunteer battalions.
102 Pomerantsev, *Nothing is True and Everything is Possible*, 3244.
103 Shore, *Ukraińska noc*, 1604–1610.
104 Charles Clover, *Black Wind, White Snow. The Rise of Russia's New Nationalism*, London: Yale University Press, 2016, kindle edition, 327.
105 Wilson, *Ukraine's Orange Revolution*, 636.
106 Marlene Laruelle, "The three colors of Novorossiya, or the Russian nationalist mythmaking of the Ukrainian crisis," *Post-Soviet Affairs* 32 no. 1 (2015): 55, 56.
107 Ibid. 57, 61–66.
108 See von Twickel, *The State of the Donbass*. 1.
109 Nikolay Mitrokhin, "Infiltration, Instruction, Invasion: Russia's War in the Donbass," 232.
110 See von Twickel, *The State of the Donbass*, 2.
111 See https://twitter.com/mjluxmoore/status/1354787089255165960?s=20, a tweet with a video clip from Simonyan's address of January 28, 2021 from the twitter account of Matthew Luxmoore, RFE/RL correspondent, accessed: February 26, 2021.
112 Konstantin Skorkin, "The Demise of the Counter-Elite: How Zakharchenko's Killing Will Change Donbas," *Carnegie Moscow Centre*, September 4, 2018, https://carnegie.ru/commentary/77158, accessed: February 26, 2021.
113 See von Twickel, *The State of the Donbass*.
114 See e.g. Szymanik and Wizowska, *Po Północy w Doniecku*; Pieniążek, *Pozdrowienia z Noworosji* or Tomáš Forró, *Donbas: Svadobný apartmán v hoteli Vojna*, (Bratislava: Dennik N, 2019) for more on the daily reality of the DNR and the LNR.
115 For more on South Ossetia and other non-recognized states such as Abkhazia or Nagorno-Karabakh see Tomasz Grzywaczewski, *Granice Marzeń. O państwach nieuznawanych* (Wołowiec: Czarne 2018).
116 von Twickel, *The State of the Donbass*, remains the best source on the "People's Republics." For more on internal repression there see Nikolai Mitrokhin, *Extra-judicial and judicial methods and forms of "law implementation" used by the eastern Ukrainian "People's Republics'" "law enforcement agencies" in the period 01.06.2015 – 01.06.2016* (Berlin: DRA, 2017).
117 Norwegian Refugee Council, "Access to Pensions for Conflict Affected Persons and IDPs in Ukraine: Facts and Solutions," https://www.humanitarianresponse.info/sites/www.humanitarianresponse.info/files/documents/files/10_2020_nrc_advocacy_paper_on_pensions_eng.pdf, accessed: February 26, 2021.
118 Stanislav Secrieru, "The Silence of the Guns: Can the Cease-Fire in Donbass Last?," *PISM Policy Paper*, no. 38(140) (November 10, 2015): 6, https://pism.pl/publica-tions/PISM_Policy_Paper_no__38__140___The_Silence_of_the_Guns__Can_the_Cease_Fire_in_Donbass_Last_, accessed: March 1, 2021.
119 Author's phone interview with Dr Tomasz Lachowski, University of Lodz, expert in international law focused on the post-Soviet space, co-editor, with Witalij Mazurenko, of a research monograph: *Ukraina po Rewolucji Godności. Prawa człowieka –*

tożsamość narodowa (Lodz: Uniwersytet Lodzki, 2017) (*Ukraine after the Revolution of Dignity. Human Rights – National Identity*). Lachowski also remarked to the author, in an email exchange of May 25, 2022, that the "Minsk Agreements are dead and buried by Russia because of its recognition of the "People's Republics and Moscow's invasion of Ukraine."

120 See von Twickel, *The State of the Donbass*, 15.
121 Ibid. 19–20.
122 Author's email exchange with Sarah Lain, associate fellow at RUSI, London, December 19, 2020.

3

HOSTS OF THE FOREIGN FIGHTERS IN UKRAINE

Volunteer Battalions and Popular Militias

Introduction

To some extent the situation of the foreign fighters on either side of the war in Ukraine had many things in common – as will be shown in the "national" chapters, there was a great deal of chaos and improvisation during their process of joining the units which accepted foreigners, their front line deployments and/or administrative procedures aimed at legalizing their stay in Ukraine. Many seemed to have hinged on ad hoc connections, and some formed pre-war of individual fighters and/or their access to a non-combatant foreigner present on either side of the conflict (humanitarian workers, journalists). Both sides initially wanted these foreigners to join their ranks but quite quickly lost interest and as the war progressed, seemed to be intent on removing them from the battlefield to avoid diplomatic embarrassment.[1] What is more, the Minsk II agreement "stipulated the disarming and disbanding of all non-state and illegal armed formations, including volunteer and mercenary units, active in the territory controlled by the Ukrainian government."[2] Such a provision effectively heralded the end of the Ukrainian volunteer battalions, of some whom hosted the foreign fighters, in their sub-state form and hastened their integration into the military or the National Guard. What is more, in November 2015 Ukraine introduced a law which "allowed foreign nationals and stateless persons to be hired by the Ukrainian army on contract."[3] This gave wannabe volunteers a firmly legal and official pathway for entry into the war on the Ukrainian side and severely dampened any prospects of genuine foreign fighters appearing in the ranks of pro-Kyiv forces.

The "separatists" subsequently took steps that would limit the potential for arrivals of new foreign fighters.[4] In 2016, the "ragtag collection of militias and private armies" was molded into army corps and this severely limited the bottom-up recruitment processes into some of the units.[5] Moreover, the assassination of the

DOI: 10.4324/9781003192992-3

Donetsk People's Republic (DNR)'s "President" Zakharchenko in 2018 led to further consolidation of that "republic's" military forces, especially the ones loyal to the now deceased leader, and the units that hosted some of the foreign fighters. These were being brought under the auspices of the DNR's "ministry of internal affairs" which accepted the already serving foreigners but banned new ones from joining the ranks. These processes of "professionalization" were accompanied by the foreign fighters' growing disenchantment with the conditions in Ukraine or the fact that the war seemed to have reached a stalemate sometime in early 2015. One former Russian foreign fighter,[6] who had been a far-right blogger before the war and then went on to write books about the conflict, stated in 2020 that "the time has come to [...] part with the romantic word "militia." [...] I can say that the so-called "popular militia" has long since disappeared here. An army appeared here [...] Poorly organized, but an army. And more specifically, then part of the Russian army."[7] Such moves often equaled termination of foreign fighter recruitment as these arrived on the front lines precisely because of the chaotic and unruly (dis/mis)organization of the volunteer units.

Consequently, and as will be demonstrated in the "national" chapters, one is still able to locate foreigners in the ranks of the opposing sides of the war in Ukraine. These are usually individuals who arrived on the front lines early and chose to stay in Ukraine or what Ukraine called the "temporarily occupied territories of Ukraine" (Ukrainian: Тимчасово окупована територія України), of DNR, Luhansk People's Republic (LNR) and Crimea.[8] Some would leave Ukraine and then go back to the front – utilizing the contacts they had for a smooth redeployment in an environment which was getting more and more proscriptive towards genuine foreign fighters.[9] In fact, these redeployments would usually take them back to their old units, formations which had a track record of accepting and accommodating foreigners in their ranks. These were the main conduits for the appearance and maintenance of foreign fighters on the front lines of the war in Ukraine. They effectively hosted such fighters and the following chapter will focus on the most notable examples of such units, hubs of foreign fighting in Ukraine. First, however, one needs to take stock briefly of the battalions and militias facing each other off in Eastern Ukraine.

Battalions and Militias

Throughout the spring of 2014, the incoming foreigners came to Ukraine to fight in a war and consequently had little time to spare and did not want to go through elaborate recruitment procedures of a standing army (had it had these in early 2014). They wanted "action," or sought to lend their military skills to the war effort, on either side of the conflict. What is more, the "separatists" had no standing army and joining what effectively functioned as "militias" had been the only option for the wannabe foreign fighters on that side of the conflict.

On the Ukrainian side, the fighters' units of choice were the volunteer battalions, effectively "pro-government paramilitary groups." These began to appear in

March 2014 and initially relied on private donations for their funding (or sponsoring from the Ukrainian oligarchs), "operated independently from official state control." They also introduced their own, independent, recruitment policies that allowed for foreigners, if these were willing and were able to track down the HQ or recruitment office of a given battalion – often located in or around the Euromaidan, to enlist in the battalions.[10] In fact, the battalions were said to have constituted "a patch-work map with each battalion having their own history, approach to recruitment, sources of funding and relations with the Ukrainian central command."[11] The battalions' do-it-yourself, bottom-up approach produced units which have been "socially, linguistically, nationally and politically varied." They "comprise[d] primarily Maidan activists with a background as diverse as police or army veterans, small entrepreneurs and students, but also, admittedly, individuals with a criminal record. Volunteer battalions include[d] both Russian-speakers from the east [...] and Ukrainian-speakers from the West [of Ukraine]."[12]

To some, the battalions looked like candidates for "state parallel paramilitaries," i.e. armed formations which would prey on a weak, collapsing state and looked poised to take over power as the conflict fades.[13] What is more, their leaders, some of whom were elected to parliament on the back of their front-line exploits, sometimes seemed like "warlords" in the making.[14] Consequently, they would be seen as commanders of "pro-government anti-government armed groups" who could theoretically challenge the government on battlefield performance, security provision and ideological purity.[15] In this sense, they started on a par with the likes of the Northern Irish Ulster Defence Association (UDA), a paramilitary organization that appeared in the early 1970s to counter the real or perceived Irish republican onslaught on the Protestant majority of this part of the UK.[16] Relatively quickly, however, the battalions grew in strength and operational capabilities and, unlike in the UDA's case, also with the state's support. The political success of their commanders, and the formation of political parties recruiting heavily amongst the veterans of the battalions, such as the National Corps (*Natsionalnyi korpus*), gave the impression that these could be in fact turning into Ukrainian mini-Hezbollahs, i.e. powerful multi-faceted armed socio-political movements or states within a state.[17] As time was passed, however, the politicized volunteer battalions proved unable and unwilling to challenge the state's monopoly of violence and their political projects failed to secure meaningful political success.[18] A worry that they or some of their members could instead copy the actions of the French OAS (Secret Army Organization, *Organisation Armée Secrète*) – a vanguardist paramilitary-terrorist organization, which challenged the French government in the early 1960s over granting Algeria's independence,[19] was not totally baseless, however. The uncompromising rhetoric of their leaders and their deep-seated antagonisms towards the post-2014 Ukrainian governments theoretically signaled some willingness to play the role anti-systemic political spoilers, with some of their individual members potentially opting for direct action to express their displeasure with the political reality in Ukraine.[20]

The battalions were able to capitalize on the army's real shortcomings to build up their legitimacy and standing in the country and amongst the Ukraine citizens.[21] As Pavel Polityuk and Natalia Zinets noted, "at the outbreak of the war in eastern Ukraine in 2014, the Ukrainian army was so poorly equipped that ordinary citizens were knitting socks, donating scrap metal and even crowd-funding a tank for soldiers at the front line."[22] Thus, in the spring and summer of 2014, it looked as without the battalions the Ukrainian war effort would have been dramatically less successful. The underfunded and initially badly led Ukrainian army proved unable at first to arrest the early "separatist", or at that time Novorossiyan, gains. Nonetheless, with the passage of time, and especially after the heavy defeat in the battle of Ilovaisk of August 2014,[23] the significance of the battalions as a lone standing, standard bearers of the post-Euromaidan enthusiasm and patriotism, began to wane. Their drive and eagerness to fight proved insufficient in a fight with the Russian soldiers and full regular army units deployed into the Eastern Ukraine to help stave off the collapse of the "People's Republics."[24] By March 2015, i.e. after the ending of major hostilities on the front lines, all but two of the initial 40+ battalions (with some having hundreds of members, others dozens at most) were "regularly registered" and found themselves incorporated either into the Ukrainian army or the National Guard, a paramilitary formation under the auspices of the ministry of internal affairs.[25]

On the other side of the front line, the "separatists" organized themselves into "local militias," effectively proxies of the Russian war effort, and at times criminal structures which were sanctioned to transform into ad hoc paramilitary units. There was no single organizational model behind this bottom-up process (with a strong input of minders and curators sent by Moscow, or even officers, organizers and rank and file soldiers who arrived from Russia). One thing was certain, however, "the units all tend[ed] to be mixed in nature, and [were] willing to accept whoever [… was] willing to join."[26] It seems that the larger DNR was able to instill more discipline and control over "its" militias than the smaller LNR, which saw bouts of significant infighting between rival commanders, and possibly, hidden interventions by Moscow to remove those deemed less obedient.[27] Such an approach ensured that the militias would not turn into anti-"state" challengers of the Moscow sanctioned and supported leadership of the DNR and the LNR. Thus, these formations had no chance to evolve into quasi-Hezbollah structures. A case in point was politically and socially radical Aleksei Mozgovoy ("most radical politically [...] than the other field commanders") and his *Prizrak* (Ghost) Brigade, known for acceptance of foreign fighters, which "[kept] aloof both from the Luhansk authorities and from the other autonomous armed formations."[28] This, however, proved short-lived as *Prizrak* lost its radical edge and independence after Mozgovoy's assassination, blamed either on Ukrainian "saboteurs" or on the Russian military intelligence service, the GRU, in May 2015.[29] Similar questions concerned the death of Alexander Zakharchenko, the leader of the DNR, widely seen as a figure partially independent of Moscow and personally in control of certain military formations, when he died as a result of a bombing in August 2018. His death hastened the installation of a more pro-Moscow-oriented leadership set up in the "republic" and saw "his" formations amalgamated into the so-called First Army Corps, allegedly run by the Russian military.[30]

Hubs – Ukraine Side

As mentioned above, prior to the 2015–16 decisions to amalgamate the volunteer battalions into the Ukrainian army and mold "separatist" militias into "army corps," the foreign fighters present on the front lines were mostly associated with several units on each side. These, in fact, acted as hubs or conduits for the foreign fighters, who were relatively free, if they could get themselves to either Kyiv or Rostov in Russia (the main embarkation point for individuals wanting to enter the DNR or the LNR), to join or at least pitch themselves as members of either the battalions or the militias. The next section will specifically focus on these groups, both on the Ukrainian and on the "separatist" side.

As will be shown below, the three units most friendly to Western foreign fighter on the pro-Ukraine side of the war, all had their own distinct features that made them attractive to prospective foreign recruits. The Georgian National Legion (GNL) advertised itself in English and seemed straightforwardly accessible via its social media accounts. Moreover, it has not only been a unit for foreign fighters but also set up by the foreign fighters themselves, i.e., Georgians. This might have swayed some of the wannabe fighters to join the legion. The Right Sector seemed like an ideal choice for individuals who were keen on getting their fighting experience as soon as possible, with relatively few questions asked – it had a decentralized structure and resisted calls for integrating into the Ukrainian security sector. Finally, the Azov Battalion/Regiment seemed like a viable fighting option on the one hand, and on the other had a captivating back story. Azov was born out of a radical political organization professing a transnational extreme right-wing ideology, disciplined, fought early and successfully in the war in Ukraine,[31] and accepted foreign fighters who sometimes also acted as its recruitment poster boys.

The Georgian National Legion (GNL)

As will be shown below, Azov was often associated with the effort of recruiting foreigners as fighters for its ranks. However, its "couple of dozen Westerners," as indicated to an author by a Azov based foreign fighter,[32] were no match for recruitment results of another unit, which was the only one on the Ukrainian side led by foreigners and which featured representatives from around 20 countries – the GNL.

Had it not been for Mamuka Mamulashvili, the GNL's founder and commander, the unit would not have been operational on the front lines. He is a veteran of the Georgian military and worked at the local ministry of defense.

Georgians knew "there were Ukrainian volunteers who fought for us [against the Russians in South Ossetia and Abkhazia in the early 1990s]" and felt that in 2014 they had a chance "to repay this debt."[33] Moreover, from his experience of being involved in the 2008 Georgian-Russo war, they also felt that "we knew the Russian [hybrid] scenario" and were therefore well-positioned to advise the Ukrainians.[34] In April 2014, Mamulashvili appeared in Ukraine with a small group of Georgian military instructors. This group formed the core of the future GNL which "grew from there [...] and became a contact point so people online would reach out to us via the social media."[35] The GNL initially existed as another volunteer battalion but, from February 2016, it became the 3rd company, 25th battalion and 54th brigade of the Armed Forces of Ukraine. In this sense, it paved the way as a first group of non-Ukrainians was admitted into the ranks of the Ukrainian army.[36]

The legion's online multilingual media operation, Mamulashvili's availability, his fluent English and general openness towards recruitment of foreigners who would then fight under the aegis of a Georgian unit allowed the "legion" to punch above its weight in terms public relations and recognition.[37] Consequently, it allowed for a construction of a truly multinational unit which featured up to 200 individuals (roughly half of whom had been Georgian) with a separate "English-speaking group" of fighters in its ranks ("we had 20 other countries and also exotic at that – Japan, Korea, Indonesia").[38] Up until 2021, the GNL would announce its new recruits publicly through its social media channels, stressing their previous military experience and whether they would be coming from a country not yet represented in the legion's ranks, such as Albania or Montenegro.[39] At one point in the 2017, the GNL sought to increase its size so that it would eventually "become a kind of 'foreign legion' within the Ukrainian forces, with a total of 150 soldiers of various nationalities." However, it never reached that number and, at the beginning of 2018, it had up to 80 soldiers in its ranks.[40]

Regardless of its size, the recruitment efforts and the openness of its commander also brought some trouble upon the unit. Mamulashvili's English enabled him to recruit Americans into its ranks,[41] or to even tour the U.S. and enjoy meetings with elected representatives in Washington, D.C.[42] At the same time, however, he effectively outsourced the recruitment effort to some of his subordinates and that put the unit under an unprecedented spotlight, as its individual recruits were public-relations embarrassments to the GNL.[43] The GNL was keen on stressing that there was "no place for nationalists, nazis, soldiers of fortune" in the legion,[44] but allegedly "questionable characters spent time with the GNL."[45] One such case concerned Ethan Tilling, an Australian citizen who first wished to join the Kurdish forces in Syria but changed his plans after learning that such individuals are threatened "with charges under foreign fighter laws in Australia." This led him to Ukraine and the GNL. His commander described him as "motivated" and a "good soldier" but was dismayed by his past as a "neo-Nazi militant" in Australia.[46] Tilling initially made the link with the GNL through Craig Lang, a discharged combat veteran and an now infamous American foreign fighter,[47] who appeared in Ukraine in 2015 and hopped between units which hosted foreign fighters, namely the Right Sector and the GNL.[48] Lang brought much unwanted attention onto the other foreign fighters in general as he was "wanted in connection with a double killing in Florida and is fighting extradition from Kyiv" to the U.S. and was amongst "seven American fighters" investigated by the U.S. Department of Justice "under the federal war crimes statute."[49] The accusations against Lang centered on his time with the Right Sector and not the GNL but still cast an unfavorable light on any unit in Ukraine that had him in its ranks. Mamulashvili praised Lang as a soldier ("a very good specialist")[50] but admitted he had not known of his legal troubles in the U.S. At the same time, Lang's case made the GNL shut down any later attempts by Americans to join the unit.[51]

Apart from the issues concerning the recruitment of "questionable characters" into its ranks, the GNL also found itself increasingly at odds with its Ukrainian hosts. In early 2018, the legion accused the 54th brigade command, i.e., the unit to which the company sized GNL belonged, of "incompetence and illegal actions" and effectively left the above-mentioned mother unit.[52] In exchange, the one of the advisors to the President Poroshenko of Ukraine called them a "banal infantry platoon", which made "some statements" during the Christmas holiday season. Moreover, this "platoon" was like one of "hundreds" Ukraine possessed on the front line. He also stressed that the GNL was "not more heroic, not more voluntary and not more patriotic" than other such units.[53] Such statements aimed on the one hand to dissolve the tension around the legion but also belittled its contribution to the Ukrainian war effort. These were also followed by accusations of indiscipline, i.e., drunkenness and hooliganism at the legion's base after its return from the front line to Kyiv,[54] or scavenging the base for scrap materials which were then allegedly sold off to Russia.[55]

While these accusations were raging, the GNL found itself restless as it was withdrawn from the front and was not allowed to come back. This obviously frustrated its foreign recruits who specifically came to Ukraine and joined this international unit because they were itching for a fight. Emile Ghessen caught the GNL on camera in this period as it was nonetheless still accepting foreigners as this would boost the morale of its members while proving the ongoing attractiveness of the legion.[56] These recruits, however, were often frustrated because "the Ukrainians don't really appreciate us," "they don't want us here at all" and "[there are] a lot of hiccups, a lot of red tape."[57] Some recruits, like Joachim Furholm of Norway (more on him in the Western European chapter), gravitated from the GNL to the Ukrainian army and one (Bari Bonen of Israel) later died in mysterious circumstances in Kyiv.[58] In addition to the restlessness, the GNL also had to address the issue of its alleged connections to Mikheil Saakashvili, former president of Georgia who was first brought by President Poroshenko into the Ukrainian government, awarded Ukrainian citizenship and made governor of Odessa. He later fell out with his erstwhile Ukrainian backers, including Poroshenko, whom he accused of supporting "criminal and corrupt [...]

clans."[59] The GNL felt that their unit "was blamed for this whole Sakashvili imbroglio," especially as Mamulashvili sister, Nona Mamulashvili, is an Member of Parliament with a political force formerly led by Sakashvili.[60] Eventually, the GNL effectively ceased to function as a separate unit and its members, as volunteers, would be helping, e.g. as reconnaissance specialists in different units of the Ukrainian army on the front lines.[61]

The Right Sector

The Right Sector (*Pravyi Sektor*) was another unit on the Ukrainian side of the war which opened its doors to foreign fighters. To some extent, it became a brand as it has been granted a "disproportionate amount of attention" by the media because of its far-right radicalism.[62] Some even perceived it, exaggeratedly, as a "right-wing" equivalent of the Islamic State of Iraq and Syria (ISIS), i.e. an entity willing to take on almost any ideologically allied radical from abroad into its ranks.[63] In fact, the Right Sector "was a broad coalition of [Ukrainian] far-right organizations and groups that came together at the end of November 2013, a few days after the start of the pro-European [Euromaidan] protests."[64] What united the radicals in the ranks of this multifaceted hydra was their rejection of the then President of Ukraine, Viktor Yanukovych, "widely considered as anti-Ukrainian and pro-Kremlin" and their preference for a militarized "national liberation," cleansing Ukraine of foreign dominations and influences.[65] Right Sector' spokesman stated: "a Ukraine for Ukrainians, run by Ukrainians, and not serving the interests of others" and a "national democracy."[66] Its audio-visual materials spoke of a coalition which was for "honour and justice" and against "corruption, totalitarian liberalism [...] integration with whoever." Moreover, it also promised a "great Ukrainian Reconquista" amidst "rebuilding Ukraine, Russia and Europe" – a process which started at "our [Ukrainian] Maidan."[67] The organizations equated "joining with Europe" (a goal of the Euromaidan, initiated in support of the association agreement with the EU) with the "death of Ukraine", as it would spell "the death of the nation state and the death of Christianity" via the EU's "totalitarian liberalism."[68] The Right Sector proclaimed it stood for "brotherhood of European nations" and the "Baltic-Black Sea Alliance" of Central-Eastern European countries.[69]

Such language could and did appeal to foreign, especially Western, far-right militants or radicals, but the coalition, which evolved into a marginal political party,[70] was a nationalist Ukrainian affair which also included many (some suggest that made up to 40 per cent of the whole movement)[71] "ethnic Russians/ Russian-speakers."[72] Despite its later allegedly "ramshackle" nature,[73] its militancy, militaristic image and perceived efficiency during the Euromaidan, and alleged threat it posed to the Ukrainian authorities as a "pro-government anti-government armed group," allowed it to punch above its weight as far as public relations and recruitment into the future volunteer battalions were concerned. However, it also brought some unwanted media attention onto its actions and members.[74] The Right Sector also drew its legitimacy from its participation in the war with its leader, Dmytro Yarosh, who was wounded in battle and subsequently won a seat in the Ukrainian Parliament.[75]

Simultaneously with the Right Sector earning battle fame, the movement also found itself in trouble with the Ukrainian state. The Right Sector claimed the government tried to "destroy the volunteer movement" as it attempted to bring all the battalions under its control.[76] What is more, its members found themselves in shoot-outs with both the security forces and members of private security companies allegedly over spoils from the illicit smuggling of cigarettes from Ukraine to the EU.[77] Some of its leading lights, such as Oleksandr Muzychko, himself a foreign fighter in the Chechen ranks in the war against Russia in the mid-1990s, irked many in Ukraine with his displays of radicalism such as threatening lawmakers with an AK-47 or rabid hostility to the post-Euromaidan Ukrainian authorities, and criticism of their lackluster performance during the Crimea and Donbas crises.[78] Ironically, however, it had been this brazenness and being seen as involved in conflict with the government that augmented the Right Sector's standing as an almost a rogue entity, which alone could claim the title of a truly independent force.[79] Its units functioned seemingly illegally on the front lines but were tolerated by their military neighbors who, at times, directed some of their supplies to the Right Sector fighters.[80] Such an organized-disorganized approach, and the ability to hop on and off from a given section of the Right Sector, enamored it to some of the wannabee foreign fighters keen on getting battlefield experience.[81] At the same time, however, the Right Sector, unlike Azov, failed to communicate a transnational socio-political vision which could act as a magnet for a higher number of external recruits. Moreover, the Right Sector's recklessness – the do or die attitude ("it is more revolutionary and radical out here [in our unit]"),[82] which attracted the likes of the above-mentioned Craig Lang into its ranks,[83] could also have been off-putting to some who wished to travel to Ukraine in the first place.

Eventually, the Right Sector split and its section, the Ukrainian Volunteer Army, UVA (Українська добровольча армія, UDA in Ukrainian), continued to man the front line via its two battalions up until late 2018.[84] Its members saw the Ukrainian army as "non-committed," a system that "would swallow us up." Its non-compromising ideological stance and the makeshift conditions in which it operated made it into a magnet for reporters who years after the war started could report on a "rogue" militia fighting on Ukraine's side.[85] Regardless of this, however, the original rump Right Sector is still present on the front lines, and apparently "enjoys" its grey status of not being a part of the Ukrainian military or of its National Guard.[86] It seems that the unruly, chaotic, disorganized but independent anti-systemic radicals of the Right Sector have not moved on from the heady days of the Euromaidan.

Azov

The Azov Battalion, later Regiment, has often been associated as the main foreign fighter hub on the pro-Ukraine side.[87] It is true that if one was to consider the Russians and the Georgians who fought in its ranks, and their mobilizations are not the subject of this monograph, then Azov would be the key unit as far as pro-Ukraine foreign fighters were concerned. At the same time, Azov's standing in this respect, as will be shown, was augmented by its political in general and international ambitions in particular and these seem to have elevated this one of many volunteer battalions in Ukraine to the role of a transnational bogey-man, allegedly recruiting unsavory, mostly far-right characters into its ranks, as Al-Qaeda did with the jihadists.[88]

In the popular imagination, Azov or "Azov Battalion" and later regiment, but also the social movement which originated from this (para)military unit, has been reduced to as an "international white supremacist group,"[89] "greatest threat [to Ukraine due to ...] the far right, even neo-Nazi, leanings of many of its members."[90] This reading of Azov saw it as a far-right equivalent of Al-Qaeda or a transnational violent, terrorist organization which inspires, recruits and trains like-minded individuals to potentially commit acts of violence outside of Ukraine.[91] It also spawned a discussion on whether the regiment or the social movement that grew out of it should be designated as a "foreign terrorist organization" by the U.S. Department of State with some American law-makers arguing for the designation.[92] Moreover, the trouble did not stop there and consequently the whole Azov movement continued to court it via political violence meted out by its members in the streets of Ukraine,[93] its transnational connections to far-right figures in Europe and the U.S.,[94] its alleged plans to set up what appeared to have looked like subsidiary organization (a "European legion") in the countries like Croatia,[95] and its continuous usage of controversial imagery (including uniforms, torches and flags) at its publicized events.[96]

Given all this, one can confidently state that Azov became the most famous of all of the original Ukrainian volunteer battalions and a seeming hub for hosting foreign fighters who wished to fight on the side of Ukraine in the Russo-Ukraine war. As will be shown, its seeming orientation towards recruitment of foreigners into its ranks lagged behind that of the GNL for instance.[97] However, due to its "white supremacist militia" status,[98] and alleged recruitment of individuals from within the "global network of white supremacist extremists that stretches across North America, Europe and Australia,"[99] Azov was pushed to the fore. It seemed like the quintessential, and most covered by the media, foreign fighter-friendly entity from the war in Ukraine.

The original Azov Battalion evolved from what Andreas Umland called "a distinctly marginal [far-right] lunatic fringe group largely unknown even among many experienced journalists and analysts writing on Ukraine."[100] It was the far-right Ukrainian milieu in general but the Patriot of Ukraine (PU, *Патріо́т Украї́ни*), a Kharkiv-based far-right organization and the "micro-party" Social National Assembly (SNA) set up by the PU,[101] in particular which in the spring of 2014 mobilized its men and meagre resources to set up Azov as a fighting unit. PU activists played a key role in the process but, had it not been for the hidden hand of the ministry of internal affairs, which favorably looked at transforming a group of Kharkiv militants into a paramilitary organization, and the Eastern

Ukrainian oligarchs, who helped with bankrolling the operation, this process would never have been successfully accomplished.[102] Interestingly enough, the future fighters were at first reluctant to cooperate with the hated state, which put many of them in jail right until the Euromaidan, and often felt the 2013/2014 revolution in Ukraine did not go far enough or that it steered the country in the wrong direction. Statements such as "we did not care about the EU and the European values, we would rather be called opponents to these values" put the Azovians on a collision course with other participants of the Euromaidan but would certainly endear them to their Western ideological brethren.[103] Yet, the state allowed this particular bottom-up mobilization to take place and Azov developed from there.

The support from the state was forthcoming even when it was clear that Azov had not been just a military or a paramilitary entity but from the outset was also designed as an overtly political organization. Early recruitment materials for foreigners who wished to join Azov from the start stressed the fact that this unit effectively is the military wing of a political party, the SNA, with a specific nationalist, far-right agenda. This was recognizable to non-Ukrainian members of ideologically comparable entities from other countries. The fact that some of its propaganda was conducted in foreign languages by its early foreign recruits also gave the unit a transnational audience from its inception. Its spokespersons openly advertised the possibilities of joining the battalion stressing that they were dealing with numerous applications from wannabe fighters from all around the world.[104] This advertised battalion/regiment was later to give birth to "the Azov Movement," of which it remained a "renowned military wing." The movement also included a political party, the National Corps, which arose out of the "volunteer support network for the Azov Volunteer Battalion" and was headed by Biletskyi, Azov's first commander and its founder.[105] To some extent, its radicalism mellowed as its original leaders turned or attempted to turn into elected officials as a result of their political involvement.

As Azov was turning less anti-systemic, or anti-state, it, nonetheless, kept the imagery and the rhetoric which accompanied its transformation from the PU to a unit of the National Guard of Ukraine (NGU). It marketed itself an effective fighting unit which was known for successfully re-capturing of the port of Mariupol.[106] Azov, in the eyes of the arriving foreign fighters, had been "the shit," i.e., the most serious and successful of the volunteer battalions which would have foreigners.[107] This in turn paved the way for its societal "legalization" and "lionization" as "the best volunteers units in the eyes of the leadership of the [ministry of internal affairs]."[108] In fact, Azov would maintain the line of "of not being just a gendarmerie but in fact, the most prolific regiment" in the whole of the Ukraine (both in the army or as a part of the National Guard) in its public relations throughout the following years.[109] The focus on the high level of training, which included e.g., hosting Western instructors with military backgrounds,[110] or mixed martial arts fighters teaching soldiers basics of that sport,[111] remained a constant feature of Azov. The mantra of keeping up or developing up to "NATO standards" was also maintained at the National Corps' latest Intermarium Conference, where the party hosts its international guests.[112] This reliance on maintaining high preparedness and readiness as far as the military side of the movement's functioning is also visible if one takes into account initiatives such as the regiment's very own "sergeant school," for development of its own non-commissioned officer (NCO) corps, devised by the regiment's officer with experience in similar institutions in the U.S.[113]

According to Vyacheslav Likhachev, "Azov was interested in foreigners as far as their experience was concerned, they wanted them to help the battalion up their game." It would, however, later stop putting its pre-war Russian connections to the fore. Azov was reshaping itself as a standard bearer for Ukrainian patriotism and nationalism, supercharged in response to the Russian invasion of Ukraine and effectively shut down "transnational" recruitment once it formally became part of the Ukrainian National Guard.[114] This relative indifference to the transnational aspect was confirmed to the author by an anonymous Western European former member of the battalion/regiment, once intent on participation in Ukrainian politics, who stressed that he "had been there from the start. 30–35 [Western] Europeans stayed with us long enough, others, a similar number, returned home quickly after deciding it was not for them. Neo-Nazis amongst them? I could count them on the fingers of one hand. Conservative? Yes, but not neo-Nazis."[115] However, the fact that that Azov featured e.g. an alleged, a "white power warrior from Sweden" in the ranks of Azov,[116] initially attracted a great deal of media attention to himself and other foreign members of the battalion, and helped transform this relatively small unit into a seemingly powerful transnational coalition of far-right fighting extremists.[117]

It should be noted here that, at times, Azov looked as if it had been attempting to do just that, while e.g., outsourcing some of its alleged recruitment to Misantrophic Division (MD), an "international neo-Nazi association."[118] MD's Russian members effectively infiltrated the SNA prior to Euromaidan and then "participated on the [Euro] Maidan demonstrations, in clashes with [Euro] Maidan opponents in Kharkiv, and some of them took part in the Donbas hostilities on Kiyv's side. Over a dozen of [… them] fought in Azov."[119] However, before Azov was able to crack down on the MD influence in its ranks,[120] it allegedly attempted to recruit foreign fighters into Azov ranks from the UK[121] and Germany.[122] The former connections proved especially embarrassing, as these resulted in visits to the Azov movement's Kyiv HQ by members of the British far right and later was proscribed as a terrorist organization, National Action.[123] On top of such efforts, Azov also stood accused of "courting" American wannabe foreign fighters, themselves member of the infamous American neo-Nazi organization, the Atomwaffen Division.[124]

Other transnational links also looked troubling, e.g., these with the so-called Russian Centre, umbrella groupuscule for Russian far-right members fighting in Ukrainian ranks, but especially *Wotanjugend*, a self-described "hammer of National Socialism," whose members effectively migrated from Russia to Ukraine.[125] Its esoteric Nazi influences and at times outright neo-Nazi posturing at, e.g., its own *Asgardsrei*, national socialist black metal festival organized in Kyiv, baffled many observers.[126] Regardless of Wotanjugend's radicalism, Azov also took under its umbrella other controversial Russian far-right individuals connected with *Restrukt!*, a "notorious Russian neo-Nazi movement."[127]

The above-mentioned links are connected to Azov's early days and its performance in the Russo-Ukraine war when it either recruited certain individuals or attempted to do so. It allowed external observers to conclude that it had been "the Ukrainian militant group that has trained and inspired white supremacists from around the world."[128] Unsurprisingly, the regiment vehemently denied these accusations while stressing that these focused on activities of non-sanctioned and fake "recruiters,"[129] for which Azov cannot be held responsible. Moreover, it also objected to being called a "militia" and not a regiment of the NGU under the ministry of internal affairs. This fact was to act as a check on attempts by over-eager foreigners who simply wished to join the unit, as was possible in its early days, i.e., before Azov's incorporation into the NGU. In its refutations Azov reiterated the position that "only foreigners who are legally on the territory of Ukraine can serve in the NGU" so that an ad hoc recruitment process by wannabe members would simply be unsuccessful.[130]

This exchange of accusations and Azov's responses to them is emblematic of the problem at hand, namely the regiment and the movement's alleged and real international ambitions. The Azov movement has run, at least before the onset of the Covid-19 pandemic, a wide-ranging transnational strategy of outreach to like-minded organizations and potential allies from abroad. Its aim, however, was not to build up a cadre of foreigners who would then join the Azov regiment, nor to train them so that they would get involved in political violence or terrorism at home, but to increase the movement or the National Corps' party standing in nationalist or far-right circles in the broader West. Moreover, this outreach was geared especially towards an "'increase [in] the volume' of Ukrainian strategic communication in general, and of Ukrainian nationalists in particular, and counter Russia's inroads into the XRW [extreme right wing] scenes of the West."[131]

The transnational outreach of Azov would be based on two ideological pillars, first the *reconquista*, regaining something that was lost, a term that "harks back to the liberation of medieval Spain from Muslim rule." This reading of the situation saw "Ukraine as the new Andalusia, from which the liberation of Europe from migrants, liberals and cosmopolitans will begin,"[132] and, secondly, *intermarium*, i.e., the area in between the seas. This term, in turn, harks back to the existence of Poland's First Republic (i.e., Rzeczpospolita, 1569–1795), a Central-Eastern European country encompassing the territories of today's Poland, Belarus, Ukraine, Lithuania and Latvia, and the interwar Polish concept of *Międzymorze*, literally: in between the seas.[133] Seen through this prism, this part of Central Europe was regarded by Azov as a "defensive Eastern European buffer against Russia and the matrix of a new Europe in which the restoration of the values of the past would be reconciled with the technological values of the future."[134]

Azov's transnational outreach activities would see the movement controversially host e.g. pro-"white ethno state"[135] American figures such as Greg Johnson[136] at the movement's more highbrow, academic/expert like conferences in Kyiv. At the same time, members of the Rise Above Movement, "a white supremacist group,"[137] themselves veterans of the infamous "Unite the Right" rally in Charlottesville, Virginia, the U.S.,[138] would also visit Azov with its leader fighting in an Azov-linked mixed martial arts club in Kyiv.[139] Both of these connections were described as a public relations "clusterfuck" by the above quoted Western veteran of Azov, who vehemently objected to issuing such invitations).[140] At the same time, the movement's members, and especially the international secretary of the National Corps, Olena Semenyaka, traveled to "[popularize Azov's intermarium] project in Western Europe and [to establish …] cooperation with both friendly Western European parties and those influenced by pro-Russian lobbyists," especially in the 2018–19 period.[141] Amongst these potential collaborationists, one could find the German Nationaldemokratische Partei Deutschlands (National Democratic Party) or NPD, the Der III Weg (Third Way) party in Germany, Norwegian Autonomous Nationalists, identitarian groups and organizations in Finland, Germany, Italy (CasaPound) and Portugal, Eesti Konservatiivne Rahvaerakond (The Conservative People's Party of Estonia) or EKRE. Moreover, she also addressed the public in fora such as the Pan-Scandinavian Scandza Forum or the Awakening II Conference in the Finnish city of Turku.[142]

Hubs – "Separatists"[143]

As much as both sides of the war initially would not mind the "internationalization" of recruitment into the respective volunteer battalions or militias, and subsequently seemed to have changed their minds on the issue,[144] it had been the "separatists" who won the proverbial race for more foreign fighters in their ranks. Of course, these had predominantly been Russians, but the most accurate estimates put the number of their non-Russian fighters at approximately 1,300 versus approximately 900 for the Ukrainian side.[145] The haphazard nature of the "separatist" forces, and their makeshift nature prevented that side from developing many foreign fighter hubs comparable to the likes of the GNL, Right Sector or Azov. It seemed that fluidity of troops across units was greater, as will be shown in the chapter detailing the travails of the French contingent on the "separatist" side. Similarly, this did not help creation of "national" units as e.g. Serbs were dispersed across up to nine different units.[146] In such conditions, stable and permanent structures openly advertising for foreign volunteers, and able to maintain them in their ranks, were rare.

One caveat, however, must be mentioned here – much of the research and attention brought onto the above-mentioned Ukrainian hubs was due to the increased media interest in spotting the proverbial neo-Nazis in Ukrainian ranks, and account for the allegedly "fascist" nature of the Euromaidan revolution (more on this in the "war" chapter of this monograph). At the same time, the "separatists," often keen on pushing to the fore their "red," i.e., far left, and internationalist credentials of some of their local and foreign fighters, seemed to have enjoyed being regarded as an anti-thesis to the "Banderite" Ukrainians. Moreover, it must be stated that for many a foreign journalist getting to Donetsk and/or Luhansk was a more troublesome process than flying into Kyiv and literally stumbling upon the likes of Right Sector or Azov offices within the broader Euromaidan area. All of the above might contribute to the fact that even today, more than seven years after the beginning of the war, the state of knowledge on what was actually happening within the "militia" ranks in the DNR and LNR is still sketchy. This disparity, however, might partially explain the source gap on foreign fighter hubs on the Ukrainian and the "separatist" side. As mentioned above, it is very likely that more of these fighters fought on the latter side, but one is able to draw upon a higher number of sources related to the former.

Certain "separatist" units initially featured a high number of Russians, also individuals from the North Caucasus, such as the veterans of the Chechen wars whose task would be to toughen but also to control the more rowdy locals.[147] This was the case with the Vostok battalion which in the later stages of the conflict underwent a "Ukrainization" phase in which its local, Donbas members were pushed to the fore.[148] Interestingly, Vostok also featured a small contingent of Western foreign fighters, from the likes of Spain, of largely far-left backgrounds associated with the organization Essence of Time, Суть времени, and Sut' vremeni, a nationalist-communist Russian entity.[149]

A more genuinely foreign fighter-oriented unit, comparable if not more significant than the Ukrainian hubs, had been the so-called Pyatnashka unit, first within the Vostok battalion, then with the DNR's the Republican Guard. Initially, it was started by "a few people. The backbone of this 'Pyatnashka' was mostly people who came from Abkhazia [a non-recognized pro-Russian statelet in Georgia]. People who went through the Abkhaz war [of 1992–1993]."[150] The Brigade's Vkontakte page mentions "15 volunteers from Russia, who simply could not watch what was happening, cooperated, kissed their daughters, wives, mothers, and went to defend the Russian land and the Russian people." They named their unit after their number – Pyatnashka means "the fifteen" in Russian.[151] The Brigade's logo featured both the 15 stars, as a reference to its name, and also not only the DNR but the Abkhaz flag as well.[152] With the passage of time, the unit also drew in Ossetians, both northern, Russian citizens, and southern, citizens of the non-recognized statelet of South Ossetia, into its ranks.[153]

The name Pyatnashka, and the symbolic usage of the number fifteen could not have been incidental. It was set up by foreign fighters and was welcoming to other such individuals. Of course, in the case of Pyatnashka the foreignness of the initial group of volunteers, albeit undisputed, was less of an issue – they were war veterans and so were deemed useful to the "separatist" war effort, spoke the local language (Russian) and might have had contacts in the "militia" milieu of the DNR from the era of the above-mentioned Abkhaz war when Russia supported the Abkhaz separatists. Nonetheless, the name of the unit evoked events, the significance of which significance went beyond Abkhazia, Russia or Donbas, namely the Spanish Civil War of the 1930s. It would be hard to miss the fact that the international brigades of that war, fighting on the governmental, republican side, also featured the XVth Briagade, which "included the English-speaking units, the British Battalion, the Irish Connolly Column, the Canadian Mackenzie-Papineau Battalion, and the American Abraham Lincoln and George Washington Battalions, as well as the 59th Battalion, Spanish speakers from Cuba, Mexico, and the rest of Latin America [...] It also included the mixed Balkan Dimitrov Battalion."[154] In this sense, the 2014 Pyatnashka, which later featured a loose collection of individuals from different parts of the world, styled itself as a logical continuation of the original XVth and seemingly augmented the myth of the "international brigades" present at the front on the "separatist" side.[155] Yet, the not unsympathetic observers of *Russia Today* commented that its troops were "ragtag," and

> [...] Most of them have never even heard of the Spanish Civil War where the term "International Brigade" springs from. [... They thought of] Joseph Stalin as the epitome of order. They have no idea that it was Stalin who stopped aiding the International Brigades in the middle of the Spanish Civil War.[156]

Despite its internationalist pretentions, Pyatnashka was a Russian-speaking unit,[157] allegedly supported by the Russian far-right "Rodina" (Fatherland) party and the authorities of the non-recognized statelet of South Ossetia. It also would be more "Ukrainized" after the death of its Ossetian commander.[158] The unit's new "local" commander, appointed in mid-2018, stressed that they "treat foreign volunteers with great warmth. We are the local guys, we had nowhere to go, and they came from far away to help. They risk their health, their lives, and they deserve a lot of respect. And mutual respect is a good basis for mutual understanding."[159]

Regardless of the scale of its internationalism, the brigade (effectively a company within Zahkarchenko's Republic Guard,[160]) with its open door policy, served as a reference point for the incoming foreign fighters and a hub or an umbrella detachment which would be ready to host them. Such was the case with the Serbian fighters in "separatist" ranks,[161] but also Czechs or Slovaks,[162] and especially the French of the then decaying Unité Continentale unit (see the French chapter for more on its travails), alongside single members from the likes of Italy, Slovenia, and the U.S.[163] Later on, the unit would also feature a "foreign section," led by a Russian-speaking French foreign fighter, which included "Brazilians, French [... and] Finnish" members.[164] Michael Sheldon saw Pyatnashka as a unit "subject to multiple command structure reforms."[165] Gradually, however, it was being brought under the control of the "DNR

Ministry of Internal Affairs" so that it no longer formed a part of a praetorian guard of the "republic's" leader,[166] and would no longer have license to partake in what effectively was a coup in the neighborly LNR in late 2017.[167]

January 2017 brought the news of a disbandment of the so-called InterUnit, or International Unit, which fought on the "separatist" side in the ranks of the *Prizrak* (Ghost) Brigade. Its fighters, including a Finn and a Pole (both used to be a couple) posed for a final photo underneath the portrait of Che Guevara, which featured a mere 12 individuals.[168] The InterUnit has been described as an "internationalist anti-fascist unit within the Prizrak Battalion [brigade]"[169] or a "a ragtag band of European, Latin American, and Indian anti-imperialist foreign fighters who had ventured to the region, drawn in by the rhetoric of defending the 'People's Republics' against Ukrainian fascism."[170] Led by an Italian fighter, call sign "Nemo," a self-described "anti-fascist," InterUnit took "the heritage of the Spanish Civil War, the Resistance and the internationalism inspired by Ernesto 'Che' Guevara."[171] It was allegedly made up of "anti-fascist and communists from Spain, Italy, Israel and USA," which, like other units covered in this chapter, saw itself as "a military and political subject, the military activity is carried out exclusively in Ukraine, while the political activity is addressed to all countries of the world, especially to the European countries, where it is still alive [in] the memory of Nazi-fascist violence."[172] The latter might have been miniscule in practice and bear no significance on the overall conflict, but instances of the unit's members actively seeking out potential recruits were reported. The InterUnit also allegedly underwent internal purges which saw its "communists [... boot out] the Duginists," so that the entity remained purely on the red side of the brown-red cocktail.[173]

The InterUnit and other short-lived foreign fighter creations such as Team Vikernes, consisting of French and Brazilian members which will be addressed in more detail in the French chapter of this monograph,[174] were operating within the confines of the above-mentioned *Prizrak* (Ghost) Brigade. It was led by a "political soldier," i.e., Aleksei Mozgovoy and "kept aloof both from the Luhansk authorities and from the other autonomous armed formations."[175] It was seen as a "maverick" unit,[176] staffed with soldiers from "other parts of the USSR,"[177] whose commander "opposed the 'LPR/LNR' leadership under both 'presidents,' Valery Bolotov and Igor Plotnitsky," and had also been "the most radical politically."[178] His anti-ceasefire approach, attacks on "political-financial-oligarchic corrupt authorities" and his desire to "liberate the people" in the whole of Ukraine put him in the cross-hairs of his Moscow or "separatist" peers or superiors,[179] and endeared him to brown-red foreign fighters who flocked to his brigade, either in their individual capacities or as a part of makeshift foreign sub-units.[180] His independence, however, had been short-lived as, in the spring of 2015, Prizrak was forced into amalgamation with "regular" LNR formations,[181] and Mozgovoi died as a result of an assassination shortly thereafter, with multiple theories emerging as to who was behind the assassination, possibly some Moscow "curator" who wanted to get rid of an unruly field commander.[182] The unit, however, maintained some notional modicum of a connection to its past as the "separatist" communist parties still lauded its members,[183] and would e.g., take on returning foreign fighters.[184]

A fate similar to that of Prizrak awaited the so-called LNR's rapid reaction group/battalion "Batman," named after the callsign of its commander, Aleskandr Bednov.[185] The commander was killed in internecine LNR fighting on January 1, 2015 and his battalion was disbanded.[186] Prior to his death, Bednov found himself in a power struggle against the incumbent "president" of the LNR, Igor Plotnitsky.[187] "Batman's" members stood accused of running an illegal detention center out of Luhansk and this fact had been used against the commander and his men in the process of the battalion's disbandment.[188] The unit initially featured the so-called "Rusich, a diversion, assault and reconnaissance group (DShRG)" which withdrew from Donbas in the summer of 2015.[189] As will be shown in the French chapter, Rusich earned itself admiration and respect for arriving early on the battlefield, its martial proficiency (but also brutality)[190] and degree of autonomy it enjoyed in the "separatist" ranks. As it had been led by foreign fighters, a Russian far-right militant and a Russian who spent his formative years in Norway, and allegedly featured a Pole, a Bulgarian and Serbs in its ranks,[191] it became a reference point for many of the arriving foreign fighters. "Rusich" also "has attracted a great deal of attention, not least due to [...] its commander's infamously sadistic [pre-war in Ukraine] behaviour." Moreover, it had a "clear neo-Nazi aesthetic, making use of the *kovlorat* symbol, which, while claiming to be of ancient Slavic origin, is clearly intended to resemble a doubled swastika."[192] Alexei Milchakov, "Rusich"'s commander, later allegedly worked as a private military contractor in Syria and ran paramilitary training camps with his "Rusich" colleagues in Russia.[193]

Conclusions

This chapter has demonstrated the centrality of hubs, i.e., units which accepted foreign fighters into their ranks, to the overall recruitment of foreign volunteers for the war in Ukraine. At first, such units asked few questions of their foreign recruits and would either host them for a prolonged time or allow them to return to the front lines. The latter, as will be shown in the "national chapters," was also happening against the backdrop of both Ukraine and the "separatists" clamping down on the bottom-up, improvised, if not chaotic character of their respective volunteer battalions and "popular militias." Thus, neither of these battalions or militias ever had a chance to develop into "state parallel paramilitaries," as some had initially feared. Moreover, as these units were becoming more professional, the chances for foreign fighters to join in a truly off the books manner were becoming less pronounced. The above-mentioned hubs, however, still kept some of their original 2014–2015 fighters in their ranks.

The Ukrainian hubs were to be found in three volunteer units which all functioned or styled themselves, due to their low initial numbers, as "battalions." The GNL proved accessible and offered a way into the Ukrainian army, the Right Sector asked few questions and seemed to promise a quick fight and Azov styled itself as the most professional offer on the market and had, to some, an enticing back story. Of these three, a part of the old Right Sector still holds a similar promise. Its fighters continue to function outside the nominal Ukrainian governmental control but its turbulent history, alleged criminal connections and seemingly chaotic command and control model discouraged many outsiders from joining. The GNL has been defunct but, as will be shown in the chapter focusing on the re-escalation of war in 2022, it successfully re-established itself. Finally, Azov, seen as a hub for far-right foreign fighters, recruited relatively few of these for the actual fighting and continued to be preoccupied with the political, and not militant or martial, outreach of its political projects to like-minded organizations in the West. As a result, many commentators joined the two activities together and wrongly saw any attempt by an Azov political spokesperson to travel abroad as an attempt to recruit far-right foreign fighters into its ranks.

The "separatists" hosted more Western foreign fighters in their ranks but had fewer foreign fighter hubs. Their chaotic and disorganized structures must have accommodated these in piecemeal fashion, i.e., a few to a unit, and these individuals would often shift between different host structures (as will be shown in the French chapter on the travails of such fighters). Moreover, less is known about the "separatist" units such as the DNR and the LNR, which, to some extent, enjoyed less scrutiny from outsiders who found it more difficult to visit their "territories." Nonetheless, some units, especially the Pyatnashka, the so-called international brigade, functioned along the same lines as the Ukrainian hubs as it welcomed many of the foreign volunteers on the "separatist" side.

Notes

1 See e.g. sections on the Italian, Croat or Serbian fighters. Their host countries saw lobbying, either from Ukraine or Russia, to retrieve "their" fighters from the front lines and/or calls for their subsequent prosecution as mercenaries, organized criminals, terrorists etc.
2 Adam Potočňák and Miroslav Mareš, "Georgian Foreign Fighters in the Conflict in Eastern Ukraine, 2014–2017," *The Journal of Slavic Military Studies* 32, no. 2 (2019): 166.
3 Ibid.
4 Documentaries which focused on the foreign fighters in the war in Ukraine amply demonstrate the precarious legal position in which they would find themselves while deployed or attempting to deploy to the front. What is more, these also shed a light on the haphazard or improvisational nature of their host units, and the attitude towards them from their commanders. See e.g. *Polite People* by Kat Argo, available here: https://www.amazon.com/Polite-People-Not-Specified/dp/B01H7VJBZO; *Ukraine: Europe's Forgotten War: Robin Hood Complex Official Documentary* by Emile Ghessen, available here: https://www.youtube.com/watch?v=5BXYZqgDelw' or, albeit a more uplifting and at times hagiographical account a one foreign fighter's war, *A Sniper's War* by Olya Schechter, available here: https://www.youtube.com/watch?v=tH_nbsvch0g, all accessed: October 14, 2021.

5 Mark Galeotti, *Armies of Russia's War in Ukraine* (Oxford: Osprey Publishing, 2019), 27.

6 Anya Hrytsenko, "Adventures of Russian Right Radicals in the Ukrainian War," *REFT<>LIGHT*, December 16, 2016, http://reftlight.euromaidanpress.com/2016/12/16/adventures-russian-right-radicals-ukrainian-war/, accessed: November 22, 2021.

7 "There is no militia, here the Russian army: 'DPR' activist Alexander Zhuchkovsky has admitted that Russia is sending its soldiers to the Donbass," *Techtumble*, April 24, 2020, https://techumble.com/there-is-no-militia-here-the-russian-army-dpr-activist-alexander-zhuchkovsky-has-admitted-that-russia-is-sending-its-soldiers-to-the-donbass/, accessed: November 22, 2021.

8 See https://zakon.rada.gov.ua/laws/show/1085-2014-%D1%80#Text for the text of the relevant Ukrainian law of November 7, 2014 which introduces the terminology, accessed: October 14, 2021.

9 The author is aware of numerous such cases on both sides of the war – some will be covered in detail in the "national" chapters of this monograph.

10 Montana Hunter, "Crowdsourced War: The Political and Military Implications of Ukraine's Volunteer Battalions 2014-2015," *Journal of Military and Strategic Studies* 18, no. 3 (2018): 90–92.

11 Tetyana Malyarenko and David J. Galbreath, "Paramilitary motivation in Ukraine: beyond integration and abolition," *Southeast European and Black Sea Studies* 16, no. 1 (2016): 121.

12 Rosaria Puglisi, "Heroes or Villains? Volunteer Battalions in Post-Maidan Ukraine," *IAI Working Papers*, (March 8, 2015); 7–8, https://www.iai.it/sites/default/files/iaiwp1508.pdf, accessed: October 15, 2021. See Volodymyr Ischenko, "Denial of the Obvious: Far Right in Maidan Protests and Their Danger Today," *Vox Ukraine*, April 16, 2018, https://voxukraine.org/en/denial-of-the-obvious-far-right-in-maidan-protests-and-their-danger-today/, accessed: October 20, 2021 for a view stressing the significance of the Ukrainian far right amongst the Euromaidan protestors, and their subsequent over-representation in the volunteer battalions and the post-Maidan political forces. Puglisi, ibid, 4 notes that the battalions indeed included far-right individuals but such an ideology is not "held by most of [the members]."

13 Huseyn Aliyev, "Strong militias, weak states and armed violence: Towards a theory of 'state-parallel' paramilitaries," *Security and Dialogue* 47 no.: 6 (2016): 498–516.

14 Adrian Karatnycky, "Warlords and armed groups threaten Ukraine's rebuilding," *The Washington Post*, December 30, 2014, https://www.washingtonpost.com/opinions/the-rise-of-warlords-threatens-ukraines-recovery/2014/12/30/a23b2d36-8f7b-11e4-a412-4b735edc7175_story.html?postshare=2811425686483358, accessed; October 15, 2021.

15 Huseyn Aliyev, "Pro-government Anti-government Armed Groups? Toward Theorizing Pro-government 'Government Challengers'," *Terrorism and Political Violence*, DOI: 10.1080/09546553.2020.1785877.

16 Henry McDonald and Jim Cusack, *UDA: Inside the Heart of Loyalist Terror* (Dublin: Penguin Ireland, 2004); Ian S. Wood, *Crimes of Loyalty: A History of the UDA* (Edinburgh: Edinburgh University Press, 2006).

17 Aurelie Daher, *Hezbollah: Mobilisation and Power* (London: Hurst, 2019).

18 The community of and around some of the battalions, however, would at times constitute a powerful pressure group within Ukraine, usually forcing the state not to alter its hawkish positions of non-recognition of the "separatist" republics. Moreover, some of their members sometimes acted as "muscle" for different Ukrainian business or political forces which would effectively "hire" the veterans for specific events. Kacper Rekawek, *Looks can be deceiving: Extremism meets paramilitarism in Central and Eastern Europe* (Berlin: Counter Extremism Project, 2021), https://www.counterextremism.com/sites/default/files/2021-06/CEP%20Report_Looks%20Can%20Be%20Deceiving_Extremism%20Meets%20Paramilitarism%20in%20CEE_June%202021_1.pdf, accessed: October 19, 2021.

19 See Alistair Horne, *A Savage War of Peace: Algeria 1954-1962* (London: Macmillan, 1977) for more on the OAS origins and its evolution.

20 In this context, the author was surprised to learn that one of his interviewees from the ranks of the Azov movement, the instigator of the Azov Regiment (one of the initial volunteer battalions) and the above-mentioned National Corps political party, is a fan of Frederick Forsyth's *The Day of the Jackal*, a fictional account of the OAS's attempts to kill the French president, Charles de Gaulle.

21 Vyacheslav Likhachev, "The Far Right in the Conflict between Russia and Ukraine," *Russie.Nei.Visions*, no. 95 (July 2016): 13, https://www.ifri.org/sites/default/files/atoms/files/rnv95_uk_likhachev_far-right_radicals_final.pdf, accessed: October 28, 2021 for a more nuanced view of the battalions: "The mere fact that these volunteer formations materialized had a propaganda value in the first weeks of the conflict, but, on the whole, the media has seriously exaggerated the role of the volunteers in the anti-terrorist operation. They did not actually play a significant role during the military operations."

22 Pavel Polityuk and Natalia Zinets, "Battle-hardened and better funded, Ukraine's army knocks on NATO's door," *Reuters*, April 14, 2021, https://www.reuters.com/business/aerospace-defense/battle-hardened-better-funded-ukraines-army-knocks-natos-door-2021-04-14/, accessed: October 15, 2021.

23 The Ukrainian military saw the battalions as brave but underequipped and undisciplined, understaffed formations who had little chance of standing up to Russian troops. Michał Klimecki, *Krym, Donieck, Ługańsk 2014-2015* (Warszawa: Bellona, 2021), 142.

24 Michael Cohen and Matthew Green, "Ukraine's Volunteer Battalions," *Infantry* (April–July 2016), https://www.benning.army.mil/infantry/magazine/issues/2016/APR-JUL/pdf/16)%20Cohen_UkraineVolunteers.pdf, accessed: October 15, 2021.

25 Ibid. 7.

26 Galeotti, *Armies*, 29–32.

27 On the killings of rebel commanders see e.g.: Andrew E. Kramer, "Assassins Are Killing Ukraine's Rebel Chiefs, but on Whose Orders?," *The New York Times*, February 8, 2017, https://www.nytimes.com/2017/02/08/world/europe/ukraine-russia-mikhail-tolstykh-dead.html?smid=tw-share, accessed: October 20, 2021. The two "republics" were even involved in a "brewing conflict." which effectively was a "coup" attempt by pro-DNR forces within the LNR in 2017. See Balázs Jarábik, "Escalation in the Donbas: Ukraine Fights for the Status Quo," *Carnegie Endowment for International Peace*, February 8, 2017, https://carnegieendowment.org/2017/02/08/escalation-in-donbas-ukraine-fights-for-status-quo-pub-67943, accessed: October 20, 2021; Nikolaus von Twickel, "Explaining the coup in Luhansk," *openDemocracy*, November 24, 2017, https://www.opendemocracy.net/en/odr/explaining-coup-in-luhansk/, accessed: October 20, 2021; Maxim Vikhrov, "The Luhansk Coup: Why Armed Conflict Erupted in Russia's Puppet Regime," *The Moscow Times*, December 1, 2017, https://www.themoscowtimes.com/2017/12/01/the-luhansk-coup-why-armed-conflict-erupted-in-russias-puppet-regime-a59763, accessed: October 20, 2021.

28 International Centre for Defence and Security, "Armed Formations in the Secessionist 'Luhansk Republic'," *ICDS Commentary*, January 10, 2015, https://icds.ee/en/armed-formations-in-the-secessionist-luhansk-republic/, accessed: October 19, 2021.

29 Radina Gigova, "High-ranking separatist commander killed in eastern Ukraine," *CNN*, May 25, 2015, https://edition.cnn.com/2015/05/24/europe/ukraine-separatist-commander-killed/index.html, accessed: October 20, 2021.

30 Thomas de Waal and Nikolaus von Twickel, *Beyond Frozen Conflict Scenarios for the Separatist Disputes of Eastern Europe* (Brussels: CEPS, 2020), 72–73, https://www.ceps.eu/ceps-publications/beyond-frozen-conflict/, accessed: October 20, 2021.

31 Vyacheslav Likhachev, "The Far Right in the Conflict between Russia and Ukraine," *Russie.Nei.Visions*, no. 95 (July 2016): 16, https://www.ifri.org/sites/default/files/atoms/files/rnv95_uk_likhachev_far-right_radicals_final.pdf, accessed: October 28, 2021.

32 Author's WhatsApp interview with a foreign member of the Azov Battalion/Regiment who wished to remain anonymous, January 28, 2020.

33 Author's WhatsApp interview with a foreign fighter from the Georgian National Legion who wished to remain anonymous, March 2, 2020. This motivation, as will be shown in different "national" chapters, has been key for many of the foreign fighters who deployed to Ukraine, e.g. Serbs who wanted to thank the Russians for their support in the Balkan wars of the 1990s so they opted for joining the "separatists" militias.

34 Ibid.

35 Ibid.

36 Ruslan Rudomskyi, "Грузинський бунт в АТО: Що насправді відбувається в 54-й бригаді," *depo.ua*, January 16, 2018, https://www.depo.ua/ukr/war/gruzinskiy-bunt-v-ato-scho-naspravdi-vidbuvayetsya-v-54-y-brigadi-20180116709276, accessed: October 21, 2021.

37 See https://www.facebook.com/GeorgianNationalLegion, accessed: October 21, 2021. As of this date, the profile has + 17,000 followers. See Mamulashvili's profile at https://www.facebook.com/MamukaLegion, accessed: October 21, 2021 has + 10,000 followers. The GNL would announce its newest recruits on the Facebook page; see e.g. Emma Vardy, "The Briton fighting 'other people's wars'," *BBC News*, April 29, 2018, https://www.bbc.com/news/uk-43899959, accessed: October 21, 2021.

38 Author's WhatsApp interview with a foreign fighter from the Georgian National Legion who wished to remain anonymous, March 2, 2020.

39 See Mamulashvili's Facebook entry of March 24, 2021: https://www.facebook.com/MamukaLegion/posts/10226223994052784, accessed: October 21, 2021.

40 Potočňák and Mareš, "Georgian Foreign Fighters," 169–70.

41 Nicholas Waller, "American Ex-Paratrooper Joins Georgian Legion Fighting in Ukraine," *Georgia Today*, February 26, 2016, http://gtarchive.georgiatoday.ge/news/3112/American-Ex-Paratrooper-Joins-Georgian-Legion-Fighting-in-Ukraine, accessed: October 21, 2021.

42 See https://twitter.com/kooleksiy/status/1179532577767645185?s=20, accessed: October 21, 2021 for a critical re-appraisal of his U.S. visit by Oleksyi Kuzmenko.

43 Author's interview with Christopher Miller, currently with *Politico*, previously reported on Ukraine for various outlets including *BuzzFeed News* and *RFE/RL*, 12 March 12, 2021.

44 Author's WhatsApp interview with a foreign fighter from the Georgian National Legion who wished to remain anonymous, March 2, 2020.

45 See: https://twitter.com/kooleksiy/status/1179532561640562688?s=20, accessed: October 21, 2021 for Oleksyi Kuzmenko's comments on the matter.

46 Sean Rubinsztein-Dunlop, Suzanne Dredge, and Michael Workman, "From Neo-Nazi to militant: The foreign fighters in Ukraine who Australia's laws won't stop," *ABC News*, April 30, 2018, https://www.abc.net.au/news/2018-05-01/foreign-fighters-return-to-australia-with-military-training/9696784, accessed: October 22, 2021.

47 Christoper Miller, "Soldier of Misfortune," *BuzzFeed News*, April 21, 2021, https://www.buzzfeednews.com/article/christopherm51/craig-lang-ukraine-far-right-extremists-true-crime, accessed: October 22, 2021 for his in-depth profile.

48 Jordan Green, "Combat Vet. Ukrainian Freedom Fighter. Alleged Murderer: Craig Lang Was Always Looking for a War," *INDY Week*, November 26, 2019, https://indyweek.com/news/longform/craig-lang-ukraine-murder-white-supremacist/, accessed: October 22, 2021.

49 Christopher Miller, "The DOJ Is Investigating Americans for War Crimes Allegedly Committed While Fighting with Far-Right Extremists in Ukraine," *BuzzFeed News*, October 8, 2021, https://www.buzzfeednews.com/article/christopherm51/craig-lang-ukraine-war-crimes-alleged, accessed: October 22, 2021.

50 Mike Eckel and Christopher Miller, "Former U.S. Soldier Who Fought With Ukrainian Far-Right Militia Wanted for U.S. Murder," *Radio Free Europe/Radio Liberty*, September 26, 2019, https://www.rferl.org/a/former-u-s-soldier-who-fought-with-ukrainian-far-right-militia-wanted-for-u-s-murder/30185448.html, accessed: October 22, 2021.

51 Christopher Miller and Roman Stepanovych, "An American Who Fought with Extremists in Ukraine Will Be Extradited to Face Double Murder Charges in Florida," *BuzzFeed News*, March 15, 2021, https://www.buzzfeednews.com/article/christopherm51/american-soldier-extradition-florida-murders-ukraine, accessed: October 22, 2021.

52 "'Georgian Legion' leaves Ukrainian Armed Forces," *UAWire*, January 6, 2018, https://uawire.org/georgian-legion-left-the-ukrainian-armed-forces, accessed: October 22, 2021.

53 See https://www.facebook.com/yuri.biriukov/posts/2016396708629136 for his statement of January 6, 2018, accessed: October 22, 2021.

54 "Грузинський легіон: від героїзму до мародерства?," *Ura Inform*, June 20, 2019, https://ura-inform.com/dajdzhest-ru/2019/06/20/gruzinskij-legion-vid-geroyizmu-do-maroderstva/, accessed: October 22, 2021.

55 Oleg Rimini, "Грузинський легіон: Історія брехні та ганьби добігає кінця," *Компромат1*, September 2, 2019, https://kompromat1.pro/articles/127657-gruzinsjkij_legion_istorija_brehni_ta_ganjbi_dobigaje_kintsja, accessed: October 22, 2021.

56 Emile Ghessen, "Ukraine: Europe's Forgotten War: Robin Hood Complex Official Documentary," YouTube, June 17, 2019, https://www.youtube.com/watch?v=5BXYZqgDelw, accessed: October 22, 2021.

57 Ibid.

58 *MEMO Middle East Monitor*, "Israel foreign fighter found dead in Ukraine," September 12, 2019, https://www.middleeastmonitor.com/20180912-israel-foreign-fighter-found-dead-in-ukraine/, accessed: October 22, 2021.

59 *BBC News*, "Georgian Saakashvili quits as Ukraine Odessa governor," November 7, 2016, https://www.bbc.com/news/world-europe-37895588, accessed: October 22, 2021.

60 Author's WhatsApp exchange with a foreign fighter from the Georgian National Legion who wished to remain anonymous, February 25, 2021.

61 Author's WhatsApp interview with a foreign fighter from the Georgian National Legion who wished to remain anonymous, March 2, 2020.

62 Vyacheslav Likhachev, "The 'Right Sector' and Others: National Radicals and the Ukrainian Political Crisis of Late 2013–Early 2104," *Communist and Post-Communist Studies* 48, nos. 2–3 (June–September 2015); 257–71.

63 Alexander Clapp, "Why American Right-Wingers Are Going to War in Ukraine," *Vice*, June 20, 2016, https://www.vice.com/en/article/exk4dj/nationalist-interest-v23n4, accessed: October 22, 2021.

64 Anton Shekhovtsov, "The Ukrainian Far Right and the Ukrainian Revolution," *New Europe College Black Sea Link Program Yearbook 2014-2015* (2015); 224.

65 Ibid. 225.

66 Shaun Walker, "Ukrainian far-right group claims to be co-ordinating violence in Kiev," *The Guardian*, January 23, 2014, https://www.theguardian.com/world/2014/jan/23/ukrainian-far-right-groups-violence-kiev-pravy-sektor, accessed: October 22, 2021.

67 *Nacjonalista.pl*, "Prawy Sektor: Wielka Ukraińska Rekonkwista," February 21, 2014, https://www.nacjonalista.pl/2014/02/21/prawy-sektor-wielka-ukrainska-rekonkwista/, accessed: October 22, 2021.

68 Walker, "Ukrainian far-right group."

69 Paweł Piwowar, "Should Poles be afraid of the Right Sector? A Polish journalist found out," *Euromaidan Press*, February 22, 2018, http://euromaidanpress.com/2018/02/22/poland-journalist-talks-nationalism-with-ukraine-right-sector-leader/, accessed: October 22, 2021.

70 Taras Tarasiuk and Andreas Umland, "Unexpected Friendships: Cooperation of Ukrainian Ultra-Nationalists with Russian and Pro-Kremlin Actors," *Illiberalism Studies Program Working Papers*, no. 8 (September 2021), https://www.illiberalism.org/wp-content/uploads/2021/09/ILLSP-Working-Paper-no.-8-September-2021-Tarasiuk-Umland-1.pdf, accessed: October 22, 2021.

71 Shekhovtsov, *The Ukrainian Far Right*, 225.

72 Huseyn Aliyev, "Unlikely Recruits": Why Politically Irrelevant Ethnic Minorities Participate in Civil Wars?, *Studies in Conflict & Terrorism*, July 2020, DOI: 10.1080/1057610X.2020.1793457, http://eprints.gla.ac.uk/219984/, accessed: October 22, 2021 for more on the Russian-speakers in the Right Sector.

73 Clapp, "Why American Right-Wingers Are Going to War in Ukraine."

74 "The far-right group threatening to overthrow Ukraine's government," BBC Newsnight, YouTube, July 23, 2015, https://www.youtube.com/watch?v=sEKQsnRGv7s, accessed: October 22, 2021.

75 Andreas Umland, "The far right in pre-and post-Euromaidan Ukraine: from ultra-nationalist party politics to ethno-centric uncivil society," *Demokratizatsiya* 28, no. 2 (Spring 2020), https://www.proquest.com/docview/2395280907?OpenUrlRefId=info:xri/sid:primo&accountid=14699, accessed: October 22, 2021.

76 *Nacjonalista.pl*, "Ukraina: Prawy Sektor ruszy na Kijów?," August 17, 2014, https://www.nacjonalista.pl/2014/08/17/ukraina-prawy-sektor-ruszy-na-kijow/, accessed: October 22, 2021.

77 "Armed groups and smuggling in Ukraine's west," DW News, YouTube, July 29, 2015, https://www.youtube.com/watch?v=h0zoK61RHyU, accessed: October 22, 2021.

78 Daisy Sindelar, "Profile: Who Was Right Sector's Oleksandr Muzychko?," *Radio Free Europe/Radio Liberty*, March 25, 2014, https://www.rferl.org/a/ukraine-oleksandr-muzychko-dead-profile/25308993.html, accessed: October 22, 2021.

79 Jack Losh, "Ukraine turns a blind eye to ultrarightist militia," *The Washington Post*, February 13, 2017, https://www.washingtonpost.com/world/europe/ukraine-turns-a-blind-eye-to-ultrarightist-militia/2017/02/12/dbf9ea3c-ecab-11e6-b4ff-ac2cf509efe5_story.html, accessed: June 24, 2021.

80 Clapp, "Why American Right-Wingers Are Going to War in Ukraine."

81 Losh, "Ukraine turns a blind eye."

82 "Out of Control: Ukraine's Rogue Militias," *Vice*, YouTube, https://www.youtube.com/watch?v=wMMXuKB0BoY, accessed: October 27, 2021.

83 Christoper Miller, "Soldier of Misfortune."

84 *Hromadske International*, "Ukraine's "Invisible" Volunteer Fighters," YouTube, November 18, 2018, https://www.youtube.com/watch?v=ZgDloPIWqwI, accessed: October 27, 2021.

85 "Out of Control: Ukraine's Rogue Militias."

86 Author's messenger exchange with Vyacheslav Likhachev, October 28, 2021.

87 Tess Owen, "House Democrats Just Demanded These Neo-Nazi Groups Be Prosecuted as International Terrorists," *Vice News*, October 16, 2019, https://www.vice.com/en/article/59nqmq/house-democrats-just-demanded-these-neo-nazi-groups-be-prosecuted-as-international-terrorists, accessed: October 21, 2021.

88 Max Rose and Ali H. Soufan, "We Once Fought Jihadists. Now We Battle White Supremacists," *The New York Times*, February 11, 20202, https://www.nytimes.com/2020/02/11/opinion/politics/white-supremacist-terrorism.html, accessed: October 21, 2021.

89 Ibid.

90 Shaun Walker, "Azov fighters are Ukraine's greatest weapon and may be its greatest threat," *The Guardian*, September 4, 2014, https://www.theguardian.com/world/2014/sep/10/azov-far-right-fighters-ukraine-neo-nazis, accessed: October 27, 2021.

91 The Soufan Center, *White Supremacy Extremism: The Transnational Rise of the Violent White Supremacist Movement*, (September 2019), https://thesoufancenter.org/wp-content/uploads/2019/09/Report-by-The-Soufan-Center-White-Supremacy-Extremism-The-Transnational-Rise-of-The-Violent-White-Supremacist-Movement.pdf, accessed: November 1, 2021.

92 Kacper Rekawek, "Don't Designate Azov. Why the U.S. should not include the Azov Movement on the Foreign Terrorist Organizations (FTO) list," *The CounterPoint Blog*, April 14, 2021, https://www.counterextremism.com/blog/dont-designate-azov, accessed: October 29, 2021 for the author's input into the debate.

93 Marc Bennetts, "Ukraine's National Militia: 'We're not neo-Nazis, we just want to make our country better'," *The Guardian*, March 13, 2018, https://www.theguardian.com/world/2018/mar/13/ukraine-far-right-national-militia-takes-law-into-own-hands-neo-nazi-links, accessed: October 27, 2021; Christopher Miller, "With Axes and Hammers, Far-Right Vigilantes Destroy Another Romany Camp in Kyiv," *Radio Free Europe/Radio Liberty*, June 8, 2018, https://www.rferl.org/a/ukraine-far-right-vigilantes-destroy-another-romany-camp-in-kyiv/29280336.html, accessed: October 27, 2018.

94 Christoper Miller, "Azov, Ukraine's Most Prominent Ultranationalist Group, Sets Its Sights on U.S., Europe," *Radio Free Europe/Radio Liberty*, November 14, 2018, https://www.rferl.org/a/azov-ukraine-s-most-prominent-ultranationalist-group-sets-its-sights-on-u-s-europe/29600564.html, accessed: October 27, 2021.

95 Michael Colborne, "Croatia Key to Ukrainian Far-Right's International Ambitions," *BalkanInsight*, July 18, 2019, https://balkaninsight.com/2019/07/18/croatia-key-to-ukrainian-far-rights-international-ambitions/, accessed: October 27, 2021.

96 See e.g. this thread by Oleksyi Kuzmenko on the foundation of another paramilitary organiation within the wider Azov movement: https://twitter.com/kooleksiy/status/1289994301087178753?s=20, accessed: October 27, 2021.

97 For example, Azov allegedly only featured 20 foreigners in June of 2014, when it was already making its name on the front lines of the war. See Klimecki, *Krym*, 115.

98 "Inside A White Supremacist Militia in Ukraine," *TIME*, January 8, 2021, YouTube, https://www.youtube.com/watch?v=fy910FG46C4, accessed: October 27, 2021.

99 Rose and Soufan, "We Once Fought Jihadists."

100 Andreas Umland, "Irregular Militias and Radical Nationalism in Post-Euromaydan Ukraine: The Prehistory and Emergence of the 'Azov' Battalion in 2014," *Terrorism and Political Violence* 31, no.1 (2019): 122–123.

101 Umland, "Irregular Militias" 111.

102 Ibid. 117–120.

103 Call sign "Woland," *Valhalla-Express*, 29.

104 *Youtube*, "Battalion AZOV :Gaston Besson il reclutatore /Full interview English," November 18, 2014, https://www.youtube.com/watch?v=2Gd0vmfXiJg, accessed: January 14, 2021.

105 See: https://nationalcorps.org/history-2/, accessed: November 8, 2021, for the party's own take on its history.

106 The author is familiar with a foreign fighter from the ranks of Azov, who used the line of "liberator of Mariupol" in his self-description on twitter.

107 Author's WhatsApp interview with a foreign member of the Azov Battalion/Regiment, January 28, 2020.

108 Likhachev, "The Far Right in the Conflict between Russia and Ukraine," 14–15.

109 Author's interview with Vlad Kovalchuk, member of the National Corps international department, February 20, 2020.

110 Ghessen, *Ukraine*.

111 Author's WhatsApp interview a foreign member of the Azov Battalion/Regiment who wished to remain anonymous, January 28, 2020.

112 Šeler's remarks were based on his experience from Croatia whose armed forces were also at first shunned by NATO but that attitude changed as the years passed by. He maintained that a similar process would happen for Azov in Ukraine. See Intermarium Support Group, *The Fourth Online Conference of the Intermarium Support Group took place in Kyiv, 24 December 2020*, https://intermarium.org.ua/en/the-fourth-online-conference-of-the-intermarium-support-group-took-place-in-kyiv/, accessed: November 10, 2021 for a video of his remarks, from 02:41:58.

113 See https://azov.org.ua/military-school/, accessed: November 10, 2021 for more on the issue.

114 Author's interview with Vyacheslav Likhachev, March 12, 2020.

115 Author's WhatsApp interview with a foreign member of the Azov Battalion/Regiment who wished to remain anonymous, January 28, 2020.

116 Dina Newman, "Ukraine conflict: 'White power' warrior from Sweden," *BBC News*, July 16, 2014, https://www.bbc.com/news/world-europe-28329329, accessed: November 10, 2021.

117 This mostly concerns French and Italian recruiters for the battalion. For more see Kacper Rekawek, *Foreign Fighters in Ukraine: The Brown-Red Cocktail* (Abingdon: Routledge, 2023).

118 See https://web.archive.org/web/20151115000032/https:/ukrainiancrusade.blogspot.com/2015/03/14-points-of-misanthropic-division.html for "14 The Points of Misanthropic Division International," March 26, 2015, https://web.archive.org/web/20151115000032/https:/ukrainiancrusade.blogspot.com/2015/03/14-points-of-misanthropic-division.html, accessed: November 3, 2021. See especially point 8, which reads: "Misanthropic Division main purpose is the immediate support of military in ATO [Anti-Terrorist Operation]: AZOV and DUK [Ukrainian Volunteer Corps, the Right Sector's paramilitary arm] – without forgetting that they are fighting and representing our cause."

119 Natalia Yudina, "The New Exile Strategy of Russian Nationalists," *Illiberalism Studies Program Working Papers*, no. 2 (December 2020), https://www.illiberalism.org/the-new-exile-strategy-of-russian-nationalists/, accessed: November 3, 2021.

120 This happened in late 2015–2016 period. See the author's interview with Vyacheslav Likhachev, March 12, 2020.

121 See Hope not Hate, *State of Hate 2018*, no. 35 (January–February 2018) 20–21, https://hopenothate.org.uk/wp-content/uploads/2021/09/State-of-Hate-2018.pdf, accessed: November 3, 2021.

122 Christian Fuchs, "Rechte Kämpferlandverschickung," *Die Zeit*, February 11, 2021, https://www.zeit.de/politik/ausland/2021-02/rechtsextremismus-neonazis-sachsen-urlaub-veteranen-ukraine/komplettansicht, accessed: November 11, 2021.

123 Hope not Hate, *State of Hate 2018*.

124 Tim Lister, "The Nexus Between Far-Right Extremists in the United States and Ukraine," *CTC Sentinel* 13, no. 4 (April 2020), https://ctc.usma.edu/the-nexus-between-far-right-extremists-in-the-united-states-and-ukraine/, accessed: November 11, 2021.

125 Michael Colborne, "The "Hardcore" Russian Neo-Nazi Group That Calls Ukraine Home," *Bellingcat Anti-Equality Monitoring*, September 4, 2019, https://www.bellingcat.com/news/uk-and-europe/2019/09/04/the-hardcore-russian-neo-nazi-group-that-calls-ukraine-home/, accessed: November 3, 2021.

126 Michael Colborne, "Most neo-Nazi Music Festivals Are Closely Guarded Secrets: Not This One in Ukraine," *Haaretz*, December 12, 2019, https://www.haaretz. com/world-news/europe/.premium-most-neo-nazi-music-festivals-are-closely-guarded-secrets-not-this-one-1.8260218, accessed: November 3, 2021.

127 Anya Hrytsenko, "Misanthropic Division: A Neo-Nazi Movement from Ukraine and Russia," *REFT< > LIGHT*, September 30, 2016, http://reftlight.euromaidan-press.com/2016/09/30/misanthropic-division-a-neo-nazi-movement-from-ukraine-and-russia/, accessed; September 14, 2021.

128 Simon Shuster and Billy Perrigo, "Like, Share, Recruit: How a White-Supremacist Militia Uses Facebook to Radicalize and Train New Members," *TIME*, January 7, 2021, https://time.com/5926750/azov-far-right-movement-facebook/, accessed: October 29, 2021.

129 See the chapter focusing on Western European foreign fighters for more on him.

130 "УВАГА! ВІДПОВІДЬ ПОЛКУ «АЗОВ» НА ЗВИНУВАЧЕННЯ, ОПУБЛІКОВАНІ У ВИДАННІ TIME," *Time*, January 10, 2021, https://azov.org.ua/zayava-polky-azov/, accessed: October 29, 2021.

131 Kacper Rekawek, *Career Break or a New Career? Extremist Foreign Fighters in Ukraine* (Berlin: Counter Extremism Project, April 2020), 27, https://www.counterex-tremism.com/sites/default/files/CEP%20Report_Career%20Break%20or%20a%20 New%20Career_Extremist%20Foreign%20Fighters%20in%20Ukraine_April%20 2020.pdf, accessed: October 29, 2021.

132 Leonid Ragozin and Sanita Jemberg, "Azov Movement's Race War Plans Find Sympathetic Audience in Latvian Government Party," *re:baltica*, December 13, 2019, https://en.rebaltica.lv/2019/12/azov-movements-race-war-plans-find-sympathet-ic-audience-in-latvian-government-party/, accessed: November 2,2021.

133 Piotr Okulewicz, *Koncepcja „Międzymorza" w myśli i praktyce politycznej obozu Józefa Piłsudskiego w latach 1918–1926* (Poznań: Wydawnictwo Poznanskie, 2001).

134 Adrien Nonjon, *Olena Semenyaka*, "The 'First Lady' of Ukrainian Nationalism," *Illib-eralism Studies Program Working Papers* (September 2020), https://www.illiberalism. org/olena-semenyaka-the-first-lady-of-ukrainian-nationalism/, accessed: November 1, 2021.

135 Dawid Lewis, "We Snuck into Seattle's Super Secret White Nationalist Convention," *The Strangler*, October 4, 2017, https://www.thestranger.com/news/2017/10/04/25451102/ we-snuck-into-seattles-super-secret-white-nationalist-convention, accessed: November 1, 2021.

136 See https://archive.vn/ciW28, accessed: November 1, 2021. Johnson was highlighted as one of "the key thinkers of the radical right." See Graham Macklin, "Greg Johnson and Counter-Currents," in Mark Sedgwick, ed., *Key Thinkers of the Radical Right: Behind the New Threat to Liberal Democracy* (London: Oxford University Press, 2019) 204–23.

137 Anti-Defamation League, "Rise Above Movement (R.A.M.)," https://www.adl.org/ resources/backgrounders/rise-above-movement-ram, accessed: November 1, 2021.

138 A.C. Thompson, Ali Winston, and Darwin Bond Graham, "Racist, Violent, Unpun-ished: A White Hate Group's Campaign of Menace," *ProPublica*, October 19, 2017, https://www.propublica.org/article/white-hate-group-campaign-of-menace-rise-above-movement?utm_campaign=sprout&utm_medium=social&utm_ source=twitter&utm_content=1508514998, accessed: November 1, 2021.

139 Christoper Miller, "Azov, Ukraine's Most Prominent Ultranationalist Group, Sets Its Sights on U.S., Europe."

140 Author's WhatsApp interview a foreign member of the Azov Battalion/Regiment who wished to remain anonymous, January 28, 2020.

141 See https://archive.vn/ciW28, accessed: November 1, 2021.

142 Ibid.

143 See the "national" chapters for more on the purely foreign fighter entities which had still been embedded with larger units on the "separatist" side, such as the French led

Unité Continentale (UC). As will be shown, Pyatnashka, although it looked like a purely foreign fighting outfit, had been a different operation. Its foreign fighters stressed their "Russianness," i.e., connection to the "separatists," some of who they had known from before the war. The unit functioned as a stand-alone formation but also featured locals who eventually took over its command.

144 Kacper Rekawek, "Neither 'NATO's Foreign Legion' Nor the 'Donbass International Brigades': (Where Are All the) Foreign Fighters in Ukraine?"

145 See the estimates by Arkadiusz Legiec, in which early manifestations the current author had also been involved: The Soufan Center, *White Supremacy Extremism* November 1, 29.

146 See the Western Balkan chapter of this monograph for more information on this issue.

147 Alec Luhn, "Volunteers or paid fighters? The Vostok Battalion looms large in war with Kiev," *The Guardian*, June 6, 2014, https://www.theguardian.com/world/2014/jun/06/the-vostok-battalion-shaping-the-eastern-ukraine-conflict, accessed: November 19, 2021.

148 Galeotti, *Armies*, 37.

149 *Essence of Time*, "Essence of Time unit in Donbass. Donetsk airport. November-December 2014. Volga," November 5, 2016, http://eu.eot.su/2016/12/07/essence-of-time-unit-in-donbass-donetsk-airport-november-december-2014-volga/, accessed: November 19, 2021.

150 *112.ua*, "'Coup' in Sukhumi: How 'Donetsk People's Republic' militants in Abkhazia overthrew 'president'," January 21, 2020, https://112.international/politics/coup-in-sukhumi-how-donetsk-peoples-republic-militants-in-abkhazia-overthrew-president-47714.html, accessed: November 22, 2021.

151 See https://vk.com/brigada_15, accessed: November 22, 2021.

152 See https://www.facebook.com/photo?fbid=3088880417801311&set=pb.100000 381483237.-2207520000. For the unit's logo with Abkhaz and DNR flags and 15 stars see also "brigade's" profile on VKontakte for its short history: https://vk.com/brigada_15.

153 Michael Sheldon, "Embassy Donetsk: the Donbas dacha," *DFRLab*, April 16, 2020, https://medium.com/dfrlab/embassy-donetsk-the-donbas-dacha-6d46966131a4, accessed: November 22, 2021.

154 David Malet, *Foreign Fighters* (New York: Oxford University Press, 2013), 99.

155 Kacper Rekawek, "Neither 'NATO's Foreign Legion' Nor the 'Donbass International Brigades" for a discussion of this issue. For recent scholarship on the international brigades see Giles Tremlett, *The International Brigades: Fascism, Freedom and the Spanish Civil War* (London: Bloomsbury, 2020).

156 Nadezhda Kevorkova, "'Donbass' International Brigade," *Russia Today*, November 17, 2014, https://www.rt.com/op-ed/206187-donbass-international-brigade-fighters-ukraine/, accessed: November 22, 2021.

157 See Pyatnashka's YouTube channel at https://www.youtube.com/watch?v=SAYp6FtJ4Mo, accessed: November 22, 2021 for evidence on this.

158 The North Ossetian commander was preceded in his post by an Abkhaz, a citizen of another non-recognized but Russia supported statelet in Georgia. See: UNIAN Information Agency, "Another commander of Russian-led fighters killed in Donbas," May 18, 2018, https://www.unian.info/war/10121609-another-commander-of-russian-led-fighters-killed-in-donbas.html, accessed: November 22, 2021.

159 Erwan Castel, "Svarog à la barre," *Donbas!*, June 8, 2018, http://alawata-rebellion.blogspot.com/2018/07/svarog-la-barre.html, accessed: November 22, 2021.

160 Galeotti, *Armies* 33. See Pyatnashka family photo from its *Vkontakte* profile at https://vk.com/photo-79511509_456240388?all=1 of May 9, 2017, which features 46 individuals, accessed: November 22, 2021.

161 Maja Zivanovic, "Donbass Brothers: How Serbian Fighters Were Deployed in Ukraine," *balkaninsight*, December 13, 2018, https://balkaninsight.com/2018/12/13/donbass-brothers-how-serbian-fighters-were-deployed-in-ukraine-12-12-2018/, accessed: November 19, 2021.

162 *SPUTNIK International*, "Czechs and Slovaks Form 'Czechoslovak' Volunteer Fighting Unit in Donbass," June 9, 2015, https://sputniknews.com/20150609/1023135080.html, accessed: November 22, 2021.

163 Erwan Castel, "Pyatnashka," *Donbas!*, June 19, 2015, http://alawata-rebellion.blogspot.com/2015/06/piatnashka.html, accessed: November 22, 2021.

164 Erwan Castel, "Volontaire français sur le front," *Donbas!*, January 25, 2017, http://alawata-rebellion.blogspot.com/2017/01/volontaire-francais-sur-le-front.html, accessed: November 22, 2021.

165 Michael Sheldon, "The Small World of French Foreign Fighters," @DFRLab, February 4, 2019, https://medium.com/dfrlab/the-small-world-of-french-foreign-fighters-f53799ee3673, accessed: January 4, 2020.

166 Author's interview with Nikolaus von Twickel of June 25, 2021, analysts for the "People's Republics" and an editor with the Center for Liberal Modernity in Berlin.

167 *DFRLab*, "Chaos in Luhansk, Explained," November 29, 2017, https://medium.com/dfrlab/chaos-in-luhansk-explained-aaba800f4a01, accessed: November 22, 2021.

168 See the author's twitter handle for this photo: https://twitter.com/KacperRekawek/status/821476509214973953?s=20, published on January 17, 2017, accessed: November 18, 2021.

169 Martina Bortolani, "Donbass e neonazismo ucraino: a Reggio Emilia illustrata resistenza antifascista alle porte dell'Europa di cui nessuno parla. Intervista ad Alberto Fazolo," *Next Stop Reggio*, November 14, 2018, https://nextstopreggio.it/donbass-e-neonazismo-ucraino-a-reggio-emilia-illustrata-resistenza-antifascista-alle-porte-delleuropa-di-cui-nessuno-parla-intervista-ad-alberto-fazolo/, accessed: November 18, 2021.

170 Aaron Lake Smith, "Light in the Donbass Window," *Harper's Magazine*, November 21, 2018, https://harpers.org/2018/11/light-in-the-donbass-window-tankies-and-anti-imperialist-fighters-in-east-ukraine/, accessed: November 18, 2021.

171 *Donbassföreningen*, "Interview with Italian Volunteer 'Nemo'," October 17, 2015, https://donbassforeningen.wordpress.com/2015/10/17/eng-interview-with-italian-volunteer-nemo-2/, accessed: November 18, 2021.

172 Ibid. Different leftist factions or groups have given some vocal support to the Russian war effort in Donbas, in the name of opposing American imperialism. See Lake Smith, "Light in the Donbass Window;" see also https://eot.su/, the website of Essence of Time, a Stalinist-nationalist entity recruiting far-left individuals from the likes of Spain or the U.S. for the war in Donbas or the Facebook profile of a ska-punk band Banda Bassotti from Italy, which organized convoys/caravans for support of the "People's Republics," https://www.facebook.com/bandabassottiband.

173 Lake Smith, "Light in the Donbass Window."

174 More on them in the French chapter of this monograph.

175 International Centre for Defence and Security, "Armed Formations in the Secessionist 'Luhansk Republic'," *Commentary*, January 10, 2015, https://icds.ee/en/armed-formations-in-the-secessionist-luhansk-republic/, accessed: November 18, 2021.

176 Galeotti, *Armies*, 49.

177 Elvia Politi, "Alberto Fazolo: 'La soluzione in Donbass? Aiutiamo l'Ucraina a liberarsi'," *sakeritalia.it*, http://sakeritalia.it/ucraina/alberto-fazolo-la-soluzione-in-donbass-aiutiamo-lucraina-a-liberarsi/, accessed: November 19, 2021.

178 International Centre for Defence and Security, "Armed Formations in the Secessionist 'Luhansk Republic'."

179 Ibid.

180 Author's exchange with a French foreign fighter over Facebook Messenger, August 28, 2015. The French led Unité Continentale was also for some of its Eastern Ukrainian existence affiliated with Prizrak.

181 *East/West*, Бригада "Призрак" Алексея Мозгового вошла в состав "Народной милиции" "ЛНР," April 4, 2015, http://www.ostrovok.lg.ua/news/agrozona/brigada-prizrak-alekseya-mozgovogo-voshla-v-sostav-narodnoy-milicii-lnr, accessed: November 18, 2021.

182 Orlando Crowcroft, "Ukraine crisis: Who killed rebel leaders Alexei Mozgovoy and Alexandr 'Batman' Bednov?," *International Business Times*, June 4, 2015, https://www.ibtimes.co.uk/ukraine-crisis-who-killed-rebel-leaders-alexei-mozgovoy-alexandr-batman-bednov-1504388, accessed: November 18, 2021.

183 *Communist Party of the Donetsk People's Republic*, "Statement of the Central Committee of the CP of the DPR in connection with the tragic death of Alexey Markov," October 25, 2020, http://wpered.su/2020/10/25/statement-of-the-central-committee-of-the-cp-of-the-dpr-in-connection-with-the-tragic-death-of-alexey-markov/, accessed: November 18, 2021.

184 Maja Zivanovic, "Donbass Brothers: How Serbian Fighters Were Deployed in Ukraine," *balkaninsight*, December 13, 2018, https://balkaninsight.com/2018/12/13/donbass-brothers-how-serbian-fighters-were-deployed-in-ukraine-12-12-2018/, accessed: November 19, 2021.

185 The unit also featured Russian foreign fighters. One of these, from St. Petersburg, later fought in the ranks of the YPG in Syria and died in 2018. See Jafe Arnold, "Former Lugansk 'Batman' Fighter Killed in Syria," *FRN*, September 30, 2015, https://fort-russ.com/2015/09/former-lugansk-batman-fighter-killed-in/, accessed: November 19, 2021.

186 "Secessionist Forces in Luhansk 'Republic': Order out of Chaos?," *International Centre for Security and Defence*, January 10, 2015, https://icds.ee/en/secessionist-forces-in-luhansk-republic-order-out-of-chaos/, accessed: November 19, 2021.

187 "Ukrainian Separatist Commander Reportedly Killed By Fellow Separatists," *Radio Free Europe/Radio Liberty*, January 3, 2015, https://www.rferl.org/a/ukraine-luhansk-bednov-plotnitsky-assassination-russia-torture-arrest/26775163.html, accessed: November 19, 2021.

188 Justice for Peace in Donbas, "The Prisons of Luhansk: The Batman's Basement," February 25, 2016, https://jfp.org.ua/rights/porushennia/violation_categories/nezakonni-mistsia-nesvobody/rights_violations/pidval_betmena?locale=en, accessed: November 19, 2021.

189 Catherine A. Fitzpatrick and Pierre Vaux, "Russian Neo-Nazi Paramilitary Group, Rusich, to Withdraw: Freezing of Conflict or a Feint?," *The Interpreter*, July 10, 2015, https://pressimus.com/Interpreter_Mag/press/9072, accessed: November 19, 2021.

190 See No Ro, "Dshrg 'Rusich' Support from Poland. GDSW 'Rusicz' Wsparcie z Polski. РУСИЧ," YouTube, January 26, 2015, https://www.youtube.com/watch?v=kJx4F5EewEY, accessed: November 19, 2021 for a video advertising their battlefield activities.

191 No Ro, "Dshrg 'Rusich' training camp 2015. Dsgw Rusicz: obóz szkoleniowy," YouTube, April 26, 2015, https://www.youtube.com/watch?v=RC-U7Poi3E4, accessed: November 19, 2021.

192 Fitzpatrick and Vaux, "Russian Neo-Nazi Paramilitary Group, Rusich, to Withdraw."

193 "Russian neo-Nazi who tortured Ukrainian prisoners shows off his holiday in Belarus," *Belsat.eu*, November 11, 2018, https://naviny.belsat.eu/en/news/russian-neo-nazi-who-tortured-ukrainian-prisoners-shows-off-his-holiday-in-belarus/, accessed: November 19, 2021. The story of his deputy, Yan Petrovsky, who returned to Norway, was arrested, and then resurfaced in St. Petersburg in Russia, was published by *Aftenposten* on December 10, 2021.

4

"TWO SIDES OF THE SAME COIN"? IDEOLOGICAL (NON-)SPLIT ON THE EUROPEAN FAR RIGHT VIS-À-VIS THE WAR IN UKRAINE

Brown-Red Postmodernism Ascendant

A picture is worth 1,000 words. One should remember this old English adage while studying some of the images from the war in Ukraine, especially those which tell us a great deal about the ideology of the foreign fighters involved in the conflict. A perfect example could be a snapshot of one of the "separatist" bases in Donetsk, probably from early 2015, which features a foreign fighter posing, with a string of flags stretched out on the wall behind him. One, uncontroversial, is the Donetsk People's Republic (DNR)'s black, blue and red, the other features an orthodox flag, and the third features Joseph Stalin.[1] It seems that in this war a newly emerged "statelet," Orthodoxy and communism can co-exist freely, without any hindrance, and no one sees any contradiction. Confusion seems to reign as one of the interviewed French foreign fighters from the "separatist" ranks admitted to the author that the war in Ukraine had truly been a "postmodern" war, with fighters engaged on either side more attached to symbols than ideologies.[2] For other foreign fighters, war should be "take[n] with a big bright smile, a bit of craziness."[3] Alternatively, it should be taken with a pinch of salt, as the fighters would also admit that "in some very f#%^ed up way [were] products of post-modernity."[4]

Such alleged postmodernism and propensity for ridiculing war, perhaps in an attempt to secure a mental escape from its hardships and horrors, does not render any attempt to discuss the ideological backgrounds of foreign fighters involved in the conflict easy or straightforward. To complicate matters further, and as will be shown, fighters on both sides had often known one another as members of broader "nationalist" or far-right milieus in their respective countries. The fact that they had often been so similar to one another was referred to by a Swede in the Azov's ranks as a "mental brain fuck" – a ridiculous issue which should

DOI: 10.4324/9781003192992-4

not, but did, happen.[5] Theoretically, their common political roots should allow for a neat and clear-cut study of fighters' ideological backgrounds. In reality, however, this is grossly complicated by their propensity to project their often individual expectations, struggles and wishes onto the conflict first and only later reconciling these with the reality on the ground. Such an approach allowed people who wished for "Paris to be like Donetsk – clean, with normal people, with traditions, with sense of values, respect for patriotism" and wishing for their country to be "just like the DNR" to join the "separatists."[6] Simultaneously, others joined an allegedly "1000 year struggle in which Ukraine guards Europe against 'Muscovy'."[7] Whether Donetsk had truly been clean or whether Ukraine actually fought Muscovy/Russia for a millennium seemed beyond the point. The follow up – deployment to a conflict in a "tribal war," with "nationalists on both sides zone because their ideology is less important than the side and symbols they identify with," [8] and making a stand – was what ultimately mattered.

Such a turn of events in relation to foreign fighters in Ukraine adds to David Malet's thorough analysis of what motivates foreign fighters. Indeed, those who flocked to either side in Ukraine heard the call that people with whom they apparently had something in common (ideology, religion, ethnicity, skin color etc.) "were under existential threat." This propelled them onward as they thought it as their "duty [...] to do something" and become "heroes," plus gain meaning in their lives. Malet would also indicate that it would have been local belligerents' recruitment messaging, playing on "identity" of the prospective fighters, that would kickstart the process. This messaging would be aimed at and crafted especially for "people marginalised in [a given] society."[9] This should sound more than familiar to all familiar with studies of the jihadist foreign fighters, whose kinship with e.g. Syrian Sunnis prompted them to join the civil war in Syria.[10] These included the marginalized Western Europeans, effectively redeemed outlaws, who saw foreign fighting as a chance for a fresh start.[11]

As will be shown, the latter – recruitment of the "marginalized," i.e. individuals coming from ideological backgrounds often beyond the pale for the majority of their compatriots, had successfully taken place, and the Western far right but also far-left extremists successfully trekked to Ukraine to take part in a war. One would be obliged, however, to question the extent to which this process had been successful as the foreigners had hardly been warmly welcomed in the conflict zone. As it turned out, and as the next chapters will demonstrate, neither side was keen on accepting too many foreign volunteers and performed only a miniscule effort to recruit abroad. When they did, they sometimes ended up with "errors in casting," such as the original French recruits for the cause of the "People's Republics."[12] It seems that the ideological mismatches or the fighters' deflated expectations upon arrival often rendered the whole affair meaningless as far as the result of the war in Ukraine was concerned. Nonetheless, the fighters, who may not have fitted into the reality of this conflict, were ready, to use Malet's term, to play on their identity and lend it to a given side in the war or even a particular unit. They thus demonstrated unprecedented, if not postmodern, flexibility, which led to a development of a brown-red cocktail.

In order to deconstruct this from an ideological point of view, and understand how the postmodernity triumphed amongst the foreign fighters in Ukraine, one must look east where Russia "nudges" those intent on "destroying the West." While doing so it casts, according to one of the most astute observers of the conflict in Ukraine, a "wide net: [...] and give[s] priority to those that are themselves directed at the destruction of the modern European civilizational identity. Groups that can act in this capacity include totalitarian sects, separatist movements, neo-Nazi and racist movements, anarchists and anti-globalists, radical ecologists, Euro-sceptics, isolationists, illegal migrants, etc."[13] In fact, Russia wages a political form of its hybrid war, described in the previous chapters. This hybrid war, however, does not include "polite people" or takeover of government buildings in the West. What it includes, however, is Russia presenting itself as an eclectic friend to all of the West's rebels or rejects who, unlike the Ukrainians, would not feel threatened by the more physical aspects of hybridity as Russia is far and cannot, and will not, invade their countries. In such a scenario, any group – brown, red or brown-red – is not beyond the pale and turns into a potentially useful conduit toward undermining the West. As will be shown, a key feat in this approach is its deniability as a great deal of the "nudging" is not done by the government of the Russian Federation but by individuals or organizations which are, seemingly but not completely, independent of the Kremlin's control. These might have existing links in the West which only facilitate their status of conduits. As far as the conflict in Ukraine is concerned, a key role, especially in relation to the most brown-red contingent of foreign fighters – the French – was played by the ideology of Eurasianism and its twenty-first century most acclaimed propagator, Alexander Dugin.

Dugin as Conduit of the Brown-Red Cocktail

Eurasianism is a philosophical/ideological trend that came to prominence in the 1920s circles of Russian emigrés.[14] It rejected "Eurocentrism" and Europe-Asia division and saw Russia as the epicenter of a "third continent," Eurasia, and looked favorably on the result of the 1917 revolution, which effectively established a Eurasian giant, the Soviet Union.[15] The ideology, driven underground during the Soviet Union, enjoyed a comeback after the Soviet Union's collapse. Alexander Dugin, also a political operator of the National Bolshevik Party (NBP, Национал-большевистская партия), which attempted to mix the far right and the far left ideas, became the ideology's public face.[16]

Dugin holds the informal title of the "best-marketed of all Russian ideologists,"[17] a feat mostly achieved on the back of him being referred to as "Putin's philosopher."[18] As will be shown in later chapters, this characterization is not accurate, as such a title belongs to Ivan Ilyin.[19] Dugin shot to a wide international but also Russian fame in the period preceding the war in Ukraine:

> [w]hen Dugin reached a new peak of success between 2012 and early 2014, when the Kremlin opened the door for all conservative ideologues to appear more visibly on state-controlled media. The government's first objective was to drown out the liberal opposition that emerged during the anti-Putin protests of 2011–12, and then to legitimize its position on the Ukrainian crisis, the annexation of Crimea, and the Donbas insurgency. Dugin rapidly became one of the main proponents of Novorossiya—the notion that eastern Ukraine's destiny is to (re)join Russia.[20]

It was an astonishing culmination of a career of an alleged GRU, *Гла́вное управле́ние Генера́льного шта́ба Вооружённых сил Росси́йской Федера́ции, Glavnoje upravlenije General'nogo shtaba Vooruzhonnykh sil Rossiyskoy Federatsii*, Main Directorate of the General Staff of the Armed Forces of the Russian Federation) a Soviet military intelligence officer's son but also a member of countercultural/dissident circles of the 1970s and 1980s Moscow,[21] who dabbled in esoterism, mysticism, paganism, occultism and later earned the title of "St. Cyril and Methodius of fascism," or a bedrock for this ideology in modern-day Russia.[22] In the meantime, he became "a professional conspiracy theorist"[23] who, after a period of anti-state activities directed at the post-1991 Russian Federation (such as participation in what effectively was an attempted coup d'état in 1993; co-founding of a nationalist-Bolshevik political party and running as its candidate in elections), made his peace with the "regime" in the late 1990s.[24] Bizarrely, while still involved in these political activities, he was allowed to lecture at the Academy of the General Staff in Moscow. This fact neatly symbolized the 1990s alliance between the seemingly irrelevant Russian nationalists and the military, which felt humiliated and discarded after it was blamed for failures of the Soviet state's interventions into Georgia and Lithuania in the late 1980s and the early 1990s.[25] Simultaneously, Dugin, the nationalist "hip" author, writer, editor and philosopher, was able to double down on his strategy effectively to transplant the tenets of the French new right (more on this school of thought below) into Russia, while "upgrading" Eurasianism, and in return marketing the latter to Western audiences.[26] This success, however, clearly had its limits as Dugin's touted intellectual, but less practical, connection or even cooperation, with luminaries of the American far-right was less than impressive,[27] and his moment of fame in Russia also came to an end after he "vehemently criticized" the Putin regime for refusing to organize a "national revolution," and create a Novorossiya and not "just" the two people's republics of Donetsk and Luhansk.[28]

As focusing too much on Dugin or his philosophy is beyond the scope of this book, the author will concentrate on issues pertaining to his seeming relevance to the Western anti-systemic circles, brown but also brown-red in general and the war in Ukraine in particular.[29] These circles had included individuals who during the war flocked not only to the "People's Republics" but also to the Ukrainian side – as will be shown in later chapters, prominent Swedish members of the Ukrainian Azov Battalion or even Azov's international secretary, Olena Semenyaka, who had her article published in a volume edited by Dugin in 2011. Dugin apparently wanted to work with individuals like her "to open up new forms of cooperation between Russia and its western periphery."[30] At the same time, this international 360 degree flexibility did not stop him from preaching that his country, Russia, should be seen "as a fighting post-liberal revolutionary force in favor of alternative [i.e. non-liberal and multipolar] future for all the people of the planet."[31] This future will see the construction of an "Eurasian empire" which would protect "us" from a "post-modernist dissolution," as testified by "loss of identity, not only national or cultural identity but also sexual and, soon, human identity" which is a natural end result of the "liberal globalization."[32] Such an approach, mixing far-left anti-Americanism or anti-imperialism with traditionalism, Christian orthodoxy and far-right authoritarianism and nativism, enabled him to cast a truly "wide net." In fact, despite his alleged opposition to postmodernism, his volatile brown-red (and white – for tsarist/orthodox nostalgia) turned him into a prophet of postmodernism, potentially all things to all men amongst the opponents of "liberal globalization."[33]

Regardless of his amorphous flexibility, however, he made his mark especially while liaising with the European far right. This was only made easier by the fact that his views are allegedly "comparable to the German inter-war 'Conservative Revolution,' and owe much to various international schools of geopolitical, proto-fascist and conspirological [conspiratorial] thought including, for instance, Julius Evola or Jean Parvulesco as well as to the post-1968 West European 'New Right.'"[34] What is more, he is known as a compiler of "European far-right ideas"[35] and their subsequent communicator, also to non-Russophone audiences, which might have smoothed some of his Western peers' pro-Russia turn in the late twentieth and early twenty-first centuries.[36] His opposition to "Atlanticism" aimed at containing Russia, regardless of what type of government (communist, democratic or nationalist) controlled the country,[37] won him a faithful audience in the West, especially on its far right which opposed the post-1945 political domination of Western Europe by the U.S.

Dugin and French Far-Right Convergence

Dugin might have been especially popular in Italy,[38] but his postmodernism seemed to strike a chord especially in neighboring France. France is the birthplace of the above-mentioned "new right" (*Nouvelle Droite*, ND), a political movement/school of thought which emerged in the late 1960s. It is a "combination" of leftist influences and "conservative revolutionary world view" and waged a cultural struggle against the American-led "soft totalitarianism" of liberalism and capitalism,[39] and opposed the "ethnocide of European civilization for the sake of Americanization, on one side, and Islamization and Afro-Maghrebization, on the other."[40] ND is fond of Russia – a counterweight to "external (read: American) supervision and interference," and this allowed for a construction of "an intellectual and cultural bridge with the Russian political geographer/ philosopher Alexander Dugin."[41]

This bridging exercise had become all the easier because, since the 1960s, the French far right was not only developing along the lines suggested by the ND intellectual patrons but also in a truly brown-red, or national-Bolshevik direction, which was especially close to Dugin's heart. Such development was the result of a thorough soul-searching as the milieu felt humiliated by France's debacle in Algeria and its failed attempt to take power in a *coup d'état* in 1961. The failure of the far right's one nation nationalism made it consider its wider, European variant, and to embrace revolutionism, i.e. opting for "fascism of the left, economically socialist, pro-Soviet during the Cold War and often pro-Maoist." Adherents of such new "revolutionary nationalism" would be called "the leftists of the right, national communists, fascists of the left, Nazi-Maoists, the red browns" or "Leninists of the right." This "ideological oscillation," puzzling to many external observers less versed in the travails of the far right, was symbolized by the movement's adoption of a "horseshoe" as its symbol – as "extremes [i.e. far right and far left] would come together."[42]

The revolutionary nationalists might not have been the most successful element of the French far right but, with cooperation from the more intellectual ND, dragged the milieu out of its anti-communist or anti-Soviet positions. This then made the pro-Russia turn easier for the likes of Jean Marie le Pen's National Front, and implanted the ideas of "anti-immigration, anti-Americanism, anti-Zionism, the defense of 'identity' in the face of the 'System'" onto the wider French far-right scene.[43] In fact, the National Front, itself a "union of the chapels," a broad-based organization with many currents, allowed for a convergence of traditional French nationalism, the 1960s revolutionary nationalism, 1970s "identitarian" nationalism (i.e. not connected to language, soil or blood, and aiming for a conservative revolution), regional or European nationalism, paganism and fervent Christianity.[44] On top of all that, from the 1990s onward, the French far right was introduced to Eurasianist ideas via *Dissidence Française*, a small political party which stood in favor of geopolitical and civilizational "continental resistance" against the perceived Anglo-Saxon domination.[45]

No matter how "fragmented" and internally competitive the milieu of the French far right might have seemed,[46] it was united in its rejection of the American influence in Europe,[47] with Alain de Benoist, the ND's founding father, writing that "Europe [...] must reorganise itself [...] in close continental association with Russia."[48] In his view, the U.S. would be behind any crisis which pitted the West against Russia and, in this reading of the international reality, the Ukraine conflict is simply another confrontation manufactured by Washington in order to weaken Moscow's hold on its immediate neighborhood and putting a proverbial spanner in the works of the Eurasianists.[49] Consequently, it is of little wonder that other ND ideologues called for Russia's "integration" into "the greatest imperial ensemble that humanity will have ever known – Eurosiberia."[50]

Such calls were being made in parallel with a growing appreciation of Russia as a symbolic "anti-pole" of the U.S., fighting for and not against conservative values.[51] Simultaneously, Dugin was turning into an activist, fundraising for the "separatists" and inciting violence against those loyal to the Ukrainian government.[52] This intellectual-practical French far-right Dugin convergence helped nurture the French mobilization for the "People's Republics." It had been the most numerically significant and most closely attached to the postmodern brown-red cocktail in terms of ideology. Moreover, its significance extends beyond the ideology as it had been the French who attempted to form the only genuine "international brigade" of the war – the so-called *Unité Continentale* (UC).[53] Its uniqueness, unlike the likes of the Azov Battalion or the Right Sector on the other side of the front line, was signified by the fact that it would only include foreign fighters in its ranks and not mix them with the locals. As such, it would constitute a realization of Jean Thiriart's idea of a "European brigade."

Thiriart's Influence: UC as a "European Brigade"

The revolutionary nationalists of the UC might not have known about Thiriart, a seemingly obscure Belgian far-right ideologue of the second half of the twentieth century, a former Nazi collaborationist, for which he was imprisoned up until 1948. As argued by Macklin, it was during the war that Thiriart had his first taste of transnationalism when he effectively worked for a collaborationist Belgian or Walloon organization which opted for the latter's inclusion into "an expanded German confederation."[54] He returned to this idea in the early 1960s when, alongside the stalwart of the British far right, Oswald Mosley, he played an important role in the establishment of "national European" political parties.[55] Bringing together post-Nazi Europeans into a pan-European fascist alliance, however, proved easier said than done.[56] Thiriart also attempted but failed in his quest of "forming European Revolutionary Brigades to start the armed struggle against the American occupier, and searched for external support in Europe as well as among Third World revolutionaries." In a move which would have pleased ND luminaries and Dugin, he was said to have pivoted "his entire political project on the precondition of a liberation of Europe from the control of America, which he considered the principal enemy of Europe."[57] In order to accomplish this, he had a vision of a post-nationalistic "extreme rightwing," no longer dominated by petty "squabbles" over borders, but a milieu intent on establishing "Europe" as an "empire," from Brest to Vladivostok – or in the 1980s, when he took a pro-Soviet turn – from Vladivostok to Dublin.[58] Regardless of whether the impetus for the "empire" was to come from the west (Brest) or the east (Vladivostok), one thing remained constant: opposition to "the totally foreign colonialism represented by the American occupation of Europe, and more particularly by the strong arm of this colonialism, NATO."[59] In order to build this "empire," Thiriart searched for an "outside lung" or "outside springboard," or – in other words – a sympathetic and anti-American government based outside the future borders of his "Europe," where "European national-revolutionaries" would prepare themselves, and form the above-mentioned "European brigades" to return home and instigate "the European revolution."[60] Throughout the 1960s, Thiriart shopped for support for his ideas in the MENA region, including Algeria, Egypt, Romania and China, and introduced far-left elements into his ideology – "national-European communism."[61]

Thiriart's failure to form such brown-red and anti-U.S. "European brigades" in the 1960s did not, however, completely kill his revolutionary dream. In 2014, almost 50 years later and for a brief period, his ideas, the French far right, and Dugin came together in the above-mentioned UC, which published a manifesto heralding its foundation.[62] The name was possibly influenced by that of a 1940s far-right French organization in favor of an internationalist nationalism of four "continental" powers (France, Germany, Italy, Russia) which could dominate Europe.[63] Some of the 2014 UC members, as will be shown, have come through the ranks of leading French far-right organizations, including those revolutionary-nationalist in nature such as the *Troisième Voie* (Third Way), itself a radical off-shoot of the National Front formed in 1985. Nicolas Lebourg associated the UC's manifesto with a political position akin to that of Francois Duprat, one of the founders of the National Front and a leader of its hardline faction, former leftist, anti-Zionist and a pro-Arab author.[64]

The UC might have been the practical embodiment of Thiriart's message but the current author found no references to him or his activities or written work in the pronouncements, interviews and social media statutes of the group or its individual members. It is thus ironic that his "vision" was effectively being put into practice without the Belgian far-right theoretician being recognized as the initiator of the "European brigade" concept. As it turns out, Thiriart was not the only far-right intellectual left out and under-appreciated by the UC. Dominique Venner, one of the pioneers of transnational European nationalism,[65] dismayed by "Europe's civil war" of 1914–1945, who argued that Europe's iden-tities, including the "continental," could only be regained in a "struggle" against an America-led "abstract model that homogenizes all differences,"[66] was another such case. Thus, effectively, while the UC mentioned or quoted Dugin, and pontificated on the East's response to a "liberal" and "globalist," "Atlanticist" and "decadent" West,[67] it was in reality furthering the ideas of Thiriart and Venner. The unit's manifesto, anti-EU and anti-American in tone, spoke of a "new cold war." This pitted the liberal and globalist West against "the East," or "Russia from which Europeans arose millennia ago," where "free men, think-ers, diplomats, activists and ordinary citizens are trying to thwart aggression." It embraced "continentalism" or "Eurasianism,"[68] and its members saw themselves as proponents of "regime change in the West." Consequently, as Russia was regarded as "the designated enemy of these regimes, [then] being on the side of Russia" seemed like an "obvious" choice to them.[69] The UC preached the need for a "unity – and not the fusion – of free peoples" in the most "international of nations." These individuals were to provide a "riposte" in the fight against "Brussels mafia."[70] Thus, Donbass in Eastern Ukraine, firmly in Europe but on the borders of the EU and NATO, was to act as the "outside springboard" for the realization of their anti-American vision. The UC, "an autonomous international brigade," was to act as a vanguard in that struggle.[71]

This choice of struggle mirrors to a large extent that made by the UC's counterparts on the far left, who would also be animated by vehement anti-U.S., anti-NATO, rhetoric. Their fixation with fighting American imperialism, but not other imperialisms, would at times lead them into alliances or understandings with "militant Islam,"[72] and, even more surprisingly, with far-right members of the UC on the front lines in Ukraine. As a result, the Spanish far-left foreign fighters who fought on the side of the "separatists," and rubbed shoulders with the French of the UC, felt no contradiction in stating that they "fought together, communists and Nazis alike, for the liberation of Russia [from a Ukraine, pro-Western, pro-American aggression]."[73] This statement, amplified by the views of the interviewed UC members who would state that "this is not about right or left. It is to fight the common enemy of both – American imperialism,"[74] was in fact a realization of the ND's long-term ambitions of establishing an "anti-American front," regardless of the differences amongst its participants and the complexities of the issue which was meant to bind them."[75]

"Two Sides of the Same Coin"[76]

As shown above, the UC, Thiriart's dream of a "European brigade" came true, and also attempted to function, in a truly national-Bolshevik fashion, as a bridge between the far right and the far left. Interestingly, its ideological background and some of the influences behind this unit were not alien to some of the individuals on the other side of the front line. A UC member was calling for "unity of Europe" in the ongoing "World War III" which "began in Libya, then in Syria, and now in the Donbass." In his view, this was a *reconquista* of Europe and the UC is "to help Russia in this fight."[77] Ironically, the Ukrainian Azov movement – the political home of the Azov Battalion/Regiment which hosted foreign fighters in its ranks, also saw itself as involved in a *reconquista*.[78] This concept, central to the identitarian movement which adopted it from Venner,[79] as the UC had done too, centered on the idea of "winning back something that had been lost"[80] or a "reversal" of Europe's current decline.[81] The "reconquest" was to be led by nationalists, outsiders in the liberal and globalist mainstream, and was intent on radically transforming the socio-economic and political future of the continent. Here, however, the similarities between Azov and the UC's *reconquistas* ended. The former saw Central-Eastern Europe (the *Intermarium* – in between the seas: Adriatic, Baltic and Black), more traditional, Christian and conservative than the liberal West, with Ukraine at its core, as the epicenter of this movement, but the latter opted for Russia as the instigator of the reconquest. The Azov movement did not mind "reconquering" Russia, with its nationalists overcoming the hated Putin regime but was not anti-Atlanticist as the Azov Regiment modeled itself on the units in NATO armies and sought professional recognition from the Alliance.[82] At the same time, Azov's outputs positioned the regiment as an heir to a Viking, i.e. Northern European, tradition of the Kievan Rus,[83] which put it on a collision course with Dugin's non-Eurocentric Eurasianism. The regiment spoke of its defense of Europe against Asiatic Russia, which was once again on the march.[84] This would, of course, be anathema to the pro-Russian UC but the two sides had more in common while looking at the EU – in their view, epicenter of the liberal political project which undermined the traditional European values.[85]

Notwithstanding such ideological similarities-differences, and as will be shown in later chapters, many of the foreign fighters present on either side of the conflict had many things in common on a more practical level. The author's interviews with these individuals uncovered people with a traditional, patriarchal view of the family, "not keen on" but not overtly hostile to LGBT rights, sometimes devout Christians but, in other cases, pagans, "European patriots" in Thiriart's vein who mostly did not mind the domestic policies of Putin's authoritarian and nativist Russia, but who were not nationally chauvinist as they saw themselves as a part of a European brotherhood of "free men," i.e. those who took a stand by participating in the Ukraine war, and fought for their beliefs. Most of them are anti-immigrant and anti-Muslim and some are antisemitic, and question e.g. the Holocaust but "are adamant they want nothing to do with either the American alt-right or white supremacist movements."[86] In fact, as one of the leading foreign fighters in the Azov's ranks opinionated, these similarities and the fact that many had known each other from before the war, turn them into "two sides of the same coin." A leading Hungarian far-right operative with strong opinions on the war in Ukraine wryly commented on this issue:

> [T]he skinheads who are currently fighting on the side of Ukraine, ideologically speaking, may be going against Russian aggression, but they are also sacrificing their lives in the interest of advancing U.S. geopolitical aims. And this goes directly against national socialist principles. And then you have Russian rebels, who are fighting viciously against the advancement of Zionist and U.S. geopolitical aims, and while they do this [it is done] under a sickle-and-hammer flag."

This, however, does not break "the symbiotic" unity of the "nationalists" present on both sides of the front line as even those displaying a red hammer and a sickle, or the brown-red hammer and a sickle replacing a swastika on Nazi Germany's red flag with a white disk, are still fighting against the "greatest enemy," i.e. Zionism."[87]

As demonstrated above, the major difference between the brown, brown-red or red fighters on either side had been their approach to Russia. The Azov or other unit's pro-Ukraine foreign fighters would not, unlike some of the French on the "separatist" side, see Russia as a force of "metaphysical patriotism," which was neither Soviet, democratic nor nationalist in nature. It is, in fact, eternal and represents the "Eastern world" in its world war with "liberal dictatorships," which are responding to the "diktat of the market."[88] The French fighters and their supporters, such as musical ensemble *Les Brigands* who visited Donetsk, continued to frame the war as a black versus white titanic clash which pitted "natural," "Christian," "traditional" Russia against the "artificial," "plastic" West, embodied here by Ukraine.[89] They thus identified the war as proxy in nature and saw themselves as allies if not agents of an "active international force," i.e. Russia, and the only one opposing the West.[90] In such conditions, they minded less the Russian alleged aloofness from the conflict as they fought, propagandized about the war or sent humanitarian assistance. Interestingly, their fascination with Russia gave the lie to the myth that Ukraine's "separatists" had been a genuinely local force which only counted, and did not totally depend on, Moscow's support.

Conclusion

The French-led UC, although also featuring Brazilian, Serbian and Spanish foreign fighters, had been the conflict's successful attempt at forming an "international brigade." Its later failures and effective dissolution and reconstitution will be discussed in more detail in the "French" national chapter. Its modest size, however, puts into context the claim that either side had a sizeable internationalist foreign following. Consequently, neither "Donbass international brigade" nor (Ukrainian) "NATO's foreign legion" ever existed.[91] The UC was amorphous in nature and its mobilization cut across ideological boundaries in a truly revolutionary nationalist or national-Bolshevik fashion, and elements of its platform did appeal to some of the foreign volunteers for the other side who had much in common with their brethren in the "separatist" ranks or the other "side of the same coin."

Notes

1 See the author's twitter feed from April 4, 2015, https://twitter.com/KacperRekawek/status/584325571787759616/photo/1, accessed: January 26, 2021.

2 Kacper Rekawek, *Career Break or a New Career? Extremist Foreign Fighters in Ukraine* (Counter Extremism Project, April 2020), 12, https://www.counterextremism.com/sites/default/files/CEP%20Report_Career%20Break%20or%20a%20New%20Career_Extremist%20Foreign%20Fighters%20in%20Ukraine_April%202020.pdf, accessed: January 12, 2020.

3 See the author's twitter feed from May 7, 2015, https://twitter.com/KacperRekawek/status/596197364462919680?s=20, accessed: January 26, 2021.

4 See the author's twitter feed from May 17, 2015, https://twitter.com/KacperRekawek/status/600054114928750592?s=20, accessed: January 26, 2021.

5 Author's interview with a Swedish member of the Azov Regiment (#1) who wished to remain anonymous over twitter Messenger, April 3, 2015.

6 *Vice News*, "Volunteer Soldiers Fighting in Ukraine: Russian Roulette (Dispatch 102)," March 18, 2015, https://www.youtube.com/watch?v=epz-eBXHKIQ, accessed: January 26, 2021.

7 *ІНФОРМАТОР*, "Нинішня війна на Донбасі: це війна двох цивілізацій: Андрій Білецький," April 25, 2015, https://www.youtube.com/watch?v=vkhIE-sAb1c#t=33, accessed: January 26, 2021.

8 Rekawek, *Career Break*, 12, https://www.counterextremism.com/sites/default/files/CEP%20Report_Career%20Break%20or%20a%20New%20Career_Extremist%20Foreign%20Fighters%20in%20Ukraine_April%202020.pdf, accessed: January 12, 2020.

9 See e.g. Malet's discussion of these issues in "An Intelligent Look at Terrorism with Phil Gurski," November 17, 2020, https://borealisthreatandrisk.com/podcast-68-david-malet-western-foreign-terrorist-fighters/, accessed: January 26, 2021.

10 Jytte Klausen, *Western Jihadism: A Thirty Year History* (Oxford: Oxford University Press, 2021) for more on the totality of this phenomenon.

11 Olivier Roy, *Jihad and Death: The Global Appeal of the Islamic State* (London: Hurst, 2017) for more on the criminals turned terrorists amongst the ranks of the jihadist foreign fighters in Syria.

12 Mathieu Molard and Paul Gogo, "Ukraine: Les docs qui montrent l'implication de l'extrême droite française dans la guerre," *Street Press*, August 3, 2016, https://www.streetpress.com/sujet/1472465929-donetskleaks-implication-extreme-droite-francaise-ukraine, accessed: January 4, 2020.

13 Andrew Wilson, "Russia's 'nudge' propaganda," *eurozine*, March 11, 2015, https://www.eurozine.com/russias-nudge-propaganda/, accessed: March 7, 2021.

14 Charles Clover, *Black Wind, White Snow: The Rise of Russia's New Nationalism* (New Haven: Yale University Press, 2016) for more on the issue.

15 Michel Eltchaninoff, *Inside the Mind of Vladimir Putin* (London: Hurst, 2018), 1169–1200.

16 Victor Yasmann, "National Bolsheviks, the Party of 'Direct Action'," *Radio Free Europe/Radio Liberty*, https://www.rferl.org/a/1058689.html, accessed: March 11, 2021 for a profile of the NBP.

17 Marlene Laruelle, "Alexander Dugin and Eurasianism," in Mark Sedgwick, *Key Thinkers of the Radical Right Behind the New Threat to Liberal Democracy* (Oxford: Oxford University Press), 155.

18 Alex Hearn, "Aleksandr Dugin: The sinister ideologue who's Putin's favourite philosopher," *The Jewish Chronicle*, March 11, 2022, https://www.thejc.com/lets-talk/all/aleksandr-dugin-the-sinister-ideologue-whos-putins-favourite-philosopher-3829SiTsfS8P7UK19PwT4k, accessed: March 25, 2022.

19 Eltchaninoff, *Inside the Mind of Vladimir Putin*.

20 Laruelle, "Alexander Dugin and Eurasianism," 157–158.

21 Andreas Umland, "Post-Soviet 'Uncivil Society' and the Rise of Aleksandr Dugin: A Case Study of the Extraparliamentary Radical Right in Contemporary Russia," Dissertation submitted to the Faculty of Social and Political Sciences of the University of Cambridge for the degree of Doctor of Philosophy (January 2007), 97–99, https://papers.ssrn.com/sol3/papers.cfm?abstract_id=2892325, accessed: March 25, 2022.

22 Clover, *Black Wind*, 174.

23 Ibid. 186.

24 Dmitry Shlapentokh, "Dugin Eurasianism: A Window on the Minds of the Russian Elite or an Intellectual Ploy?," *Studies in East European Thought* 59, no. 3, (September 2007): 217.

25 Clover, *Black Wind*, 185.

26 Ibid. 181–186.

27 Benjamin R. Teitelbaum, *War for Eternity: The Return of Traditionalism and the Rise of the Populist Right* (Harmondsworth: Penguin Books, 2021), Edition 70 Kindle.

28 Laruelle, "Alexander Dugin and Eurasianism," 157–158.

29 Andreas Umland, "Post-Soviet 'Uncivil Society' and the Rise of Aleksandr Dugin: A Case Study of the Extraparliamentary Radical Right in Contemporary Russia," Dissertation submitted to the Faculty of Social and Political Sciences of the University

of Cambridge for the degree of Doctor of Philosophy, (January 2007), https://papers. ssrn.com/sol3/papers.cfm?abstract_id=2892325, accessed: January 6, 2020, for a thorough study of Dugin's philosophy.

30 See: Adrien Nonjon, "Olena Semenyaka, The 'First Lady' of Ukrainian Nationalism," Illiberalism Studies Program Working Papers (September 2020), https:// www.illiberalism.org/olena-semenyaka-the-first-lady-of-ukrainian-nationalism/, accessed: January 18, 2021.

31 See Unité Continentale's, which is described in "the French" chapter of this, Facebook page, where it quotes Dugin: https://www.facebook.com/unite.continentale/ photos/pb.681941775182139.-2207520000../700031180039865/?type=3&theater, accessed: January 5, 2020.

32 Eltchaninoff, *Inside the Mind of Vladimir Putin*, 1215.

33 Liberalism, according to Dugin, is one of the three big ideologies that dominated the 20th century – alongside communism and nationalism. Only liberalism, however, is said to have been victorious internationally. In Dugin's view, the response to these artificial ideologies or constructs, the world needs to embrace "the fourth political theory" – a concept which overcomes "the limits of Western, post-Christian modernity [...] a multi-polar ideology which is not universalist [...] fir for local conditions." It allows for the maintenance of peculiarities and "unites and not divides" humanity and e.g. allows Russians to maintain being Orthodox and Slavs simultaneously. See: *Xportal.pl*, "Alexandr Dugin: Polskość musi przezwyciężyć globalizm," March 5, 2019, https://xportal.pl/?p=34351, accessed: March 24, 2021.

34 Andreas Umland, "Post-Soviet 'Uncivil Society' and the Rise of Aleksandr Dugin. A Case Study of the Extraparliamentary Radical Right in Contemporary Russia," Dissertation submitted to the Faculty of Social and Political Sciences of the University of Cambridge for the degree of Doctor of Philosophy (January 2007), 93–94, https://poseidon01.ssrn.com/delivery.php?ID=910024021106117092095099077108100126039006020032019035067000092010126087094064076007039055026029057040105067025116113093069080119055089076076122110103071091064016072033041079097117004124065065116116101088085012111088090000011102126088030126098094081096&EXT=pdf&INDEX=TRUE, accessed: January 6, 2020. In fact, Dugin's fondness for the above-mentioned "Conservative Revolution" is not unique to the philosophical patron and influence of the UC, but cuts across the frontline and is shared by the likes of the Azov movement, a nationalist socio-political entity whose members fought on the Ukrainian side in the discussed war. See e.g. a speech by Olena Semenyaka, "International Secretary of the National Corps, the parliamentary wing of the Azov movement," *Counter Currents*, May 1, 2019, https://counter-currents.com/2019/05/the-conservative-revolution-right-wing-anarchism/, accessed: January 6, 2020.

35 Anton Shekhovtsov and Andreas Umland, "Is Aleksandr Dugin a Traditionalist? 'Neo-Eurasianism' and Perennial Philosophy," *The Russian Review* 68, no.4 (2009): 675, quoted in Patrik Hermansson et al., *The International Alt-Right. Fascism for the 21st Century?* (Abingdon: Routledge, 2020), 224.

36 Teitelbaum, *War for Eternity*, 70.

37 Clover, *Black Wind*, 233–239.

38 Teitelbaum, *War for Eternity*, 69.

39 Tamir Bar-On, *Where Have All the Fascists Gone?* (Abingdon: Routledge, 2016), 191–192.

40 Guillaume Faye, *Why We Fight. Manifesto of the European Resistance* (London: Arktos, 2011), 41. Tamir Bar-On quotes from Pierre-Andreé Taguieff's French expert on ND, classification of tendencies within the movement to describe ND's "intellectual tendencies." These include, amongst others, both the "red brown" revolutionary nationalism and the GRECE's (ND think tank: Research and Study Group for the European Civilization, set up by de Benoist) "neo-fascists and neo-pagans." See Bar-On, *Where Have All the Fascists Gone?*, 138.

41 José Pedro Zúquete, *The Identitarians. The Movement Against Globalism and Islam in Europe* (Notre Dame, Indiana: University of Notre Dame Press, 2018), 231–232.

42 Nicolas Lebourg, *Le monde vu de la plus extrême droite: Du fascisme au nationalisme-révolutionnaire* (Perpignan: Presses universitaires de Perpignan, 2010), 7–10.

43 Nicolas Lebourg, "Qu'est ce que le nationalisme-révolutionnaire?," *#FTP*, https://tempspresents.com/2013/06/07/nicolas-lebourg-definir-le-nationalisme-revolutionnaire-2/, June 7, 2013, accessed: January 15, 2021.

44 Nicolas Lebourg, "La reconfiguration des extrêmes droites françaises, des marges sociales à l'offre politique," in Jérôme Jamin, ed., *L'Extrême droite en Europe* (Bruxelles: Bruylant, 2016), 167–168.

45 Nicolas Lebourg, "The French Far Right in Russia's Orbit," *Carnegie Council for Ethics in International Affairs*, May 15, 2018, https://www.carnegiecouncil.org/publications/articles_papers_reports/the-french-far-right-in-russias-orbit/_res/id=Attachments/index=1/Lebourg-EN%20revised%203.pdf, accessed: January 15, 2021.

46 Author's email exchange with Professor Stéphane François, expert on the French far right, May 18, 2020.

47 Jean-Yves Camus, "Alain de Benoist and the New Right," in Mark Sedgwick, ed., *Key Thinkers of the Radical Right. Behind the New Threat to Liberal Democracy* (Oxford: University Press, 2019), 86.

48 Alain de Benoist and Charles Champetier, *Manifesto for a European Renaissance* (London: Arktos, 2012), 38.

49 Zúquete, *The Identitarians*, 234.

50 Faye, *Why We Fight*, 52.

51 Hermansson et al., *The International Alt-Right*, 220–221.

52 Teitelbaum, *War for Eternity*, 155.

53 This unit is extensively covered in the "French" chapter of this book.

54 Graham Macklin, *Failed Fuhrers. A History of Britain's Extreme Right* (Abingdon: Routledge, 2020), 139–140.

55 Ibid. 138–142.

56 Anton Shekhovtsov, *Russia and the Western Far Right. Tango Noir* (Abingdon: Routledge, 2018), 58.

57 Alexander Jacob, "Introduction," in Jean Thiriart, *Europe, An Empire of 400 Million* (London: Arktos, 2021), 4–5.

58 Shekhovtsov, *Russia and the Western Far Right*, 60–61.

59 Jacob, "Introduction," 9–10.

60 Shekhovtsov, *Russia and the Western Far Right*, 58–59.

61 Ibid. 57.

62 See https://www.facebook.com/pg/unite.continentale/about/?ref=page_internal; accessed: January 15, 2021.

63 Lebourg, "The French Far Right in Russia's Orbit."

64 Ibid.

65 Jean-Yves Camus, "Alain de Benoist and the New Right," in Mark Sedgwick, ed., *Key Thinkers of the Radical Right. Behind the New Threat to Liberal Democracy* (Oxford: University Press, 2019), 78.

66 Zúquete, *The Identitarians*, 1–2, 19, 21.

67 See UC's "Manifesto" at https://www.facebook.com/pg/unite.continentale/about/?ref=page_internal; accessed: January 15, 2021.

68 His name would later come up in the author's interviews with different members of the UC. No other philosopher would be mentioned by the members.

69 Rekawek, *Career Break*, 17.

70 See UC's "Manifesto."

71 See interview with Viktor Lenta, where he recounts his Donbass adventure upon returning to France, available at http://alawata-rebellion.blogspot.com/2015/10/lanalyse-de-victor-lenta.html?m=0, accessed: January 5, 2020.

72 Nick Cohen, *What's Left? How the Left Lost its Way* (New York: Harper Perennial, 2007).

73 Patricia Ortega Dolz, "We fought together, communists and Nazis alike, for the liberation of Russia," *El País*, February 27, 2015, http://elpais.com/elpais/2015/02/27/inenglish/1425051026_915897.html, accessed: February 3, 2021.

74 Author's exchange with a French foreign fighter over twitter Messenger, February 22, 2015.

75 Bar-On, *Where Have All the Fascists Gone?*, 110.

76 See Mikael Skillt tweet of May 5, 2015: https://twitter.com/MikaelSkillt/status/595507421948354560?s=20, accessed: March 12, 2021.

77 Sergei Safronov, "Боевые ряды ополченцев ДНР пополнились первыми французами," *RIA Novosti*, August 21, 2014, https://ria.ru/20140821/1020867138.html, accessed: January 5, 2020.

78 See chap. 3 in this volume.

79 Zúquete, *The Identitarians*, 1.

80 Anton och Jonas, "The First Lady of Ukraine with Anton and Jonas," YouTube, March 30, 2019, https://www.youtube.com/watch?v=GkaF9xwzr2M, accessed: March 12, 2021.

81 Rekawek, *Career Break*, 27.

82 This was evident to the author during the Azov movement's Fourth Online Conference of the Intermarium Support Group (December 2020) which featured presentations on the military prowess of the regiment, and how it would be looking forward to a direct link with NATO, and how the Alliance would also benefit from it. See: https://intermarium.org.ua/en/the-fourth-online-conference-of-the-intermarium-support-group-took-place-in-kyiv/, accessed: March 11, 2021 for a write up on the above-mentioned conference.

83 See the author's twitter feed of April 1, 2015, https://twitter.com/KacperRekawek/status/583241768143060994?s=20, accessed: March 11, 2021, for a sample of such propaganda.

84 See e.g. a speech by the commander of the Azov Battalion: ІНФОРМАТОР, "Нинішня війна на Донбасі - це війна двох цивілізацій: Андрій Білецький," YouTube, April 24, 2015, https://www.youtube.com/watch?v=vkhIE-sAb1c#t=33, accessed: March 12, 2021.

85 Jonas, "The First Lady of Ukraine."

86 Rekawek, *Career Break*, 9–10.

87 Attila Juhász et al., *"The Truth Today Is What Putin Says It Is:" The Activity of Pro-Russian Extremist Groups in Hungary* (Budapest: Political Capital, 2017), 12, https://www.politicalcapital.hu/pc-admin/source/documents/PC_NED_country_study_HU_20170428.pdf.

88 Représentation France RPD, "Le Volontaire français Erwan Castel dans l'armée de la République Populaire de Donetsk," YouTube, December 4, 2017, https://www.youtube.com/watch?v=tofbb8gr3zQ%3B+http%3A%2F%2Falawata-rebellion.blogspot.com%2Fp%2Fqui-suis-je.html, accessed: January 14, 2021.

89 Radio Brigandes, "Les Brigandes au Donbass: Reportage sur une guerre pour la Liberté (R.B. VI: Décembre 2016)," YouTube, December 12, 2016, https://www.youtube.com/watch?v=izSAwGydgfI, accessed: January 14, 2021.

90 Rekawek, *Career Break*, 10.

91 Rekawek, "Neither 'NATO's Foreign Legion' Nor the 'Donbass International Brigades.'"

5

FRANCE

"To Fight American Imperialism"

French Foreign Fighters in Ukraine: An Introduction

The French foreign fighters in Ukraine are responsible for the author's introduction to the subject and his subsequent fascination with it. Their representatives constituted the first group of fighters present on the front lines in Ukraine whom the author saw on the news back in the summer of 2014. As he wrote elsewhere: "[h]ere I was, sitting in my office in Warsaw, Poland [at the Polish Institute of International Affairs, PISM], seeing a report about the French citizens traveling to a neighboring country, Ukraine, to fight alongside pro-Russian "separatists."[1] The above-mentioned news report was both shocking and illuminating.[2] Shocking as it was deeply perplexing to witness young Western Europeans travel to a war in a country on the other side of Europe, for a cause they had theoretically very little understanding of or familiarity with. This is illuminating, as it immediately became clear that these individuals were, at least initially – as they were later said to have been receiving renumeration from the "separatist" authorities[3] – foreign (but not terrorist) fighters. As the world was mostly fixated on such fighters in the ranks of the Islamic State of Iraq and Syria (ISIS), here was a different case of a seemingly similar phenomenon.

The report named "the Frenchmen, [...] Michel [Mickael Takahashi], Victor [Lenta], Nicolas [Perović] and Guiyom [Guillaume Cuvelier]" who allegedly came "to Donetsk in mid-August 2014 to assist the local population and help 're-inform' the French public about the conflict." This re-information was, in their view, needed as the narrative in France depicted Russia and not the "army of Kiev" (presumably, Ukraine) as "the aggressor," and attacks the "pro-Russian population" of Donbas. This very army was said to have been unable to fight for much longer and certainly not into 2015.[4] The fact that the Ukraine's capital and not the name of the country was used in description of its alleged "attack" on this country's legally held

DOI: 10.4324/9781003192992-5

territory was probably meant: (a) to disparage the opponent of the "separatists,"; and (b) to strengthen the "separatist" narrative of a non-viable Ukrainian state splintering along regional lines with the allegedly "pro-Russian" East perfectly entitled to choose its own future. As for the capacities of the Ukrainian army, the French fighters were making their statement while it was suffering one of its worst defeats on the front in the battle of Ilovaisk.[5]

The French fighters in the report had fresh uniforms, neatly pressed, with abundant Ribbons of Saint George (a Russian military symbol present in military decorations, also used by the "separatists") attached to them. On top of that, they also sported badges of their *Unité Continentale* (Continental Unity, UC) and the black-blue and red of the Donetsk People's Republic. Only Lenta, their leader, spoke to the camera. He was flanked by Cuvelier, who – at the beginning of the video – looks around nervously, with Takahashi and Perović right behind the other two and at times sitting down on what looked like a disused tank turret, parked right next to a military truck with a flat tire.

The fact that the interview takes place in an area akin to a public park, with trees and benches clearly visible in the background, adds a surreal dimension to the whole episode. On the one hand, you have a group of foreigners concerned about the war, with another newsman filming the group from behind them but, on the other hand, one can also spot a local civilian inspecting what looked like an abandoned truck in the background. This, in fact, is a photoshoot with the four almost lined up like a rock back with the vocalist (Lenta), and an outspoken lead guitarist (Cuvelier, educated, with fluent English, who stood for the far-right Parti de la France in the 2010 regional elections,[6] and later openly spoke about his experiences in Donbas)[7] conveniently positioned at the front, and the less centerstage drummer and influential bass guitar player (silent Takahashi, and Perović who later quarreled with Lenta as to who should lead the UC)[8] standing back. Interestingly, the fighters themselves confirmed to the author that his conviction of this appearance being a staged event was right:

> They would take us out in front of the cameras, show us around, and try to put into "safety" [mode] in a boring second line position. We, however, understood what was going on and we always managed to break their balls to get what we wanted. But it was tiring. I told them – "no interviews if you don't get us weapons and missions." That is how we got in a Recon [reconnaissance] group in Donetsk [...] usually, we just ignored their orders after a while and mounted our own patrols, raids, scouting. What were they going to do? Shoot us?[9]

Such appearances showcased the arrival of the French foreign fighters in the ranks of the "separatists," of whom up to 40 passed through the ranks between the summers of 2014 and 2016.[10] Simultaneously, the tension amongst the fighters themselves and their self-confessed, and "very tiring" almost constant struggle with the locals "to build up schemes so we could go into combat" allegedly prevented them from doing "soldier's work correctly." Eventually, there was "nothing left to do [t]here [in Donbas]" as "the war of movement changed into war of positions" and the fighters went home.[11]

Brown-Red UC: Roots and Pre-Lives

Viktor Lenta, the self-confessed leader of the UC, claimed his unit was formed back in January of 2014 in Belgrade.[12] Moreover, UC members are photographed brandishing colors of Partizan Beograd, Serbia's second most successful football club, while putting up posters with the words "Free Vojislav Seselj. Stop the American Dictatorship" in different French towns.[13] Moreover, the UC's number two, Perović, is of Serbian-Montenegrin origin and his ancestry and connections in the Balkans were said to have been used in the recruitment of Serbs into the UC.[14] The UC featured former soldiers: Lenta, who claimed that the war in Donbas was his fourth, after Chad, Afghanistan and the Ivory Coast, and Perović who fought in Afghanistan (according to his UC superior – with valor, an opinion not shared by his colonel from the French army),[15] and two others "who served in Afghanistan as part of the army but were not engaged in hostilities."[16]

Apart from the Serbian overtures, the UC leaned towards anti-American, anti-EU, anti-Israeli but pro-Russian discourse, e.g. via pro-Assad or pro-Qaddafi imagery on its Facebook page which depicts the U.S. as responsible for the wars in Iraq, Syria, Libya, Ukraine and violence in Venezuela.[17] It also quotes from Alexander Dugin's, leading Eurasianist of the twenty-first century, "Fourth Political Theory." The book lays down a seemingly new political concept which would, in the words of Dugin, supersede the trio of political theories which dominated the twentieth century, i.e. liberalism, Marxism and fascism. It is an attempt to set modernity against itself while returning to traditionalism and rebelling against commercial universalism, and opting for cultural diversity.[18] Lenta himself admitted that the UC is full of "political soldiers" (individuals fanatically devoted to a far-right political cause – a term originally developed in the UK to describe National Front's uncompromising young radicals)[19] and a geopolitical movement, based on Alexander Dugin's works" working towards developing a "multipolar world" which would be "anti-mondial" (or anti-global, anti-universal or, in practice, anti-American), traditional in terms of values, anti-oligarchic or revolutionary.[20] The UC denounced "our submission to NATO, the European Union and the United States" and called from Donbas for "engagement in resistance, here, at home, now."[21]

The UC's embrace of Dugin is telling. While interviewed, the group's members would attempt to downplay the "right-left" political divide ("this is not about right or left. It is to fight the common enemy of both – American imperialism")[22] and their pre-war "nationalist" views ("I was not just a nationalist. I had a view on geopolitics, on history, etc. [...] but once you are on the ground, you stop focusing on politics so much. Instead, you focus on the military work [...] but I stopped seeing the world like that. I shall support whatever cause I feel is just").[23] Other, non-UC affiliated Frenchmen, saw themselves as "idealist[s] seeking to transcend 'political politics'."[24] And yet, they still evoked Dugin, a Russian "red nationalist" (or national-Bolshevik), and the alleged "St Cyril and Methodius [read: the alpha and omega] of Fascism."[25] His "neither left nor right" approach, and association with the Russian national-Bolsheviks, allowed UC members to portray themselves as "patriots" or "realists" who were beyond "yesterday's" petty political divisions and were intent on abolishing the current "oligarchic" system in France. Labels of being on the "far right" were dismissed as tags or slurs produced by mainstream politicians such as Nicolas Sarkozy or Emmanuel Macron.[26] All of this, however, could not mask the fact that the UC's leaders had a rich history of involvement in the French militant far right and pre-Ukraine war membership of organizations such as *Jeunesses Identitaires*, *Jeunesses Nationalistes*, *Lys Noir*,[27] or later association with *Les Zouaves* (a far-right militant groupuscule in existence between 2018 and 2022),[28] or as shown, running as candidates for far-right parties. Their supporters, with whom they later shared platforms at events, also openly referred to the UC as proponents of the neo-fascist "third way."[29] What is more, some were photographed giving a Nazi-style salute while holding a flag with a Celtic cross while in Donbas,[30] and due to their far-right views were even later termed "errors in casting" on behalf of the Donetsk People's Republic (DNR)/Luhansk People's Republic (LNR) by other Frenchmen (but not foreign fighters) present in Donbas.[31] In short, the UC was the quintessential brown-red unit present on the front lines of Donbas.

The UC's Arrival and Everyday Reality in the Conflict Zone

Lenta, who effectively blazed the trail for the French foreign fighters in the DNR/LNR ranks, later recounted his ordeal on the way to Donetsk. It took him and the other trio of Frenchmen almost two months to finally get to Donbas, and their journey there was, at times, farcical in nature. The French got to Rostov in South Western Russia, the convergence point for Russian involvement in Donbas and later also for the foreign volunteers. They traveled there via Moscow and Budapest,[32] where they were hosted by the local far-right sympathizers with links to the French radical right milieu. While in Russia, the group allegedly encountered suspicion on behalf of the authorities ("your visa is wrong") and were deported to ... Ukraine.[33] Another member of the UC admitted that they had been arrested while in Russia both on the way in and out of Donbas ("the Russians didn't expect any foreign volunteers"),[34] and one member was charged with illegally crossing the Russian border. Their Eurasianism and their stay in Russia, however, allowed for forging contacts in the Russian extremist milieu which provided "letters of introduction" to people in the Vostok Brigade, which was open to featuring foreign fighters, especially Russians, in its ranks.[35] Armed with such contacts, the original UC members flew to Kyiv, took a bus eastwards, and then literally crossed the front line to get into Donetsk.[36]

What happened later was far from perfect, from the point of view of the arriving fighters. As already shown, fighting was not on the menu offered by their "separatist" hosts. To add insult to injury, the Frenchmen, some of whom had military backgrounds, were often appalled by the brutality, disorganization and drunkenness in the "separatist" ranks. They were at times to participate in attacks which would merely consist of a given commander leading them into a barrage of fire with the Russian shout of "davai, davai!" – roughly translated as "come on, come on!."[37] At the same time, they would also be bullied, or attempted to be bullied, by other officers who warned that they would "shoot you and then I will train you," or wake up with their HQ surrounded by mines laid by their drunken "degenerate" local "comrades."[38] From their point of view, they "sacrificed everything they got" to deploy to Donbas but they were relegated to the status of "cool little tourists" deployed for the cameras. At the same time, the locals would not make the most of the experience of the likes of Lenta or Perović, "ex-military from elite units of Western armies, with war experience and technical knowledge." Thus, the DNR armed forces still relied on "outdated Soviet tactics used during WWII." Consequently, their experience could not be matched to that of the Azov's foreigners, including the Swedes, who, allegedly "got good equipment, they are deployed on the very front line in semi-autonomous groups. They train Ukrainian soldiers etc." The French wished their "side" would have done the same thing and were exasperated and disheartened by the mistrust that surrounded them. What is more, they would be arrested on their way in and out of Donbas by Russians who allegedly "did not expect any foreign volunteers."[39]

Looking at all this, Lenta came to the conclusion that "foreign volunteers are not being used to the full for the current hostilities. They are much talked about, their presence in the Donbas is touted in propaganda, such things I can understand, it is a feature of times; propaganda is very important, but—it isn't exactly what they expected. Brazilians, Spaniards, they travelled half-way across the world and arrived in the Donbas to fight, not to talk." He allegedly held talks with his superiors so that they would end up being sent as a group into combat missions. Otherwise, in his view, they would continue being used only up to "no more than ten percent" of their capacity.[40] This underusage of foreign fighters made the original UC, as Lenta confessed, change their unit affiliation at least three times in the opening months of their deployment to Donbas.[41] Such chaotic conditions and the general indifference to the Frenchmen's wishes and valuable experience created an explosive mix which later saw the UC effectively unravel.

The UC: The Unraveling

The fact that the life of a foreign fighter in Donbas was taking its toll on those foreigners who decided to join this war was admitted by some of the participating Frenchmen. Involvement allegedly equaled participation in an "ideological conflict, conflict with yesterday's friends, conflict with political choices, conflict with jealous people, slanderers and imbeciles, conflict finally with oneself."[42] As it later transpired, the conflict also consumed the French contingent in Donbas with some of its veterans who are now back in France hardly on speaking terms with one another,[43] although the early 2019 "Yellow Vests" demonstrations in Paris seemed to have brought some of them together again.[44] There is reluctance on their behalf to recollect the events of late 2014/early 2015 in detail, when the internal conflict in the French or foreign ranks in the Donbas had been at its most acute. The documentary *Polite People*, the most close-up look at some of the fighters involved, is not helpful in this regard as it catches some of the Frenchmen after the split in the ranks.[45] Its director, however, admitted to the author that in the early 2015 most of the UC's members, be it French, Spanish or Serbian, basically abandoned the Lenta-Perović duo of leaders.[46] The way they ran their organization was said to have been "villainous" and "criminal" by another, non-UC, foreign fighter, with the commanding Frenchmen accused of "mistreatment and torture" of their colleagues, being "unfit to command" and "cowardice."[47]

Later in 2015, some of the protagonists seemed to have mended fences as Lenta thanked only some, but not all, of his subordinates for their service. Other Frenchmen's critiques zoomed in on Perović as the main instigator of strife and a source of incompetence in the ranks.[48] The UC's former commander blamed the actual collapse of his unit on the fact that he and his men associated themselves with Donbas "political soldiers" like Igor Girkin, Aleksey Mozgovoi or Arsen Pavol-Motorola, independently minded and no favorites of the Russian "curators" of the "People's Republics." Lenta acknowledged his unit was effectively a brown-red amalgam, "a synthesis of big ideas [such as nationalism or communism] of the twentieth century" as it featured communists from Spain and nationalists from France or Serbia. What brought them together was their alleged desire to "fight the U.S." and its imperialism. At the same time, their eagerness to fight got them into trouble with the more cautious DNR commanders, who seemed to have been content with the September 2014 ceasefire and looked down on units literally spoiling for a fight.[49] The UC, as Lenta acknowledged, fought at Shyrokyne in the winter of 2015 where it suffered four wounded (two French and two Brazilian) and this allegedly contributed to the unit's collapse.[50]

The UC, or what was left of it, devoid of its Serbian, Spanish or Brazilian members,[51] and with the French deeply divided, was effectively integrated into the International Brigade ("Pyatnashka" literally "the 15," which was a reference to its initial membership),[52] a unit set up by Abkhaz DNR volunteers,[53] which included Czech, Serbian or Slovak members, and was later itself integrated into DNR's national guard.[54] A French conduit into "Pyatnashka" had been Erwan Castel, former soldier, "a Breton, polytheist and European" in his late 50s who joined the unit in early 2015.[55] Castel admitted that he decided to abandon French Guiana where he worked as a guide after watching the news of the Odessa clashes in May 2014 when more than 40 people died.[56] Castel is allegedly a veteran of the Karen militias in Myanmar who, alongside Gaston Besson, a French recruiter for the Azov Regiment, a nationalist unit on the side of Ukraine. Such a "coincidence" is, according to one author, a caricature of the "narrowness" of the foreign fighter milieu in France.[57] This narrowness becomes even more evident with information that Besson allegedly provided references, for future "employment," to some of his compatriots who fought on the pro-"separatist" side.[58]

The other part of the UC, call it the anti-Lenta group, sought refuge in attempting to mold its unit on the "Subversive Assault Reconnaissance Group Rusich." Rusich, as was shown in Chapter 3 in this volume, was led by Russian extreme right wing (XRW) individuals. They allegedly had it easier in "People's Republics" for a variety of reasons: "they speak Russian. We don't and locals tend to treat anyone who doesn't speak Russian as a retarded Mongolian or a tourist, [... they arrived there] at the beginning of the war when it was still a war of movement."[59] This allegedly allowed them to be more flexible and improvise while e.g. waging their own hit and run campaign on the enemy.[60] Subsequently, the unit was to gain respect amongst the "separatists" and was tolerated as a semi-autonomous special purpose team.

The French, according to the fighters interviewed by the author, had no such possibility as their brown-red UC effectively came into being in the late summer of 2014, that is after the first ceasefire, when the so-called Minsk Protocol was signed.[61] Moreover, "the commanders of the French volunteers [presumably Lenta and Perović], French themselves [...] had a much more regular traditional approach to war, and they obeyed the chain of command." This was hardly surprising as the two above-mentioned individuals had been French soldiers before journeying to Eastern Ukraine. At the same time, some of their subordinates were keen on doing things differently in general, and on being deployed to the front line in particular: "the DNR command said: don't do anything, wait, tomorrow – 'zavtra'."[62] These tensions facilitated the splits in the UC and two of the original four Frenchmen joining "Team Vikernes [TV,] a group of foreign volunteers fighting on the pro-Russian side in the Donbas war since August 2014."[63] TV, of which the most illustrious member was a Russia educated Brazilian – Rafael Lusvarghi,[64] later came to train with Rusich which allegedly "worked the same way, wanted to the same things, acted the same, and encountered the same exact problems."[65] This short-lived cooperation was captured on camera in the documentary *Polite People*, directed by an American journalist effectively embedded with TV, and features one TV member calling Rusich "an excellent team."[66] Interestingly, Lusvarghi, visibly uneasy while training with Rusich in *Polite People*, later allegedly had a completely different view of the better known "team": "I hate those guys [...] They are a shame to all of us [...] They are nazis."[67] Such a divergence of opinions, with Lusvarghi who himself dabbled in far-right politics and named his team after a convicted neo-pagan and neo-Nazi Norwegian killer (Varg Vikernes),[68] vividly testifies to the fact that on many occasions solidarity amongst the fighters was an illusory concept. What is more, some shades of brown seemed even beyond the pale for the ingredients of the brown-red cocktail.

The UC's Second Life

Interestingly, the idea of "continental unity," and a (para)military force supporting it, did not vanish with the slow departure of the original French members throughout 2015. In 2018, the UC reconstituted itself under the command of

Philippe Khalfine, who was married to a teacher of French at the university in Donetsk. Khalfine who was present in Donbas from at least 2016 onwards as a journalist working for the DNR's press service,[69] and was photographed on the front lines with a firearm in 2017.[70] He "decided to come [to Donetsk] when I saw the images of people taking up arms to defend themselves, with a lot of courage and solidarity. France has lost all its sovereignty vis-à-vis Brussels. Today, I consider the People's Republic of Donetsk [DNR] as my adopted homeland."[71]

Khalfine stressed that "this time" the UC would no longer be a "militia" but an "official unit," utilizing the logo, colors and legacy of its 2014–2015 predecessor. Moreover, Lenta was still left in charge of the group's social media profiles, thus providing continuity to the group's messaging. Khalfine hoped that this new development would allow the Slavic and European people "to work together and effectively against our common and real enemy [globalism]."[72] Interestingly, the new commander stressed that the Frenchmen who stayed in Donbas, after the original departure of UC members, were all from "the extreme-left."[73] Indeed, some had the Soviet flag and Stalin's photographs as their Facebook cover photos but also posted photos of President Trump,[74] and had allegedly nothing to do with the far-right tropes of their predecessors. This paved the way for the term "errors in casting" – describing the "wrong" type of volunteers for the first UC, which allegedly assisted the "separatists" in a fight against Ukrainian "fascism."[75]

This new UC acknowledged only four of its members openly (two Frenchmen, a Serb and a Belgian),[76] and would, at times, also introduce other Frenchmen present in the ranks, outside the UC.[77] The group stopped publishing front line updates at the end of 2018, its Belgian member abandoned Donetsk and, in September 2018, the UC announced the DNR's effective freeze of recruitment of foreigners into the unit (Republican Guard in General and the UC in particular).[78] This was allegedly caused by the change in the Guard's chain of command – from then on it fell under the ministry of internal affairs, which would not allow foreigners to serve in the ranks of its troops.[79] Ironically, a similar reality exists in Ukraine and is responsible for the fact that no new soldiers can join e.g. the Azov Regiment, which falls under the country's ministry of internal affairs. This restriction, however, did not terminate the UC's existence as, in February 2019, it was rumored that the UC was led by a Serbian foreign fighter, Darko Pavlovic.[80]

Fighting vs. Non-Fighting French in the Service of the "Separatists"

As was demonstrated, a significant chunk of the French contingent in the ranks of the "separatists" consists of former French soldiers (e.g. Lenta, Perović, Castel, Munier, former French Foreign Legion member Aleksandre Nabiev,[81] artilleryman and former far-right militant Renaud Regeard[82] – praised by Lenta for his exploits on the front lines,[83] plus former soldiers in non-combatant roles such as François Mauld d'Aymée – more on him below). They had not all known each other before the war but nonetheless gravitated to DNR or its cause. This might mean that sections of the French military were at least susceptible to the ideological message emanating from Moscow. Arnaud Danjean, a French Euro MP specializing in defense and foreign affairs, commented on this to Nicolas Henin:

> The army is in no way affected by a structural ideological [pro-Russian] bias. But it should not be denied that there is a significant concentration of pro-Putin individuals in certain circles of the army. 'He has balls,' we hear people say. He fascinates. He vigorously defends Russian national interests. For a certain very Bonapartist right wing, this is the leader we would like to have. This leadership crisis is accompanied by a fracturing of society, in particular profiting from the anti-Muslim sentiment that takes hold, takes over and complements traditional anti-Americanism [...] But it is more, I think, a question of circumstances (the famous vacuum of Western leadership in the face of the cold determination of the Kremlin's master) reinforced, however, it is true, by two concomitant phenomena: the militarization of the post-terrorist counter-terrorism response [...] (with the army at the forefront, at least in public communication) and Russian interventionism in Syria, reinforcing the idea of a realistic Moscow strategy in the face of Western cowardice. The martial rhetoric, in my opinion excessive, which accompanies the [French] deployment [...] in the Sahel, and all anti-terrorist communication, singularly echoes the Russian position and strategic choices.[84]

At the same time, this sentiment, potentially shared by dozens if not hundreds of soldiers and veterans in France who had decided not to be involved in Donbas, is often not enough to transform a given individual from a regular Frenchmen to a foreign fighter in Eastern Ukraine. A set of contacts or a network was needed to complete one's journey from Paris to Donetsk. Here, the French did not disappoint, with the likes of Christelle Néant, "an activist defending human rights [...] revolted [by] what is happening here [Eastern Ukraine]," who had been present in Donetsk since March 2016, and was employed by DoniPress (DNR's press agency).[85] The agency would also organize commercial tours of Donbas for the French-speaking "friends of Donbas" and would issue invites to French politicians and foreign affairs experts to come and visit Donetsk. The French were assisted in the process by French-speaking locals operating either out of Donetsk (such as Svetlana Kissileva)[86] or out of Russia (Elena Sydorova).[87] The French involvement with Donbas also extended to "musical groups" such as Les Brigands,[88] who visited Donetsk in 2016, and their exploits were later presented in a self-produced documentary which featured four French foreign fighters and Néant.[89] Another possible link into Donbas could have been operationalized via Serbia. Perović, UC's original second in command, is of Serbian origin. Although he lived in Montenegro, Perović was said to have been responsible for some of the UC's recruitment in Serbia[90] – the UC originally included a Serbian contingent.[91] The UC's legend has it that it had been originally formed in Belgrade, some members allegedly received training there before deploying to Donbas,[92] and crowdsourcing donations received by its members were said to have financed travel of some of its Serbian volunteers to Donbas.[93]

The original UC allegedly had been in touch with individuals from NGOs who sent humanitarian assistance to Donbas. The UC member "met them on Facebook or VKontakte, chatted, and they agreed to meet and help us when we spoke to them in real [life]." Unfortunately, the contacts were not all smooth as the UC's interlocutors had "difficulties" accepting its preference for involvement in war. For the humanitarians, unsurprisingly, "it was a concept impossible to accept [... as] Westerners go [to places like Donbas] and do tourism or humanitarian aid."[94] This discussion and the differences in views produced a dichotomy in the French involvement on the "separatist" side in the war in Ukraine – on the one hand, the fighters and, on the other, the non-combatant personnel, mostly involved in producing media output in French from Donetsk. As we have seen, however, some individuals – like UC second commander, Philippe Khalfine, and to some extent Erwan Castel – who in December 2017 announced he was returning into the ranks[95] – were able to transcend this divide by alternating their media and fighting stints. Consequently, such an approach begs the question of how truly objective they could be as reporters of the now defunct channel *Novorossiya Today*, styling itself as a "national" and "public" broadcaster of the "separatist" statelets.

The third component of the French involvement with the "separatists" was on display via organizations present in France, who either effectively fundraised for DNR/LNR causes in France or wished to represent the "People's Republics" in France. These included *Urgence Enfants du Donbas* (Emergency Aid for the Children of Donbas), led by former Marine Le Pen's adviser, Emmanuel Leroy,[96] *Vostok France Solidarité Donbas* (East France – Solidarity with Donbas),[97] or Novopôle (co-led by French "nationalist" figures and the above-mentioned Svetlana Kissileva), styling itself as a "representative of Novorossiya in France."[98] The DNR has, in fact, opened up its "Representative Centre," a de facto quasi-consulate, in Marseille in 2017,[99] set up as an association, which saw the French ministry of foreign affairs attempted to dissolve in both 2018 and 2021 but failed to do so due to arguments over the legality of such a move.[100] This "diplomatic" mission came on top of an earlier attempt to set up an "embassy" in Paris.[101]

Post Lives

Some of the French still remain in the "separatist" territories. Those are mostly the veterans of UC (Khalfine) or "Pyatnashka" (Castel). No Frenchmen present in Donetsk, however, could rival François Mauld d'Aymée as far as success in their new, adopted homeland was concerned. Singer Mauld d'Aymée[102] arrived in Donetsk in 2015 and, since 2018, has been working at the Donetsk State Academic Philharmonic and teaching at the DNR's State Music Academy.[103] He is a former French soldier, veteran of the Iraq war, sympathizer of Eurasianism [and a] supporter of continental alliances," in reality an anti–American coalition of like-minded Europeans, including Russian, forces and states.[104] As a French citizen, he acted as an "international observer" of the widely regarded as fraudulent elections in the DNR in November 2018.[105] On the back of his newly granted citizenship, he later became a deputy to DNR's youth parliament.[106]

The most illustrious post-war story, however, is that of Cuvelier, one of the original four members of the UC who made it to Donetsk in the summer of 2014. While on the way out of Donbas, he and his fellow TV members, Takahashi and the Brazilian Lusvarghi, were decorated with medals in Moscow by none other than Igor Girkin himself, effectively the man who started the war in Donbas.[107] The first two, in line with "Western foreign fighter society" theory, which stipulates that fighters know one another and gravitate toward the next conflicts,[108] quickly joined the film-maker Kat Argo, herself a former U.S. army soldier, in the Iraqi Kurdistan where they set up *Qalubna Ma'kum* ("Our hearts are with you"), part rapid reaction team, part medical team assisting the Kurdish Peshmerga in their fight with ISIS.[109] The unit was quickly "disinvited" by its hosts, Peshmerga's 9th brigade, as accusations of its alleged misappropriation of donations it received mounted.[110]

In April 2017, Cuvelier's social media profile carried a photo from his "graduation," as it later turned out, as an infantryman from Fort Benning in Georgia, United States. Unfortunately for him, the fact that he himself publicized his fact of joining the U.S. army (he has a dual French/American citizenship), allowed journalists to pick it up, and subsequently interview him about the episode. According to Cuvelier, "The [U.S.] army is my only chance of moving on and cutting with my past. I realized I like this country, its way of life and its Constitution enough to defend it. By publishing a story on me, you are jeopardizing my career and rendering a great service to anyone trying to embarrass the Army. My former Russian comrades would love it [...] so, I please ask you to reconsider using my name and/or photo."[111] Four weeks later he was discharged.[112]

Lenta, it seems, had a quieter post-Ukraine war. According to some of his foreign colleagues, Viktor "milks his Donbas days" by frequenting places where the "nationalist milieu" or "its tribes" gather.[113] This is where he would routinely bump into some of his French colleagues or "colleagues" from the opposing UC faction. Consequently, he and at least three others resurfaced in early 2019 as an alleged "security detail" of the so-called "yellow vests," who were protesting in downtown Paris against the French government's economic policies.[114] This action also won him some media coverage, due to his past and the way he carried himself (red beret of the paratroopers and a "Poirot"-like moustache), as he became one of the faces of the protest.[115] Serge Munier, another French veteran, born in Luhansk, who had served with "Pyatnashka,"[116] and is currently living in Moscow and has not been a member of the UC, wrote that the yellow vests were "were genuine French people, an endangered species, the rearguard of modern society." They came out to resist "all kinds of parasites, both those who arrive by the thousands by boat and those who sit on the assembly and

boards of banks." What is more, he compared the protests to "a popular uprising, almost comparable to the revolutionary atmosphere of the Donbas in the
spring of 2014. A taste of freedom."[117] Such a statement echoes that of another
French veteran who spoke to the author about his and his colleagues' "dream
of a 'French Donbas,' even though it is quite obvious we don't have the means
to achieve it."[118] In this sense, one could wonder if the veterans would be ready, to
paraphrase the American white supremacists, to "bring the war home" if they
had a chance.[119] The same fighter professed his lack of belief in the efficacy of
"terrorism or mass shooting or assassinations." In his view, armed activity would
only harm the cause of the "nationalists," as it would "unite the society behind
the police and the state, [and] justify the strengthening of security and authoritarian laws." This, in his view, rendered terrorism or insurrection useless.[120]

French on the Other Side

The French mobilization for the Ukrainian side was paltry, to say the least.[121]
Only GUD (*Groupe Union Défense*), a marginal force on the French far right, came
out in support of Ukraine in its conflict with Russia.[122] This transpired despite
protestations of the volunteers on the other side, such as Castel, or views expressed
by the other pro-"separatist" fighters in interviews with the author, who claimed
that the "nationalist" milieu was more deeply and evenly split.[123] Consequently,
some reports indicated the presence of individual Frenchmen in the likes of the
then Azov Battalion.[124] It had not been the fighters, however, but a single French
recruiter allegedly made the biggest mark for the pro-Ukraine side.

Gaston Besson, a former French parachutist, based in Croatia, was alleged
a companion of Castel from Myanmar. A veteran of other wars, especially the
Yugoslav wars of the 1990s where he fought on the pro-Croat side with "hundreds of other foreigners,"[125] Besson used his vast contact book, accumulated
while fighting in foreign wars,[126] to drum up the number of experienced foreign
volunteers, who would pay for their own ticket to Kyiv, and who would have
been destined for the ranks of the Azov Battalion. He later claimed he would be
getting 15–16 emails a day but would only continue conversations with two or
three potential volunteers, "serious people," people without commitments who
would be ready to stay in Ukraine for a prolonged period of time.[127] His call for
volunteers, released on his Facebook page in June 2014, stated that "all foreign
volunteers are now, more than welcome to join our revolution" but they need
to get to Kyiv before being looked after by the nascent unit. He gave a choice
to the prospective volunteers of a short-term training deployment or a four to
six month one, which would see a given foreign involved in actual fighting.
Upon landing, a volunteer would be provided "a telephone number, an email
address, and a name of an English speaking person part of the S.N.A. [Social
National Assembly], Political branch of the Azov Bataillon." He warned that
this unit is a "military wing of the S.N.A." and that it is "socialist, nationalist
and radical" in outlook,[128] or "anti-communist, but the spirit is the same as that

of the International Brigades that fought [against Fascism] in Spain in the thirties."[129] Besson maintained that he had "nothing against the Russians" but since they "invaded" Ukraine, he and others had to fight them. As for his politics, he gave a rather convoluted brown-red statement of being "with the anarchists, the communists, the people of the extreme right," and "idealist," and would not care as long as "the fight is worthy."[130] He stressed that his unit would not want nor take "trigger-happy fanatics, drug addicts, or alcoholics [...] or extremists." Ironically, the final goal, mirroring that of the UC counterparts, some of whom Besson allegedly had known from before the war, was "to create an international brigade."[131] The extent to which he succeeded has been addressed in the chapter devoted to Azov and other foreign fighter-friendly units of the Ukrainian battalions, but Besson hardly succeeded in enlisting any French compatriots into Azov's ranks.[132]

Conclusion

The French were not the most numerous of the foreign fighters in the war in Ukraine. They predominantly fought on the "separatist" side and theirs was one of the, if not the, most influential foreign fighter contingents on the front line. Its members started the UC, a genuine "international unit," set up by non-locals and to be staffed by foreigners only. Moreover, it was ideological in nature and effectively brought to life Thiriart's vision of a "European brigade" and put together "political soldiers" of both the far right and the far left, while attempting to put into practice Dugin's "fourth political theory." For a while it looked as if the UC could integrate other, e.g. Serbian, Spanish or Brazilian, foreign fighters for the "separatists" into its structure and a present a wide transnational, pro-Continental, i.e. pro-Russian, front which would fight the allegedly pro-U.S. and pro-NATO Ukraine. The unit's relatively quick demise marked a symbolic end of "separatist," or in fact, Russian, attempts to construct quasi-viable "Donbas international brigades." The story of the French in the war in Ukraine, however, is far from over. April 2022 brought the news of François Mauld d'Aymée's – one of the 2014 originals – involvement in the siege of Mariupol in the ranks of the DNR troops.[133] This veteran of the French army and a singer now found himself besieging the hated Azov Regiment defending this southern Ukrainian town. It is to be expected that other pro-Russia Frenchmen, and veterans of the war in Ukraine, will sooner or later resurface in different trouble spots of the world.

Notes

1 Kacper Rekawek, "Why 'Not Only Syria?' How an Idea Was Born and Put into Practice," in K Rekawek, ed., *Not Only Syria? The Phenomenon of Foreign Fighters in a Comparative Perspective* (Amsterdam: IOS Press, 2017), V.
2 *Russia Today*, "French Donbas fighters: We came to inform people of the reality of this war," August 29, 2014, https://www.youtube.com/watch?v=ahdROttr_o8, accessed: January 4, 2020.

3 Mathieu Molard and Paul Gogo, "Ukraine: Les docs qui montrent l'implication de l'extrême droite française dans la guerre," *Street Press*, August 3, 2016, https://www.streetpress.com/sujet/1472465929-donetskleaks-implication-extreme-droite-francaise-ukraine, accessed: January 4, 2021.

4 See n 2.

5 Paweł Pieniążek, "Pieniążek z Iłowajska: Upadek ukraińskiego frontu," *Krytyka Polityczna*, August 31, 2015, https://krytykapolityczna.pl/swiat/pieniazek-z-ilowajska-upadek-ukrainskiego-frontu/, accessed: January 4, 2020.

6 See "List PDF en Seine-Maritime. Dans l'Eure," https://parti-de-la-france.forumactif.org/t472-liste-pdf-en-seine-maritime-dans-l-eure," accessed: January 4, 2020, originally mentioned on Anton Shekhovtsov's blog, "French Eurasianists join (pro-)Russian extremists in Eastern Ukraine," August 27, 2014, http://anton-shekhovtsov.blogspot.com/2014/08/french-eurasianists-join-pro-russian.html, accessed: January 4, 2020.

7 Thomas Joly, "Compte-rendu de la conférence de Guillaume Cuvelier à Amiens," *Le Blog de Thomas Joly*, September 6, 2015, http://www.thomasjoly.fr/2015/09/compte-rendu-de-la-conference-de-guillaume-cuvelier-a-amiens.html, accessed: January 4, 2020.

8 Michael Sheldon, "The Small World of French Foreign Fighters," *@DFRLab*, February 4, 2019, https://medium.com/dfrlab/the-small-world-of-french-foreign-fighters-f53799ee3673, accessed: January 4, 2020.

9 Author's exchange with a French foreign fighter over Facebook Messenger, August 28, 2015.

10 Molard and Gogo, "Ukraine."

11 Author's exchange with a French foreign fighter over Facebook Messenger, August 28, 2015.

12 Andrey Borodulin, "French volunteer fighters for DPR: "We want to come back to Donbas soon and start an offensive," *Slavyangrad.org*, November 30, 2014, https://slavyangrad.org/2014/11/30/french-volunteers-we-want-to-come-back-and-start-an-offensive/?fbclid=IwAR1mYPzXnbGCIGM9Xb3M7f2iDMm9Icw3JSK-CIe9QFTwuenvrkyy28Hm54VA, accessed: January 5, 2020. The group's links with Serbia were very visible on its now almost empty Facebook page: it featured photos from demonstrations of Serbian far-right groups such as Dveri (Doors) or Srpska stranka Zavetnici (Serbian Party Oathkeepers). These disappeared in one of the periodic "far-right" purges conducted by Facebook.

13 See https://www.facebook.com/unite.continentale/?ref=nf&hc_ref=ARS1iae0P-dEpfrAZW2k79PVAuJubM3L7VafYs8XbALY7dqNcsWmJg5MKPX3e97RX8x0, accessed: January 5, 2020. Vojislav Šešelj is the founder of the Serbian Radical Party (SRS), and a former convict of the International Criminal Tribunal for the former Yugoslavia (ICTY). For Seselj's indictment by the ICTY see https://www.icty.org/x/cases/seselj/ind/en/ses-ii030115e.pdf, accessed: January 5, 2020.

14 For more on the issue see videos featuring Viktor Lenta, where he recounts his Donbas adventure upon returning to France, see http://alawata-rebellion.blogspot.com/2015/10/lanalyse-de-victor-lenta.html?m=0, accessed: January 5, 2020. The website is in fact a blog of a French foreign fighter but not a member of the UC, Erwan Castel. Castel was initially critical of Lenta and the UC but the two seemed to have mended fences while the former thanked the latter for "opening up the way [to French and foreign fighters] to Donbas."

15 Jacques Leleu, "Nikola Perović, de la Savoie au Donbas," *Le Dauphiné*, September 1, 2014, https://www.ledauphine.com/france-monde/2014/08/31/nikola-Perović-de-la-savoie-au-Donbas, accessed: January 5, 2020.

16 Borodulin, "French volunteer fighters for DPR."

17 For more on UC's ideology see the "ideological" chapter preceding the "national" chapters. See https://www.facebook.com/unite.continentale/photos/pb.681941775182139.-2207520000../685349161508067/?type=3&theater, https://www.facebook.com/

unite.continentale/photos/pb.681941775182139.-2207520000../688850801157903/
?type=3&theater, accessed: January 5, 2020.

18 See: https://www.facebook.com/unite.continentale/photos/pb.681941775182139.-
2207520000../700031180039865/?type=3&theater, accessed: January 5, 2020.

19 For more on the concept see: Nigel Copsey, *Contemporary British Fascism: The British
National Party and the Quest for Legitimacy*, Basingstoke: Palgrave Macmillan, 2004.

20 Andrey Borodulin, "French volunteer fighters for DPR."

21 Leleu, "Nikola Perović."

22 Author's exchange with a French foreign fighter over twitter Messenger, February
22, 2015.

23 Author's exchange with a French foreign fighter over Facebook Messenger, August
28, 2015.

24 Erwan Castel, "Du partisan métapolitique," *Donbas!*, January 9, 2016, accessed:
January 6, 2015.

25 Charles Clover, *Black Wind, White Snow: The Rise of Russia's New Nationalism*
(New Haven and London: Yale University Press, 2016), 11.

26 For an example of such an approach see an interview with Lenta: *Nous Voulons Vivre!*,
"Victor Alfonso Lenta: La crainte du pouvoir," May 7, 2019, https://www.youtube.
com/watch?v=L9NQSiLYvU4, accessed: January 6, 2020.

27 Pierre Sautreuil, "Meeting Them in the Field: A Closer Look at French Foreign
Fighters in Ukraine," in K Rekawek, ed., *Not Only Syria? The Phenomenon of Foreign Fighters in a Comparative Perspective*, (Amsterdam: IOS Press, 2017), 93. For more
on the above-mentioned French organizations see: Jean Yves Camus, *Extrémismes
en France: faut-il en avoir peur?* (Toulouse: Éditions Milan, "Milan actu," 2006) and
Nicolas Lebourg, *Le Monde vu de la plus extrême droite. Du fascisme au nationalisme-
révolutionnaire* (Perpignan: Presses universitaires de Perpignan, 2010).

28 Maxime Macé, "Victor Lenta, le paramilitaire d'extrême droite qui tente de manipuler les
Gilets jaunes," *FranceSoir*, February 5, 2019, https://www.francesoir.fr/politique-france/
victor-lenta-le-paramilitaire-extreme-droite-qui-tente-de-manipuler-les-gilets-jaunes,
accessed: January 6, 2020.

29 See quotes from Alain Beajam in Molard and Gogo, "Ukraine."

30 Erwan Castel, "A propos des mots 'Libre' et 'Liberté'," *Donbas!*, January 28, 2018,
http://alawata-rebellion.blogspot.com/2018/01/a-propos-des-mots-libre-et-liberte.
html, accessed: January 6, 2020.

31 Molard and Gogo, "Ukraine."

32 Pierre Sautreuil, "Des paras français dans le Donbas," *Le Monde*, August 26, 2014,
https://www.lemonde.fr/europe/article/2014/08/26/des-paras-francais-dans-le-
Donbas_4476646_3214.html, accessed: January 11, 2020.

33 See http://alawata-rebellion.blogspot.com/2015/10/lanalyse-de-victor-lenta.html?m=0,
accessed: January 5, 2020.

34 Author's exchange with a French foreign fighter over Facebook Messenger, August
28, 2015.

35 See http://alawata-rebellion.blogspot.com/2015/10/lanalyse-de-victor-lenta.html?m=0,
accessed: January 5, 2020.

36 Alternative theory has it that UC members were smuggled into Donbas from Rostov,
after receiving training, by individuals associated with the *Novorossiya* movement in
Russia, including associates of Igor Girkin. See e.g. Miroslav Mareš, Martin Laryš,
and Jan Holzer, *Militant Right-Wing Extremism in Putin's Russia: Legacies, Forms and
Threats* (Abingdon: Routledge, 2019), chap. 9 or Anton Shekhovtsov, "French Eurasianists join (pro-)Russian extremists in Eastern Ukraine," August 27, 2014, http://
anton-shekhovtsov.blogspot.com/2014/08/french-eurasianists-join-pro-russian.
html, accessed: January 4, 2020.

37 Author's exchange with a French foreign fighter over Facebook Messenger, August
28, 2015.

38 See Kat Argo's documentary *Polite People* at https://www.amazon.co.uk/Polite-People-Not-Specified/dp/B01H7MDI9S, accessed: January 5, 2020.

39 Author's exchange with a French foreign fighter over Facebook Messenger, August 28, 2015.

40 Borodulin, "French volunteer fighters for DPR."

41 See http://alawata-rebellion.blogspot.com/2015/10/lanalyse-de-victor-lenta.html?m=0, accessed: January 5, 2020.

42 Erwan Castel, "Volontaires européens," *Donbas!*, http://alawata-rebellion.blogspot.com/2019/02/volontaires-europeens.html?m=1, accessed: January 7, 2020.

43 Author's exchange with a French foreign fighter over Facebook Messenger, April 22, 2020.

44 See e.g. https://www.facebook.com/photo.php?fbid=1510486915654450&set=ecnf.100000794687829&type=3&theater for a photo from the demonstrations featuring former UC members. The profile belongs to Ghislain Lagrega, another French foreign fighter from the conflict. Accessed: January 7, 2020.

45 Kat Argo's *Polite People* is available at https://www.amazon.co.uk/Polite-People-Not-Specified/dp/B01H7MDI9S, accessed: January 5, 2020.

46 Author's exchange with an anonymous journalist, embedded with foreign fighters for the "separatists" in 2015 and 2016, over Facebook Messenger, August 17, 2015.

47 Erwan Castel, "Le Donbas prêt pour la Victoire finale," *Donbas!*, February 22, 2015, http://alawata-rebellion.blogspot.com/2015/02/le-Donbas-pret-pour-la-victoire-finale_22.html, accessed: January 7, 2020.

48 Erwan Castel, "En attendant l'orage," *Donbas!*, September 11, 2015, http://alawata-rebellion.blogspot.com/2015/09/en-attendant-lorage.html, accessed: January 7, 2020.

49 One of UC members commented on this to the author: "Of course, some commanders were willing to take us into action. It was usually a conflict between commanders, the one who were willing to take us into combat and attack, and the ones who are implementing the ceasefire and just want to use us as propaganda tools." See author's exchange with a French foreign fighter over Facebook Messenger, August 28, 2015.

50 See http://alawata-rebellion.blogspot.com/2015/10/lanalyse-de-victor-lenta.html?m=0, accessed: January 5, 2020.

51 See the chapters devoted to the Western Balkans and other international volunteers in this volume.

52 See https://www.facebook.com/photo?fbid=3088880417801311&set=pb.100000381483237.-2207520000. For the unit's logo with Abkhaz and DNR flags and 15 stars see also the "brigade's" profile on VKontakte for its short history: https://vk.com/brigada_15, accessed: January 12, 2020. For more on the unit see the chap. 3 in this volume.

53 *112.ua News Agency*, "'Coup' in Sukhumi: How 'Donetsk People's Republic' militants in Abkhazia overthrew 'president'," January 21 2020, https://112.international/politics/coup-in-sukhumi-how-donetsk-peoples-republic-militants-in-abkhazia-overthrew-president-47714.html, accessed: January 11, 2020.

54 Sergey Sukhanin, "Foreign Mercenaries, Irregulars and 'Volunteers': Non-Russians in Russia's Wars," *The Jamestown Foundation*, October 9, 2019, https://jamestown.org/program/foreign-mercenaries-irregulars-and-volunteers-non-russians-in-russias-wars/, accessed: January 11, 2020.

55 Erwan Castel, "Qui-suis je?," *Donbas!*, http://alawata-rebellion.blogspot.com/p/qui-suis-je.html, accessed: 1January 4, 2021.

56 Représentation France RPD, "Le Volontaire français Erwan Castel dans l'armée de la République Populaire de Donetsk," YouTube, December 4, 2017, https://www.youtube.com/watch?v=tofbb8gr3zQ%3B+http%3A%2F%2Falawata-rebellion.blogspot.com%2Fp%2Fqui-suis-je.html, accessed: 1January 4, 2021.

57 Sautreuil, "Meeting Them in the Field," 94.

58 Kacper Rekawek, *Career Break or a New Career? Extremist Foreign Fighters in Ukraine* (Counter Extremism Project, April 2020), 15, https://www.counterextremism.com/sites/default/files/CEP%20Report_Career%20Break%20or%20a%20New%20Career_Extremist%20Foreign%20Fighters%20in%20Ukraine_April%202020.pdf, accessed: January 12, 2020.

59 Author's exchange with a French foreign fighter over Facebook Messenger, August 28, 2015.

60 For more on the controversies and travails of Rusich and other Russian XRW individuals who fought in the war, see Central-Eastern European "national" chapter.

61 *United Nations Peacemaker*, "Protocol on the results of consultations of the Trilateral Contact Group (Minsk Agreement)," September 5, 2014, https://peacemaker.un.org/UA-ceasefire-2014, accessed: January 5, 2020.

62 Author's exchange with a French foreign fighter over Facebook Messenger, August 28, 2015.

63 See Team Vikernes VKontatke profile, https://vk.com/public93628709, accessed: January 5, 2020.

64 See *Counter Extremism Project*, "The Afterlives of Extremist Foreign Fighters in Ukraine," YouTube, November 30, 2020, https://www.youtube.com/watch?v=peP5L2EJyUs, accessed: January 5, 2020 for the author's video explainer on Lusvarghi.

65 Author's exchange with a French foreign fighter over Facebook Messenger, August 28, 2015.

66 Kat Argo's *Polite People* is available at https://www.amazon.co.uk/Polite-People-Not-Specified/dp/B01H7MDI9S, accessed: January 5, 2020.

67 Author's exchange with a Brazilian foreign fighter in Ukraine who wished to remain anonymous, over Facebook Messenger, August 28, 2015.

68 *Russia and the World*, "The Eurasian Movement in Brazil: trajectory and arrest of Rafael Lusvarghi," November 24, 2016, http://arussiaeomundo.blogspot.com/2016/11/the-eurasian-movement-in-brazil.html, accessed: January 5, 2020. For more on Vikernes see Michael Moynihan and Didrik Soderlind, *Lords of Chaos: The Bloody Rise of the Satanic Metal Underground* (Port Townsend: Feral House, 2003).

69 See Khalfine's Facebook profile at https://www.facebook.com/photo?fbid=1713336605405501&set=pb.100001875353241.-2207520000, accessed: January 11, 2020.

70 Ibid.

71 Hugo Boursier, "Ukraine : la République Populaire de Donetsk, nouvelle patrie d'adoption de quelques francophones," *TV5Monde*, November 22, 2018, https://information.tv5monde.com/info/ukraine-la-republique-populaire-de-donetsk-nouvelle-patrie-d-adoption-de-quelques-francophones, accessed: January 11, 2021.

72 See the annoucement on Khalfine's Facebook profile: https://www.facebook.com/photo.php?fbid=2028218830583942&set=pb.100001875353241.-2207520000..&type=3, accessed: January 11, 2020.

73 Boursier, "Ukraine."

74 See Facebook profile of Sebastien Hairon at https://www.facebook.com/sebastien.hairon, accessed: January 11, 2020.

75 Molard and Gogo, "Ukraine."

76 One of these fighters is running a blog, see: http://combattre-et-agir.blogspot.com/2018/, accessed: January 11, 2020.

77 See Khalfine's profile at https://www.facebook.com/photo?fbid=3444457518960059&set=ecnf.100001875353241, accessed: January 11, 2020.

78 The Republican Guard, of which "Pyatnashka" and consequently the UC were parts, had been under the personal command of the DNR's "head of state," Alexander Zakharchenko. After his assassination in August 2018, "all hitherto independent formations were forcibly integrated into the "First Army Corps," thought to be under the command of Russian military officers, or into the Interior or State Security Ministries, believed to be controlled by the [Russian] FSB." See: Nikolaus von Twickel, "The State of the Donbas: A study of eastern Ukraine's "separatist"-held areas," in

Thomas de Waal and Nikolaus van Twickel, *Beyond Frozen Conflict. Scenarios for the "separatist" Disputes of Eastern Europe* (Brussels: CEPS, 2020), 73. See also Castel's teary tribute paid to Zakharchenko: Erwan Castel, "Que le souvenir des morts soit la force des vivants!," *Revue Méthode* http://www.revuemethode.org/m091801.html, accessed: 1 January 4, 2021.

79 See UC Facebook profile, https://pl-pl.facebook.com/unite.continentale/photos/pb. 681941775182139.-2207520000../1995071370535833/?type=3&theater, September 23, 2018, accessed: January 11, 2020.

80 Sheldon, "The Small World of French Foreign Fighters."

81 *InformNapalm*, "Les masques du 'monde russe' en France," February 10, 2016, https:// informnapalm.org/fr/les-masques-du-monde-russe-en-france/, accessed: January 13, 2021.

82 Andy Barréjot, "Tarbes: Un ex-para tarbais en guerre en Ukraine," *Ladepeche.fr*, November 28, 2014, https://www.ladepeche.fr/article/2014/11/28/2000462-l-ex-para-tarbais-en-guerre-en-ukraine.html, accessed: January 13, 2021.

83 See: http://alawata-rebellion.blogspot.com/2015/09/en-attendant-lorage.html?m=0 for Lenta's correspondence with another French foreign fighter, Erwan Castel from September 2015, accessed: January 13, 2021.

84 Nicolas Hénin, *La France Russe. Enquête sur les réseaux Poutine* (Paris: Fayard, 2016), 58.

85 Boursier, "Ukraine."

86 Molard and Gogo, "Ukraine."

87 Editor in chief of the journal *Méthode*. See her profile at http://www.revuemethode. org/sydorova.html, accessed: 1January 4, 2021.

88 Les Brigandes describe themselves as a "fraternal community" fighting "against the social and spiritual standardization of industrial socjety [...] opposed to any form of standardizing globalism and to the financial, political and religious lobbies [...]." See Les Brigandes, "Qui sommes nous?," https://communaute-rose-epee.fr/ce-que-nous-sommes/, accessed: 1January 14, 2021.

89 Radio Brigandes, "Les Brigandes au Donbas : Reportage sur une guerre pour la Liberté (R.B. VI - Décembre 2016)," YouTube, 12 December 2016, https://www. youtube.com/watch?v=izSAwGydgfI, accessed: January 14, 2021. One of the fighters is sniper Tonio, member of "Pyatnashka," featured by Erwan Castel on his blog on 3 November 2015: http://alawata-rebellion.blogspot.com/2015/11/tonio.html, accessed: January 14, 2021. He admits to starting a new family in Donetsk and indicates he would not be coming back to Paris.

90 Lenta makes this admission in videos featured on Erwan Castel's blog: http:// alawata-rebellion.blogspot.com/2015/10/lanalyse-de-victor-lenta.html?m=0, accessed: January 14, 2021.

91 See UC "family photo" from 28 September 2014 which features Perović and four others, out of a group of 26 men, making the traditional Serbian "three finger salute," https:// www.facebook.com/unite.continentale/photos/a.681959115180405/792515807458068/? type=3&theater, accessed: January 14, 2021.

92 Barréjot, "Tarbes."

93 Author's interview with a Serbian jounalist, an expert on the country's far right, who wished to remain anonymous, June 3, 2020.

94 Author's exchange with a French UC foreign fighter over Facebook Messenger, September 14, 2015.

95 Représentation France RPD, "Le Volontaire français Erwan Castel dans l'armée de la République Populaire de Donetsk," YouTube, December 4, 2017, https://www. youtube.com/watch?v=tofbb8gr3zQ%3B+http%3A%2F%2Falawata-rebellion.blogspot. com%2Fp%2Fqui-suis-je.html, accessed: January 14, 2021.

96 See the organization's (now largely dormant) website at: https://urgence-enfants-Donbas.fr/?fbclid=IwAR35iy2Es-eUm6PcLXGQzhG_WdDQiQM1UjD2yPDX-CxJxRyEgVD3bdrsmNsw, accessed: January 13, 2021.

97 See the organization's website at: https://vostokfrance.wixsite.com/vostok, accessed: January 14, 2021.

98 *InformNapalm*, "Les masques du 'monde russe' en France."

99 *People's Council of the Donetsk People's Republic*, "Vladislav Berdichevsky: DPR Representative Centre in France will help Europeans learn truth about civil war in Donbas," September 26, 2017, https://dnrsovet.su/vladislav-berdichevsky-dpr-representative-centre-in-france-will-help-europeans-learn-truth-about-civil-war-in-Donbas/, accessed: January 13, 2021.

100 See the Centre's Facebook profile at: https://www.facebook.com/donetskFrance/posts/2799178183654334, message from January 13, 2020, accessed: January 13, 2021.

101 Author's interview with Paul Gogo, a French journalist, who reported from the DNR and later wrote about the French foreign fighters in the ""separatist"" ranks, May 8, 2020.

102 See Kath, "Spotlight: François Mauld d'Aymée," *Fault*, April 4, 2012, https://fault-magazine.com/2012/04/spotlight-francois-mauld-dalymee/, accessed: January 13, 2021.

103 *Donetsk News Agency*, "Frenchman who received DPR citizenship announces plans for Youth Parliament," March 20, 2019, https://dan-news.info/en/world-en/frenchman-who-received-dpr-citizenship-announces-plans-for-youth-parliament.html, accessed: January 13, 2021.

104 See his profile at *Sans Frontières*, an official journal of the French-Russian Institute of Donetsk, set up by another former French soldier, Francois Maurice, a veteran of the conflict in Bosnia, and "passionate about geopolitics" who lives, according to his Facebook profile, in Lons, France (https://www.facebook.com/francois.maurice.7/, accessed: January 13, 2021): http://sf.donntu.org/maulddaymee.html, accessed January 13, 2021. Maurice also leads the journal *Méthode*, published by the above-mentioned Institute (see e.g. its September 2018 issue: http://www.revuemethode.org/pdf/m0918.pdf?fbclid=IwAR2ITlm0pUWflVu0xYlEctXUZC24JUTszJ9H-5b4WpMAoZ-WfYVi7S7fwbdM). The journal's editor in chief is a Russian national, and an academic at the University of Novocherkassk in Russia, Elena Sydorova, decorated in 2020 by the French ministry of education and youth for her "for services rendered to the French culture." See https://www.facebook.com/photo.php?fbid=10222219653550879&set=pb.1551030698.-2207520000..&type=3, accessed: January 13, 2021. The journal publishes contributions from Erwan Castel, French foreign fighter in DNR and "Pyatnashka" member." See http://www.revuemethode.org/castel.html, accessed: January 13, 2021.

105 *Euromaidan Press*, "Far right and left, conspiracy theorists among "foreign monitors" at Russia's sham Donbas elections: Report," November 16, 2018, http://euromaidan-press.com/2018/11/16/far-right-and-left-conspiracy-theorists-among-foreign-monitors-at-russias-sham-donbas-elections-report/, accessed: January 13, 2021.

106 Author's interview with Paul Gogo, a French journalist, who reported from the DNR and later wrote about the French foreign fighters in the ""separatist"" ranks, May 8, 2020.

107 See his picture with Igor Girkin: *Ucrânia em África*, "O terrorista franco-americano é expulso do exército americano," May 31, 2017, https://ucrania-mozambique.blogspot.com/2017/05/o-terrorista-franco-americano-e-expulso.html, accessed: January 12, 2020.

108 Rekawek, *Career Break*, 15.

109 Adam Lucente, "Foreign volunteers in Kurdistan Region shift focus to medical aid," *Al-Monitor*, January 12, 2016, https://www.al-monitor.com/pulse/originals/2016/01/foreign-volunteers-medical-assistance-peshmerga-iraq.html, accessed: January 12, 2020.

110 Kurt T, "Qalubna ma'kum: foreign-fighter frauds in Kurdistan," *SOFREP*, https://sofrep.com/news/qalubna-makum-foreign-fighter-frauds-in-kurdistan/, April 4, 2016, accessed: January 12, 2020.

111 Thomas Gibbons-Neff, "He fought with Russian-backed militants in Ukraine. Now he's a U.S. soldier," *The Washington Post*, May 1, 2017, https://www.washingtonpost.com/news/checkpoint/wp/2017/05/01/he-fought-with-russian-backed-militants-in-ukraine-now-hes-a-u-s-soldier/, accessed: January 12, 2020.

112 Thomas Gibbons-Neff, "U.S. soldier who fought with Russian-backed militants has been discharged from the Army," *The Washington Post*, May 1, 2017, accessed: January 12, 2020.

113 Author's exchange with a French foreign fighter over Facebook Messenger, April 24, 2020.

114 Pierre Tremblay, "Un milicien du Donbas au service d'ordre des gilets jaunes," *HUFFPOST*, January 18, 2020, https://www.huffingtonpost.fr/2019/01/18/un-combattant-du-Donbas-dans-le-service-dordre-des-gilets-jaunes_a_23645055/, accessed: January 12, 2020.

115 *Nous Voulons Vivre!*.

116 Tremblay, "Un milicien du Donbas."

117 See Munier's Facebook profile at https://www.facebook.com/photo?fbid=529018 774231775&set=pb.100013709702247.-2207520000.

118 Rekawek, *Career Break*, 17.

119 Kathleen Belew, *Bring the War Home. The White Power Movement and Paramilitary America*, (Cambridge: Harvard University Press, 2018), 30.

120 Rekawek, *Career Break*, 25.

121 There is some conflicting evidence on this issue with one of the author's interviewees, Pierre Sautreuil of the *La Croix* newspaper, who wrote about the French foreign fighters in Ukraine on the "separatist" side, indicating to the author that one of his trusted sources confirmed that up to 30 Frenchmen secretly fought on the pro-Ukraine side in this war (author's telephone conversation with Pierre Sautreuil, March 1, 2022). This was contradicted by a former French member of Azov, who asked the author to remain anonymous. According to him, in 2014, that is at the height of the war and the peak of foreign fighter recruitment, only four Frenchmen went through the ranks of Azov, supposedly a key conduit for foreign fighters in this war (author's email exchange with the above-mentioned fighter, March 30, 2022).

122 Nicolas Lebourg, "Comment le FN est devenu si pro-russe," *Slate.fr*, May 30, 2018, http://www.slate.fr/story/162369/fn-extreme-droite-francaise-guerre-ukraine-russie-lobby, accessed: January 14, 2021. See tumblr page dedicated to Azov's international outreach to appreciate the very few inroads the movement, and subsequently the regiment, were able to make in France: https://interregnum-intermarium.tumblr.com/, accessed: 1January 4, 2021.

123 At least two such fighters indicated that their immediate nationalist circles were split on the Ukraine-Russia conflict with some of their former friends terminating contacts upon learning of their deployment in Donbas.

124 Christopher Allen, "Meet the European Fighters Who Have Gone to War in Ukraine," *Vice*, August 25, 2015, https://www.vice.com/en/article/xd7axz/european-british-fighters-in-ukraine-920, accessed: January 14, 2021.

125 *Études Géostratégiques*, "Gaston Besson: parcours d'un volontaire armé," November 9, 2013, https://etudesgeostrategiques.com/2013/11/09/gaston-besson-parcours-dun-volontaire-arme/, accessed: January 14, 2021.

126 Laetitia Moreni, Gaëtan Vannay, and jzim, "J'en ai marre de tuer des gens. J'ai passé l'âge!," *RTS*, April 9, 2015, https://www.rts.ch/info/monde/6686719-jen-ai-marre-de-tuer-des-gens-jai-passe-lage.html, accessed: January 14, 2021.

127 YouTube, "Battalion AZOV: Gaston Besson il reclutatore/Full interview English," November 18, 2014, https://www.youtube.com/watch?v=2Gd0vmfXiJg, accessed: January 14, 2021.

128 See the call on Besson's Facebook profile at https://www.facebook.com/gaston.besson/posts/688220024584939, accessed: January 14, 2021. While writing this, in mid-January 2021, it has 78 likes, and Besson has 4.000+ friends on Facebook.

129 Fausto Biloslavo, "Ukraine: Far-Right Fighters from Europe Fight for Ukraine," *eurasianet*, August 6, 2014, https://eurasianet.org/ukraine-far-right-fighters-from-europe-fight-for-ukraine, accessed: January 14, 2021.
130 Moreni et al., "J'en ai marre."
131 YouTube, "Battalion AZOV."
132 Nicolas Lebourg, "The French Far Right in Russia's Orbit," *Carnegie Council for Ethics in International Affairs*, May 15, 2018, https://www.carnegiecouncil.org/publications/articles_papers_reports/the-french-far-right-in-russias-orbit/_res/id=Attachments/index=1/Lebourg-EN%20revised%203.pdf, accessed: January 15, 2021.
133 See https://twitter.com/guicorneau/status/1516387423474888715?s=20&t=iA7VzE6Cy7BSV_jBEetFvw, accessed: April 20, 2022.

6

SWEDEN

"Fight Them There So They Don't Come Here"

Introduction: Mikael Skillt's Contingent

The Swedish contingent of foreign fighters, almost exclusively consisting of people who deployed on the pro-Ukraine side,[1] came to be dominated by a single individual – Mikael Skillt. His early arrival in Ukraine, recruitment of others into the ranks of the Azov Battalion, service on the front line, interviews he gave to the world media looking for an English-speaking spokesman, turned him into an icon as far as foreign fighter deployment in this war was concerned. His career since parting ways with the Azov movement only adds to this myth and further strengthens his reputation. It would be wrong, however, to assume that other fighters, in general, and his compatriots in particular, had much in common with Skillt. Many came from different backgrounds, hid their faces when journalists were around, and did not start a private military company in the war's aftermath. Some, as the author learnt, resented Skillt – not for his media availability – but for his later public repudiation of elements of his pre-war far-right ideology.[2]

One thing, however, is certain: Skillt and another Swede arrived in Kyiv "three months before any foreigner arrived," i.e. in late February 2014.[3] At the time, no Azov Battalion existed, French UC members – trailblazers for foreign fighters intent on joining the "separatist" forces, were months away from starting their journey to Donetsk. The big recruitment call of Gaston Besson, a Frenchman recruiting foreigners for the Ukraine side,[4] arrived almost four months later. Skillt preceded all of this and later organized, fought and became a public face of a recruitment effort. He literally reset his life while in Ukraine, largely cut his ties to native Sweden, cleansed himself of some of the controversial aspects of his past and also became a success story – to some extent, settling down in Ukraine with a job in a coveted private military contracting. In the meantime, his Swedish contingent, mostly in the ranks of the Azov Battalion/Regiment,

DOI: 10.4324/9781003192992-6

had a much happier existence in Ukraine than many of the Frenchmen on the separatist side. There were fewer Swedes but they wasted relatively less time on photo shoots or arguments on whether they could fight. Moreover, despite sometimes profound differences amongst them. They also argued less with each other, and genuinely felt they participated in some of the war's most iconic moments.

Skillt was effectively a trailblazer, one of the very first foreigners who arrived in Ukraine with an intention to fight.[5] Later on, he would, alongside the above-mentioned Besson and Francesco Fontana of Italy, emerge as the key international poster boy for Azov, and the key interviewee for all foreign journalists wanting to write either about the conflict, involvement of foreign fighters or his unit.[6] It seems that he had been preparing for this role almost from the beginning of the conflict, while allegedly working on establishing an "international centre where nationalists from other countries can go and get to know like-minded Ukrainians [...] They could come and get an understanding of what has happened here and what is happening in other countries."[7] This project, as it later transpired, never came to fruition but, instead, Skillt played a key role in recruitment, training and integration of foreigners into the Azov Battalion (later Regiment).

Swedish Foreign Fighters in Ukraine: Introduction

Beginnings were humble to say the least. Skillt recalled that with a "loose group of friends [...] all nationalists" he established "Swedish Volunteers for Ukraine" (*Svenska Ukrainafrivillige*),[8] a Facebook page which later acted as a recruitment tool for his efforts in Ukraine. The group decided to send an emissary to Ukraine,[9] a Swede nicknamed "Sonic," and simultaneously decided to utilize the connections Skillt, as the then representative of the neo-Nazi Party of the Swedes (*Svenskarnas parti*, SvP), forged with the Ukrainian nationalists of *Svodoba* (Liberty), who won more than 10 percent of the votes in the 2012 parliamentary election.[10] This led the nascent Swedish group to involvement with *Sich* (literally: administrative and military center of the Zaporozhian Cossacks between the sixteenth and eighteenth centuries), formerly *Svodoba's* youth wing. This group, widely accused of neo-Nazi sympathies,[11] hosted the Swedes who in their ranks patrolled the streets of post-Euromaidan Kyiv. Later on, however, Skillt and others decided to change their colors and opted for joining the nascent Azov Battalion. In their view, Azov offered more chances of front line experience. Allegedly, while stumbling upon the unit for the first time, Skillt and another Swede immediately recognized its determination to be deployed to the emerging front lines and came away satisfied that they had found "the shit" they had been looking for in Ukraine.[12]

Skillt later remarked that "some Swedes who [made contact after reading his tweets on twitter and said] that they have military experience and view us as a serious organization. We then exchange emails and explain the rules of [Azov]. Then it's 'Welcome to Kiev'. When they arrive we have a little chat, and if they are found useable we go to one of the bases around Mariupol." Such an approach would sometimes lead to super rapid deployments of Swedes onto the battlefields – one, a self-confessed liberal who had informed his colleagues of his non-right wing views beforehand, was nonetheless accepted, and found himself "on a mission" two days after arrival.[13] According to Skillt's long-time companion from the ranks of the Swedish far-right organizations, such events established him as the "go to guy," "the pull" for other Swedes who wanted to fight in Ukraine. In this sense, his network of contacts in Sweden and Ukraine "merged" and was put to use in recruitment of fighters for Azov. The fact that Skillt was doing it publicly was also supposed to have helped – it made attempts to reach him easier as he made a conscious decision to sever ties with Sweden. Some of his companions had, however, other ideas and therefore would never speak publicly or even show their faces.[14] Regardless of one's outlook on whether going to Ukraine equaled a "reset" or had simply been a "career break,"[15] one must ask about the motivations of different Swedes. In short, what were they looking for in (Eastern) Ukraine?

Skillt allegedly made the transition from Sweden to Ukraine while having a steady job ("on track to make about $65,400" a year).[16] He also served in the Home Guard, a reserve for the Swedish Armed Forces but also had a troubled past with stints in jail.[17] Moreover, he had a rich political CV – the Swedish Resistance Movement,[18] precursor to the Nordic Resistance Movement, National Democrats, and finally the SvP. Despite five years in the Home Guard, though, he never deployed to a war but was aghast watching the shooting of Ukrainian protestors on the Maidan. He allegedly felt "angry" and thought that the pro-government snipers would not fare so boldly if he was up against them in the ranks of the other side – "Let's see if they have any counter-sniper training, he thought. Let's see if they can survive me."[19]

Skillt and his compatriots, the third biggest national subgroup in the Azov Battalion/Regiment (after Ukrainians and Russians), with representatives of 16 other nationalities present in the ranks.[20] The Swedes in total, according to different source numbered fewer than 10,[21] five to 10,[22] or around a dozen,[23] or around 30 individuals.[24] They were a mixed group, to say the least, with the non-combatant group numbering as many as 50 who passed through Ukraine because of the war, more significant in size.[25] The contingent has been, rather excessively and simplistically, compared to the Swedish volunteers who joined the Waffen SS during World War II. The comparison hardly stands as the latter might have been up to 10 times more numerous.[26]

These seemingly feeble numbers were most probably beefed up by the involvement of Swedes who would hide their nationality (nicknamed "the ghosts" by the current author in another of his publications on the topic),[27] some of whom had military experience or literally would take a leave of absence from the Swedish armed forces and secretly deploy to Ukraine.[28] Some Azov members would later admit to being contacted by active Swedish soldiers.[29] Ideologically, the Swedish contingent was a bizarre mixture of lone liberals who nonetheless joined Azov, former criminals "wanting to start afresh"[30] and "extremists" of whom some had known each other from before the war, and other liberals who supported the Ukrainian war effort materially.[31] Thus, one should not speak of a "profile," a "typical" Swedish volunteer for the war in Ukraine.[32] At the same time, however, the most visible element was that around Skillt – involved with a "highly political unit" which espoused far-right imagery.[33] While doing so, the Swedes, "although they will not admit it," indirectly fed the Kremlin's narrative of a "fascist" or "neo-Nazi" international forming to support Ukraine's "aggression" against Donbas.[34] As will be shown, this was happening against the background of the Swedish far-right milieu taking a decisively pro-Russia turn. Moreover, the mere existence of this "unit" was also a key feature of the Russian narrative on the need to "de-Nazify" Ukraine in the aftermath of the February 24, 2022 (re-)invasion of the country.[35]

Sweden's Far Right and Russia

Russia helped instigate the conflict, transformed it into a war and, finally, directly intervened in Donbas in the summer of 2014. This internationalization of what started as an internal Ukrainian political crisis transformed attitudes on the conflict. No longer was the discussion along the pro- or anti-Euromaidan lines. It became a Ukraine versus Russia duel. This development had a sizeable impact on the Western far right but also far-left internal politics as both the brown and the red, and the brown-red, actors were taking sides in this Eastern European war. As was demonstrated in the "ideological" chapter (Chapter 4), Russia, often via seemingly non-official and independent channels, has been working to undermine the socio-political integrity of the West. Consequently, some sections of the Western right and left wing radicals saw it as the only viable counterbalance to the hated "Atlanticist" or "imperialist" U.S. Discussions on these issues were also taking place in the Swedish radical circles, especially on the far right, and these will be analyzed first before continuing with the story of the Swedish foreign fighters in Ukraine.

Sweden is a country which is separated from Russia solely by the Baltic Sea, and the two have a long history of inter-state conflict (especially in the sixteenth to eighteenth centuries). For this reason, the Swedish "radical nationalists" had a dim view of the USSR/Russia during the Cold War, and saw the country as a "threat to the Swedish sovereignty." More recently, however, Russia has been seen more as an "anti-thesis" to the EU and the U.S., and this provided an opening which the Nordic Resistance Movement (NRM, a transnational, Scandinavian but headquartered in Sweden, extreme right organization) fully utilized to forge links with the Russian Imperial Movement (RID), a leading far-right Russian entity.[36] At the same time, according to one of the Swedes involved in Ukraine in a non-combatant role, the Swedish "establishment" or "mainstream" has traditionally remained wary of Russia. Consequently, seeing NRM's Russian overtures, plus growing sympathy for President Putin amongst the Swedish nationalists, including amongst the members of the parliamentary Swedish Democrats, the "mainstream" allegedly gladly smeared its anti-systemic, nationalist or far-right opponents with the label of being "pro-Russia."[37]

Undoubtedly, seeds of a pro-Russia turn amongst the Swedish far right had been sown early in the 2010s, when the RID developed its own Swedish branch and forged contacts with the Swedish Resistance Movement (SRM), which became the NRM in 2015.[38] The political collapse of the above-mentioned SvP, which suffered a humiliating electoral setback in the 2014 parliamentary elections (winning barely over 4,000 votes), emboldened the SRM, which successfully united different extreme right trends in the country and from then on became a "key to the white power movement" in Sweden and in Scandinavia.[39] As the NRM was consolidating, it apparently hosted a high level RID delegation and received "a gift of money" from the Russians. Moreover, it got invited into RID's loose network of the "World National Conservative Movement," which also featured the French UC, fighting on the "separatist" side in the war in Ukraine.[40] Interestingly, RID also opened its paramilitary "Partizan" program to NRM members, who were keen to join but their first preference had allegedly been teaming up with their compatriots in the ranks of the then Azov Regiment, on the pro-Ukraine side. The NRM leadership worked hard to diffuse this sentiment and channeled "its" fighters into the RID's program.[41]

One of the unfortunate, from the NRM and RID's points of view, by-products of this "channeling" had been a spate of bombing attacks against targets associated with refugees and a "gathering spot of a left-wing organisation" carried out by what was described as a "rogue" NRM cell in the area around Gothenburg in the winter of 2016/2017.[42] The fact that the two of the three bombers had trained with the RID in Russia,[43] even though bomb-making was allegedly not on the curriculum of their training,[44] had since been used as a testament to a strengthening NRM–RID connection, and a one of the key reasons why the latter was "designated" by the U.S. State Department as "a Specially Designated Global Terrorist."[45] The RID's leaders basked in the attention this brought them and treated it as a "reward," but the NRM, which was anti-U.S. but operated in Scandinavia which enjoyed friendly relations with the U.S. and NATO, had less to be pleased about.[46]

Such a designation of the NRM's Russian conduit, whose "alumni" seemed to have been staging terrorist attacks in Europe, created an image of a robust and vehemently militant far-right Swedish milieu. This, in the words of individuals studying it, is not an accurate picture. Its extreme actors, the SvP and the NRM, were structured like political parties and suffered whenever they tried to contest parliamentary elections, which were usually followed by a split within the ranks by the most militant members.[47] At the same time, the milieu is "the most closely monitored entity in Sweden" with "the police, the security service, political groups, left wing extremists, the media, left-wing NGOs [...] all in on the action" to monitor "2000 believers of whom 500 max. march down the street."[48] The smallness of the milieu was to some extent underscored by two events, one pre-Ukraine war, the other taking place after it erupted. In 2012, Alexander Dugin spoke at "Identity and Geopolitics: Towards a Multi-Polar World" seminar which was held in Sweden. The attendees included a "who's who" of the Swedish far right, including Mikael Skillt, future member of the Azov Regiment,[49] and his later pro-Russian adversaries.[50] 2017 saw the establishment of Free Sweden (*Det Fria Sverige*), an association intent on building "parallel structures" for "the Swedish minority" in Sweden whose board included the likes of former NRM members and an Azov veteran simultaneously.[51] The above-mentioned smallness also extends to other Scandinavian countries with the likes of Skillt chatting on social media with a Russian-Norwegian fighting in the "separatist" ranks whom he had known from before the war.[52]

Skillt's SvP, which was disbanded in 2015, was "the ideological home" of the far-right element amongst the Swedes attracted to the war in Ukraine.[53] The party's archived program spoke of the fact that "only people who belong to the Western genetic and cultural heritage, which includes the ethnic Swedes, should be able to be Swedish citizens" and that "Sweden shall be governed by the Swedes: Non-Swedes shall not be allowed to hold positions of power within Swedish society."[54] Skillt was a prominent member and so was Patrik Fridén, who stood in elections for the party.[55] Fridén later fought, unlike most of his compatriots, in the ranks of the less well-known Aidar Battalion in Ukraine, a unit whose leaders entered the Ukrainian Parliament as deputies for Ukrainian nationalist parties.[56] While Skillt and Fridén deployed to Ukraine, the SvP collapsed and the Swedish extremist wing of the far-right milieu became dominated by the NRM, a more pro-Russian organization. Consequently, as the likes of Skillt, and figures like Carolus Andersson or Carolus Löfroos, another Swedish Azov member, were returning to Sweden (either permanently or for a brief spell), they would be questioned by the Swedish Security Service, SÄPO, about the NRM, "an organisation that is directly hostile to us."[57] Indeed, NRM members would allegedly refer to Skillt as an "Arab Jew or Mike – nigga lover."[58] This was supposedly an end result of their pro-Ukraine involvement, and the fact that some of the leading Ukrainian politicians or oligarchs sponsoring the likes of the Azov Battalion were Jewish.

This split amongst the Swedish nationalists/far right, with members of the NRM allegedly going as far as to threaten Skillt, who was said to have responded in kind,[59] turned into a construct resembling the "Israel-Palestine conflict," with both sides increasingly more entrenched on their partisan, either pro-Russia or pro-Ukraine, positions.[60] Initially, however, Ukraine seemed to have had the upper hand as in the eyes of the Swedish far right it had been originally settled or effectively founded by Scandinavians or "ancient Swedish colonists" in the 9th century Kyivan Rus. This admittedly far-fetched link produced a seeming "sentiment of kinship" with Ukraine amongst some of the Swedes, who regarded the Ukrainian struggle as a clear-cut nationalist defense of the homeland against external aggression.[61]

Motivations of the Swedish Foreign Fighters

Regardless of the Russia-Ukraine split and discussions of the Swedish far right, some of the Swedish foreign fighters traveled eastward because of a straightforward desire "to stop Russia [...] as there will always be a group of people who will fight

Russia, whomever it starts the war with."[62] One of the later arrivals perceived the war as "a bigger game," which potentially, due to Russian actions, could spread as it was not just about Ukraine or Donbas. Consequently, for him, joining the fight was a matter of solidarity as he "would have wanted someone to come and help" Sweden had it been attacked.[63] This amounted to, as one observer put it to the author, their own "domino theory" in which "if Ukraine was to fall then they [Russia] would come for all of us."[64] Bizarrely, such a reading of a situation mirrored the black and white, us versus them, Russia versus the U.S. understanding of the war in Ukraine by some of the Frenchmen deployed in the "separatist" ranks.

The Swedish contingent, mostly based in a "highly political unit" (Azov), with members such as Skillt in its ranks, often stood accused of vividly contributing to the "fascist" or "neo-Nazi" image of the Ukrainian volunteer battalions in general and Azov in particular. At the same time, however, Swedes were adamant that they would be able to count "neo-Nazis in Azov [...] on the fingers of one hand." Interviewed Swedish fighter agreed that his fellow Swedes had indeed been "conservative" but not extreme and their main motivation was to join a "professional unit,"[65] or "soundest choice" as far as its fighting capabilities were concerned. Others Swedes would agree they had "always been on the right side of the [political] spectrum"[66] but also objected to being called "white supremacists,"[67] "neo-Nazis" and would state their apolitical status.[68] They were appalled with "persecution" by liberal media after they returned home – "leftists wanted us to be officially compared to the Islamic State of Iraq and Syria (ISIS)."[69] Some confessed they had to move abroad "to find work outside Sweden after this."[70] They also admitted that they found living in Sweden difficult for individuals like themselves, i.e. "those who don't fully accept the politically correct way of life."[71]

The difficulty, in their view, stemmed from the fact that a socio-political construct akin to "thought control" prevails in their country where even the nationalist opposition party – the Sweden Democrats – is forced to put forward "dark skinned" or "Jewish" members so they would convince everyone they were not racist.[72] Sweden, allegedly, is desperate not to receive a "bad press" internationally and since the local media focused on the Swedish "conservative" foreign fighter returnees from Ukraine, the state would not then allow them a chance "to regain a normal life." In this reading of the situation, the small group of returnees had to be sacrificed on the altar of political correctness and stability but this would not, in the words of one fighter, stop the slow creep toward an "open civil war" in Sweden as "gangs, factions, groups" would fight each other within the next 10 years. Some of the rationale for this war is also to be derived from the fact that Sweden is unable to put "a reasonable cap on migration [... and] welfare being more readily available for non-citizens now." It is allegedly even unable to deal with the criminal migrants of today with its law enforcement underfunded and lax penalties for petty criminality.[73] Moreover, in their view, Sweden is a part of "culturally Marxist" EU which allows for excessive public demonstrations of "poison" such as public endorsement of homosexuality. The "gay minority," as one fighter stated, should not be molested but "must stay in the closet"[74] Such views, as demonstrated by the author elsewhere,[75] often mirrored those of the fighters deployed on the other side of the conflict who would also call themselves "nationalists," and belonged "to the same family, with the same values."[76]

As much as some if not all of the above-mentioned views could be seen as beyond the pale by some readers, one must admit that the fighters' "bad press" argument received some support from seemingly unexpected quarters when Kajsa Norman, a London-based investigative Swedish reporter, scrutinized "the repercussions of the Swedish herd mentality" and the effect of "brand and ideology" triumphing over "free speech, real debate, and true pluralism of opinion."[77] Her book, *Sweden's Dark Soul*, was an indictment of a society which is obsessed with external appearances and public relations, and chooses not to confront controversial issues such as immigration when more than 160,000 asylum seekers entered a country of approximately 10 million inhabitants in 2015 alone.[78] Such an influx was bound to create a backlash amongst the ethnic Swedes but its proponents would be scorned by the country's establishment. This, in Norman's view, exposed the fact that Sweden is not a model democracy as it ostracizes those who do not comply with the official worldview, which portrays Sweden as one of the happiest countries in the world, and rewards conformity, uniformity and alleged overarching, but – in reality – enforced, consensus.[79] The discussed fighters certainly felt excluded and no longer "happy" in their country.[80]

Their unhappiness also stemmed, however, from the controversy surrounding their real political affiliations, and how these were later expressed in conversations or communication with individuals from outside their social circles. Thus, in Skillt's eyes he and his colleagues had been nothing more than "conservatives," and he later repudiated his "Nazi" views,[81] but observers would bring out his statements in favor of "racial segregation,"[82] or fighting for "white Ukraine."[83] One would find it difficult to square their alleged "apolitical" status with their demand for "an open discussion on holocaust [... as] some things [might have been] fabricated [... and] but one cannot discuss it because 'money rules the world.'"[84] Their dislike for Nazism would be noted but so would statements on preferring it to communism "in a kind of a civil war setting," as would their references to *The New York Times* as "Jew York Times," or their praise of World War II fascist militias (in this case, Slovakia's *Hlinkova Garda*) on their social media.[85]

Some of such statements, as the author investigated elsewhere, might have constituted, to some extent, a self-chosen "shock and awe" tactics which was meant to dumbfound or outright scare others with extremist imagery. Moreover, they could also be the end result of historical naivete or an attempt to relive or recreate the long gone conflicts, such as that on the Eastern front of World War II. One of the French fighters in the "separatist" ranks, undoubtedly a partisan observer of the foreigners in Azov's ranks, observed that for his opponents it had been enough to see "a couple of runes [on Azov's uniforms] and think it is a re-enactment of the 1941-45 Eastern Front," with their regiment, Azov, on the side of the then Nazi Germany. Usage of such symbols, in his view, would of course "piss off Russia [which fought the Nazi Germany between 1941–45]" and thus allow e.g. the Azov's Swedes to further "troll the Russians" and the "separatists."[86] Notwithstanding the *schadenfreude* of the French in the separatist ranks, as demonstrated, some of their contingent, allegedly fighting it out with "fascist" Kyiv government, held views dangerously similar to that of the most extreme Swedes in the Azov ranks.

Regardless of their political convictions, some of the Swedish fighters, like Skillt or Fridén, had been known members of a party widely seen as "neo-Nazi." Their preference for being directly referred to as "conservative," "nationalist," "patriotic" or even "Christian fundamentalist" to a large extent enabled the outsiders to treat it as an invitation-provocation to seek out and concentrate on their most extreme statements, and consequently regard them as proponents of the far or the extreme right. In turn, the above-mentioned media and the Swedish establishment allegedly felt justified in "prosecuting"[87] them and, more controversially, discussing their return home against the backdrop of (dis)similar returns of ISIS' foreign fighters, 300 of whom came from Sweden.[88]

Despite the pain associated with returning to Sweden and disagreeing with the mainstream views back at home, the fighters felt they fought for Europe and to "protect our European heritage."[89] Their preferred option would be for Sweden to maintain its tradition and cherish its history.[90] Consequently, this was the reason why most of them joined Azov – a unit also keen on similar issues for Ukraine, a country that, in their view, can chart its own path, neither pro-Russian nor in the EU, but admiring, albeit grudgingly, as it did not offer much help in the war, the military prowess and standards of NATO.[91]

Swedish Foreign Fighters at War in Ukraine

The French UC members had a tough time adjusting to the reality on the front lines in the ranks of the "separatists" and to some extent the Swedish experience had not been so much different while fighting for Ukraine. "Incompetence," "lack of organization," "lack of initiative" they witnessed amongst some of the Ukrainian colleagues instinctively made them band together and make the most of their pre-war experiences and training. Moreover, they neither spoke Russian or Ukrainian and thus had to operate together as otherwise they would be treated as a "backpack" for an English-speaking local Azov fighter.[92] Azov Swedes confessed to the author that the language barrier made communication with their colleagues difficult. This was especially an issue when the battalion moved into Mariupol in June 2014 and "bullets flew around us." The scene, as one fighter remembered, was a bit "fuzzy" and also resembled "a film" but this time he found himself right in its midst, not just a bystander. In the aftermath of the battle, his battalion "felt well received" but remembered a group of around 100 "pro-Russian" civilians who "ended up screaming at us in Mariupol after we liberated it." He admitted that this was not surprising as civilians were not keen on "men with guns of any sort" in their streets.[93]

At the same time, the Ukrainian side was said to have appreciated the Swedes' efforts and regarded them as good fighters.[94] The French pro-"separatist" fighters had actually been convinced that "foreign volunteers in Azov regiment got good equipment, they are deployed on the very front line in semi-autonomous groups. They train Ukrainian soldiers etc."[95] Almost all of it, as the author was told by the Swedish interviewees, had been true but it also took a lot of "hassle" to put in place. What is more, the Ukrainian side showed its most post-Soviet bureaucratic nature when by the time of writing this, it failed settle the status of the Swedes in its ranks. These, effectively, overstayed their visas and theoretically had been in the country illegally. They were promised Ukrainian citizenship as a way out of this limbo and the author would exchange messages with one fighter on "his application" for a Ukrainian passport as early as in the spring of 2015. Almost six years later, the issue still has not been resolved, as attested by the given fighter's archived social media statuses.[96]

The Aftermath and the Lives of Others (Non-Foreign Fighters)

Skillt neatly summarized the situation of his fellow countrymen, veterans of the war in Ukraine by saying that that they were neither "[private military] contractors but are not homeless either. Some made good, some made a clusterf&★^ upon returning home." He admitted knowing one veteran who sought a career in PMC companies but ended up "driving trucks in Norway."[97] Others also spoke to the author of their need to abandon Sweden as they could not find a job there[98] or felt hounded by the press.[99] At least one, at the time of writing this, is still deployed in Eastern Ukraine in the ranks of the Azov Regiment.[100] At the same time, others initially reporting from Ukraine for alternative media, returned to Sweden and a played a key role in setting up the above-mentioned Free Sweden. No castigation or hounding was reported in cases of other Swedes, including the "liberals," who seemed to have returned to their pre-war routine.

As for Skillt, a self-confessed pagan suffering from PTSD, he married a local woman and revealed he wanted to run for parliament in Ukraine.[101] In 2017–2018, he acted as the Azov movement's advisor and reportedly fell out with its leaders over some of the connections they were making in the U.S., e.g. with the Rise Above Movement (RAM), "a US white supremacist group that trains in mixed martial arts,"[102] or Greg Johnson, "an alt-right ideologue."[103] Some foreign Azovians were scathing in his criticism of these connections in his interview with the author: "I told them – you have other conservatives, e.g. in Europe. Keep the right wing ideology, you will have partners." In their view, Azov wanted "a forward operating base for them in the U.S." but its connections there resulted in the movement attracting a lot of negative publicity and consequently, now entering U.S. for them is a "no-go."[104] What is more, for Skillt personally being politically associated with a movement making friends with "U.S. racialists" was "bad for his job," i.e. private military contracting in co-operation with the

Americans which took him to places like Libya or Somalia. Simultaneously, he allegedly also abandoned his intention of becoming active in Ukraine politics – he allegedly "came to Ukraine to fight corruption but [would be …] damned if he went into corruption."[105]

The fact that some, like Skillt, actually chose to stay in Ukraine after the war might have been influenced by the fact that the Swedish justice system, also at the behest of Russia,[106] had been looking into the activities of the Swedish "neo-Nazis" in relation to their alleged war crimes in Donbass.[107] Simultaneously, the "separatists" were rumored to have offered an award for Skillt's "head."[108] His colleague wryly commented that he could "see it coming" from the beginning of their Ukraine deployment as "Mike" (Mikael) gave too many interviews "without a balaclava."[109] As was mentioned, the Swedish SÄPO would "check on" the returnees – some commented that they did not mind this kind of scrutiny.[110] Some fighters were even convinced that the security service, with advanced knowledge of a given fighter's trip, attempted to "sabotage" these through administrative measures.[111]

Other, non-combatant, Swedes appeared in Ukraine at an early stage of the conflict, in February 2014 – just like Mikael Skillt. Activists of the Nordic Youth, a far-right organization active between 2010 and 2019, met with Svoboda representatives; so did "representatives" of *Fria Tider* (online right wing news media) and Motgift (alternative media website). They had also reported from the Maidan and one of them, Robin Holmgren, later joined the Azov Battalion.[112] One interviewee admitted to the author that this group – activists supporters, "reporters" of sympathetic media, trainers like himself or outright military instructors,[113] might have been higher in number than the fighters and include up to 50 individuals.[114] Some, as mentioned above, quietly slipped in and out of the country, while others even managed literally to smuggle dogs out of the country.[115]

Conclusion

To an extent, the Swedish contingent of the foreign fighters in Ukraine is a mirror image of the French, described in the previous chapter. It is by far not the most numerous but because of the fact that its leading light, Mikael Skillt, arrived early to Ukraine and then fronted the foreign recruitment for the Azov Battalion/Regiment, it proverbially punches above its relatively minor numerical strength. It was at least partly brown in nature as it featured Swedish individuals from the country's broader far right. These, however, while deploying to the Ukrainian side effectively crossed many of their ideological comrades who opted for Russia and the "separatists" in 2014 after a rather unexpected pro-Moscow turn on behalf of some of the country's most radical far-right individuals. The story of the Swedes in Ukraine does not, however, end with the 2014–15 phase of the war, before it "froze" as, almost eight years later, in the spring of 2022, some of them are still fighting in Ukraine and one of them has been trapped in the besieged city of Mariupol. He was later involved in the prisoner exchange with Russia and at the time of writing this is undergoing rehabilitation in Saudi Arabia, which helped broker the exchange.

Notes

1 The author heard of one, maximum two, Swedes who, in a clandestine manner, were to feature in the ranks of the "separatists." See author's interview with Lars Gyllenhaal, Swedish author, expert on the Swedish military history, Stockholm, February 18, 2020.

2 Author's interview with a Swedish foreign fighter, not a member of Azov, who wished to remain anonymous, over Facebook Messenger, February 17, 2020.

3 Author's interview with a Swedish member of the Azov Regiment (#1) who wished to remain anonymous over twitter Messenger, March 11, 2015.

4 See the "French" chapter for more on him and his actions in Ukraine.

5 *Fria Tider*, "Swede Patrols Ukraine's Streets with Right-wing Paramilitaries," March 26, 2014, https://www.friatider.se/swede-patrols-ukraines-streets-with-right-wing-paramilitaries, accessed: January 20, 2021.

6 Fausto Biloslavo, "Ukraine: Far-Right Fighters from Europe Fight for Ukraine," *eurasianet*, August 6, 2014, https://eurasianet.org/ukraine-far-right-fighters-from-europe-fight-for-ukraine, accessed: January 14, 2021.

7 *Fria Tider*, "Swede Patrols."

8 *Hate Speech International*, "Ukraine's far-right forces," February 3, 2015, https://www.hate-speech.org/ukraines-far-right-forces/, accessed: January 20, 2021.

9 Ibid.

10 Author's WhatsApp interview with a foreign member of the Azov Battalion/Regiment who wished to remain anonymous, January 28, 2020.

11 *BBC Newsnight*, "Neo-Nazi threat in new Ukraine: Newsnight," YouTube, February 28, 2014, https://www.youtube.com/watch?v=5SBo0akeDMY#t=226, accessed: January 20, 2021.

12 Author's WhatsApp interview with a foreign member of the Azov Battalion/Regiment who wished to remain anonymous, January 28, 2020.

13 *Hate Speech International*.

14 Author's interview with Jonas Nilsson, member of the non-combatant contingent, MMA fighter, who taught wrestling to the members of the Azov Regiment, Stockholm, February 16, 2020.

15 See Kacper Rekawek, *Career Break or a New Career? Extremist Foreign Fighters in Ukraine* (Counter Extremism Project, April 2020), https://www.counterextremism.com/sites/default/files/CEP%20Report_Career%20Break%20or%20a%20New%20Career_Extremist%20Foreign%20Fighters%20in%20Ukraine_April%202020.pdf, accessed: January 12, 2020.

16 Nolan Peterson, "How a Swedish Sniper Found Redemption in the Ukraine War," *The Daily Signal*, August 10, 2015, https://www.dailysignal.com/2015/08/10/meet-the-former-neo-nazi-spokesman-who-now-fights-for-freedom-in-ukraine/, accessed: January 20, 2021.

17 Author's interview with an anonymous Swedish policeman who had known Skillt from before his move to Ukraine, January 28, 2020.

18 Skillt was said to have been active in the Swedish Resistance Movement's "hang the paedophiles campaign," which saw the organization's members patrol areas around schools in different parts of Sweden. See Magnus Ranstorp and Filip Ahlin, eds., *Från Nordiska motståndsrörelsen till alternativhögern En studie om den svenska radikalnationalistiska miljön* (Stockholm: CATS, 2020), 160 https://www.fhs.se/download/18.aa44b1740d51053bc784/1599031490867/Fr%C3%A5n%20Nordiska%20motst%C3%A5ndsr%C3%B6relsen%20till%20alternativh%C3%B6gern%20-%20en%20studie%20om%20den%20svenska%20radikalnationalistiska%20milj%C3%B6n.pdf, accessed: January 20, 2021.

19 Peterson, "How a Swedish Sniper Found Redemption."

20 Author's WhatsApp interview with a foreign member of the Azov Battalion/Regiment who wished to remain anonymous, January 28, 2020.

21 See: Magnus Ranstorp, Filip Ahlin, eds., *Executive summary: From the Nordic Resistance Movement to the Alternative Right. A study of the Swedish radical nationalist milieu* (Stockholm: CATS, 2020), 6 https://www.fhs.se/download/18.23f6da6b173f8bed598498cc/1598877052261/Summary%20-%20From%20the%20Nordic%20Resistance%20Movement%20to%20the%20Alternative%20Right%20%E2%80%93%20a%20Study%20of%20Radical%20Nationalistic%20Environments%20in%20Sweden.pdf.

22 Author's exchange on twitter direct messaging with a Swedish fighter who twice deployed to the frontline in Ukraine January 28, 2020.

23 Author's interview with Lars Gyllenhaal, Swedish author, expert on the Swedish military history, Stockholm, February 18, 2020.

24 Author's interview with an anonymous police officer whose job is to monitor his country's far-right extremists, Stockholm, February 12, 2020.

25 Author's interview with Jonas Nilsson, member of the non-combatant contingent, MMA fighter, who taught wrestling to the members of the Azov Regiment, Stockholm, February 16, 2020.

26 *Hate Speech International.*

27 Rekawek, *Career Break*, 19.

28 Author's interview with Diamant Salihu, a Swedish journalist who covered the story of the Swedish foreign fighters in Ukraine, Stockholm, February 12, 2020.

29 It is worth noting here that Carolus Löfroos, the Azov member who received the communication, was himself expelled from the Home Guard upon returning from Ukraine in late 2014. See Daniel Olsson, "Soldat ville strida mot Ryssland – köps ut," *Expressen*, January 9, 2019, https://www.expressen.se/gt/soldat-ville-strida-mot-ryssland-kops-ut/, accessed: January 20, 2021.

30 Author's WhatsApp interview with a foreign member of the Azov Battalion/Regiment who wished to remain anonymous, January 28, 2020. The discussed individual, Leo Sjöholm, was the only Swedish casualty in the conflict – he later died in a car accident. See Yuliana Romanyshyn, "Swedish volunteer with Azov Battalion dies in car accident," *Kyiv Post*, January 24, 2015, https://www.kyivpost.com/article/content/war-against-ukraine/swedish-volunteer-with-azov-battalion-dies-in-car-accident-378284.html?cn-reloaded=1,Accessed: January 25, 20201.

31 An example of such an individual would be Jonas Ohman, founder of the Lithuania-based NGO Blue/Yellow. His organization has been active in helping Ukraine since the summer of 2014.

32 Lars Gyllenhaal, a Swedish author and an expert on Swedish military history, confirmed this point to the author while stating that he "believes that only half of the Swedish persons in question can be said to have been political activists/extremists." Author's email exchange with Gyllenhaal, May 30, 2022.

33 Interestingly, other Swedes, such as Patrik Fridén who fought in the ranks of the Aidar Battalion and not the more visible Azov, had also been an SvP member before deploying to Ukraine.

34 Gyllenhall.

35 See the poscript chapter for more on the situation after February 24, 2022.

36 Ranstorp and Ahlin, *Från Nordiska*, 453.

37 Author's interview with Jonas Nilsson, member of the non-combatant contingent, MMA fighter, who taught wrestling to the members of the Azov Regiment, Stockholm, February 16, 2020. Sweden Democrats' splinter group, the Alternative for Sweden (AfS), is said to have a more pro-Russia-friendly position. See Ranstorp and Ahlin, *Från Nordiska*, 456.

38 Morgan Finnsiö, "Sweden," in K. Rekawek, H. J. Schindler, and A. Ritzman. eds., *Violent Right-Wing Extremism and Terrorism – Transnational Connectivity, Definitions, Incidents, Structures and Countermeasures* (Berlin: Counter Extremism Project, November 2020), 115, https://www.counterextremism.com/sites/default/files/CEP%20Study_Violent%20Right-Wing%20Extremism%20and%20Terrorism_Nov%202020.pdf, accessed: January 25, 2021. See also Ranstorp and Ahlin, *Från Nordiska*, 193–194.

39 Author's interview with Morgan Finnsiö, expert on the Swedish far right, associated with EXPO foundation, February 12, 2020, Stockholm.

40 Ibid. 115.

41 Ibid.

42 J. Lester Feder, Edgar Mannheimer, and Jane Lytvynenko, "These Swedish Nazis Trained in Russia Before Bombing a Center for Asylum Seekers," *Buzzfeed News*, July 22, 2017, https://www.buzzfeednews.com/article/lesterfeder/these-swedish-nazis-trained-in-russia, accessed: January 25, 2021.

43 The Swedish duo were said to have appeared on the social media profiles of RID (VKontakte). See Ranstorp and Ahlin, *Från Nordiska*, 454.

44 Author's interview with an anonymous police officer whose job is to monitor his country's far-right extremists, Stockholm, February 12, 2020.

45 See the Department's designation of April 6, 2020 at: https://www.state.gov/designation-of-the-russian-imperial-movement/, accessed: January 25, 2021.

46 Robyn Dixon, "Inside white-supremacist Russian Imperial Movement, designated foreign terrorist organization by U.S. State Department," *The Washington Post*, April 13, 2020, https://www.washingtonpost.com/world/europe/russia-white-supremacist-terrorism-us/2020/04/11/255a9762-7a75-11ea-a311-adb1344719a9_story.html, accessed: January 25, 2021. See also Ranstorp and Ahlin, *Från Nordiska*, 193–194.

47 Author's interview with Morgan Finnsiö, February 12, 2020.

48 Author's interview with an anonymous police officer whose job is to monitor his country's far-right extremists, Stockholm, February 12, 2020.

49 Author's WhatsApp interview with Benjamin R. Teitelbaum, expert on the Swedish far right and the associate professor of ethnomusicology, international affairs at the University of Colorado, Boulder, January 28, 2020.

50 Benjamin R. Teitelbaum, *Lions of the North: Sounds of the New Nordic Radical Nationalism* (New York: Oxford University Press, 2017), X–XV.

51 Ranstorp and Ahlin, *Från Nordiska*, 348.

52 Tim Hume, "Far-Right Extremists Have Been Using Ukraine's War as a Training Ground. They're Returning Home," *Vice News*, July 31, 2019, https://www.vice.com/en/article/vb95ma/far-right-extremists-have-been-using-ukraines-civil-war-as-a-training-ground-theyre-returning-home, accessed: January 25, 2021.

53 Author's interview with an anonymous police officer whose job is to monitor his country's far-right extremists, Stockholm, February 12, 2020.

54 See https://web.archive.org/web/20110808231900/http://www.svenskarnasparti.se/punktprogram/, accessed: January 20, 2021.

55 Ida Gustafsson, "Patrik Fridén går kvar på utbildningen," *Aftonbladet*, April 24, 2014, https://www.aftonbladet.se/nyheter/a/wExwzA/patrik-friden-gar-kvar-pa-utbildningen, accessed: January 20, 2021.

56 *112UA*, "Ex-commander of Aidar battalion released from custody in Greece," March 3, 2020, https://112.international/politics/ex-commander-of-aidar-battalion-released-from-custody-in-greece-49142.html, accessed: January 20, 2021.

57 Author's exchange on twitter direct messaging with an anonymous Swedish fighter who twice deployed to the frontline in Ukraine January 28, 2020.

58 Author's WhatsApp interview with a foreign member of the Azov Battalion/Regiment who wished to remain anonymous, January 28, 2020.

59 Ibid.

60 Author's interview with Jonas Nilsson, member of the non-combatant contingent, MMA fighter, who taught wrestling to the members of the Azov Regiment, Stockholm, February 16, 2020.

61 Author's interview with Morgan Finnsiö, February 12, 2020.

62 Author's interview with a Swedish member of the Azov Regiment (#1) who wished to remain anonymous over twitter Messenger, March 11, 2015.

63 *Svt Nyheter*, "Carolus från Sundsvall strider i Ukraina," January 30, 2015, https://www.svt.se/nyheter/utrikes/carolus-fran-sundsvall-strider-i-ukraina, accessed: January 21, 2021.

64 Author's interview with an anonymous Swedish policeman who had known Skillt from before his move to Ukraine, January 28, 2020.

65 Author's WhatsApp interview with a foreign member of the Azov Battalion/Regiment who wished to remain anonymous, January 28, 2020.

66 Hume, "Far-Right Extremists."

67 Author's interview with a Swedish member of the Azov Regiment (#1) who wished to remain anonymous over twitter Messenger, July 13, 2015.

68 *Yle.fi*, "Finnish fighter in Ukraine: "I'm not a Nazi," January 31, 2015, https:// yle.fi/uutiset/osasto/news/finnish_fighter_in_ukraine_im_not_a_nazi/7772719, accessed: January 21, 2021.

69 Author's interview with a Swedish foreign fighter, not a member of Azov, who wished to remain anonymous, over Facebook Messenger, February 17, 2020.

70 Author's interview with a Swedish member of the Azov Regiment (#2) who wished to remain anonymous over twitter Messenger, January 28, 2020.

71 Author's interview with a Swedish member of the Azov Regiment (#1) who wished to remain anonymous over twitter Messenger, July 13, 2015.

72 Ibid.

73 Author's interview with a Swedish foreign fighter, not a member of Azov, who wished to remain anonymous, over Facebook Messenger, February 17, 2020. Another fighter, this time a member of the Azov, endorsed the anti-immigrant vigilante "Soldiers of Odin" but mused on the effectiveness of their patrolling, hinting that more radical measures would be needed to control immigration into Sweden. See author's interview with a Swedish member of the Azov Regiment (#1) who wished to remain anonymous over twitter Messenger, February 28, 2015.

74 Author's interview with a Swedish member of the Azov Regiment (#1) who wished to remain anonymous over twitter Messenger, March 23, June 6, July 13, 2015.

75 Rekawek, *Career Break*.

76 Author's exchange with a French foreign fighter over Facebook Messenger, August 28, 2015.

77 See Kajsa Norman's author page at http://www.kajsanorman.com/en/index.html, accessed: January 21, 2021.

78 For statistics on immigration see Sweden's official website at https://sweden.se/ migration/#, accessed: January 21, 2021.

79 Kajsa Norman, *Sweden's Dark Soul. The Unravelling of a Utopia* (London: Hurst, 2018).

80 Cathrine Thorleifsson, "The Swedish dystopia: violent imaginaries of the radical right," *Patterns of Prejudice* 53, no.5 (2019): 518 for more on the issue. Thorleifsson discusses a "dual Swedish dystopia" which permeates the thinking of the country's far right as it simultaneously longs for a "white" utopia of the Sweden of the past and is terrified by the "civil war"-like vision of a country overran by Muslim immigrants.

81 Nolan Peterson, "Putin's War: A Swedish Sniper in Ukraine," *Newsweek*, August 15, 2015, https://www.newsweek.com/putins-war-swedish-sniper-ukraine-362883, accessed: January 25, 2021.

82 Diamant Salihu, Svenskarna som strider i Ukraina, *Expressen*, December 10, 2014, accessed: January 21, 2021.

83 Anna-Lena Laurén, "Svensk nynazist deltar i striderna," *Svenska Dagbladet*, July 23, 2014, https://www.svd.se/svensk-nynazist-deltar-i-striderna, accessed: January 21, 2021.

84 Author's interview with a Swedish member of the Azov Regiment (#1) who wished to remain anonymous over twitter Messenger, April 3, 2015.

85 Author's interview with a Swedish foreign fighter, not a member of Azov, who wished to remain anonymous, over Facebook Messenger, February 26, 2020.

86 Rekawek, *Career Break*, 12–13.

87 The case of Fridén also received ample coverage before his apperance in the ranks of Aidar. He had been training as an explosives technician and due to his running for office in the ranks of SvP, this caused a minor scandal in Sweden. See Gustafsson, "Patrik Fridén."

88 Linus Gustafsson and Magnus Ranstorp, *Swedish Foreign Fighters in Syria and Iraq* (Stockholm: CATS, 2017) http://www.diva-portal.org/smash/get/diva2:1110355/ FULLTEXT01.pdf, accessed: January 21, 2021.

89 Ibid.

90 Author's interview with Diamant Salihu, a Swedish journalist who covered the story of the Swedish foreign fighters in Ukraine, Stockholm, February 12, 2020.

91 Author's interview with a Swedish member of the Azov Regiment (#1) who wished to remain anonymous over twitter Messenger, September 15, 2015.

92 Ibid.

93 Ibid.

94 Author's interview with an anonymous police officer whose job is to monitor his country's far-right extremists, Stockholm, February 12, 2020.

95 See: the chapter on the French fighters in the war. Author's exchange with a French foreign fighter over Facebook Messenger, August 28, 2015.

96 The author possesses these in his archive but since the fighter asked for anonymity, the author will not be sharing links to them.

97 Author's WhatsApp interview with a foreign member of the Azov Battalion/Regiment who wished to remain anonymous, January 28, 2020.

98 Author's WhatsApp interview with a foreign member of the Azov Battalion/Regiment who wished to remain anonymous, January 28, 2020.

99 Ibid.

100 See https://twitter.com/mikolaswed, accessed; January 26, 2021, for his twitter account.

101 Salomon Garage, "Interview with AZOV-volunteer Mikael Skillt," YouTube, August 14, 2016, https://www.youtube.com/watch?v=2HLpBRswZcU&feature= youtu.be, accessed: January 20, 2021.

102 Karim Zidan, "RAM's revival and the ongoing struggle against MMA's far-right fight clubs," *The Guardian*, November 27, 2019, https://www.theguardian.com/ sport/2019/nov/27/rams-revival-and-the-ongoing-struggle-against-mmas-far-right-fight-clubs, accessed: January 26, 2021.

103 Oleksyi Kuzmenko, "'Defend the White Race:' American Extremists Being Co-Opted by Ukraine's Far-Right," *bellingcat*, February 15, 2019, https://www. bellingcat.com/news/uk-and-europe/2019/02/15/defend-the-white-race-american-extremists-being-co-opted-by-ukraines-far-right/, accessed: January 26, 2021.

104 Author's WhatsApp interview with a foreign member of the Azov Battalion/ Regiment who wished to remain anonymous, January 28, 2020. For a U.S. view on Azov see e.g. Max Rose and Ali H. Soufan, "We Once Fought Jihadists. Now We Battle White Supremacists," *The New York Times*, February 11, 2020, https:// www.nytimes.com/2020/02/11/opinion/politics/white-supremacist-terrorism. html, accessed: January 26, 2021.

105 Author's WhatsApp interview with a foreign member of the Azov Battalion/ Regiment who wished to remain anonymous, January 28, 2020.

106 *Interfax.ru*, "МИД РФ призвал расследовать действия шведских неонацистов в Донбассе," August 12, 2015, https://www.interfax.ru/world/459729, accessed: January 25, 2021.

107 *Stalker Zone*, "The Investigation into the Crimes of Swedish Mercenaries in Donbass Resumed," https://www.stalkerzone.org/investigation-crimes-swedish-mercenaries-donbass-resumed/, accessed: January 25, 2021.

108 Ilaria Morani and Salvatore Garzillo, "In Ucraina il cecchino più ricercato dai russi: 'Combatto insieme a soldati italiani'," *Corriere della Sera*, accessed: January 25, 2021.

109 Author's interview with a Swedish member of the Azov Regiment (#1) who wished to remain anonymous over twitter Messenge, August 12, 2015.

110 Author's WhatsApp interview with a foreign member of the Azov Battalion/Regiment who wished to remain anonymous, January 28, 2020. At the same time, the Swedish justice sector was said to have been unhappy with the lack of co-operation coming

from its Ukrainian counterpart in relations to these investigations. The Swedes, as the author was told, were becoming convinced that the Ukrainians did not want them to find out about potentially controversial or outright criminal activities of the Swedish fighters on their territory. See author's interview with an anonymous police officer whose job is to monitor his country's far-right extremists, Stockholm, February 12, 2020.

111 Author's interview with a Swedish member of the Azov Regiment (#1) who wished to remain anonymous over twitter Messenger, September 30, 2015.
112 *Hate Speech International.*
113 Author's interview with Diamant Salihu, a Swedish journalist who covered the story of the Swedish foreign fighters in Ukraine, Stockholm, February 12, 2020.
114 Author's interview with Jonas Nilsson, member of the non-combatant contingent, MMA fighter, who taught wrestling to the members of the Azov Regiment, Stockholm, February 16, 2020.
115 See the author's twitter feed from June 18, 2015, https://twitter.com/Kacper Rekawek/status/611624872024907776?s=20, accessed: January 26, 2021.

7

THE BALKANS

Repeating the 1990s War in Yugoslavia?

Introduction

In the past, the author would often perceive the participation of the foreign fighters from Croatia and Serbia in the conflict in Ukraine as an almost logical continuation of the war of the 1990s when the countries clashed with one another during the Yugoslav wars. According to such a reading of the situation, some of the nationalistically minded veterans of these wars simply wished to settle the old scores with their arch rivals when an opportunity presented itself. Consequently, the pro-Russian Serbs joined up with the "separatists" and the Croats appeared in the ranks of the Ukrainian volunteer battalions. As the research leading to the production of this book progressed, however, the author realized that such an approach to Croat and Serbian foreign fighters in the war in Ukraine is inaccurate and simplistic. As will be shown, the issue of "repayment of debts" owed to some foreign friends was key in this process and not some illusory desire to continue the unfinished conflicts from the 1990s. What is more, the Serbian contingent dwarfed the Croat and one should not consider the two as actively competing against one another. At the same time, deployments of both groups of fighters put their two countries of origin in politically embarrassing situations vis-à-vis the EU and Russia. For this reason, they took an active interests in the travails of "their" fighters, and called on their citizens to return home. Such calls did not fall on deaf ears, as these contingents suffered some problems while trying to get to Ukraine (the Croats) or went through thorough and long-lasting internal rivalries and splits (the Serbs), which made the allure of continuing the fighting much less rewarding than previously thought.

DOI: 10.4324/9781003192992-7

Serbia

The Serbian contingent in the war in Ukraine was possibly the biggest of all of the European ones present on the front lines. Its members were to be found entirely in the ranks of the "separatists." It certainly had been a multifaceted hydra, with its members arriving in the Donetsk People's Republic (DNR)/Luhansk People's Republic (LNR) via different routes, with varying backgrounds and motivations for joining the fight. It encompassed not only Serbs from Serbia but also Bosnian and potentially Montenegrin Serbs. Moreover, just like the French contingent in the "separatist" ranks, it had its own share of drama as its members allegedly embezzled funds earmarked for sustaining Serbian fighters in the field and plotted assassinations against each other. In addition to this, many of them had illustrious post-war careers, which saw some of them (a) involved as private military contractors (PMCs) in Syria,[1] (b) others plotting a coup in Montenegro and, finally, (c) some returning back home to face the threat of jail terms which usually went away after they concluded plea agreements with the prosecutors and received paltry jail sentences for their foreign fighting, which had been illegal since 2014.

Mobilization of Fighters and Motivations

The Serbian foreign fighters in Ukraine seemed to have originated from three distinct sources. First, some actually appeared in Ukraine prior to the eruption of the war in Donbas. Dejan Berić, who after the collapse of his construction business in Serbia, was working on construction sites in Sochi right before the 2014 winter Olympics, first appeared in Crimea[2] before deploying to Donbas where he fought alongside Girkin's unit in Slavyansk.[3] The same could be said some other Serbian fighters who also traveled to Donbas from Russia or Belarus, where they worked on construction sites.[4] Secondly, the French-led Continental Unity (UC, *Unité Continentale*) organizations, and a foreign fighter unit present in the "separatist" forces, which included Nikola Perović, a part Serbian/Montenegrin former French soldier, was also conducting some recruitment in Serbia.[5] It asked for funds from its sympathizers from around the world and was to sponsor travel of the wannabe Serbian fighters to Donbas.[6] This, according to Serbian sources, went awry and Perović ended up owing money to the individual Serbian fighters.[7] Thirdly, the Serb fighters came from the ranks of the Chetnik movement. Chetnik is literally a member of an irregular band/company who styled himself as a participant of a nationalistic movement harking back to the World War II when the collapse of the Yugoslav army gave birth to a largely unstructured, "amorphous" movement of "insurgent bands."[8] By the early twenty-first century, the Chetniks were effectively a collective of some of the Serbian veterans of the Yugoslav wars of the 1990s – nationalist, religious and ultra-conservative in their ideological outlook.[9]

Around a dozen of such Chetniks also appeared in Crimea and were later to be found in Donbas – allegedly on the invitation of the Cossacks, themselves veterans of the war in Yugoslavia in the 1990s.[10] In the meantime, their leader, Bratislav Živković, was accused by some of his men of misusing his Serbian unit's funds.[11] He nonetheless returned to Serbia, allegedly to organize further departures and displayed a knack for self-publicity often present amongst the Serbian foreign fighters in Ukraine when the Serbian media "accidentally" caught up with him at Belgrade airport in June 2014.[12] In the later years, Živković was first banned from Montenegro for his alleged subversive activities, then "expelled from Romania and given a 15-year entry ban after authorities accused him of spying on NATO military bases in the country's southeast," arrested in Serbia in 2018 "on suspicion of organizing the participation of Serb fighters in the war [in Ukraine]," then released, before finally resurfacing in Donetsk.[13]

The above-mentioned three recruitment sources of Serbian foreign fighters must be studied alongside the motivations of such individuals, which also point out the mechanics of how they were mobilized or convinced to deploy eastward. What strikes any student of the Serbian contingent in Ukraine is the often repeated assertion that the Serbs deployed to Donbas to repay some debt they had to the Russians from the 1990s or by invitation of their former Russian comrades from the Yugoslav wars.[14] As underscored by Milos Popović, back then numerous Russian fighters deployed to the Western Balkans were motivated by "Pan-Slavic and Pan-Orthodox sentiments."[15] Years later, "many among Bosnian Serbs and those from Serbia who joined the fight on the Russian/'separatist'/Donbas side did so because they saw the war as an anti-establishment fight, against the West, against NATO. The fact that they were Eastern Orthodox helped too."[16] Indeed, some of them, such as Živković, had a track record of anti-systemic ("Serbia is not free") outbursts related not only to the broader West but to their more immediate political, Western Balkan surroundings.[17] As will be shown later, they continued in their often conspiratorial radical manner after they returned from Serbia, with some allegedly involved in the plot to oust a pro-Western government of Montenegro and/or to assassinate a pro-EU Serbian President, Aleksandar Vučić.

These fighters might not have been far right in the traditional or Western sense – not always did they belong to militant, fascist or neo-Nazi political outfits and largely functioned outside the microcosm of the transnational far right or the local, Serbian outfits which would aspire to membership in this milieu (for some the link had been the UC and Perović). At the same time, they held nationalistic views, and many were war veterans who were motivated by religion and would not accept non-"pure Serbs" into their immediate company back at home.[18] On top of that, and this was also said to have been the key behind their motivation to join DNR/LNR forces,

> there is a long private military contracting (PMC) tradition in the region which involves the veterans of the 1990s' wars. It predates the Ukraine conflict – look at the White Legion which fought in Zaire, full of Serbs.

They [the Serbian foreign fighters] also went to Ukraine for the money. Some expected a new, good life out there but found themselves stuck in Donetsk or Luhansk,[19]

with one going back to Serbia and redeploying back to the conflict in 2018.[20] In the words of Ljubodrag Stojadinović, a prominent Serbian security and defense commentator,

> this area [the Western Balkans] has produced many packs of war dogs and there are probably some in different places today. I think some are still in prison in countries that have suffered a disaster, I'm talking about Libya in the first place and some other countries. It is certain that these people are not harmless. But, I think that their influence on the events is minor and that they appear there primarily because of themselves. For some of their personal reasons, regardless of whether those reasons are, in that perverse sense, emotional or material or adventurous, there have always been such people.[21]

In this sense, the Serbs in Ukraine hardly were foreign fighters as it had been the pecuniary award that was said to have motivated them. The monthly salaries allegedly offered varied but some reported that initially even up to €10,000 per month was promised. Such sums, if truly offered, were unsustainable in the long run and the fighters arriving later were paid far less – sometimes around €200–250 a month.[22] Thus, their perceived mercenary exploit rapidly turned into a more mundane, regular foreign fighting one as such sums hardly sustained them while in the DNR/LNR, nor did they allow for making savings and simply profiting from the war in Eastern Ukraine. Simultaneously, their foreign counterparts who fought on either side of the war, in all sorts of (para)military units, were also receiving renumeration – just like the foreign fighters in the ranks of the Islamic State of Iraq and Syria (ISIS).[23]

Numbers

The Ukrainian Служба безпеки України, *Sluzhba bezpeky Ukrayiny* (SBU), Security Service of Ukraine, allegedly produced a number of 300 Serbs involved in the war in Ukraine on the side of the DNR/LNR. This was said to have been "an inflated figure and 100 is a more realistic number for the Serbian foreign fighters there"[24] and, as will be shown, some had been Serbs residing outside of Serbia in Bosnia-Herzegovina or Montenegro. Bratislav Živković allegedly led 15 Chetniks in the ranks of the LNR troops,[25] and the rest were to be found in at least eight units of the "separatists."[26] There was no attempt to form a Serbian-led equivalent of the predominantly French UC, although this outfit featured some Serbs in its ranks. As the fighters were coming to the front via different connections and routes, any desire to mold them into a single unit (although Serbian smaller units such as the Chetnik "Jovan Šević" existed in Ukraine) would prove hard and potentially, politically costly for the "separatists." It could also have produced some embarrassing consequences for the Serbian government, which was not keen on inflating the roles of its nationals on the front lines in Ukraine.[27]

This resulted in an unprecedented approach by the Serbian justice system to hold, or allegedly hold, the fighters accountable for their actions in Ukraine. No other country launched such a process as, by the end of 2018, the Serbian courts identified 45 Serbian citizens who "have had legal proceedings started against them for allegedly going to fight on the battlefields of Ukraine," and 29 were convicted – as pertaining to the 2014 law which criminalized foreign fighting. This law, allegedly adopted as a result of EU and U.S. pressure,[28] "went well beyond the requests from the UN Security Council resolutions, and opted to criminalize foreign fighting irrespective of its connection to terrorism," i.e. it was not solely drafted with the Serbian jihadi contingent in Syria in mind. It forbids "organization, recruitment, logistical support, public incitement to travel abroad, and the participation in an armed conflict abroad [in the ranks of a foreign army or a paramilitary formation]" – punishable by up to 10 years of imprisonment – but steers clear of criminalizing "providing public support for travelling."[29] At the same time, this seemingly stringent law provided the returning Serbs, and the Belgrade authorities, with, literally, a "get out of jail card" as the convicted fighters predominantly accepted plea agreements and received paltry, suspended sentences for their activities.[30]

Unhappy Endings and Drama Contingent

In March 2021, a Russian newspaper covered the case of Slavisha Mitrović, a former Serbian fighter in the ranks of the LNR's Prizrak Brigade, led by Aleksey Mozgovoy, a commander cherished by the French fighters in the "separatist" ranks.[31] Mitrović, a Croatia-born Serb and a veteran of the wars of the 1990s, who joined the fight in Ukraine in 2014 and was later wounded, feared arrest if he was to return to Serbia. He gained the "citizenship" of the LNR but had trouble finding employment in Russia and saw little success on his path to Russian citizenship. His compatriot, Vladimir Stanimirović, a Kosovo war military veteran, who also arrived in "the People's Republics" in 2014, got married while there and fathered a child, met a worse end as October 2016 brought the news of his death on the front.[32] Allegedly, this event, coupled with other mysterious events concerning the Serbian contingent led to an increased number of disillusioned Serbian volunteers' trickling back home.[33]

The above mentioned Beric, and Dejan Vujic, another Serbian fighters, allegedly targets of assassination plot by their countryman, Radomir Počuča, spoke openly to the press of their allegations and suspicions vis-à-vis some of their countrymen present in "the People's Republics." They alleged that some were effectively involved in starting or launching a unit, full of "children" who would come to Donetsk to "wave flags." This was meant to convince their erstwhile, possibly Russian, sponsors that the enterprise of sending foreign fighters to the Donetsk People's Republic

(DNR)/Luhansk People's Republic (LNR) was functioning like clockwork and that further investment, allegedly pocketed by Počuča, was needed to sustain the flow of such individuals from Serbia to "the People's Republics."[34] Vujić, an experienced former Serbian paratrooper who worked at a construction site in Belarus when the war in Ukraine started,[35] and Berić, a media superstar of the DNR forces – his exploits later to be covered in a documentary,[36] had a good reputation in Donetsk and saw to the fact that Počuča and his alleged Serbian sidekick were arrested. Interestingly enough, his arrest must have ruffled some feathers in both "the People's Republic," Russia, and possibly – given Počuča's former job at the Serbian ministry of the interior – also Serbia. He consequently "resurfaced" in Moscow,[37] only later to return to Serbia and receive a paltry 18-month suspended sentence for his foreign fighting.[38] In the meantime, via the media, he traded insults with Berić, whom Počuča accused of being the agent of the Ukrainian security service, SBU.[39] In return, Berić called him "a liar, a thief and a traitor."[40] As the two squared up against one another, it was becoming apparent that their rivalry sustained itself because of their preference to have it out in the open, e.g. on their Facebook profiles, where they were posting about their exploits from the war in Ukraine.[41] In this field, Berić rather successfully rivaled Počuča, a former TV anchor, as he "published a book, worked for a small TV station and even appeared at a press conference in Moscow which was held by [Russian] foreign ministry spokeswoman Maria Zakharova."[42]

Regardless of their spat, Počuča, who was allegedly close to Serbs involved in the preparation of the coup in Montenegro,[43] was seen "in a very down town [area] of Belgrade [...] walking freely and proudly [after his return]."[44] Given the fact that the coup potentially also had a Serbian angle – i.e. a strike against Serbia's leaders whose then pro-EU foreign policy choices might not have been to the taste of "powers from outside the country"[45] – his ability to roam the streets of his country's capital seemed remarkable. At the same time, Berić, the alleged SBU agent, and by extension, hostile to Russia, which enjoys very good relations with Serbia, was also back in his country. In the spring of 2021, he announced he would be returning to the DNR to fight on its behalf in the renewed Eastern Ukrainian hostilities.[46] In the meantime, he somehow withstood accusations of participation in the above-mentioned Montenegrin coup and his alleged plotting an attack on the Serbian prime minister.[47] All of such exploits suggest that the Serbian contingent might have been infiltrated by the Serbian security services which (a) wanted to keep an eye on a genuine, or Russia instigated – as is suggested by some,[48] mobilization of foreign fighters for the war in Ukraine, and (b) ensure that no negative fall-out for Belgrade arises from the activities of such fighters.[49] In this concept, both Berić and Počuča, and all the other Serbs, could have been allowed to function in the DNR/LNR and count on relatively lenient sentences, if any, for their activities upon their return, provided they followed the general guidelines for their behavior from the Serbian authorities. This might have been a pragmatic strategy of which Belgrade could have informed Moscow, especially given the fact that some Serbs would drift to the front lines regardless of any interest or involvement of the Serbian or Russian security services. This, as was shown, was their "repayment of debts," as mentioned by the likes of Berić or Mitrović in their post-war reminiscences.[50] Živković also hinted at the bottom-up recruitment process of fighters while reminiscing about his war exploits – he admitted him and his men were actually stopped on the way out of the DNR/LNR by the Russian internal security service, FSB. They were allowed to continue on their way to Moscow, and then to fly back to Belgrade. Had they been organically recruited for the war by the FSB, or other Russian intelligence agency, then there would have been a lesser chance of any controls on the way back home.[51]

Non-Serbia's Serbs and the Post-War Fall Out

Amongst the Serbs, a small contingent of 11[52] individuals came from Bosnia and Herzegovina. Again, these included veterans of the wars of the 1990s, some allegedly escaping punishment e.g. for their activities in Kosovo.[53] These allegedly left for Ukraine in 2014 and returned home without any hindrance, and some were said to have been assisted in their travel by the Serbian Chetniks and traveled to Russia from Belgrade airport.[54] As Bosnia, like other Western Balkan countries, also bans foreign fighting, the fact that only one of the fighters, Gavrilo Stević, had so far been charged with "joining foreign paramilitary or parapolice formations," and acquitted in 2020,[55] might have been a sign of the authorities' preoccupation mostly with the Syrian returnees[56] or potentially their "hiding," often in plain sight in the Serbian part of Bosnia – Republika Srpska. This entity would have little inclination to assist in the Bosnian prosecutions of pro-Russian fighters from Ukraine.

Apart from the now seemingly classic story of going there and returning, with or without facing prosecution, which seems to be the standard fare for most of the Serbs involved in the conflict in Ukraine, the story of another Bosnian-Serb, Davor Dragolobović Savičić, offers a snapshot of another phenomenon connecting the war in Ukraine and its Western Balkan participants. As it turns out, some Serbs decided to further cultivate their PMC tradition – this time in the ranks of the infamous private military contractors of the. The Wagner Group is a private military company which is often used by Russia as a deniable force in conflicts around the world.[57] Savičić, by 2016 officially living in Russia and claiming to be working on a construction site, with battlefield experience from the Bosnian war, Kosovo, and Ukraine all allegedly under his belt, was said to have led a Wagner's Serbian platoon in the attack on Palmyra in Syria.[58] His subordinates potentially included other Serbian veterans of the war in Ukraine who, as was alluded by the head of the Ukrainian SBU,[59] first joined the company while fighting in Donbas and then deployed to Syria where one of them died.[60]

The post-Ukraine PMC developments amongst the Serb, or Bosnian-Serb, veterans underscore another key feature of the Serbian foreign fighter contingent, namely its above-mentioned links and connections to Russia. These are operationalized via organizations such as *Zavet* (Oath), a Serbian-Russian association with offices both in Republika Srpska and in Russia, which enjoys strong ties with the Union of Donbass Volunteers (UDV), a Russian organization grouping the volunteers of the war in Ukraine.[61] The former organizes "cultural exchange with Russia, such as sending kids to Rostov-on-Don to learn Russian." At the same time, the latter e.g. sends delegations to war cemeteries in Bosnia which feature graves of Russian foreign fighters from the war in Bosnia – in Visegrad or outside Sarajevo. Around 50 Russians allegedly fell in the conflict in Bosnia while fighting in the ranks of the *Vojska Republike Srpske* (VRS, Army of Republika Srpska). These Russian fighters were mostly veterans of the wars in Georgia or Moldova[62] and were grouped in their own, semi-autonomous of VRS, units. Some had fought earlier in the Croat-Serb forces or gravitated toward the conflict in Kosovo.[63] It is also worth noting that the Russian veterans of the Bosnian war, some of whom later also fought in Ukraine – such as Igor Girkin, are eligible for military compensation in Republika Srpska.[64] Moreover, the UDV is allegedly spreading its activities into the Balkans via esoteric outfits such as "the Balkan Cossack Army," which, according to Maria Kucherenko, an analyst at the Centre for Research of Civil Society in Kyiv, is to assist the mother organization in "recruit[ment], supply and cover [for] the activities [of] foreign mercenaries in the Russian war against Ukraine."[65] The UDV also has a track record of erecting monuments to Russian soldiers who died during the Serbian-Turkish wars of 1876–78 in Serbia.[66]

The final element of the Serb-Russian connection which predated and will outlast the war in Ukraine was fully visible during the autumn 2016 attempted coup in Montenegro. This little Western Balkan country had its five foreign fighters present in the ranks of the pro-Russian "separatists" – all five returned but only one, the most well-known due to his prominent social media presence, got convicted for foreign fighting (the activities of the others predated the changes in the criminal code).[67] At the same time, at least one veteran of the Montenegrin armed forces fought on the other side, in the ranks of the Georgian National Legion (GNL).[68] Regardless of the country's meagre, although – per capita – rather impressive (one fighter per 100,000 inhabitants = six for approximately 600,000),[69] statistics, it was meant to become a platform for a post-war deployment of the Serbian fighters from Ukraine. One of these, "who did not face prosecution for foreign fighting" in Serbia, was "suspected of playing a key organizational role in the failed coup."[70] He was to recruit a core group of Serbian and Montenegrin fighters, including those with experience from the war in Ukraine, but allegedly acted on the orders of the Russian military intelligence – GRU,[71] a security service whose training center is in the same village in Russia as those of Wagner, the PMC company which shipped some Serbian and Bosnian-Serb fighters from Ukraine to Syria.[72]

Croatia

Croatian authorities looked at the issue of foreign fighting from a relatively unique perspective. Their approach was guided, in the words of the country's minister of justice, by Croatia's experience from the 1990s, "when volunteers from around the world came and fought on our side, and we were very grateful that they came and helped us."[73] Consequently, Zagreb seemed not to have minded if its citizens were to repay this international debt in a war of their choice. This bore a striking resemblance to the situation in Serbia, with the exception that, in the latter country, it had been the fighters themselves, and not their government, who expressed such opinions.

French, British, German, Finnish, Dutch, Hungarian and Italian foreign fighters all fought in the Croatian War of Independence between 1991 and 1995 on the Croat side.[74] According to most reliable estimates, 550 such individuals were involved and around 90 died in the conflict.[75] Many apparently had very little idea about Yugoslavia or Croatia but cited their willingness to assist a small nation (Croatia) fight off an alleged yoke of communism, and since they were either military or military veterans, were bored with their uneventful military service which often offered no prospect of actual deployment to a war in the reality of a post-Cold War Europe.[76]

Amongst the foreign fighters "who came and fought" on Croatia's side was the above-mentioned Gaston Besson, who two decades later became one of the early stalwarts of recruitment of foreign fighters into the ranks of the proto-Azov Battalion.[77] Besson later settled in Croatia, received the country's citizenship and a veteran's pension, and had been a natural conduit for Croats who wanted to join the war in Ukraine. His efforts had by far not been the only transnational connection available to Croats who wished to fight in foreign wars – the country's armed forces feature (or featured) former French foreign legionnaires who in the 1990s returned home to fight in the Croatian War of Independence. Their skills but also their contact books proved invaluable to the nascent Croat army of the early 1990s.[78] These would be in demand more recently as one of them was rumored to have been involved in the, now abandoned, project of creating Azov's so-called "foreign legion,"[79] allegedly an official recruitment channel for foreigners who wished to fight in Eastern Ukraine.[80]

The Croat non-denial of its citizens involvement in the war in Ukraine, which was mixed with some irritation at suggestions that these were not prohibited or prevented ("If you or I go there [to Ukraine] and fight on one side, so what? What does it have to do with the Republic of Croatia?" asked the country's justice minister),[81] put the country in a unique position vis-à-vis the issue of returning foreign fighters. Unlike other former Yugoslav republics, which criminalized foreign fighting,[82] it refrained from doing so but also rejected the predominant Central-Eastern European (CEE) path of "denial" in which the authorities would not concern themselves with the returnees and chose to look the other way and downplay their presence or returns so that these would attract as little public attention as possible.[83] It did not deny and, as was shown, even took some pride from the fact that foreign fighting "benefited" Croatia in the past,[84] but did not turn its citizens' fighting in Ukraine into a national *cause célèbre*. In 2015, the authorities "called on [the fighters] to return from Ukraine," allegedly under the Russian pressure.[85] In this sense, Croatia moved on to resemble the approach of the Baltic states which chose not to advertise the presence of their nationals on the front lines so that this would not provoke Russia,[86] or other CEE countries vis-à-vis their small but existing jihadi contingents in the ranks of ISIS which would not be discussed much so that "no unnecessary [social] anxiety would be caused."[87]

Little is known about the political background of the Croat volunteers but statements such as the following, by Denis Šeler – their main on the ground organizer in Croatia and later the most well-known Croat foreign fighter in the war – firmly place at least some of them within the broader brown-red cocktail that was attracted to the war in Ukraine:[88] "[Ukraine witnesses] a struggle for European freedom […] A struggle for the white European race, its culture and history […] Ukraine is the last bastion of Christian right-wing Europe."[89] Others, however, were far less ideological in their pronouncements, insisting that they left behind well paid jobs in Croatia "to come to help a country that has been attacked by a stronger enemy." They also rejected the "mercenary" label as they allegedly were receiving €170 salary in Ukraine, and turned back many volunteers who wanted to join the fight but lacked military experience.[90]

Tomislav Sunić, a Croatian-American writer and an alleged "intellectual guru" of Croatia's far right, remarked that "on a more sentimental, subconscious level, for Croats, Ukraine is a friend."[91] Šeler, who spoke at Azov's Intermarium Conference in late 2020, confirmed this and compared the Ukrainian experience from 2014 to that of Croatia in 1991–92. In his view, neither country had a "big brother" type of a supporter, unlike their immediate adversaries – the Serb nationalists in Croatia (supported by the then Yugoslavia and especially Serbia) or the "separatists" in Ukraine (backed by Russia). In short, both Ukraine and Croatia had been the weaker side in the conflict and this was allegedly evident to all the Croat volunteers who eventually linked up with Azov. Šeler was adamant that he heard the slogan of "Russia exists wherever Russians live" but in his experience this concerned the Serbs, and for this reason he could easily relate to Ukraine's predicament from the Euromaidan and afterwards. What is more, he also drew more parallels between the two countries – in his view, Azov, just like the units of the Croat armed forces in the 1990s, had been built from scratch, in a bottom-up fashion. As the years passed by, Croat forces, at first considered beyond the pale for their alleged atrocities in the Balkan Wars, came to be accepted by the Western military partners, including NATO, which Croatia eventually joined in 2009. Šeler expressed confidence that the same would happen to Azov, a military unit with a vast fighting experience against Russia, a feat unmatched by any of the NATO's forces.[92]

Šeler's evolution toward a feted former member of the Azov regiment, and a speaker at its trademark Intermarium conference, was not straightforward to say the least.[93] A self-confessed leader of on one of Dinamo Zagreb's football ultras,[94] a former soldier who fought in the 1990s' wars, divorcee with an 11-year-old son, approached Azov via the social media as early as May 2014 but received no reply from them. Eventually, he sold his car, closed his company and, with a few other Croats, who all fitted in just two cars laden with medical supplies, trekked eastward and presented themselves at the Azov's recruitment center in Kyiv. Afterwards, they featured in the ranks of the foreign detachment of the Regiment, coordinated by Mikael Skillt, the poster boy of Azov's international recruitment.[95] Šeler admitted that just seven Croats rotated as fighters through Ukraine, most in Azov with one moving to the Organization of Ukrainian Nationalists (OUN), Організація українських націоналістів, *Orhanizatsiya ukrayins'kykh natsionalistiv*) volunteer battalion,[96] as some had been prevented from deploying to Ukraine by "the political intrigue on the part of Ukrainian officials."[97] Moreover, he was also instrumental, alongside "Croat Ukrainians," in bringing children of the deceased Ukrainian soldiers for holidays in Croatia.[98] After his front line involvement, Šeler continued to be involved in some of the political initiatives fronted by the National Corps (NC), the political arm of the Azov movement, an entity which also featured the above-mentioned Azov Regiment. He hosted an NC delegation which visited Croatia in 2019 when, apparently, a decision was made to hold the next Intermarium conference (a trademark NC/Azov annual event) in Croatia. Its 2020 conference featured, apart from Šeler, another Croat speaker – an MP of the Croat Conservative Party (HKS, *Hrvatska konzervativna stranka*), Marko Milanović Litre. Milanović Litre, who in November 2020 made a speech in the Croat parliament asking it to recognize the Ukrainian "terror famine" or *Holodomor* of 1932–33 as genocide,[99] was called "our friend" by the NC during the conference. Just like Šeler, he stressed the Croat-Ukrainian similarities – both suffered from exploitation at the hands of their communist oppressors, and both in the early 1990s abandoned "artificial alliances" of Yugoslavia and the Soviet Union, respectively. He was also quick to point out that both countries used to be battlegrounds between Western and Eastern powers and for this reason must "empower" themselves, while forming an alliance of an effective in-betweeners – in line with Azov's much touted concept of the Intermarium, i.e. an anti-Western and anti-Russian alliance of former CEE states.[100]

Conclusion

The Ukraine war attracted a sizeable group of former Yugoslav foreign fighters. These, however, did not deploy because of their desire to continue their 1990s wars within a different conflict. Many came to "repay the debts" allegedly owed to foreigners, mostly Russians, who assisted their fight in the Yugoslav wars. Some did it out of idealism – to assist the weaker side in the conflict. A sizeable group thought this was an opportunity to restart their lives and earn a decent salary. Others seemed to have been seeking fame rather than fortune and turned themselves into social media celebrities. As was shown, the contingents had their problems while trying to get to Ukraine or while there, often because their countries' authorities and their security services were greatly interested in their exploits. The majority of the fighters moved on, while receiving paltry sentences for their foreign fighting at home, and some continued as PMCs in places like Libya or Syria and thus became fully fledged mercenaries.

Notes

1 March 2022 saw the news of Russia allegedly recruiting Syrian foreign fighters for its rekindled war in Ukraine. See Kareem Chehayeb, "In Syria, Russia leads effort to recruit fighters for Ukraine," *Al Jazeera*, April 1, 2022, https://www.aljazeera.com/news/2022/4/1/in-syria-moscow-leads-effort-to-recruit-fighters-for-ukraine, accessed: April 22, 2022.

2 Marija Ristic, "Facebook Reveals Serbian Fighters' Role in Ukraine War," *BalkanInsight*, December 27, 2017, https://balkaninsight.com/2017/12/27/facebook-reveals-serbian-fighters-role-in-ukraine-war-12-25-2017/, accessed: May 11, 2021.

3 Christopher Othen, "Serb Volunteers in Novorossiya: Part 2," October 19, 2017, in Christopher Othen, *Bad People, Strange Times, Good Books*, https://christopherothen.wordpress.com/2017/10/19/serb-volunteers-in-novorossiya-part-2/, accessed: May 11, 2021.

4 Author's interview with Predrag Petrović, program director at the Belgrade Centre for Security Policy, an independent Serbian think tank, and an author of publications on the Serbian foreign fighters, June 5, 2020.

5 See the French chapter of the book for more on the Continental Unity and its Western Balkan exploits.

6 Maja Zivanovic, "Donbass Brothers: How Serbian Fighters Were Deployed in Ukraine," *BalkanInsight*, December 13, 2018, https://balkaninsight.com/2018/12/13/donbass-brothers-how-serbian-fighters-were-deployed-in-ukraine-12-12-2018/, accessed: May 11, 2021.

7 Author's interview with Predrag Petrović, program director at the Belgrade Centre for Security Policy, an independent Serbian think tank, and an author of publications on the Serbian foreign fighters, June 5, 2020.

8 Stevan Pavlowitch, *Hitler's New Disorder. The Second World War in Yugoslavia* (London: Oxford University Press), 273–279.

9 Author's interview with Predrag Petrović, program director at the Belgrade Centre for Security Policy, an independent Serbian think tank, and an author of publications on the Serbian foreign fighters, June 5, 2020.

10 Iva Martinović, "Srpski četnici na Krimu: 'Psi rata' spremni za novi sukob," *Radio Slobodna Evropa*, March 6, 2014, https://www.slobodnaevropa.org/a/srpski-cetnici-na-krimu/25288046.html, accessed: May 11, 2021.

11 Othen, "Serb Volunteers in Novorossiya: Part 1."

12 *Pravda*, "ПОЧЕЛО ЈЕ: Четнички командант Братислав Живковић у Доњецку," June 14, 2021, https://pravda.rs/2014/6/14/pocelo-je-cetnicki-komandant-bratislav-zivkovic-u-donjecku/, accessed: May 11, 2021.

13 Maja Zivanovic, "Serbian Nationalist Flaunts Freedom with Ukraine Call to Arms," *BalkanInsight*, June 14, 2019, https://balkaninsight.com/2019/06/14/serbian-nationalist-flaunts-freedom-with-ukraine-call-to-arms/, accessed: May 11, 2021.

14 Ristic, "Facebook." Una Hajdari, a freelance journalist focusing on the Western Balkans and Central-Eastern Europe, aptly commented on the motivations of the Russians who fought in the Balkan wars of the 1990s in an email exchange with the author of May 27, 2022: "In the 1990s, there were two main motivations for Russian or former Soviet citizens fighting in Bosnia and elsewhere. First, the conservatives among them fought for the purpose of defending their fellow Orthodox and/or Slavic brothers. Second, the 'fake' or wannabe left fought to defend their 'Serb/Yugoslav communist brothers,' as pointless and absurd that is. So here we see clearly separate and even opposed set of motivations."

15 Milos Popović, "Pathways of Foreign Fighters," *leidensecurityand-globalaffairsblog*, March 28, 2021, https://leidensecurityandglobalaffairs.nl/articles/pathways-of-foreign-fighters, accessed: May 11, 2021.

16 Author's interview with Una Hajdari, May 20, 2021.

17 Miloš Teodorović, "Živković: Sinđelića nismo hteli u Ukrajini, Rusija me odlikovala zbog Krima," *Radio Slobodna Evropa*, https://www.slobodnaevropa.org/a/sindjelic-srbija-desnicari/28139283.html, accessed: May 12, 2021.

18 Ibid.

19 Author's interview with Predrag Petrović, program director at the Belgrade Centre for Security Policy, an independent Serbian think tank, and an author of publications on the Serbian foreign fighters, June 5, 2020.

20 Zivanovic, "Donbass Brothers."

21 Martinović, "Srpski četnici na Krimu."

22 See *The Insider*, "Кремлевский спрут: часть III. Как ГРУ использовало сербов для переворота в Черногории и войны в Украине," July 13, 2018, https://theins.ru/politika/108304, accessed: May 11, 2021.

23 See the introductory chapter for more on the issue of payment for foreign fighting.

24 Author's interview with Predrag Petrović, program director at the Belgrade Centre for Security Policy, an independent Serbian think tank, and an author of publications on the Serbian foreign fighters, June 5, 2020.

25 Teodorović, "Živković."

26 Zivanovic, "Donbass Brothers."

27 In 2014, the Serbian prime minister called the involvement in Serbs in Ukraine as "damaging the state." See ibid.

28 Ibid.

29 Luka Glušac, "Criminalization as Anxious and Ineffective Response to Foreign Fighters Phenomenon in the Western Balkans," *Journal of Regional Security*, (2020): 11.

30 See https://terorizam.detektor.ba/ for the Balkan Investigative Reporting Network database of the Serbian, and other Western Balkan, foreign fighters and their convictions. Accessed: May 12, 2021.

31 Дмитрий Стешин, "Какой серб нужнее России: комедиант или доброволец с Донбасса," *Комсомольская правда*, March 28, 2021, https://www.kp.ru/daily/27250/4379725/, accessed: May 11, 2021.

32 *Kurir*, "Srbin Ubijen Na Prvoj Liniji Fronta: Vladimir Stanimirović poginuo braneći Ruse u Ukrajini," October 14, 2016, https://www.kurir.rs/crna-hronika/2491845/srbin-ubijen-na-prvoj-liniji-fronta-vladimir-stanimirovic-poginuo-braneci-ruse-u-ukrajini, accessed: May 11, 2021.

33 Othen, "Serb Volunteers in Novorossiya: Part 6."

34 *Telegraf*, "Serbian Komandos in Ukraine: Pocuca wanted to kill me, he came here just for the money (Video)," April 20, 2015, https://www.telegraf.rs/english/1531430-serbian-komandos-in-ukraine-pocuca-wanted-to-kill-me-he-came-here-just-for-the-money-video, accessed: May 11, 2021.

35 Othen, "Serb Volunteers in Novorossiya: Part 5."

36 See https://www.amazon.com/Snipers-War-Olya-Schechter/dp/B07D97FSJN/ref=sr_1_1?dchild=1&keywords=Olya+Schechter&qid=1620726048&sr=8-1 for Olya Schechter's 2018 movie about Berić, accessed: May 11, 2021.

37 *Novosti*, "Radomir Počuča na slobodi, u Moskvi!," April 16, 2015, https://www.novosti.rs/vesti/planeta.299.html:543765-Radomir-Pocuca-na-slobodi-u-Moskvi, accessed: May 11, 2021.

38 Ljudmila Cvetković, "Počuča: Nagodio sam se, ne idem u zatvor zbog Ukrajine," *Radio Slobodna Evropa*, April 20, 2016, https://www.slobodnaevropa.org/a/pocuca-nagodio-sam-se-ne-idem-u-zatvor-zbog-ukrajine/27686011.html, accessed: May 11, 2021.

39 Berić was indeed captured by the Ukrainians in the mid-2014 and then mysteriously exchanged or possibly bought out from captivity. This allegedly raised eyebrows amongst his detractors and might have formed the basis of Počuča's allegations against him. See *Ukrinform*, "Sniper Deki who turned into a journalist," July 15, 2019, https://www.ukrinform.net/rubric-polytics/2740372-sniper-deki-who-turned-into-a-journaliie.html, accessed: May 11, 2021.

40 Andrijana Nešić, "Počuča Tvrdi: Imam informacije da Berić radi za Službu bezbed-nosti Ukrajine,"*Srbija Danas*, January 4, 2016, https://www.srbijadanas.com/clanak/pocuca-tvrdi-imam-informacije-da-Berić-radi-za-sbu-27-12-2015, accessed: May 11, 2021.

41 Author's interview with Luka Glušac, executive board member of the Belgrade Centre for Security Policy, an independent Serbian think tank, and an author of publications on the Serbian foreign fighters, June 1, 2020.

42 Mladen Obrenovic, "As Ukraine Conflict Intensifies, Serb Volunteers Prepare for Bat-tle," *BalkanInsight*, April 16, 2021, https://balkaninsight.com/2021/04/16/as-ukraine-conflict-intensifies-serb-volunteers-prepare-for-battle/, accessed: May 11, 2021.

43 *The Insider*, "Кремлевский спрут."

44 Predrag Petrović and Isidora Stakić, "Western Balkan Extremist Research Forum: Serbia Report," *British Council* (April 2018), 34, https://www.britishcouncil.rs/sites/default/files/erf_report_serbia_2018.pdf, accessed: May 11, 2021.

45 Christo Grozev, "Balkan Gambit: Part 2. The Montenegro Zugzwang," *bellingcat*, 25 October 2017, https://www.bellingcat.com/news/uk-and-europe/2017/03/25/balkan-gambit-part-2-montenegro-zugzwang/, accessed: May 11, 2021.

46 Obrenovic, "As Ukraine Conflict Intensifies, Serb Volunteers Prepare for Battle."

47 Petrović and Stakić, "Western Balkan Extremist Research Forum," 34.

48 *The Insider*, "Кремлевский спрут."

49 Author's interview with Predrag Petrović, program director at the Belgrade Centre for Security Policy, an independent Serbian think tank, and an author of publications on the Serbian foreign fighters, June 5, 2020.

50 Ristic, "Facebook."

51 Teodorović, "Živković."

52 Obrenovic, "As Ukraine Conflict Intensifies, Serb Volunteers Prepare for Battle."

53 Ristic, "Facebook;" and Mladen Obrenović, "Under Cossack Banner, Russian Ties with Balkan Fighters Strengthened," *Detektor*, October 16, 2020, https://detektor.ba/2020/10/16/balkanska-kozacka-vojska-poveznica-za-veterane-ratova-u-ukra-jini-i-bih/?lang=en, accessed: May 11, 2021.

54 Avdo Avdić, "Na Putinovom Putu: Sedam državljana BiH ratovalo u Ukrajini – niko nije procesuiran," *Žurnal*, October 16, 2017, https://zurnal.info/novost/20736/sedam-drzavljana-bih-ratovalo-u-ukrajini-niko-nije-procesuiran, accessed: May 12, 2021.

55 Obrenović, "Under Cossack Banner."

56 Glušac, "Criminalization," 23.

57 Zbigniew Parafianowicz, Prywatne armie świata. Czyli jak wyglądają współczesne konflikty (Kraków: Mando, 2021) for more on Wagner.

58 Marija Ristic, "Serb Fighters' Mercenary Path from Ukraine to Syria," *BalkanIn-sight*, April 22, 2016, https://balkaninsight.com/2016/04/22/bosnian-serb-fighters-mercenary-path-to-syria-04-22-2016/, accessed: May 12, 2021.

59 *Прямий канал*, "У складі ПВК "Вагнер" на Донбасі воювали вісім громадян Сербії: СБУ," February 2, 2018, https://prm.ua/u-skladi-pvk-vagner-na-donbasi-voyuvali-visim-gromadyan-serbiyi-sbu/, accessed: May 12, 2021.

60 Ristic, "Facebook."

61 Semir Mujkić, "Ukraine War Veterans Bind Russia and Bosnian Serbs," *BalkanIn-sight*, May 22, 2019, https://balkaninsight.com/2019/05/22/ukraine-war-veterans-bind-russia-and-bosnian-serbs/, accessed: May 12, 2021.

62 Stanislav Secrieru, "Come and Go: Trajectories of Foreign Fighters in and out of Moldova" in Kacper Rekawek, ed., *Not Only Syria? The Phenomenon of Foreign Fighters in a Comparative Perspective* (The Hague: IOS Press, 2017) for the most comprehensive discussion of the foreign fighters who gravitated to and from Moldova, and some later reappeared in Bosnia or Donbas.

63 Author's interview with Milos Popović, a post-doc researcher at the Leiden University researching the foreign fighters in the Balkan wars of the 1990s, May 25, 2021.

64 Author's interview with Semir Mujkić, Balkan Insight journalist who covered the travails of the Bosnian Serb foreign fighters in Ukraine, June 9, 2020.

65 Obrenović, "Under Cossack Banner."

66 *Новороссия*, "Союз Добровольцев Донбасса почтил память русских защитников Сербии," September 3, 2017, https://novorosinform.org/410983, accessed: May 12, 2021.

67 Vlado Azinović and Edina Bećirević, *A Waiting Game: Assessing and Responding to the Threat from Returning Foreign Fighters in the Western Balkans* (Sarajevo: Regional Cooperation Council, 2017), 41, https://www.rcc.int/pubs/54/a-waiting-game-assessing-and-responding-to-the-threat-from-return-ing-foreign-fighters-in-the-western-balkans, accessed: May 11, 2021.

68 See chap, 3 in this volume for more on the GNL. See also the Facebook profile of the GNL's commander where he announced volunteers from which countries joined his unit - https://www.facebook.com/MamukaLegion/posts/10226223994052784, March 24, 2021, accessed: May 11, 2021.

69 French foreign fighter contingent would amount to 670 fighters had it matched the per capita value of that from Montenegro.

70 Azinović and Bećirević, *A Waiting Game*, 43.

71 Роман Доброхотов, "Кремлевский спрут. Часть 2. Как ГРУ пыталось организовать переворот в Черногории," *The Insider*, March 24, 2017, https://theins.ru/politika/49316, accessed: May 12, 2021.

72 Ristic, "Serb Fighters' Mercenary Path."

73 Sven Milekic, "Some Croats Fighting in Ukraine Army, Pusic says," *Balkan Insight*, February 12, 2015, https://balkaninsight.com/2015/02/12/croatia-not-prosecuting-fighters-in-foreign-wars/, accessed: May 24, 2021.

74 Author's interview with Milos Popović, a post-doc researcher at the Leiden University researching the foreign fighters in the Balkan wars of the 1990s, May 25, 2021.

75 See https://www.facebook.com/groups/874106455981393/permalink/1270495226342512/ for a post on this in the Facebook group dedicated to foreign volunteers in the Croatian ranks in the Croatian War of Independence *Zahvala stranim dragovoljcima Domovinskog rata* (Thank you to the foreign volunteers in the Homeland War) maintained by Tomislav Šulj, who has been researching this issue for years.

76 Author's interview with Milos Popović, a post-doc researcher at the Leiden University researching the foreign fighters in the Balkan wars of the 1990s, May 25, 2021.

77 See the French chapter of this monograph.

78 Author's interview with Sven Milekic, Balkan Insight contributor and a PhD student at the Maynooth University, May 27, 2020.

79 The alleged leader of this "legion" had been a speaker at Azov's Intermarium Conference in early 2019. See archived page on Azov's international outreach: https://interregnum-intermarium.tumblr.com/post/184469943719/the-azov-movement-in-the-west-achievements-in/embed, accessed: May 24, 2021.

80 This "legion" would not have recruited individuals into the Azov Regiment itself as it bars foreigners from joining its ranks. If this scheme was to become reality then it might have concerned the Ukrainian army which, theoretically, allows for a contractual recruitment of foreigners into its ranks. See: Michael Colborne, "Croatia Key to Ukrainian Far-Right's International Ambitions," *Balkan Insight*, July 18, 2019, https://balkaninsight.com/2019/07/18/croatia-key-to-ukrainian-far-rights-international-ambitions/#gsc.tab=0, accessed: May 24, 2021 for the story on the alleged "legion."

81 Milekic, "Some Croats Fighting in Ukraine Army, Pusic says."

82 Glušac, "Criminalization," 10.

83 Egle E. Murauskaite, *Foreign Fighters in Ukraine: Assessing Potential Risks* (Vilnius: Vilnius Institute for policy analysis, 2020), 17, https://vilniusinstitute.lt/wp-content/

uploads/2020/02/foreign-fighters-in-ukraine-assessing-potential-risks.pdf, accessed: May 24, 2021.

84 Milekic, "Some Croats Fighting in Ukraine Army, Pusic says."

85 Hikmet Karcic, "The Balkan Connection: Foreign Fighters and the Far Right in Ukraine," *Newlines Institute for Strategy and Policy*, May 1, 2020, https://newlinesin-stitute.org/eurasia/the-balkan-connection-foreign-fighters-and-the-far-right-in-ukraine/, accessed: May 24, 2021.

86 See the Central-Eastern Europe chapter of this research monograph.

87 Andrzej Gurba, "Ismail Slo, Polak w ISIS, pochodził z Pomorza. Zwerbowano go przez internet," *Polska Times*, August 12, 2015, https://polskatimes.pl/ismail-slo-polak-w-isis-pochodzil-z-pomorza-zwerbowano-go-przez-internet-kim-byl-jacek-s/ar/5868602, accessed: May 24, 2021.

88 For more on Šeler's "conservative, nationalist or patriotic" views see his inter-view at На Два Слова, "Деніс Шелер: Україна готова до військової операції з повернення своїх територій," YouTube, July 13, 2020, https://www.youtube.com/watch?v=IGbe5CMiYZc, accessed: May 25, 2021.

89 Jovana Georgievski, "Своё 'Междуморье:' Зачем объединяются ультраправые Украины и Хорватии," *Radio Free Europe/Radio Liberty*, February 9, 2020, https://www.svoboda.org/a/30420644.html, accessed: May 24, 2021.

90 Ivica Kristović, "Dao sam otkaz, ostavio ženu i djecu te krenuo pomoći Ukra-jincima," *Večernji List*, February 11, 2015, https://www.vecernji.hr/vijesti/hrvatski-dobrovoljci-ne-mrzimo-srbe-ni-ruse-pomazemo-ukrajinskom-narodu-989338, accessed: May 24, 2021.

91 *Danas.hr*, "Ekstremno Desni Militantni Pokret Azov Tijesno Surađuje S Hrvatskom Desnicom: U Zagrebu planiraju osnovati svoju 'legiju stranaca'?," net.hr, July 19, 2019, https://net.hr/danas/svijet/ekstremno-desni-militantni-pokret-azov-tijesno-suraduje-s-hrvatskom-desnicom-ove-jeseni-u-zagrebu-planiraju-osnovati-svoju-legiju-stranaca/, accessed: May 24, 2021. Una Hajdari, a journalist focusing on the Western Balkans and the Central-Eastern Europe, commented on the Croat pref-erences in the Russo-Ukraine war in an email exchange with the author of May 27, 2022: "Croat foreign fighters joined the Ukrainian side because they hate com-munists and see all iterations of the modern Russian state to be a successor of the Soviet Union and because they compare themselves to Ukrainians, see themselves as being victims to the Serb aggression just like Ukrainians are the victims of Russian aggression."

92 See https://youtu.be/bQ4zJTTy-ps for the recording of the Azov's "The Fourth Online Conference of the Intermarium Support Group" during which Šeler spoke, accessed: May 24, 2021.

93 See https://ko-kr.facebook.com/ifnotwar/posts/denis-croatiaregiment-azovi-was-born-in-december-1975-in-zagreb-croatia-i-studie/1106383916120990/ for Šeler's September 21, 2016 statement to @ifnotwar Facebook site, accessed: May 24, 2021.

94 These ultras had a track record of supporting Ukraine in general and Azov in par-ticular. See *football24.ua*, "Фанаты Динамо Загреб провели акцию с плакатом 'Слава Украине'," July 11, 2018, https://football24.ua/ru/chm_2018_tag51275/ https://football24.ua/ru/fanaty_dinamo_zagreb_proveli_akciju_s_plakatom_slava_ukraine_n475179/, accessed: May 24, 2021.

95 Denis Šeler, "The History of Croats in Defense of Ukraine and Interview with Croatian volunteer of 'AZOV' Denis Šeler (Pena)," http://rozum.info/news/2015-09-03-418, September 3, 2015, accessed: May 24, 2021.

96 See https://ko-kr.facebook.com/ifnotwar/posts/denis-croatiaregiment-azovi-was-born-in-december-1975-in-zagreb-croatia-i-studie/1106383916120990/ for Šeler's September 21, 2016 statement to @ifnotwar Facebook site, accessed: May 24, 2021.

97 Šeler, "The History of Croats in Defense of Ukraine."

98 Ibid.

99 *Intermarium Support Group*, "National Corps' visit to Zagreb bears first fruits: Croatian parliament might recognize the Holodomor as genocide," November 30, 2020, https://intermarium.org.ua/en/national-corps-visit-to-zagreb-bears-first-fruits-croatian-parliament-might-recognize-the-holodomor-as-genocide/, accessed: May 25, 2021.

100 See https://youtu.be/bQ4zJTTy-ps for the recording of the Azov's "Fourth Online Conference of the Intermarium Support Group," accessed: May 24, 2021.

8

OTHER WESTERN EUROPEANS (AND AMERICANS)

A Few Here, a Few There

Introduction

Previous chapters of this research monograph provided detailed accounts of the two most influential Western European contingents of foreign fighters in the war in Ukraine – French (pro-"separatist") and Swedish (pro-Ukraine).[1] This chapter will account for the participation of individuals from further nine Western European countries, i.e. Austria, Denmark, Finland, Germany, Italy, the Netherlands, Norway, Spain and the UK. These will be "ranked" from the biggest of these contingents (Italy), to the smallest (Norway), which effectively amounted to just two fighters.[2] While discussing these national contingents, the author will not only focus on the brown or brown-red fighters in their ranks – present but not always dominant – but also previously unseen fighters with more unusual background, i.e. far left (outright red) or from amongst the asylum seekers present in a given Western European country.

As will be shown, the small numbers of the far-right fighters involved showcase a general disinterest in the war on behalf of the wider Western European and American milieu. Its members, groups, organizations and parties took sides, quarreled but would not have prompted into actually deploying eastward to fight on the either side of the conflict. Nowhere was this contrast more striking than in Germany where, as will be shown, the far-right milieu enjoys a plethora of transnational connections, and some of its political actors were said to have developed pro-Russia and pro-Ukraine wings. However, it has produced very few actual fighters or even militants, whose connections to the likes of Ukrainian radicals went beyond political engagements.

As this monograph concentrates, as is most often the case in studies of political violence, on those who "did" or "joined" a given violent entity, or "went" to fight somewhere, this chapter will not feature a detailed analysis of the reasons

DOI: 10.4324/9781003192992-8

behind the relatively feeble numbers of fighters from certain Western countries. However, one can risk a theory related to trailblazers discussed in the French and Swedish chapters. The lack of such individuals, true foreign fighting pioneers with connections in their home countries, could have nullified chances for recruitment of a significant number of fighters from a given country. If this was to be the case, then one must also look at the proverbial other side of the coin – the war's pull. It must be stated that, especially in the light of the Syrian civil war, this pull was modest, to say the least. The war, as was demonstrated in the chapter on the conflict in Ukraine, seemed incomprehensible to many outsiders (was it a civil war or a state-on-state conflict?) and its seemingly lesser brutality than that of Syria could have also contributed to less passionate reactions amongst the Western public. Moreover, Ukrainian diasporas, although numerous in certain Western countries, failed to act as recruitment sergeants for non-Ukraine related individuals wanting to join the conflict. They might have collected money and sent equipment to Ukraine but failed to inflame the imagination of their "new" countrymen, who largely seemed disinterested. This state of affairs could be regarded as surprising given the fact Donetsk is actually closer to major Western countries than Damascus in Syria, and seemingly should have generated more interest in the West than a country in the Middle East. Nonetheless, it did not and things changed only in 2022 when Russia overtly invaded Ukraine.

Italy – "Both Right and Left"

Anyone wishing to fully account for the involvement of the Italians in the war in Ukraine, predominantly on the "separatist" side, is immediately struck by the fact that they are dealing with one of the largest Western European contingents which is very much red-brown in nature. Moreover, its members were being prosecuted by the police for their Ukrainian sojourn as late as in 2021.[3] At the same time, this contingent spawned no organization or unit in the mold of the French led UC or different Serbian, if ephemeral, outfits. There was no attempt to justify one's fighting along ideological, Eurasian, brown-red, lines, although Italians present in Donbas produced two memoirs (the seemingly larger French contingent "only" managed one book). Instead, it seems that there had been a ring of wannabe fighters who recruited or inspired their followers. Some of these "originals" had had previous Russian or mercenary connections (and legal problems at home on top of that) which might have helped or influenced their decisions to deploy eastward.

According to some 2017 Ukrainian sources, there had been up to 37 "Italian mercenaries and accomplices of the Donetsk People's Republic (DNR)/Luhansk People's Republic (LNR) terrorists." Out of these, the activities and sometimes affiliations of 19 had been detailed. Additionally, a further 10 were named as activists, propagandists or supporters who appeared in the "separatist" territories for at least a short while. Finally, the published data featured a compendium on high level visits of Italian politicians to either Crimea or "separatist" territories, and names of allegedly Italian organizations (it included organizations that were Spanish) that supported the DNR and the LNR.[4] A year later, in August 2018, after the first arrests of the alleged Italian recruiters who sent people to Eastern Ukraine, Ukraine officially handed in a list of 25 alleged Italian fighters to the latter country's officials.[5]

While discussing the origins and the make-up of the Italian contingent in Ukraine much is made of Andrea Palmeri, both a former football hooligan and a far-right militant, with a conviction for knife crime. Palmeri was a member of *Forza Nuova* (New Force, a far-right Italian political party), nicknamed "generalissimo," who seemingly ideally fits the bill of a Western foreign fighter present in Ukraine.[6] At the same time, however, he is now safely ensconced not in Ukraine, which allegedly attracted more far-right fighters, but in the LNR, where he wanted to open up a bakery. He speaks Russian and is a Christian Orthodox convert.[7] His Facebook profile includes a photo with Irina Osipova,[8] a prominent Russian expat and a self-confessed fan of Vladimir Putin residing in Rome who herself is posting photos with far-right Italian political figures.[9] The latter also converses on social media with Gabriele Carugati, another Italian foreign fighter for the "separatists." Carugati is sought by the Italian authorities for his alleged co-recruitment of individuals for the "separatists."[10] He is a son of a Northern League's (*Lega Nord*, LN, Italian far-right party with long-standing ties with Moscow)[11] local politician.[12] Carugati neatly summarized the ideological, and at times far from far-right, motivations of the fighters in the DNR/LNR ranks. In September 2016, he posted a photo of a "separatist" militiaman with a flag combining these of the Soviet Union, the St. George's ribbon (component of Russian military decorations, also adopted by the "separatists") and the Russian imperial flag, commenting that: "[this is] incomprehensible to [...] militant anti-fascists." Osipova reinforced his point while commenting on the photo: "It is not even national Bolshevism, but it is respect for the history of one's country which was an empire in the time of the tsars and a superpower after the war. Pride of being heirs of a strong state that knows how to defend and position itself in the world."[13] Thus, it seemed as if anyone could have implanted anything onto their motivation behind joining or supporting the "separatists," allegedly not Russia's puppets but whose forces featured individuals happy to fight under Russian banners.

Other fighters displayed even more exotic motivations for their involvement in the war, such as Massimiliano Cavalleri, another Italian far-right militant,[14] who stated that: "every time I shoot a Ukrainian soldier I imagine they [bullets] will hit one of our politicians in Brussels."[15] Ultimately, however, an Italian propagandist – working for the DNR information outlets, presented with a knife by the DNR's leader in recognition of his services,[16] Vittorio Nicola Rangeloni, provided the most succinct summary of the Italian foreign fighter motivation for involvement in the war: "be careful to make it an ideological question [...] with us there are people of right and left, right and left are concepts that are lost in this war. Here we are not fighting for either communism or fascism."[17] In short, this was a blank canvas on which each fighter was able to paint his own colors.

For Rangeloni himself, the war was a chance to stand out from amongst "many young people looking for a job,"[18] and a decision to trek eastward was made easier by the fact that "one of his parents was of Russian origin."[19] Most interesting to an outside observer, however, had been the case of Antonio Cataldo, whose work for a "security agency" took him to Libya in 2011 as a mercenary. His alleged "passion for Russian martial arts" and mixing in the circles of their enthusiasts in Milan was said to have led him toward playing a pivotal role in recruitment of "mercenaries" (the earnings of between €400–500 were mentioned between the recruiting sergeants) for the LNR militias.[20] The contingent also featured a former policeman who became the target of the security authorities only in 2021 despite his numerous travels between the "separatists" territories and Italy, and his appearances in "separatist" media.[21] Finally, in a truly brown-red vein, the contingent, apart from the far-right, pro-Russian, former security personnel individuals, it also featured far-left fighters. Foremost was "Nemo," the commander of the *InterUnit* (a unit grouping communist militants within the LNR's Prizrak (Ghost) Brigade) which was said to have also include other Italians.[22] "Nemo" was allegedly a nickname of Alberto Fazolo (although he strenuously denied it) an "internationalist militant [...] journalist [... who] spent two years in Donbas carrying out political and humanitarian activities," and later published a book about his exploits.[23] In interviews, Fazolo, just like his Spanish colleagues on the "separatist" side, stressed the fact that "Donbas is first and foremost a people's war to oppose the return of fascism to Ukraine."[24] He stressed, however, that the likes of Prizrak, styling itself as a socialist militia, mostly featured non-locals, i.e. Russians from the Russian Federation, who came to fight in this unit not because of internationalist, leftist ideas but rather "for their people and their land."[25]

This motley crew of individuals seemed at first to hardly concern the Italian authorities. Things changed in 2018 when first arrests were made (and three suspects evaded capture, like Palmeri, continuing to reside in the DNR/LNR territories) and a year later were followed up with convictions for recruitment into or participation in the conflict in Donbas, and receipt of salaries for their involvement in the war.[26] This final argument might have been behind the authorities referrals to the accused as "mercenaries"[27] but this claim was laughed off by Palmeri, who stressed that their salaries as fighters (€200 per month) hardly made them into twenty-first century dogs of war.[28] Nonetheless, the investigations continued and produced more arrests of the former fighters in the spring of 2021.[29]

At the same time, the Ukrainian side also featured Italian foreign fighters. These were less numerous than their "separatist" counterparts but also attracted a fair amount of attention to themselves on the media front. Francesco Saverio Fontana, a middle aged former far-right Italian militant who "had been to Ukraine several times before [Euromaidan] in connection with his job," became one of the early faces, alongside Mikael Skillt and Gaston Besson, of recruitment of foreigners into the ranks of what later became the Azov Battalion.[30] He later claimed that apart from him 80+ other foreigners, including seven other

Italians, also served in this unit.[31] He had also confessed to have known some of the Italians fighting on the other side of the conflict and was adamant that he "respect[ed] them and would help them if they were in trouble."[32] Moreover, he claimed to have known their backgrounds and admitted that he "could have been among them myself." Like many of the other fighters he expressed dislike of the Euromaidan and the "Euro-democrats," proponents of "banker-driven Europe." He was similarly in tune with the feelings of the predominant part of the far-right milieus in Western Europe when stating that he was a "Putinist" who would have opted for Russia over America.[33] In 2015, he was spotted in the UK at extreme right rallies, allegedly while recruiting far-right British activists into the ranks of Azov, presumably under the auspices of the so-called Misanthropic Division, "the world wide front and recruiting wing for pro-Nazi militias operating in the Ukraine."[34] He was later rumored to have "retired" and enjoyed life while looking after his grandchildren.[35]

Spain – "Leftist Friends"

As was indicated by the current author elsewhere,[36] the Spanish contingent of foreign fighters in Ukraine literally shot to fame in February 2015 when eight of its members were arrested for "possessing arms and explosives, complicity in murders and assassinations, and influencing the neutrality of Spain" by joining the "separatists" in the war in Ukraine.[37] This police operation preceded similar actions by their counterparts in Italy (2018) and Czech Republic (2021), discussed either in this or other chapters of this work. It resembled coordinated actions aimed at a different type of foreign fighters – namely those destined for the Islamic State of Iraq and Syria (ISIS). In fact, the same month – February 2015 – saw exactly such operations aimed at disrupting a flow of fighters from Spain to the organization, which ended with four arrests.[38]

The arrested Spaniards, of course, had nothing to do with ISIS or jihadism. At the same time, however, they differed from the more "brown" recruits either present in the Ukrainian or the "separatist" ranks. As it later turned out, they had been "Novorossiya's Leftist Friends," individuals coming from the far-left milieus of especially Spain and "other South European countries," such as Italy, who joined the war on the side of the "separatists."[39] Such individuals, as was claimed by a source critically documenting "the actions and policies of the Russian government in both foreign and domestic spheres,"[40] "[until] 2014 [...] did not have the slightest idea of the political situation in Ukraine, let alone its history, ethnic and cultural groups populating its territory, the history of Ukraine-Russia relations, and so forth." While the Euromaidan was happening, they were said to have acquired that "knowledge" through "Russian propaganda."[41]

This reading of the situation, however, does not give full justice to the motivations and views of the "Leftist friends," especially the Spanish. A Spanish fighter, interviewed by the author, claimed that he "knew this conflict better [than others], studied it" and wished to join as he "wanted to witness a creation of a new state, and take part in an anti-imperialist struggle."[42] For him and his comrades, the war in Ukraine was preceded by "a fascist coup d'état financed by the great powers – headed by the USA."[43] The Spanish thus imagined that this war is in fact a masked repeat of "their" civil war from 1936 to 1939, which saw the Soviet Union support the republican government and the Fascist Italy and Nazi Germany rallying behind the rebels. This time, they reasoned, Ukraine, run by a fascist "junta" which came to power in coup, was fighting against the legitimate republicans located in the "People's Republics." The latter, they reasoned, aimed to restore their former Soviet glory or even re-introduce Sovietism to Eastern Ukraine.[44] Such views, steeped in anti-fascist discourse, anti-imperialist, i.e. virulently anti-American, of the Spanish far-leftists did not necessarily need the war in Ukraine, nor much of prodding from "Russian propaganda." In fact, it would have been surprising had the Spanish red milieu reacted differently to conflict which pitted a country seeking help from the West (Ukraine) and seemingly challenging the only "active international force" which was "anti-imperialist," i.e. anti-U.S.[45] With both Novorossiya, and then its successor "People's Republics" actively combining the red, i.e. post-Soviet paradigm in its imagery and propaganda,[46] the Spanish communists of different stripes and organizational affiliations could attempt to blend in more easily into the conflict and project their Spanish civil war-like reading of the situation on the reality on the ground.

In the later years, a sort of reckoning with this very reality, and their desire to join the conflict, was to be found in the Spanish fighters' reminiscences. One of the eight arrested in 2015, who were quickly released, later ended up working in a menial job in Belgium and eagerly testified to his willingness to return to the war but was also adamant that second such outing would not be forgiven by the "state."[47] Others openly toned down their expectations related to the future of the "People's Republics" and the fact that these statelets had not been in the business of "socialist revolution" which attracted the "Leftist friends" there in the first place.[48] Famously, they were even prepared to rationalize their red-brown alliance with "Nazis,"[49] whom they were allegedly fighting, but ended up sharing trenches with in Eastern Ukraine as "we all want the same: social justice and the liberation of Russia from the Ukrainian invasion."[50] This rationalization even led five "Spanish communists," including – allegedly two former military men, to join the French UC, at that time led by far-right individuals, in October 2014. The photo commemorating this union sees the French and Serbian UC members flying the flags of their respective countries, and that of Novorossiya, with the Spaniards holding the flag of the Second Spanish Republic, which perished with the conclusion of the civil war in 1939.[51] In short, it can be argued that the Spaniards approached the war with an attitude of 'it is what it is, we are here to fight the Ukrainian Nazis'" and while witnessing the arrival of far-right extremists who joined the DNR/LNR militias, felt resigned to even doubt or pose questions to their local, or Russian, comrades of commanders.[52]

The down-to-earth reckoning, followed in some cases by February 2015 arrest, must have been more difficult for the Spanish foreign fighters as many chose to advertise their presence openly in the "People's Republics"[53] and their return to Spain.[54] Thus, what might have at first looked like an adventure, a deed to support anti-imperialist struggle, turned into an experience which was far from ideal. Interestingly, for some their trek eastward was a real eye opener: "my experience [in the DNR/LNR] changed my views completely. Now I think I am starting to support NATO and Western culture."[55] This is not to suggest that such a reversal of views was universal but to indicate that, for some Western foreign fighters of the red background, the "People's Republics" hardly constituted beacons of anti-imperialism and anti-fascism as they "felt under-appreciated" by their hosts and were uneasy with the "Soviet" wastefulness, suspicions and chaos.[56]

It seems that in certain cases considerable effort was put into actually getting the Spanish fighters from Madrid to Donetsk in the summer of 2014. Some ended up in Donetsk on their own – after reaching out to a locally based "Spanish journalist who spoke Russian,"[57] others traveled with "humanitarian caravans" fronted by the Italian, but popular in leftist circles in Spain, punk band Banda Bassotti, and chose to stay in the "People's Republics."[58] Finally, the largest group, members of Spanish far-left organizations, such as the United Left of the Spanish Communist Party, were in touch with administrators of social media profiles sympathetic to the "separatist" cause, who later linked them up with contacts in Russia.[59] This, according to some sources, suggested a presence of a "pro-Russian network" which facilitated their travel eastward.[60] While it is not known which organization or group stood behind this alleged "network,"[61] the Russian neo-Soviet but also nationalist, Essence of Time movement (Суть времени; Sut' vremeni) was active in showcasing the presence of international in general, but Spanish in particular, members of its unit within the ranks of the Vostok Battalion of the DNR forces.[62] With the passage of time, the few in number Essence's Spaniards effectively constituted the last Spanish fighters present in the DNR/LNR and remained the ports of call for all Spanish-speaking activists or journalists wanting to hear from their compatriots based in "People's Republics."[63]

Finland – Propagandists and Fighters

The Finnish contingent in the war in Ukraine, numbering fewer than 10 people, was hardly the most significant in terms of size. However, the Finn's involvement in the war in Ukraine is not limited to actual fighting and in reality has been more prevailing in other fields, namely propaganda. Here, Janus Putkonen, allegedly "one of the local warlords at the Moscow's information front,"[64] definitely made a mark. He moved to Donetsk in the summer of 2015 and established *DONi News*, a media company which hardly attempted to communicate news objectively and more resembled an international mouthpiece of the DNR, e.g. Putkonen would interview people wearing t-shirts with Vladimir Putin or colors/badges of the DNR.[65] He got very close to the DNR's ruling elite,[66] at one moment even being presented with a pistol by Alexander Zakharchenko.[67]

In the meantime, he set up a cultural center which was aimed at attracting Finnish tourists to the region and possibly Finnish investment.[68] In the meantime, he would not only interview Finnish fighters who joined the "separatists" for *DONi*,[69] but also allegedly became a guide and a host for the arriving Finnish foreign fighters.[70] Interestingly, Putkonen found his service of less value to the DNR authorities after Zakharchenko was killed in the summer of 2018, and he had to flee to a neighboring LNR. He later ended up in in Luhansk.[71]

His Finland-based interviewee and to some extent, associate and counterpart, was Johan Bäckman, who arrived on the media scene in Finland, Russia and Estonia in 2007 – "when a Soviet Red Army monument was relocated from the center of the capital, Tallinn, to a large war cemetery."[72] This academic, formerly married to a Russian woman, staged pro-Soviet demonstrations and published a book on the scandal around the removal of the "bronze soldier." He became a Finland-based affiliate of a Russian Institute of Strategic Studies (RISS), a think tank closely linked to intelligence and power circles in Russia, and organized events under its affiliation in his native country.[73] Moreover, he also acted as an "electoral observer" during the Crimean "referendum," visited the DNR and the LNR, boasted about recruiting four of his compatriots for the fight in the ranks of the "separatists"[74] and, finally, set up an "embassy of Novorossiya" in Finland.[75]

Of the fighters, whether or not recruited by Bäckman, a 38-year-old Petri Viljakainen became the first Finn who appeared in the "separatist" ranks.[76] Unemployed and largely unfamiliar with Donetsk and the DNR, he nonetheless traveled eastward to "to oppose U.S. power, NATO, neo-Nazis, and 'Western propaganda'." He confessed to "seeking a purpose" as he had nothing definite in Finland. He had been clear that he opposed "fascism," that of the Azov Battalion, in particular. In his view, the fight was "against Western neoliberalism and the capitalist world order."[77] Such views positioned him closer to the red in the brown-red cocktail which appeared on the front lines in Eastern Ukraine and Viljakainen later joined the LNR's far-left *InterUnit*, which grouped like-minded radicals.[78] In 2016, he got engaged to Ludmiła Dobrzyniecka, a Polish member of the *InterUnit*,[79] but the couple quickly split with Dobrzyniecka leaving Donbas.[80]

More or less at the same time as Viljakainen was joining the LNR's Prizrak Brigade, the Ukrainian volunteer battalions in general, and Azov in particular, featured a lone known Finn in its ranks – Petteri Kääpä.[81] He spent three months in Eastern Ukraine and duly returned to Finland, possibly so that he would not overstay his visa and attract too much attention from the security services. This was a tactic favored by the conflict's "ghosts," i.e. secretive individuals who would usually not show their faces and give interviews while in Eastern Ukraine and approach the conflict as a "hop on-hop off" adventure during which they would deploy to the war-return home and then redeploy on many occasions.[82] The "ghosts," as the author was told by the interviewees from the Ukrainian volunteer battalions, would be former Swedish or Finnish soldiers who wished to "shoot up a few Ruskis while in Eastern Ukraine" and then returned home to earn some money so they could go back to front lines.[83]

The UK: "Rat Line," Non-Ideological Fighters and a Propagandist

The British far-right scene has on several occasions been branded a "failure," and in the words of an insider, "had not much to show for itself, save a few punch ups at Trafalgar Square [in London], the odd riot, several unsuccessful electoral forays and a brace of convictions for sub-revolutionary activity."[84] More recently, and by the middle of the twenty-first century's second decade – a time when the war in Ukraine was in full swing – the British National Party (BNP), the most politically successful far-right radicals in the history of the UK, "imploded" after winning "almost one million votes" in the 2009 European Parliamentary elections, and the "anti-Muslim street scene, exemplified by the English Defence League (EDL), lost momentum from 2013 onwards." In the later years, a "more youthful component of Britain's overtly national-socialist milieu," i.e. the National Action (NA), banned in 2016 as a terrorist organization, took a more prominent role in the once again "failure" of a milieu.[85] As will be shown, this development had some implications for those attempting to recruit British individuals for the war effort in Ukraine.

In fact, the British far right, and the NA itself, were allegedly reached by different "recruiters," such as non-Ukrainian Azov Battalion members,[86] but these "were incredibly frustrated by their unwillingness to join either Azov or any other groups. More often the British fascists just wanted to hang out and look tough. They would not commit to anything at all." This pattern continued "when the British police started arresting people for NA membership [and] some NA members went to the Ukraine to hide but [...] had to return because all they wanted to do was get photographs of themselves hanging out there," and as such were of no use to the Ukrainian far right or the volunteer battalions arising from that milieu.[87] At the same time, some the British far right attempted to rather unsuccessfully establish a "rat line," funneling wannabe recruits from the UK into Poland and then Ukraine – all developed with the alleged support of the British-based Polish extremists of the National Rebirth of Poland (*Narodowe Odrodzenie Polski*, NOP).[88]

At the same time, the other side – i.e. Russia and the "separatists" – fared no better in attracting Britons to "engage militarily" in its ranks. It did, however, manage to enroll the BNP's then leader, Nick Griffin, into wining and dining in Russia,[89] and attempted to have his party join the WNCM – World National-Conservative Movement, a pro-Moscow coalition of far-right entities, groups and parties from the broader West.[90]

The lack of success in recruitment of ideologically motivated Britons into the ranks of either the nationalist Ukraine volunteer battalions or the "separatist" militias does not mean, however, that the war in Ukraine saw no presence of British foreign fighters at all. Chris Garrett, spent time with the Azov Battalion, although he denied being "right-wing or a Nazi sympathizer."[91] Allegedly attracted by Azov's call for people with "any kind of knowledge with first aid, volunteering, with basic military skills, de-mining, anything,"[92] this former British cadet and a member of the Karen National Liberation Army (KNLA) in Myanmar, saw the conflict as a chance to test himself in the conditions of a major war.[93] Other Britons, allegedly as many as six and some with military experience from the ranks of the pro-Kurdish fighters in Syria,[94] flocked to the ranks of the Georgian National Legion, one of the most internationalized units on the pro-Ukraine side – "a community of people of more than 20 nations."[95] At the same time, at least two Britons were involved in the fight on the pro-"separatist" side[96] with one of them, Benjamin Stimson, jailed in 2017 under UK's terrorism laws, two years after he returned from Ukraine.[97]

The face of the British interest and to some extent, involvement in the conflict had not been the relatively few fighters but a blogger Graham Phillips. A freelancer for *Russia Today*, who seemed fearless while covering the early stages of the war, he had been living in Ukraine long before the beginning of Euromaidan, and developed a critical view of the protest movement.[98] This later on led him to both Crimea and the "People's Republics" from which he posted dozens, if not hundreds, of short gonzo journalistic clips which had a pro-Russia/pro-"separatist" tinge, if not a flavor of pro-Russian activism[99] – such as the infamous "interview" with the captured Ukrainian "saboteur."[100] At the time of writing, his YouTube channel has 273,000 subscriptions and he continues to post videos from Russia occupied Crimea or updates from Donbas.[101] Unsurprisingly, he also resurfaced in the newly Russia occupied territories of Ukraine, namely Mariupol, in 2022 and "interviewed" a British prisoner of war captured by the DNR troops.[102]

Germany – Much Ado About Nothing?

Germany possesses a "multifaceted [extremist] scene" which has a long history of violent activism, and a strong track record of transnational connectivity.[103] As was found by the author while co-writing another publication, almost any foreign extremist organization attempts to build up links with likeminded German comrades.[104] No wonder that in such conditions the broader German far right found itself in the thick of discussion on the war in Ukraine, and its leading actors were leaning either for Ukraine or for Russia in the conflict. The general European pattern of "established far-right parties desiring to strengthen their anti-mainstream credentials opting for Russia versus more extreme elements and indentitarians, not beholden materially to Moscow, opting for Ukraine" also held in Germany.[105]

Consequently, the likes of the "established" Alternative for Germany (*Alternative für Deutschland*, AfD) was increasingly moving toward the pro-Russia camp,[106] and so did the National Democratic Party of Germany (*Nationaldemokratische Partei Deutschlands* or NPD), although the Ukrainian Azov movement would claim that there was a limit to the latter's pro-Russian stance with its youth organization, and section of the party itself, actually taking a different position.[107] At the same time, the more radical German party *Der III Weg* (Third Way), was referred to as "the long-time ally of the Azov Movement,"[108] and its representatives spoke at the latter's events, with the party strenuously denying reports of its members allegedly receiving paramilitary training with the Russian Imperial Movement in Russia (*Russkoe imperskoe dvizhenie*, RID). Similar exchange of visits seemingly put the other radicals of the *Die Rechte* (the Right) also in the Ukrainian nationalists' orbit but some sources indicated that the party effectively developed a pro-Russia and a pro-Ukraine wings.[109]

This seeming multitude of actors taking a stance on the conflict, some allegedly splitting over this issue, was not, however, matched by the actual mobilization of fighters for the war itself. In fact, the single known face of the German participation in the conflict had been Margarita Seidler, a nurse and a rare female foreign fighter in this war, who moved to Ukraine in 2002 after converting to Christian Orthodoxy.[110] She later found herself in Slavyansk, controlled by a militias loyal to Igor Girkin, the de facto instigator of the war in Ukraine, and decided to fight Ukrainian "Nazis." Allegedly, 19 German individuals with an extremist background who traveled to Ukraine are known to the authorities in Germany. By mid-April 2022, it was reported that of these 19 only four are still believed to be in the area and only six went with the clear motivation to participate in the war. Some of these cases included genuine far-right militants who ventured eastward, joining either of the conflicts sides, either to "get battlefield experience or as an adventurist, adrenaline driven sojourn."[111] The scarcity of German recruits on either side was confirmed to the author by:

a. Nikolaus von Twickel, an analyst based in Germany who publishes updates on the situation in the DNR/LNR: "The only German I know of ... there was a Russian-German, whose parents had emigrated to Germany in the 1990s from Luhansk. He lasted a short time in LNR and returned to Germany in 2014. The fact that there were so few Germans is a remarkable fact, the People's Republics could not even set up one office, 'embassy' or a 'consulate' there, yet they pulled it off in France, Italy, Czech Republic."[112]

b. A Swedish member of the Azov regiment confirmed to the author a presence of a single German in the ranks, a former special forces soldier who left after a brief period in which the battalion was being stood up and trained.[113]

At the same time, author's local sources indicated that German neo-Nazis were seen and heard in LNR in conflict's early days.[114] What is more, some German media reported that around 100 "Russian Germans" joined the militias of the "People's Republics," and that the Ukrainian embassy was pressurizing Berlin to stop the inflow of fighters into the "separatists'" ranks.[115] Finally, there were reoccurring reports about Azov's or other Ukrainian nationalists attempting to lure German radicals to the front lines – the last from early 2021, which featured an interview with a German-based recruiter who claimed that three eventually made it to the front.[116] These reports complemented the news on the establishment of a German chapter of Tradition and Order, "an associate of the Azov movement,"[117] co-led by prominent Azov personnel and Denis "Nikitin"

Kapustin, "famous Russian neo-Nazi," "a key figure among right-wing extremists in Europe," founder of the White Rex clothing brand, who spent part of his youth in Germany.[118] His activities, effectively – "subcultural event management in Kyiv," helped lure some of the German extreme right radicals to full contact combat sports fights in Ukraine, and constituted a creation of an "event led cultural sphere and not a (para)military unit, e.g. Azov, the Germans would be joining. This seemed more successful and attractive to all concerned."[119] Alternatively, as will be shown in the Central European chapter of this monograph, the German "influence" was also present amongst those backing Russia in the war as allegedly a parliamentary worker the German AfD party was behind an unsuccessful attack by Polish nationalist radicals at a Hungarian cultural center in Western Ukraine.[120] Such an act was to inflame tensions between Kyiv and Budapest and further isolate Ukraine on the international stage.

Denmark – Foreign Fighters from an Unexpected Source

Denmark's far-right milieu in general, and its extreme right component in particular, had seen, like most of its European counterparts, disputes and splits related to the war in Ukraine. The Party of the Danes (*Danskernes Parti*) lined up on the side of Ukraine and its leader visited Ukraine to showcase his support. At the same time, the other elements of the milieu, the Danish chapter of the Nordic Resistance Movement (NRM) but most especially the Danish National Front (*DF, Dansk Front*), which in the past had contacts with the Slavic Union (Славянский союз; СС; Slavyanskiy soyuz) in Russia. The DF's leader later settled in Russia and became a Russian citizen, opted for the "separatists."[121] At the same time, the milieu hardly produced any foreign fighters for either of the sides of the war in Ukraine. Surprisingly, the Danish, or more precisely – Denmark's inhabitants, foreign fighters for this war emerged from a seemingly unexpected source.[122]

Isa Munayev, a legendary Chechen commander from the second Chechen war (1999-2009), who later broke with the Chechen underground due to its turn away from nationalism and toward Islamism,[123] settled as a refugee in Denmark after 2005. Years later, he and a band of fellow Chechen emigres,[124] who also lived there, resurfaced in Ukraine as the core of the Dzhokhar Dudayev battalion, named after Chechnya's first president. The unit was "not strictly Muslim, though it includes a number of Muslims from former Soviet republics, including Chechens who have fought on the side of the Islamic State in Syria. It also includes many Ukrainians. But all are fighting against what they perceive to be a common enemy: Russian aggression."[125] The battalion suffered a split that produced more "Chechen" units in the ranks of Ukraine's volunteer battalions which faced, ironically, other Chechens fighting alongside the separatists.[126] Munayev died during the battle of Debaltseve in early 2015 and a British educated fellow Chechen, Adam Osmayev, took over the command. Two years later, he was a target of an assassination attempt in Kyiv in which his wife perished.[127] Ironically, as Osmayev was taking over the command, the war in Ukraine saw a visible reduction in violence as the two sides settled for what effectively became a stalemate of trench warfare. Some of the "Chechen" units on the Ukrainian side were effectively demobilizing as they found themselves under criticism of some of the Ukrainian authorities, reluctant to support the allegedly "Islamist" or "radical" fighters.[128]

The Netherlands – Running Away from Something

Up to seven individuals from the Netherlands trekked eastward to join the conflict in Ukraine,[129] and in most cases these had been decisions connected not only with Ukraine or "People's Republics" pull but rather push factors, i.e. issues which made them leave their native country in the first place.[130] Notably, one case stands out amongst these as it involves potentially the sole family amidst the fighters trekking to Ukraine, i.e. a foreign fighter, his wife and their two young children who all relocated to the DNR. This is a phenomenon widely known amongst the fighters who traveled to Syria with their families in tow[131] but was hardly repeated in Eastern Ukraine where the fighters, as was shown in the French chapter, were more keen to start their lives alongside local spouses. Pascal Hillebrand, the Dutch fighter in question, was an exception to this rule. A former soldier and a truck driver in his late 30s, allegedly "disappointed with Western actions in countries such as Libya, Iraq and Syria," he abandoned his "Western" life to find "happiness" in the DNR, a place where "there is no corruption. Everyone helps everyone. While in the Netherlands you no longer know your own neighbor." He was said to have "recovered physical and mentally" and allegedly looked forward to leading a small farmer's life in the DNR.[132] His wife, Isle, hailed the "separatists" for their decision to break "away from the Western system of influence."[133]

Walter Klop, a 23-year-old in 2015, might have been the first Dutchman to join the war in Eastern Ukraine. He appeared in Kyiv in the summer of 2014 and barely speaking English managed to enlist in the Right Sector, which he left in early 2015. He allegedly left behind "a childhood of homes, youth care and youth prisons" and wanted to "do something good" for the Netherlands in the aftermath of the MH17 disaster, which saw the shooting down of a civilian airplane by the "separatists" with 298 dead, of which 193 were Dutch.[134] Another Dutch recruit, allegedly autistic Sjoerd Heeger,[135] found himself on the front lines with the Right Sector in early 2017.[136] Around a year later, after moving to a war "which has more meaning" and was about "freedom" and not "power," he died while fighting in the ranks of the Yekîneyên Parastina Gel (YPG) in Syria.[137]

Austria: "Violence and Adventure"

The Austrian far right has been developing ties with the Soviet Union since the early 1950s. Its currently electorally most successful incarnation, the Freedom Party of Austria's (Freiheitliche Partei Österreichs, FPÖ) links with Russia, the

Soviet Union's successor, have been documented elsewhere and need not be repeated in this volume.[138] The second decade of the twenty-first century brought the party major electoral gains – it polled circa 20 percent in the 2013 election, and 26 percent in the 2017 election – after which it joined the coalition government with the Austrian People's Party (Österreichische Volkspartei, ÖVP). Thus, given the FPÖ's popularity, the outbreak of the war in Ukraine could have potentially galvanized the country's right wing seemingly pro-Russian radicals into action and e.g. seen them trek eastward to support the fight of the "People's Republics." As it later turned out, this evidently had not been the case – the author's early counts of the foreign fighters in the war in Ukraine featured no Austrians.[139] The local observers, however, confirmed, sightings of individuals from this country in the ranks of the "separatist" militias and stressed that they had been far-right radicals, just like the other Western Europeans present in Donetsk but unlike the Southern Europeans or individuals from Latin America who had professed far-left political inclinations.[140] At the same time, some Austrians fought on the pro-Ukraine side and their stories, thanks to their being featured in the media[141] and associating with some of the most well-known foreign fighters from the war,[142] catapulted them to a considerable level of notoriety.

Out of the four alleged Austrians who joined the Ukrainian volunteer battalions, it had been the half-Austrian, half-Tunisian Ben Fischer who attracted the most attention.[143] Fischer was a former Austrian soldier who served as a peacekeeper in Kosovo, then a private military contractor in Somalia, and later twice appeared on the Ukrainian front, finally ending up with the Right Sector's Task Force Pluto, after being spurned by the Azov Battalion (allegedly due to his Arab looks – his nickname in Ukraine had been "Bin Laden").[144] In the meantime, i.e. between spells in Ukraine, he also managed to join the People's Defense Units (YPG) in Syria.[145] What allegedly drove him to these conflicts was his "automatic, instinctive [desire] to take the side of those who are attacked, who are oppressed," i.e. the Ukrainians or the Kurds.[146] At the same time, however, he once quipped to a journalist that "where death is, everything is much livelier,"[147] and that he looked for "an experience full of "violence and adventure," unlike those of his peers, and not accepting "that the only possible existence is a civilian one."[148] He left behind his "bourgeoise" persona and "multicultural" Vienna, an ironic statement given his multinational background.[149] While with the Right Sector, he was joined by a self-confessed Austrian army deserter, Alex Kirschbaum, who was to later complain of the "neutered" state of his nation which does not allow overt displays of nationalism and, unlike Ukraine, reduces it to soccer hooliganism and fanatical following of Eurovision.[150]

Fischer's "popularity," and his association with the RS, "a rogue unit with the rogue Ukrainian nationalist group"[151] attracted the Austrian justice system to his exploits in Ukraine. In 2017, when Fischer was crossing the EU's external border between Poland and Ukraine, he was arrested and later extradited to Austria, for alleged involvement in war crimes during the fight at the Donetsk airport but released upon arriving in Vienna.[152]

Norway: Few but Notable (Wannabe) Fighters

The Norwegian extreme right is relatively small but its different strands, be it the more anti-Islamist or anti-immigrant or the openly national-socialist (i.e. the local chapter of the Nordic Resistance Movement), despite relatively limited contact they enjoy with Eastern Europe and the radicals there, perceive Russia as a "well-functioning place." Moreover, due to its authoritarianism, nativism and alleged state-ordered Islamophobia, it has a "specific appeal" to the rank and file far rightists of Norway.[153] The smallness of the milieu, however, limited its members' potential contribution to the ranks of the pro-Russian separatists or the rival nationalist units in the ranks of the Ukrainian volunteer battalions. In fact, it is just two individuals who, albeit rather publicly, symbolized and epitomized the Norwegian foreign fighting in the war in Ukraine.

The first is Joachim Furholm, "a troubled man, with a child left behind in Norway,"[154] who successfully joined the regular Ukrainian army. While in Ukraine, he claimed that for him this opportunity was "a good chance to serve in the military for someone who has not [done it before]." He expressed his unwillingness to join the Norwegian army as it would "send me to the MENA (Middle East and North Africa) for wars I do not approve of, I am joining to protect people's freedom not to fuck with people's freedom."[155] His career in the military, however, had been short-lived as Furholm was later, in his view, discharged due to the political pressure from the Norwegian embassy in Kyiv. The latter, allegedly, protested with the Ukrainian authorities who allowed a seemingly well-known far-right radical to join the fight at the front in Eastern Ukraine.[156] Furholm's discharge left him stranded in Kyiv in which he befriended local far-right radicals and was said to have been "recruiting" like minded individuals, mostly Americans, into the ranks of the Azov Regiment via his personal Facebook.[157] This was strenuously denied by the Regiment, which refused to entertain the thought of allowing Furholm to join its ranks "due to a lack of military skills, training and discipline."[158] The fact that Furholm, allegedly former "bank robber,"[159] attempted to associate himself with the broader Azov movement was confirmed to the author by Olena Semenyaka, the National Corps (Azov movement's political wing) international secretary: "we are okay with people who come and want to support us. We end the 'bad connections,' a Norwegian [Furholm], some US guys. All to be counted on fingers of one hand. We now think twice as it is sometimes better to let such people go. Furholm wanted to help? Seemingly ok but it went downhill from there."[160]

The second Norwegian, or in fact – a Norwegian Russian, was Jan or Yan Petrovsky, who arrived in Norway with his mother as a teenager in 2004. He later became a self-confessed "nationalist of two countries," i.e. Russia and Norway, his adopted second homeland, and moved in circles of "Eastern European neo-Nazis" present in Oslo.[161] In 2010, he was arrested as police found "illegal weapons, military equipment, and fake documents," belonging to a Russian neo-Nazi who unsuccessfully claimed asylum in Norway, in a tattoo studio where

Petrovsky worked.[162] After the arrest Petrovsky eventually moved back to Russia where he met Aleksey Milchakov, future commander of the *Rusich*, a diversion, assault and reconnaissance group (DShRG), one of the most iconic far-right units in the ranks of the "separatists,"[163] whose members, including Petrovsky – second in command to Milchakov, were later associated with war crimes.[164] This unit, as was shown in the French chapter, rubbed shoulders with e.g. Team Vikernes while out on the front line in Donbas. The summer of 2015 saw its announcement of a "retreat" from Donbas for "regrouping and resupply." Milchakov stated that it "has fulfilled its tasks and obtained resources from this war. We will not go on fighting under these conditions for those whose interests are unclear [...] The next war awaits us."[165] As was demonstrated while discussing Team Vikernes, what bothered Rusich was the stalemate on the front line, in place since the winter of 2015, and the inability of making a mark in an increasingly frozen conflict. In the aftermath of this decision, Petrovsky drifted back to Norway where he participated in anti-immigrant patrols of the Soldiers of Odin,[166] and toured Europe sharing his exploits from the front lines.[167] In 2016, he was arrested, stripped of his permanent residence in Norway and finally deported to Russia.[168]

During Donald Trump's presidency, the threat from right wing extremists, or violent domestic extremists, was becoming the key issue for the United States of America's department of homeland security. In this context, the Christchurch attack seemed like a perfect illustration of their "nightmare scenario of globalized white supremacist terrorism [that] was coming to life."[169] Any alleged links to Ukraine which the attacker – Brenton Tarrant, was supposedly said to have had, immediately came under a lot of scrutiny and focused a lot of attention on the Ukrainian far right and its transnational dimension. Couple that with the already discussed putative contacts between the representatives of the Azov movement and members of the American alt-right or other far-right extremists,[170] and the prophecy of "white supremacy" terrorism becoming a truly global phenomenon seemed real.[171] Consequently, a lot of attention was paid to any potential American foreign fighter who attempted to join the war in Ukraine. As will be shown below, the issue of their actual participation in the war was overhyped, but consumed a great deal of attention of especially the Western media, which tied this issue to the 2014 controversies surrounding nationalist Ukrainian volunteer battalions. In this reading of the situation, these entities, such as the Right Sector but especially Azov, turned into far-right equivalents of Al-Qaeda or ISIS, i.e. entities which attracted and trained extremists, and were then to field these for terrorism missions in their home countries.[172]

The controversy surrounding Ukraine and the potential far-right foreign fighters from the U.S. was not only the fallout from the Christchurch attack. It seemed as if that midway through the twenty-first century's second decade, Ukraine, just like other parts of Central and Eastern Europe, were becoming a proverbial "Shangri-La" for the world's right-wing extremists.[173] More conservative, homogenous, seemingly anti-LGBT and less politically correct than their

Western allies and neighbors, this part of Europe attracted a lot of attention in the Western far-right circles. Its leading lights, such as the American Robert Rundo, would attempt to settle in the region and took time to extoll its heritage and tradition.[174] In addition to all that, Ukraine seemingly offered (a) a chance to rub shoulders with like-minded far-right figures who actually fought in this country's war with Russia and (b) an elusive, but some thought real, opportunity to join the Ukrainian brethren in the actual fighting in Donbas. As it later transpired, the offer was not real but remained an imaginary and illusory concept, a fantasy for most of the wannabe fighters of fanboys of different Ukrainian formations. In short, whereas allegedly "the emergence of Azov Battalion and Right Sector in Ukraine in 2014 electrified the neo-Nazi movement in the United States," this fact failed simultaneously to produce an avalanche of recruits for the Ukrainian side:[175] the most reliable estimate indicates that around a dozen Americans fought for Ukraine,[176] and another source mentioned seven U.S. "white supremacists" who either joined or visited the above-mentioned units in Ukraine.[177] One of the American fighters also died early in the war.[178] At the same time, Ukraine was said to have sought only one individual who fought in the "separatist" ranks.[179] This could have well been the Russell "Texas" Bentley, a self-confessed member of the Essence of Time far-left unit who later settled in Donetsk and was involved in "information Warfare for the Donetsk People's Republic."[180] Allegedly, there were also other Americans fighting for the *InterUnit*, a far-left entity fighting on the side of the "separatists."[181]

These humble numbers, however, do not mean that certain members of e.g. the American far-right milieu would not express "a [repeated] interest in traveling to the Ukraine to fight with nationalists there."[182] What is more, some actually made it to Ukraine as in October 2020 two Americans, said to have been members of the banned Atomwaffen Division,[183] allegedly attempted to join the Azov Regiment in Ukraine but ended up deported by Ukraine instead.[184] Such stories, and their coverage in media read globally, enabled to inflate the American-Ukrainian "white supremacy" connection which, to a large degree, remained notional or aspirational.[185] It is nonetheless undeniable that in some cases the interest in the Americans who traveled to Ukraine was completely warranted. This was evident especially in relation to stories of the Right Sector's chaotic and disorganized approach to "its" foreigners, including the Americans,[186] or the investigation of the case of Craig Lang, tackled in more detail in the chapter on units which hosted foreign fighters in Ukraine. Especially the latter, almost a ready-made story for a TV series or a movie, captured the imagination of the American public. Lang fought both in the ranks of the Right Sector and the GNL but also stands accused of a double murder allegedly committed in the U.S. and is currently fighting his extradition back to his country from Ukraine.[187] Interestingly, Lang was also allegedly responsible for recruitment of other "questionable characters" into the ranks of the latter formation,[188] including a "neo-Nazi militant" from Australia.[189]

Conclusion

The Western European foreign fighters mostly joined the "People's Republics" militias and not the Ukrainian volunteer battalions. A significant chunk of these contingents was constituted by non-ideological fighters who a) were running from trouble at home, b) sought adrenaline and/or adventure. At the same time, especially the largest Italian and Spanish contingents featured a wide-array of brown-red or red-brown personnel who seemed not to have minded sharing trenches with their ideological counterparts while in Eastern Ukraine. Moreover, well known and committed far-right militants, with no pretense of any shade of red in their backgrounds, were also to be found in the "separatist" ranks.

These fighters were recruited in numerous ways but clear patterns of how they got to Eastern Ukraine are clearly emerging, i.e. in certain cases a role of the Russian expats living in Western Europe, or Russian organizations operating there, was key; pro-Russian or outright Russian voices present on the social media acted as connectors between fighters and their future "separatist" units; the same could be said about Western journalists or activists who trekked to the DNR and the LNR, and then linked the wannabe foreign fighters from their countries with the locals.

While in the "separatist" held territories, some fighters had second doubts as to their involvement in the war but others, and that has also been the case for the foreigners on the Ukrainian side, decided to stay and start afresh by marrying local women. The Western European "separatist" contingent also featured female fighters and saw one fighter move his whole family to "People's Republic" – an unprecedented move, more akin to that practiced by ISIS fighters. In addition to that, the "separatists" also had their first foreign fighter, albeit short-lived, couple.

In certain cases, it had not been the actual fighters but rather the propagandists who were the real faces of a given contingent in the ranks of the "separatists." These individuals, most often for personal gain, produced gonzo journalistic materials from the front lines and the "People's Republics" which aimed at augmenting a pro-"fascist junta" rhetoric emanating from the Russian media amongst members of the Western public opinion. In certain cases, these propagandists were also said to have helped out with recruitment and even lodging some of their countrymen who were arriving in the DNR/LNR to join the conflict.

The Western European pro-Ukraine fighters were less numerous and their ranks also featured an array of men who seemed more "pushed" into going away from their countries than attracted or "pulled" be the conflict in Ukraine in particular. At the same time, however, these had often been far right or "conservative," as they would call themselves, individuals or well-known militants. They had known some of their counterparts who decided to align with the "separatists" or, in their words, Russia. They also co-existed on the front lines with some seemingly unlikely allies, e.g. Danish-Chechen asylum seekers who went to Ukraine to fight against the Russians. Moreover, some of these brown fighters, as well as the less ideological ones, also fought in other wars – namely in Syria, and usually in the ranks of the far from fascist Kurdish YPG. Some pro-Ukraine fighters joined the Ukrainian army and never made it to the more ideological of the volunteer battalions. Interestingly, the case which in the recent years attracted the most attention, however, was that of a Norwegian far-right radical who got into the army, which is perfectly legal in Ukraine – on contractual basis, but never made it into the ranks of the Azov Regiment, a former volunteer battalion.

Upon returning home the pro-Ukraine fighters hardly faced any legal sanctions but this development was not mirrored in the cases of their "separatist" counterparts. Some Western European countries arrested and prosecuted the veterans of the DNR/LNR militias, accusing them of mercenary or terrorist activities, or actions aimed at undermining the neutrality of their host countries vis-à-vis the Russo-Ukraine war.

Notes

1 P. Ortega Dolz, "We fought together, communists and Nazis alike, for the liberation of Russia," *El Pais*, February 27, 2015, http://elpais.com/elpais/2015/02/27/inenglish/1425051026_915897.html.

2 It must be noted, however, that beyond the larger Italian and Spanish, and very small Austrian and Norwegian contingents, it is extremely difficult to rank the remaining five in according to the numbers as there exist inconsistencies related to the final size of the contingent (see German and Danish cases) or its actual fighting character (see Finnish case).

3 It had not been the rather impressive numbers of fighters, or the Ukrainian attempts to have the Italian authorities to clamp down on their recruitment but the case of a Ukrainian soldier with Italian citizenship, Vitalyi Markiv, which was the most memorable Ukrainian-Italian story arising from the war. In 2019, after a lengthy and controversial trail, Markiv "was found guilty of complicity in deliberate murder of Andrea Rocchelli [Italian photographer who was present near the frontline in Sloviansk on May 24, 2014] and sentenced to 24 years in prison." His appeal against the verdict led to his exoneration and release in November 2020. For more on the case see Olga Tokariuk, *Battle of narratives: Kremlin disinformation in the Vitaliy Markiv case in Italy*, Kyiv: Ukraine Crisis media centre, March 30, 2021, https://drive.google.com/file/d/1sGK2lLqN46MVMN6qFKvRvJ4buJP1Fu3b/view, accessed: June 22, 2021.

4 See https://www.facebook.com/fondDMEnglish/posts/the-list-of-italian-mercenaries-and-accomplices-of-lpr-dpr-terrorist-translators/1905429726384695/ for a post on the issue from July 25, 2017 which features a re-pasted and translated list of the alleged foreign fighters, previously published by the news portal censor.net, accessed: June 22, 2021.

5 *Unian*, "For the first time, Italy arrests far-right Italians who fought in Ukraine – media," August 8, 2018, https://www.unian.info/world/10217207-for-the-first-time-italy-arrests-far-right-italians-who-fought-in-ukraine-media.html, accessed: June 22, 2021.

6 Ferruccio Pinotti, "Mercenari italiani in Donbass, a giudizio ultras della Lucchese: 'Azioni contro l'Ucraina'," *Corrierre Della Sera*, January 21, 2021, https://www.corriere.it/cronache/21_gennaio_21/mercenari-italiani-donbass-giudizio-ultras-lucchese-azioni-contro-l-ucraina-58a62c06-5bfe-11eb-9e63-4c8bcf5518af.shtml, accessed: June 22, 2021.

7 Yulia Silina, "The Italian football hooligan who fled house arrest to become a pro-Russian fighter in Ukraine," *The Local*, April 10, 2018, https://www.thelocal.it/20180410/andrea-palmeri-italian-football-hooligan-russian-separatist-lugansk-ukraine/, accessed: June 22, 2021.

8 See https://www.facebook.com/andrea.palmeri.5, accessed: June 23, 2021.
9 Anton Shekhovtsov, *Russia and the Western Far Right* (Abingdon: Routledge 2018), 6772, Kindle.
10 Tony Wesolowsky and Yaroslav Kreshko, "Italy Moves to Crack Down on its Fighters in Ukraine's Donbas," *Radio Free Europe/Radio Liberty*, August 16. 2018, https://www.rferl.org/amp/italy-moves-to-crack-down-on-its-fighters-in-ukraine-s-donbas/29437946.html?__twitter_impression=true&s=09, accessed: June 23, 2021.
11 Ibid. 5413–5419.
12 *La Provincia di Varese*, "Un varesino al fronte con i filorussi," December 1, 2014, http://www.laprovinciadivarese.it/stories/Cronaca/un-varesino-al-fronte-con-i-filorussi_1092398_11/, accessed: June 23, 2021.
13 https://www.facebook.com/photo?fbid=524861891040301&set=ecnf.100005494847635, accessed: June 23, 2021.
14 Alessandro Farruggia, "Italiani in Ucraina: 'Si battono contro l'Europa Ma non vengono per soldi'," *QuotidiaNazionale,* April 19, 2018, https://www.quotidiano.net/esteri/italiani-ucraina-1.3858948, accessed: June 23, 2021.
15 *Today Rassagena*, "Due volontari italiani combattono per Putin: 'Oggi in Ucraina, domani in Italia'," March 31, 2016, https://www.today.it/rassegna/italiani-milizie-filorusse-donbass.html, accessed: June 23, 2021.
16 Ukraine Crisis media centre, "Chi sono italiani che combattono nelle fila dei militanti in Donbas. Prima parte," August 3. 2017, https://uacrisis.org/it/59314-italiani-militanti-donbas-1a-parte, accessed: June 23, 2021.
17 Fabio Polese, "Un italiano nel Donbass: 'Combatto senza armi per aiutare i filorussi'," *il Giornale*, September 22,2015, https://www.ilgiornale.it/news/mondo/italiano-nel-donbass-combatto-senza-armi-aiutare-i-filorussi-1174222.html, accessed: June 23, 2021.
18 Ibid.
19 *Il Giorno Lecco*, "Un lecchese sotto assedio: 'Vi racconto il Donbass'," November 4, 2017, https://www.ilgiorno.it/lecco/cronaca/lecco-barzio-donbass-1.3511644, accessed: June 24, 2021.
20 Andrea Fantucchio, "Ecco come reclutavano mercenari per Putin anche in Irpinia," *Ottopagine.it*, 5 August 2018, https://www.ottopagine.it/av/cronaca/163642/ecco-come-reclutavano-mercenari-per-putin-anche-in-irpinia.shtml, accessed: June 24, 2021.
21 *ANSA.it*, "Terrorismo: indagato voleva andare a battersi per filo-russi," April 29, 2021, https://www.ansa.it/sardegna/notizie/2021/04/29/terrorismo-indagato-voleva-andare-a-battersi-per-filo-russi_5c86f897-d549-4a6a-ab14-b49f196465e6.html, accessed: June 24, 2021.
22 *Donbassföreningen*, "Interview with Italian Volunteer 'Nemo'," October 17, 2015, https://donbassforeningen.wordpress.com/2015/10/17/eng-interview-with-italian-volunteer-nemo-2/, accessed: June 24, 2021.
23 *Next Stop Reggio*, "Donbass e neonazismo ucraino: a Reggio Emilia illustrata resistenza antifascista alle porte dell'Europa di cui nessuno parla. Intervista ad Alberto Fazolo," November 14, 2018, https://nextstopreggio.it/donbass-e-neonazismo-ucraino-a-reggio-emilia-illustrata-resistenza-antifascista-alle-porte-delleuropa-di-cui-nessuno-parla-intervista-ad-alberto-fazolo/, accessed: June 24, 2021.
24 See Fazolo's interview by Olsi Krutani, sentenced after the 2018 arrests for assisting in recruitment of Italians for the war in Donbas to two years and eight months of imprisonment: Olsi Krutani, "Eliminazione leader del Donbass: Intervista allo scrittore Alberto Fazolo," *Periodico Daily*, November 9, 2020, https://www.periodicodaily.com/epurazione-leader-del-donbass-intervista-allo-scrittore-alberto-fazolo, accessed: June 24, 2021.
25 *SakerItalia*, "Alberto Fazolo: 'La soluzione in Donbass? Aiutiamo l'Ucraina a liberarsi'," June 12, 2020, http://sakeritalia.it/ucraina/alberto-fazolo-la-soluzione-in-donbass-aiutiamo-lucraina-a-liberarsi/, accessed: June 24, 2021.

26 Matteo Indice, "Mercenari filorussi dall'Italia al Donbass, le prime condanne in Italia," *La Stampa*, July 3, 2019, https://www.lastampa.it/cronaca/2019/07/02/news/mercenari-filorussi-dall-italia-al-donbass-le-prime-condanne-in-italia-1.36636396, accessed: June 24, 2021.

27 According to some, the main reason why such individuals were prosecuted, unlike those recruiting fighters for the Ukrainian volunteer battalions, was the fact that this process involved Italians as the recruited and it had been happening on Italian soil. See: author's skype interview with Pietro Castelli, Italy's prominent expert on the far right, September 10, 2020.

28 Daniele Dell'Orco, "Mai reclutato mercenari, in Donbass si combatte gratis,' intervista esclusiva ad Andrea Palmeri," *Nazione Futura*, May 28, 2021, http://www.nazionefutura.it/politica/mai-reclutato-mercenari-in-donbass-si-combatte-gratis-intervista-esclusiva-ad-andrea-palmeri/, accessed: June 24, 2021.

29 *Carabinieri*, "Sicurezza: italiano combatteva come mercenario nel Donbass (Ucraina), arrestato," May 6, 2021, http://www.carabinieri.it/cittadino/informazioni/comunicati-stampa/sicurezza-italiano-combatteva-come-mercenario-nel-donbass-(ucraina)-arrestato, accessed: June 24, 2021.

30 *Hate Speech International*, "Ukraine's far-right forces," February 3, 2015, https://www.hate-speech.org/ukraines-far-right-forces/, accessed: June 24, 2021.

31 Moreover, there was at least one Italian in the ranks of the Right Sector: Jack Losh, "Ukraine turns a blind eye to ultrarightist militia," *The Washington Post*, February 13, 2017, https://www.washingtonpost.com/world/europe/ukraine-turns-a-blind-eye-to-ultrarightist-militia/2017/02/12/dbf9ea3c-ecab-11e6-b4ff-ac2cf509efe5_story.html, accessed: June 24, 2021.

32 Ilaria Morani, "Io, italiano che combatto come "foreign fighter" per l'Ucraina," *Corriere della Sera*, February 12, 2015, https://www.corriere.it/esteri/15_febbraio_12/io-italiano-che-combatto-come-foreign-fighter-per-ucraina-93bcdefa-b2b0-11e4-9344-3454b8ac44ea.shtml, accessed: June 24, 2021.

33 *Hate Speech International*, "Ukraine's far-right forces."

34 *Hope Not Hate*, "Russian Court Sentences Members of a Neo-Nazi Terror Group Also Active in the UK," June 22, 2017, https://www.hopenothate.org.uk/2017/06/22/russian-court-sentences-members-neo-nazi-group-also-active-uk/, accessed: June 24, 2021.

35 Author's direct message exchange with a foreign member of the Azov Battalion/Regiment, who wished to remain anonymous, on twitter, May 27, 2015.

36 Kacper Rekawek, "Neither "NATO's Foreign Legion" Nor the "Donbass International Brigades:" (Where Are All the) Foreign Fighters in Ukraine?," *PISM Policy Paper*, no. 6(108), (March 2015): 1, https://www.pism.pl/files/?id_plik=19434, accessed: February 10, 2021.

37 Mirren Gidda, "Disbanded Brothers: What Happens When Ukraine's Foreign Fighters Return Home," *Newsweek*, April 11, 2015, https://www.newsweek.com/2015/11/13/disbanded-brothers-what-happens-when-ukraines-foreign-fighters-return-home-390551.html, accessed: June 22, 2021.

38 Dan Kedmey, "Spain Breaks Up ISIS Recruitment Ring Targeting Young Women," *Time*, February 24, 2015, https://time.com/3720182/spain-isis-recruitment-ring/, accessed: June 22, 2021.

39 *The Interpreter*, "'Novorossiya's' 'Leftist' Friends," May 30, 2015, https://www.interpretermag.com/novorossiyas-leftist-friends/, accessed: June 22, 2021.

40 See: https://www.interpretermag.com/about-us/, accessed: June 22, 2021.

41 *The Interpreter*, "'Novorossiya's' 'Leftist' Friends."

42 Author's Facebook Messenger interview with a Spanish fighter who wished to remain anonymous, September 24, 2015.

43 https://www.elsaltodiario.com/europa-del-este/vida-tras-kalashnikov-donbas-independiente, accessed: June 22, 2021.

44 See https://comitedeapoyoalaucraniaantifascista.wordpress.com/2014/08/20/comu-nicado-de-la-brigada-internacional-carlos-palomino/ for a summer 2014 call to action on behalf of the "Carlos Palomino Brigade" of Spanish volunteers for DNR/LNR, accessed: June 22, 2021.

45 Kacper Rekawek, *Career Break or a New Career? Extremist Foreign Fighters in Ukraine* (Counter Extremism Project, April 2020), 10, https://www.counterextremism.com/sites/default/files/CEP%20Report_Career%20Break%20or%20a%20New%20Career_Extremist%20Foreign%20Fighters%20in%20Ukraine_April%202020.pdf, accessed: January 12, 2020.

46 Marlene Laruelle, "The three colors of Novorossiya, or the Russian nationalist myth-making of the Ukrainian crisis," *Post-Soviet Affairs* 32, no. 1 (2015): 55, 56.

47 Gidda, "Disbanded Brothers."

48 Loïc Ramirez, "La vida tras el kalashnikov en el Donbás independiente," *El Salto*, January 11, 2020, https://www.elsaltodiario.com/europa-del-este/vida-tras-kalashnikov-donbas-independiente, accessed: June 22, 2021.

49 There is one documented case of a fighter from the Spanish extreme right who fought in the ranks of Team Vikernes, the unit described in detail in the French chapter. See Pep Anton Ginesta, "Neonazis a la guerra: la connexió espanyola i el seu ecosistema," *Directa*, October 23, 2019, https://directa.cat/neonazis-a-la-guerra-la-connexio-espanyola-i-el-seu-ecosistema/, accessed: June 22, 2021. Quique Badia Masoni, a free-lance journalist and a PhD student at Universitat Autonoma de Barcelona, interviewed by the author on WhatsApp on June 1, 2020 mentioned a probability of a second such case, i.e. a Spanish far-right militant, fighting in the ranks of the "separatists" is likely. The author, however, was not able to find corroborating evidence for this claim.

50 Ortega Dolz, "We fought together."

51 See https://www.facebook.com/unite.continentale/photos/pb.681941775182139.-2207520000../801174989925483/?type=3&theater, accessed: June 22, 2021.

52 Author's WhatsApp interview with Arsenio Cuenca, research associate at Cinved, "a multi-disciplinary research and study initiative that investigates a range of core questions relating to far-right parties and social movements in Europe and, especially in Spain," June 20, 2021. See e.g. https://www.youtube.com/watch?v=j-XssFTAMao, accessed: June 22, 2017 for an interview with Patxi Castellano of January 5, 2017 in which he displays such an attitude indicating that the conflict is not exactly what he thought it would be: "What took place here was a coup [...] People had no choice but to rebel. They [Ukraine] wanted to ban and deny them ["separatists"] their culture and history, and here people, unlike in the other part of Ukraine where they are softer, put up with a lot, but then explode. It is not that they make a revolution to establish the Soviet Union. They have taken up arms to defend their land and their families, their way of life, their culture."

53 Kazbek Basayev, "Spanish civil war nostalgics join fight alongside Ukrainian rebels," *Reuters*, August 8, 2014, https://www.reuters.com/article/uk-ukraine-crisis-span-iards/spanish-civil-war-nostalgics-join-fight-alongside-ukrainian-rebels-idUKKB-N0G81W120140808?edition-redirect=uk, accessed: June 22, 2021.

54 L.Á. Vega, "El brigadista gijonés en Ucrania regresa con un oído dañado por las explo-sions," *La Nueva España*, November 16, 2014, https://www.lne.es/asturias/2014/11/16/brigadista-gijones-ucrania-regresa-oido-19918285.html, accessed: June 22, 2021.

55 Author's Facebook Messenger interview with a Spanish fighter who wished to remain anonymous, September 24, 2015.

56 Ibid.

57 Ibid.

58 See https://www.youtube.com/watch?v=01Yq_OIAQdY for March 16, 2015 annou-cement of the second caravan, accessed: June 22, 2021.

59 Dolz, "We fought together."

60 Jorge A. Rodríguez, "Detenidos ocho españoles por luchar en el bando prorruso en Ucra-nia," *El Pais*, February 27, 2015, https://elpais.com/politica/2015/02/27/actualidad/1425026528_611328.html, accessed: June 22, 2021.

61 Author's WhatsApp interview with Quique Badia Masoni, a freelance journalist and a PhD student at Universitat Autonoma de Barcelona, June 1, 2020.
62 Essence of Time, "Our comrade Bali awarded with the "Internationalist Warrior" medal," August 26, 2018, http://eu.eot.su/2016/08/26/our-comrade-bali-awarded-with-the-internationalist-warrior-medal/, accessed: June 22, 2021.
63 Gonzo Blogger, "Milicianos españoles en Donetsk. 9-02-2017," YouTube, February 9, 2017, https://www.youtube.com/watch?v=HIm-KqAF8sw, accessed: June 22, 2021.
64 Hybrid Warfare Analytical Group, "The curious case of Janus Putkonen: the sequel. Finnish case of Russian disinformation continues," Ukraine Crisis media center, March 30, 2020, https://uacrisis.org/en/the-curious-case-of-janus-putkonen-the-sequel-finnish-case-of-russian-disinformation-continues, accessed: June 10, 2021.
65 Marko ES, "Janus Putkonen and the Donbas *DONi-News* – disinformation and misrepresentation, Kharkiv Human Rights Protection Group, October 18, 2017, http://khpg.org/en/1508187981, accessed: June 10, 2021.
66 See a partisan source which, however, thoroughly explores his linkages to this elite, via leaked emails: *Inform Napalm*, "EgorovaLeaks: Filtering and Control of Foreign Journalists in DPR," September 8, 2016, https://informnapalm.org/en/foreign-journalists-in-dpr/, accessed: June 10, 2021.
67 For a video of this "ceremony" see https://www.youtube.com/watch?v=y5t6W7cfGHE, accessed: June 10, 2021.
68 See https://www.youtube.com/watch?v=yePbTnH35K8 for a video from its opening of October 28, 2016.
69 See https://www.youtube.com/watch?v=2HLpBRswZcU, between 12:08 and 13:25 for a clip of such an interview by Putkonen, accessed: June 10, 2021.
70 Author's interview with Jessikka Aro, a Finnish journalist and an expert on the Russian disinformation campaigns, April 16, 2021.
71 Author's Facebook Messenger exchange with a journalist who followed and wrote about developments in the "People's Republics" but wished to remain anonymous, June 10, 2021.
72 Propaganda Relief Collective, "The Kremlin's Voice: Johan Bäckman," *Upnorth*, September 13, 2016, https://upnorth.eu/the-kremlins-voice-johan-backman/, accessed: June 10, 2021.
73 Ibid.
74 See https://www.youtube.com/watch?v=AVaUcrEIFRQ&t=1s for his interview of September 30, 2015 with one of the fighters he allegedly helped recruit, accessed: June 10, 2021.
75 Propaganda Relief Collective, "The Kremlin's Voice: Johan Bäckman."
76 Länsi-Suomi, "Ristiretkellä," July 26, 2015, https://ls24.fi/plus/ristiretkella, accessed: June 10, 2021 for his profile.
77 Ibid.
78 See https://www.google.com/url?sa=i&url=http%3A%2F%2Fredstaroverdonbass. blogspot.com%2F2016%2F10%2Fdonbass-internationalists-salute-che.html&psig= AOvVaw2QOHQjuktm6I6Wn3gCG3FD&ust=1623412193752000&source= images&cd=vfe&ved=0CAkQjhxqFwoTCLi7uuz_jPECFQAAAAAdAAAAABAD for an undated photo of the InterUnit which features Viljakainen, accessed: June 10, 2021.
79 See https://twitter.com/johanbek/status/791345941752184834 for the announcement of the engagement from October 26, 2016, accessed: June 10, 2021.
80 Author's Facebook Messenger exchange with a journalist who followed and wrote about developments in the "People's Republics" but wished to remain anonymous, June 10, 2021.
81 *Iltalehti*, "Petteri taisteli palkkasotilaana Ukrainassa," October 19, 2015, https:// www.iltalehti.fi/ulkomaat/a/2015101920534159, accessed: June 10, 2021. The case of Carolus Andersson vel Carolus Lofroos, a Finn with a Swedish citizenship who lived in Sweden, is covered in the Swedish chapter of this monograph.

82 Rekawek, *Career Break*, 19.

83 Author's email exchange with an anonymous Ukrainian member of one of the volunteer battalions, January 17, 2016.

84 Graham Macklin, *Failed Führers. A History of Britain's Extreme Right* (Abingdon: Routledge, 2020), 333–342, Kindle.

85 Graham Macklin and Shaun McDaid, "United Kingdom," in Kacper Rekawek, Alexander Ritzmann, and Hans Jakob Schindler, *Violent Right-Wing Extremism and Terrorism: Transnational Connectivity, Definitions, Incidents, Structures and Counter-measures* (Berlin, Counter Extremism Project, November 2020), 126–127, https://www.counterextremism.com/sites/default/files/CEP%20Study_Violent%20Right-Wing%20Extremism%20and%20Terrorism_Nov%202020.pdf, accessed: February 9, 2021.

86 Nick Lowles (ed.), *2018 State of Hate*, London: Hope Not Hate, January–February 2018, Issue 35, https://www.hopenothate.org.uk/wp-content/uploads/2018/03/State-of-Hate-2018.pdf, accessed: June 28, 2021 for more on the issue.

87 Author's email exchange with Matthew Collins, researcher at Hope Not Hate, June 28, 2021.

88 Matthew Collins, "Recruiting for Ukraine," *Hope Not Hate*, (January–February 2018), https://www.hopenothate.org.uk/research/state-of-hate-2018/violence/recruiting-for-ukraine/, accessed: June 28, 2021. See https://stopnacjonalizmowi.wordpress.com/2018/05/02/national-action-jak-brytyjska-organizacja-terrorystyczna-odwiedzila-wroclaw/?fbclid=IwAR09-WQ_DElb3Lslk4k9TmcqqijJXWBSui134E-FDkdegGoOTLJ_rDvr4z0;https://stopnacjonalizmowi.wordpress.com/2018/05/07/metafizyka-glupkow-rzecz-o-misanthropic-division-polska/?fbclid=IwAR37T-K5iYn9NsOSdiczOn5E1ToN6ToRMDAz-gIKFgGrC75btxIZN9jqUAts; https://stopnacjonalizmowi.wordpress.com/2018/04/22/dawid-czerwonko-neonazista-emigrant-niemile-widziany-w-anglii/ for primers on the Polish-UK extremist link and information on Dawid Czerwonko – allegedly the key player behind the NA/post-NA – NOP connections who is also featured in *Hope Not Hate* publications quoted above, all accessed: June 28, 2021.

89 Author's email exchange with Matthew Collins, researcher at Hope Not Hate, June 28, 2021.

90 Anton Shekhovtsov, "Russian politicians building an international extreme right alliance," *Anton Shekhovtsov's Blog* (September 15, 2015), https://anton-shekhovtsov.blogspot.com/2015/09/russian-politicians-building.html, accessed: June 29, 2021.

91 Mirren Gidda, "Disbanded BrothersJune 22."

92 Christopher Allen, "Meet the European Fighters Who Have Gone to War in Ukraine," *Vice*, April 25, 2015, https://www.vice.com/en/article/xd7axz/european-british-fighters-in-ukraine-920, accessed: June 28, 2021.

93 Gidda, "Disbanded Brothers."

94 Emma Vardy, "The Briton fighting 'other people's wars'," *BBC News*, April 29, 2018, https://www.bbc.com/news/amp/uk-43899959, accessed: June 28, 2021.

95 Author's interview with an anonymous member of the Georgian National Legion, March 11, 2020.

96 Tom Burridge, "Ukraine conflict: The Brits fighting with pro-Russian rebels," *BBC News*, October 19, 2015, https://www.bbc.com/news/world-europe-34568857, accessed: June 28, 2015.

97 The Czech prosecutors would use a similar approach while detaining "their" DNR/LNR foreign fighters returning from Donbas. They saw their active service in the ranks of the militias as a terrorist attacks upon an established and recognized state – Ukraine. See the Central-Eastern European chapter of this research monograph. For more on Stimson, see *BBC News*, "Oldham man jailed for Ukraine terror offence," July 14, 2017, https://www.bbc.com/news/uk-england-manchester-40612229, accessed: June 29, 2021.

98 Max Seddon, "How a British Blogger Became an Unlikely Star of the Ukraine Conflict: And Russia Today," *BuzzFeed News,* May 22, 2014, https://www.buzzfeednews.com/article/maxseddon/how-a-british-blogger-became-an-unlikely-star-of-the-ukraine, accessed: June 29, 2021.

99 Phillips allegedly attempted to break up an exhibition dedicated to the war in Georgia of 2008 which was held in the Georgian Embassy in London. See *Unian Information Agency,* "Ukraine calls on UK police to probe Graham Phillips for 'terrorist activity' in Donbas," August 8, 2018, https://www.unian.info/politics/10217576-ukraine-calls-on-uk-police-to-probe-graham-phillips-for-terrorist-activity-in-donbas.html, accessed: June 29, 2021. He also resurfaced in Kosovo and posted videos in which he called the country's leaders "war criminals and terrorists." See Die Morina, "UK Journalist Banned from Twitter Angers Some in Kosovo," *BalkanInsight,* March 11, 2019, https://balkaninsight.com/2019/03/11/uk-journalist-banned-from-twitter-angers-some-in-kosovo/, accessed: June 28, 2021

100 See https://www.youtube.com/watch?v=IuTrYXoiDgk, accessed: June 29, 2021 for the video posted by Phillips on his channel.

101 See https://www.youtube.com/channel/UCbwfUqs5Y6_jblWJwMIfRzA, accessed: April 22, 2022.

102 The "interview" was uploaded at https://www.youtube.com/watch?app=desktop&v=rNizGwjZbo0&feature=youtu.be, accessed: April 22, 2022 but quickly taken down by YouTube.

103 Rekawek, Ritzmann, and Schindler, *Violent Right-Wing Extremism and Terrorism,* 17.

104 See ibid. for a detailed account of how American, British, Finnish, French and Swedish counterparts reach out to their German brethren.

105 Author's interview with Dr Anton Shekhovtsov, expert on the Western European far right, Vienna, February 18, 2020.

106 Shekhovtsov, *Russia and the Western Far-Right,* 8701.

107 See https://archive.is/ciW28 (archived) for a summary of National Corps, Azov's political wing, international activities before mid-2019, accessed: June 28, 2021.

108 Ibid. And author's email exchange with Olena Semenyaka, the international secretary of the National Corps, June 7, 2020.

109 Adrien Nonjon, "Olena Semenyaka, The 'First Lady' of Ukrainian Nationalism," *illiberalism,* October 20, 2020, https://www.illiberalism.org/olena-semenyaka-the-first-lady-of-ukrainian-nationalism/, accessed: June 28, 2021.

110 Alexei Ovchinnikov, "Маргарита Зайдлер: Конечная цель фашистов - не Донецк, а Россия," *Комсомольская правда,* August 11, 2014, https://www.kp.ru/daily/26267.5/3145047/, accessed: June 28, 2021.

111 Author's WhatsApp interview with Daniel Koehler, director of GIRDS – German Institute for Radicalisation and De-Radicalisation Studies, April 6, 2020.

112 Author's WhatsApp interview with Nikolaus von Twickel, analysts for the "People's Republics" and an editor with the Center for Liberal Modernity in Berlin, December 21, 2020.

113 Author's WhatsApp interview witha foreign member of the Azov Battalion/Regiment who wished to remain anonymous, January 28, 2020.

114 Author's interview with a Ukrainian journalist, a native of Donbas, who reported from the frontlines throughout 2014 and 2015 and wished to remain anonymous, March 22, 2020.

115 *Frankfurter Allgemeine Zeitung,* "Mehr als 100 Deutsche sollen für Separatisten kämpfen," March 15, 2015, www.faz.net/aktuell/politik/ausland/mehr-als-100-deutsche-sollen-in-ostukraine-fuer-separatisten-kaempfen-13483893.html, accessed: June 28, 2021.

116 Kai Biermann et al., "Die braune internationale," *Die Zeit,* February 10, 2021, https://www.zeit.de/2021/07/faschismus-international-awd-neonazi-terrorimus-rechtsextremismus, accessed: June 28, 2021.

117 Kacper Rekawek, *Looks Can Be Deceiving: Extremism meets paramilitarism in Central and Eastern Europe* (Berlin: CEP Berlin, June 2021), https://www.counterextremism.com/sites/default/files/2021-06/CEP%20Report_Looks%20Can%20Be%20Deceiving_Extremism%20Meets%20Paramilitarism%20in%20CEE_June%202021_1.pdf, accessed: June 28, 2021.

118 Katerina Kovalenko, "Fight for the white race. How the Russian neo-Nazi Denis Nikitin promotes his ideas in Ukraine, and why the Azov Regiment," *Zaborona*, June 12, 2020, 17, https://zaborona.com/en/fight-for-the-white-race-how-the-russian-neo-nazi-denis-nikitin-promotes-his-ideas-in-ukraine-and-why-the-azov-regiment/, accessed: June 28, 2021.

119 Author's zoom interview with Robert Claus, expert on the German MMA scene and its extreme right connections, October 20, 2020.

120 *Deutsche Welle*, "AfD worker accused of ordering arson attack in Ukraine," January 15, 2019, https://www.dw.com/en/afd-worker-accused-of-ordering-arson-attack-in-ukraine/a-47093618, accessed: April 7, 2021.

121 Author's interview with Chris Holmsted Larsen of the Danish Centre for Prevention of Extremism, October 8, 2020.

122 For more on this see Chris Holmsted Larsen, "Danish Foreign Fighters: Past and Present Patterns," in Kacper Rekawek, ed., *Not Only Syria? The Phenomenon of Foreign Fighters in a Comparative Perspective* (The Hague: IOS Press, 2017), 12–21.

123 For more on this see e.g. James Hughes, *Chechnya: From Nationalism to Jihad* (Philadelphia: University of Pennsylavania Press, 2008).

124 Adam E. Kramer, "Islamic Battalions, Stocked with Chechens, Aid Ukraine in War with Rebels," *The New York Times*, July 7, 2015, https://www.nytimes.com/2015/07/08/world/europe/islamic-battalions-stocked-with-chechens-aid-ukraine-in-war-with-rebels.html, accessed: June 3, 2021.

125 Marcin Mamon, "The final days of a chechen commander fighting in Ukraine," *The Intercept*, February 27, 2015, https://theintercept.com/2015/02/27/isa-munayevs-war/, accessed: June 3, 2021.

126 Shaun Walker, "'We like partisan warfare:' Chechens fighting in Ukraine – on both sides," *The Guardian*, July 24, 2015, https://www.theguardian.com/world/2015/jul/24/chechens-fighting-in-ukraine-on-both-sides, accessed: June 3, 2021.

127 Emil Souleimanov, "Chechen Units Deployed in Eastern Ukraine," *The Central Asia-Caucasus Analyst*, June 4, 2014, http://www.cacianalyst.org/publications/analytical-articles/item/12990-chechen-units-deployed-in-eastern-ukraine.html, accessed: June 3, 2021; Shaun Walker, "Russia blamed for attack on Chechen pair who fought with Ukrainians," *The Guardian*, October 31, 2017, https://www.theguardian.com/world/2017/oct/31/russia-blamed-for-attack-on-chechen-couple-who-fought-with-ukrainian-forces, accessed: June 3, 2021.

128 Author's interview with Marcin Mamoń, Polish freelance journalist and an expert on the Chechen insurgents and fighters, the last reporter to interview Munayev before his death, June 7, 2021.

129 The seven included three actual fighters discussed below, plus one fighter's family (wife and two children). The seventh member of this contingent was supposed to have been found in the "Iron March" database, where an allegedly Dutch member was bragging about his participation in the war. See Cyril Rosman, "Nederlanders actief op gehackt forum voor neonazi's," *AD*, January 24, 2020, https://www.ad.nl/binnenland/nederlanders-actief-op-gehackt-forum-voor-neonazis~acf07aa8/, accessed: June 10, 2021. For more on these individuals see Gijs Weijenberg, Jeanine de Roy van Zuijdewijn, "The Forgotten Front: Dutch Foreign Fighters in Ukraine," 16 July 2021, *ICCT*, https://icct.nl/publication/the-forgotten-front-dutch-fighters-in-ukraine/, accessed: October 7, 2022.

130 See the introductory chapter of this monograph for a discussion of the push and pull factors.

131 See the introductory chapter for more on these issues and literature examples where such cases are presented.

132 Ondine van der Vleuten, "Axelaar met gouden hart sluit zich aan bij rebellenleger," *PZC*, September 30, 2017, https://www.pzc.nl/zeeuws-nieuws/axelaar-met-gouden-hart-sluit-zich-aan-bij-rebellenleger~aa00fd20/?referrer=https%3A%2F%2Fwww.diigo.com%2F, accessed: June 10, 2021.

133 Bergema and Weijenberg, "The Forgotten Front." Mid-2021 brought the news of his serious injury while attending to his farm which his wife communicated on his Facebook page. See https://www.facebook.com/pascal.hillebrand.754/posts/802112300692350, accessed: June 10, 2021.

134 For Klop's profile see Tobias den Hartog en Stefan Huijboom, "Brabander vecht in Oekraïne: 'Zo krijg ik eindelijk respect'," *AD*, January 31, 2015, https://www.ad.nl/buitenland/brabander-vecht-in-oekraine-zo-krijg-ik-eindelijk-respect~a2a80769/?referrer=https%3A%2F%2Fwww.diigo.com%2F, accessed: June 10, 2021.

135 Cyril Rosman, "Nederlander trekt met Koerden op tegen IS," *AD*, June 1, 2017, https://www.ad.nl/buitenland/nederlander-trekt-met-koerden-op-tegen-is~ad609dd1/, accessed: June 10, 2017.

136 Losh, "Ukraine turns a blind eye to ultrarightist militia."

137 Rosman, "Nederlander trekt met Koerden op tegen IS," and Cyril Rosman, "Nederlander die streed tegen IS komt om in Syrië," *AD*, February 17, 2018, https://www.ad.nl/binnenland/nederlander-die-streed-tegen-is-komt-om-in-syrie~ae86337a/, accessed: June 10, 2021.

138 For more on these ties see Shekhovtsov, *Russia and the Western Far-Right*, 262.

139 See https://pism.pl/file/885c4172-b380-4bb7-a1ea-8a334d91d9f2, accessed: June 9, 2021. This is supported by e.g. Legieć's calculations from 2017: Arkadiusz Legieć, "Profiling Foreign Fighters in Eastern Ukraine: A Theoretical Introduction" in Rekawek, ed., *Not Only Syria?*.

140 Author's interview with Eugeny Spirin, a freelance journalist, native of Luhansk, who observed the early stages of "People's Republics" at first hand, March 20, 2020.

141 Alexander Clapp, "Why American Right-Wingers Are Going to War in Ukraine," *Vice*, June 20, 2016, https://www.vice.com/en/article/nzw4pb/why-american-right-wingers-are-going-to-war-in-ukraine-id-en, accessed: June 9, 2021.

142 See e.g. Christopher Miller, "Soldier of Misfortune," *BuzzFeed*, April 9, 2021, https://www.buzzfeednews.com/article/christopherm51/craig-lang-ukraine-far-right-extremists-true-crime, accessed: June 9, 2021 for a profile of Craig Lang, who stands accused of a double murder in the U.S.

143 Paul Batruel, Thomas Trescher, and Peter Draxler, "Fischer zieht in den Krieg," *kurier.at*, February 15, 2017, http://dossier.kurier.at/de/y1nIKvJd/fischer-zieht-in-den-krieg/?page=1, accessed: June 9, 2021.

144 *hromadske international*, "Austrian Suspected of War Crimes in Ukraine. We Talked to His Co-Fighters," May 10, 2017, https://en.hromadske.ua/posts/austrian-suspected-of-war-crimes-in-ukraine-we-talked-to-his-co-fighters, accessed: June 9, 2021.

145 Clapp, "Why American Right-Wingers Are Going to War in Ukraine."

146 Борис Немировський, "Відень у «карателів» не вірить. Суд відпустив Бена Фішера, який воював за Україну Повний текст читайте тут," *Главком*, June 2, 2017, https://glavcom.ua/publications/viden-u-karateliv-ne-virit-sud-vidpustiv-bena-fishera-shcho-voyuvav-za-ukrajinu-418369.html, accessed: June 9, 2021.

147 Batruel, Trescher, and Draxler, "Fischer zieht in den Krieg June 9."

148 Clapp, "Why American Right-Wingers Are Going to War in Ukraine."

149 Batruel, Trescher, and Draxler, "Fischer."

150 Clapp, "Why American Right-Wingers Are Going to War in Ukraine."

151 Ibid.

152 *RFE/RL*, "Poland Arrests Austrian Man Suspected of War Crimes in Eastern Ukraine," April 30, 2017, https://www.rferl.org/a/ukraine-poland-arrests-austrian-war-crimes/28460416.html, accessed: June 9, 2021.

153 Author's interview with a researcher of the Norwegian far right who wished to remain anonymous, October 6, 2020.

154 Author's interview with John Faerseth, Norwegian independent journalist specializing in the topic of the far right, January 31, 2020.

155 Emile Ghessen, "Ukraine – Europe's Forgotten War: Robin Hood Complex Official Documentary," YouTube, June 17, 2019, https://www.youtube.com/watch?v=5BXYZqgDelw, accessed: June 9, 2021 for a documentary which features Furholm in Ukraine.

156 *hromadske international*, "From Oslo to Donbas: Why Was a Norwegian Kicked out of the Ukrainian Army?," October 4, 2018, https://en.hromadske.ua/posts/from-oslo-to-donbas-why-was-a-norwegian-kicked-out-of-the-ukrainian-army?fbclid=IwAR15GrmSJdTt5iIE5aE9cOml6IAcR2vdZlVkJjaed_-l62EIEODgO9ax-AM, accessed: June 9, 2021.

157 Simon Shuster and Billy Perrigo, "Like, Share, Recruit: How a White-Supremacist Militia Uses Facebook to Radicalize and Train New Members," *Time*, January 7, 2021, https://time.com/5926750/azov-far-right-movement-facebook/, accessed: June 9, 2021.

158 See https://nationalcorps.org/national-corps-statement-on-the-information-provocation-by-time-magazine/ for a statement by the National Corps, the Azov movement's political wing, on the issue, January 11, 2021, accessed: June 9, 2021.

159 Jordan Green, "The lost boys of Ukraine: How the war abroad beckoned American white supremacists," *Triad City Beat*, January 19, 2020, https://triad-city-beat.com/the-lost-boys-of-ukraine/, accessed: June 9, 2021.

160 Author's interview with Olena Semenyaka, March 20, 2020.

161 See *meduza*, "Enemy of the State or its founding element? Yan Petrovsky, Russian nationalist accused of war crimes in Ukraine, was deported from Norway," January 20, 2017, https://meduza.io/en/feature/2017/01/20/enemy-of-the-state-or-its-founding-element, accessed: June 9, 2021 for his profile.

162 Ibid. and author's interview with John Faerseth, Norwegian independent journalist specializing in the topic of the far right, January 31, 2020.

163 *The Interpreter*, "Russian Neo-Nazi Paramilitary Group, Rusich, to Withdraw – Freezing of Conflict Or a Feint?," July 10, 2015, https://pressimus.com/Interpreter_Mag/press/9072, accessed: June 9, 2021.

164 Hayla Coynash, "Russian wanted for war crimes in Donbas arrested in Norway," *Kharkiv Human Rights Protection Group*, October 21, 2016, http://khpg.org/en/1476975539, accessed: June 9, 2021.

165 *The Interpreter*, "Russian Neo-Nazi Paramilitary Group."

166 Author's interview with John Faerseth, Norwegian independent journalist specializing in the topic of the far right, January 31, 2020.

167 See the author's twitter feed for documentation of Petrovsky's tour in Poland – https://twitter.com/KacperRekawek/status/689922942545850369?s=20, https://twitter.com/KacperRekawek/status/689819664885661696/photo/1, accessed: June 9, 2021. His tour allowed him to meet pro-Russian members of the Polish far-right milieu.

168 *meduza*, "Enemy of the State."

169 Betsy Woodruf Swan, "They tried to get Trump to care about right-wing terrorism. He ignored them," *Politico*, August 26, 2020, https://www.politico.com/news/2020/08/26/trump-domestic-extemism-homeland-security-401926, accessed: March 30, 2022.

170 Tim Lister, "The Nexus Between Far-Right Extremists in the United States and Ukraine," *CTC Sentinel* 13, no. 4 (April 2020), https://ctc.usma.edu/the-nexus-between-far-right-extremists-in-the-united-states-and-ukraine/, accessed: March 30, 2022.

171 Max Rose and Ali H. Soufan, "We Once Fought Jihadists. Now We Battle White Supremacists," *The New York Times*, February 8, 2020, https://www.nytimes.com/2020/02/11/opinion/politics/white-supremacist-terrorism.html, accessed: March 30, 2022.

172 Clapp, "Why American Right-Wingers Are Going to War in Ukraine."

173 Kacper Rekawek, *Looks can be deceiving: Extremism meets paramilitarism in Central and Eastern Europe* (Counter Extremism Project, June 2021), https://www.counterextremism.com/sites/default/files/2021-06/CEP%20Report_Looks%20Can%20Be%20Deceiving_Extremism%20Meets%20Paramilitarism%20in%20CEE_June%202021_1.pdf, accessed: March 30, 2022.

174 Ibid. 25.

175 Jordan Green, "The lost boys of Ukraine: How the war abroad beckoned American white supremacists," *Triad City Beat*, January 19, 2020, https://triad-city-beat.com/the-lost-boys-of-ukraine/, accesssed, April 1, 2022.

176 The Soufan Center, *White Supremacy Extremism: The Transnational Rise of the Violent White Supremacist Movement* (New York: The Soufan Center, 2019), 29, https://thesoufancenter.org/wp-content/uploads/2019/09/Report-by-The-Soufan-Center-White-Supremacy-Extremism-The-Transnational-Rise-of-The-Violent-White-Supremacist-Movement.pdf, accessed: February 10, 2021.

177 Green, "The lost boys of Ukraine."

178 Polly Mosendz, "American Volunteer Fighter 'Franko' Dies Fighting Separatists in Eastern Ukraine," *The Atlantic*, August 20, 2014, https://www.theatlantic.com/international/archive/2014/08/american-volunteer-fighter-franko-dies-fighting-separatists-in-eastern-ukraine/378818/, accessed: April 1, 2022.

179 Author's WhatsApp exchange with Christopher Miller, a *Politico* journalist with more than a decade of experience in reporting for Ukraine, also for the likes of *BuzzFeed News* or *RFE/RL*, 29 September 2021.

180 See Bentley's website at http://www.russelltexasbentley.com/p/about.html, accessed: April 1, 2022.

181 *Donbassforeningen*, "Interview with Italian Volunteer 'Nemo'."

182 *United States District Court for the District of Maryland*, "Patrick Mathews Detention Motion," January 21, 2020, https://www.documentcloud.org/documents/6664640-Patrick-Mathews-Detention-Motion.html, accessed: March 30, 2022.

183 As it later transpired, one had actually been a former member of another far-right terrorist entity, the Base. See Ben Makuch and Marc Lamoreux, "U.S. Man Deported from Ukraine Was Marine Dropout Linked to Neo-Nazi Terror Group," *Vice News*, March 25, 2021, https://www.vice.com/en/article/g5b43y/us-man-deported-from-ukraine-was-marine-dropout-linked-to-neo-nazi-terror-group, accessed: March 30, 2022.

184 Christopher Miller, Ukraine Deported Two American Members of a Neo-Nazi Group Who Tried to Join a Far-Right Military Unit for "Combat Experience," *Buzzfeed News*, October 8, 2020, https://www.buzzfeednews.com/amphtml/christopherm51/ukraine-deports-american-neo-nazi-atomwaffen-division?__twitter_impression=true, accessed: March 30, 2022.

185 Rekawek, Ritzmann, and Schindler, *Violent Right-Wing Extremism and Terrorism*, 7.

186 Clapp, "Why American Right-Wingers Are Going to War in Ukraine."

187 See chap. 3 of this monograph.

188 See https://twitter.com/kooleksiy/status/1179532561640562688?s=20, accessed: October 21, 2021 for Oleksyi Kuzmenko's comments on the matter.

189 Sean Rubinsztein-Dunlop, Suzanne Dredge, and Michael Workman, "From Neo-Nazi to militant: The foreign fighters in Ukraine who Australia's laws won't stop," *ABC News*, April 30, 2018, https://www.abc.net.au/news/2018-05-01/foreign-fighters-return-to-australia-with-military-training/9696784, accessed: October 22, 2021. Another Australian also fought in the ranks of the Right Sector – see ibid. This meager Australian contribution was partially mirrored as far as Canadian fighters were concerned. This is a unique case as Canada hosts a diaspora of +1 million Canadian-Ukrainians, of whom some, as Ukrainians, traveled to their country of origin to fight in the war. These, however, could have hardly been regarded as foreign fighters – they might have been diaspora fighters at best since some, if not

most, still held Ukrainian passports. At the same time, the diaspora also fundraised for the Ukrainian war effort and some of that money trickled down to the volunteer battalions – see, e.g. Clapp, "Why American Right-Wingers Are Going to War in Ukraine." The situation changed in 2022 when seemingly large numbers of Canadians tried to enlist with Ukraine's International Legion. See Tom Blackwell, "Canadian infantry veteran enters 'living hell' in Ukraine to capture village from Russians," *National Post*, April 5, 2022, https://nationalpost.com/news/canada/living-hell-canadian-veteran-enters-chaotic-combat-in-ukraine-to-capture-village-from-russians, accessed: April 22, 2022.

9

CENTRAL-EASTERN EUROPEANS (CEE)

More Red than Brown?

Introduction

Post-communist countries from the Central-Eastern Europe (CEE) found them-selves in a unenviable position after the eruption of the Russo-Ukraine war.[1] In 2014, they had celebrated 25th anniversaries of ridding themselves of the Soviet dominance, which was followed by integration into the EU and NATO, respec-tively. At the same time, an attempt by Ukraine, for some of them – their Eastern neighbor, via Euromaidan, to initiate a similar trajectory for itself was met with a virulent Russian opposition and a war in Donbas. For some of these countries, such as Poland or the Baltic States, memories of a Soviet/Russian dominance of the CEE were still vivid and Moscow's policy toward Ukraine might have seemed like another example of their eastern neighbor's imperialism. Interestingly, such worries seemed more distant in the likes of the Czech Republic, Slovakia or Hungary, which all had a tradition of political forces positively attuned to Russia.[2]

The conflict also put the region's far-right scenes under pressure – on the one hand, as will be shown, these had a fair share of pro-Russian sentiment (instilled from their early days – late nineteenth/early twentieth centuries, e.g. Poland; or acquired – after 2010 in Hungary) but were at the same time concerned with Russia's dismembering of a neighboring state, and some of their members, at least initially, favored Ukraine. In their eyes, this was a country protecting its territo-rial integrity against an external aggression.[3] At the same time, the organizations from the milieu they belonged to would usually side with Russia in the Russo-Ukraine conflict but had, as will be shown, problems with outright endorsements of the "People's Republics" which harked back to communist nostalgia, a no-go for the CEE far rightists, in their external communication. Unsurprisingly, the CEE post-communist proponents had no such qualms and fans of the Donetsk People's Republic (DNR) and the Luhansk People's Republic (LNR) could be

DOI: 10.4324/9781003192992-9

found in the region's "red" organizations, i.e. amongst far-left parties in Poland or the Czech or Slovak paramilitary organizations which were largely pan-Slavic (read: pro-Russian) in nature.

The following chapter will outline these differences and take stock of the brown-red cocktail's composition in the CEE vis-à-vis the war in Ukraine, while looking at individuals who found themselves on the front lines in Eastern Ukraine and organizations who sent people to the war.

Baltic States

The far-right or the brown-red cocktail moniker does not give justice to the ideological leaning of the foreign fighters from the three Baltic States, i.e. Estonia, Latvia and Lithuania in Ukraine. According to Egle Murauskaite, an expert on these [Baltic] fighters, many of them might have been "into guns but not the far right." She divided the Baltic participants joining the cause of Ukraine since 2014 into two categories: (1) a larger, ideologically motivated group of medical personnel, psychologists, and NGO workers delivering aid, determined "to make a stand, so that Russia does not come after us [Lithuania] next," and (2) the actual fighters – individuals with some prior military training who wanted put their skills to test, or feel a rush of adrenaline.[4] Similarly to the French case, amateur adventure seekers falling into this second category, and usually operating more secretively, were looking to leverage the connections made by the first group to make it into the battlefield in Ukraine and establish links with volunteer battalions.[5] Such attempts were rarely successful as the first group was cautious in terms of sharing its address books with more combat oriented compatriots.[6] The governments, not keen on advertising the presence of such fighters in Ukraine so that Russia could not use this against them on the international scene, kept a low profile in relation to their returns. This enabled the Baltic states to maintain a degree of "deniability" vis-à-vis their existence and their trips to Ukraine.[7]

Unsurprisingly, a different approach was maintained in relation to fighters who joined the "separatists" – these individuals could count on no "see no evil, hear no evil" approach of the authorities. Consequently, Estonia extradited an ethnic Russian citizen of the country to Ukraine on terrorism charges and Latvia, which prohibits participation of its citizens in an armed conflict without the consent of the authorities, did the same with members of "separatist" militias.[8] Latvia also tried to prosecute Benes Ayo (a Latvian national, a self-proclaimed activist of "the Other Russia [party in Russia], the Communist Party of the DNR and the Headquarters for the Defence of Russian Schools in Latvia"). He was sought by the police for his alleged involvement in subversive activities in the country.[9]

Czech Republic[10] and Slovakia

The two above-mentioned states might have parted ways on January 1, 1993, when Czechoslovakia officially disappeared but this seems not to have mattered that much to the Czech and Slovak foreign fighters present in the war in Ukraine.

One of them, a Slovak, Martin "Sojka" Keprta, attempted to form a "Czecho-Slovak legion" (the name of the units consisting of Czech and Slovaks present in the ranks of the Entente armies in World War I) in the DNR but allegedly found no takers amongst the Czech and Slovak fighters.[11] Other sources, however, showed that a "Czecho-Slovak" unit, consisting of eight people within the Pyatnashka Brigade did, in fact, exist. It openly advertised on Facebook and asked for volunteers who were under the age of 40, with a track record of military service (also as former draftees in the Czech or Slovak armies) and Russian speakers to come forward. It also offered clues on the logistics – a volunteer needed to reach out, then fix a Russian visa and get himself to Rostov on the Don, where he would stay in a "verified" hotel and then would be picked up and driven to Donetsk.[12] Not that many, it seems, picked up these clues and traveled eastward but the contingents from the two countries in the "separatist" forces might have outnumbered the French one, an impressive feat given the fact that France, with a population four and a half times larger than both the CEE states, could have theoretically produced a far larger contingent. As the two contingents received joint coverage by the local media, experts and academics, these will be discussed together below but the larger Czech mobilization will occupy most of the space.

Tomáš Forró, an authority on the subject of the Czech and Slovak foreign fighters, who spent time with them during his reporting from Donetsk, divided such fighters into three categories: mercenaries-businessmen, who use the war as a chance for making money outside of their fighting on the front, thugs – former criminals (the first two categories were to overlap) and idealists.[13] As the individual cases of the Czech and Slovak fighters will be discussed and the proportion of these categories within their ranks will become clear, a few common things are visible from the outset.

1. Both the Czechs and Slovaks almost exclusively joined the "separatist" ranks – the only exception being the two Slovak members of the Azov Battalion, one a former French foreign legionnaire, the other escaping prosecution for property crime in Slovakia. Moreover, the local far-right scenes, with very exceptions, squarely lined up behind Russia and the "separatists."[14]

2. These scenes had not been the source of mobilization for the "separatist." The individuals who went to Donbas to fight rather had "communist or post-communist and pan-Slavic sympathies. They were mobilized through paramilitary pro-communist structures and not nationalist political parties."[15] At the same time, however, they expressed anti-migrant, anti-Muslim sympathies[16] and were decisively anti-Western, anti-liberal ("felt repressed by the Western culture while in the Czech Republic [...] and felt unhappy at home") in their political orientation which, paradoxically, brought them closer to the archetypal Western far-right position.[17] One would describe the Ukrainians as "demented fascists paid by Jewish oligarchs" and summarized his worldview as that of "Eastern values against Western values, against pedophilia and faggotry."[18] In short, they constituted the red in the brown-red cocktail that was present on the front lines in Ukraine.

3. Both contingents featured individuals literally "running away from trouble," including these sought by the law enforcement, a strong push factor in a decision of a potential foreign fighter who considers deploying to a war zone.[19]

The Czech fighters were said to have been avid consumers of Russian or pro-Russian media, or Facebook pages professing their pro-Russian stance, present in both the Czech and Slovak (two similar languages and both official languages of Czechoslovakia) social media environment. The latter not only provided them with narratives deployed by the "separatists" and Moscow in Donbas e.g. "fascists attacking innocent civilians in Donetsk," or Ukraine utilizing chemical weapons against its adversaries there, but also useful contacts which allowed certain Czechs to get in touch with their compatriots in Donetsk,[20] e.g.:

> I saw a "Russia is our real friend" page on Facebook, it had 12,000 members. This is where I got to know one woman whom I asked as to how I could get there [to Donetsk] and if it is worth going there. She gave me a contact to a Facebook profile of a guy who knew how things stood there [in Donetsk]. I asked him what I needed to join them [in Donetsk]. This was at the beginning of the Summer of 2015. He wrote back saying I needed a Russian visa and he would then pick me up.[21]

The first Czechs who got to Donbas, who deployed there as early as June 2014 – then acted as their compatriots first ports of call while on the way to "separatist" controlled Donetsk. The first duo, Ivo Stejskal and Vojtěch Hlinka, went there together and on their own – they had no support from paramilitary, pan-Slavic Czech groups which only appeared on the scene a year later. By September 2014, both were dead, admittedly a relatively rare occurrence amongst the foreign fighters in Ukraine.[22] Of the duo, the former, who spoke some Russian, had been better known as he was filmed giving a speech at a rally in Donetsk, and was later interviewed by the Russian TV.[23] Stejskal was already in his forties, a former physical education teacher and a gym instructor, who came to Donbas to prevent a "genocide of the Russian-Ukrainian people" and stand with the "Slavs." Him and Hlinka, who had to navigate their way through Ukraine – just like the first initial contingent of the French who trekked to Donbas, and not utilize the later Moscow-Rostov-Donetsk pipeline – effectively had been the Czech trailblazers.[24]

They were later followed by at least 10 of their known compatriots,[25] Ukrainian authorities put their number at 20,[26] and potentially as many as up to 30 with some remaining anonymous.[27] Some seemed to have been more ideologically minded, others motivated by the push factor of escaping trouble at home, and finally there was a group which allegedly searched for adventure and a bout of adrenaline.[28] Just like in other contingents, some of these had been soldiers prior to their self-deployment to Donbas, e.g. Martin Sukup, a self-declared communist who "openly rejected Czech Republic's accession to NATO," which cost him his career in the military, and later saw his business collapse. In order to improve his situation following these setbacks, he joined the "separatists" in the summer of 2014 and later rose to become a lieutenant colonel in the forces of the DNR.[29] His obtaining a high military rank disproves the above-mentioned theory on the foreign fighter's lack of battlefield experience while in Ukraine and their under-appreciation by their hosts, especially by the "separatists," as was seen in the case of the French contingent. One cannot forget, however, that for a Czech, i.e. a Slav who might even have had some knowledge of Russian prior to his arrival in Donetsk, must have had it easier while in Eastern Ukraine and could have more smoothly connected with the relevant individuals or units.

Such was most probably the case of another Czech who also rose to the rank of a lieutenant colonel, Oldřich Grund. He had worked in St. Petersburg before the war as a construction technician. He traveled to Donetsk through Russia, independently of Stejskal and Hlinka, and joined the fight in its very early days – in the ranks of the unit led by the infamous Igor Girkin, the de facto instigator of the war in Donbas.[30] He later settled in Donetsk, got married and cut off his ties to the Czech Republic, refusing to pay alimony for his Czech son.[31] His war exploits later led to his sentencing to 15 years on terrorism charges.[32] This seemingly bizarre occurrence had a legal explanation as the Czech Republic, which bans fighting in the ranks of foreign armies without the authorization from the country's president, could not have applied this law against individuals who joined armed forces of non-recognized "People's Republics." Instead, the courts came to rely on the penalties for terrorism as they interpreted the activities of Grund as joining an illegal entity and staging terrorist attacks against a recognized state – Ukraine.

A similar approach was deployed while addressing the case of Lukáš Nováček, Alexej Faděev and another, as yet unnamed Czech individual still in Donetsk.[33] The former allegedly joined DNR forces in summer of 2015. In January 2022, he received a six-year jail sentence for participation in an organized crime group.[34] He denies involvement in any fighting for the DNR and claims he only traveled to Russia to meet a girlfriend whom he conversed with on a Russian social media site, and it was her, and her friend, who convinced him eventually to travel to Donetsk and join the DNR's "armed forces." Nováček allegedly set off on his journey due to specific push factors – "a difficult breakup with his girlfriend" in the Czech Republic and lack of financial means.[35] Faděev, a Belarussian residing in the Czech Republic, is facing a similar stint in jail for his service in the DNR's Republican Guard (which featured the likes of the "International" Pyatnashka Brigade). He rejected the terrorism accusation and claimed he was there "to help people" and to oppose "fascists who took power [in Ukraine]."[36] According to an expert on the Czech far-right and paramilitary scenes, two further fighters, Pavel Botka and Jiří Urbánek, faced similar charges.[37] Allegedly former criminals, one adopted in his childhood by a Czech agent of a Russian intelligence service, and a former French foreign legionnaire,[38] had illustrious careers while in Donetsk. Botka lost his leg after stepping on a landmine[39] and both later left the DNR forces, converted to Islam and allegedly attempted to establish a Donetsk-based branch of a Czech custom made furniture producer.[40] It seems that even while in "the People's Republics" they remained businessmen at heart.

The same fate, if he was to return to the Czech Republic, could possibly await Alojz Polák and the above-mentioned Sukup, both former members of the so-called Czechoslovak Soldiers in Reserve for Peace (*Českoslovenští vojáci v záloze za mír*), a Czech paramilitary organization, who were allegedly tasked with preparing the ground for further arrivals of their comrades to Donetsk, their training and then re-deployment to the Czech Republic, potentially to engage in political violence or terrorism.[41]

"Czechoslovak Soldiers" formed in 2015 as a self-defense, bottom-up group which allegedly was happy to assist the Czech state during emergencies, such as the migrant crisis.[42] The group was led by a former high level Czech military officer who stepped down from the army and publicly called NATO a "criminal organization." Its alleged motto was the phrase: "we are against war. Our politicians and not Russian soldiers are our enemies," and its members had a history of threatening the local politicians with violence if the Czech Republic was to find itself in a conflict on the side of NATO. The group spoke of "international elite" or "economic elite" which promote the agenda of "representative democracy to further weaken the citizens' freedom and power."[43] With allegedly 2,000 active members in 2015, it might not have been the classic, in the Western sense, "far right" but its members were coming from an anti-immigrant (it rose to fame during the 2015 migrant crisis), nativist, homophobic milieu which saw itself first as pan-Slavic, pro-"peace," and peddled post-communist nostalgias. In this sense, it formally had relatively little in common with the local "nationalist" scene (with some exceptions – especially related to the Freedom and Direct Democracy, *Svoboda a přímá demokracie*, radical right/libertarian party with 22 members in the Czech parliament)[44] but shared some of its sentiments. As the years went by, however, the group lost its radical appeal and slowly became dormant or a collection of paramilitary hobbyists who sought contacts with the Czech security sector on the local level and attempted to organize public awareness or education campaigns.[45]

By 2021, the "Czechoslovak Soldiers" seemed irrelevant. One issue, however, seemed troubling – one of its members, Miloš Ouřecký, who fought in Donbas safely returned home and seemed not to have faced any legal sanctions,[46] unlike some of his colleagues whose cases were progressing through the courts (see the case of Grund discussed above),[47] or Pavel Kafka who received a three year sentence for participation in "organized crime group,"[48] or Erik Eštu, who joined the Czech army after returning from Donbas – he received a suspended sentence and the loss of his military rank).[49] This bizarre duopoly ended in April 2021 as the Czech police, on the back of a wider diplomatic spat with Russia,[50] moved in against the pro-Russian infrastructure in the country, including the "Czechoslovak Soldiers" whose five members, amongst them Ouřecký, were arrested for supporting terrorism – three of these were retained behind bars in the pre-trial period.[51] Since 2016, the country's domestic security agency (BIS) was reporting that the local paramilitary scene uses contacts with "Russian spies" while turning its members into foreign fighters.[52] This perceived connection might have been used as an excuse to go after the pro-"separatist," and by default pro-Russian, paramilitaries while tensions with Moscow were running high. At the same time, the Czech police could have waited with its move against the "Czechoslovak Soldiers" once court cases against individual foreign fighters who returned from Donbas clear through different court levels (as was the case throughout 2020). With the first sentences becoming legally binding, the theory goes, the police arrested the key members of the above-mentioned organization.[53] Prior to such arrests, in early 2021, Czech Republic also effectively banned "armed groups" described as "armed, paramilitary in nature [...] intended for the armed pursuit of goals based on political, religious or other ideologies, [handling] weapons, [seeking] to gain access to weapons, or [organizing] people who possess/handle weapons."[54]

The collapse of the paramilitary infrastructure, which supported some of the travels of Czech fighters eastward, came on top of other surprising developments related to that country's contingent in Eastern Ukraine. Some of its members who are still in Donetsk publicly traded accusations of spreading "lies" about one another and even plotting assassinations of their supposed comrades.[55] To add some spice to the accusations, such plans were allegedly instigated by Nela Lisková, a former high-level member of the paramilitary National Home Guard (*Národní domobrana*, one of the above-mentioned paramilitary groups which sprang to life in the Czech Republic around the time of the migrant crisis) and a self-proclaimed "honorary consul" of the DNR in the Czech city of Ostrava, whom the fighter marked for assassination was said to have been enamored with.[56] The illegal "consulate," effectively an NGO, was closed down following the court's decision in 2018,[57] and Lisková also lost her connections to the DNR as she was not allowed into the "People's Republic" a year later. This might have something to do with the fact that her anti-Muslim, anti-migrant and racist ("A black Muslim wave with the smell of death is rolling over us"),[58] views, could have irked her "anti-fascist" contacts in "the People's Republic" or that she failed to link up Donetsk companies with potential business partners in the Czech Republic.[59] It must be stated that the failure of her "honorary consulate" was partly mirrored by the controversy around the self-proclaimed Novorossiya's embassy in Slovakia, which allegedly failed in its advertised services of moving goods and money between the "People's Republic" and Bratislava, including ones intended for the benefit of the Slovak fighters.[60]

The similarities between the "consulate" and the "embassy's" lack of spectacular business successes are not the only ties that bind the Czech and the Slovak contingent in the "separatist" ranks. Both were effectively animated by similar motivations, and operationalized via similar, if not the same, online connections. The less numerous Slovak fighters (allegedly numbering seven)[61] also readily spoke of their "fight" against the West or the EU in the East of Ukraine,[62] or "fascist" Ukraine,[63] or "fascists" while preventing "killings of women and children."[64] Similarly, the fighters, with the exception of the likes of Mário Reitman, a self-proclaimed "racist skinhead,"[65] would have contested or have been appalled by accusations of allegedly belonging to or sharing views of the far right. Nonetheless, their most visible member and one allegedly with the highest rank in the DNR forces, Martin "Sojka" Keprta, former member of the paramilitary *Slovenskí branci* (SB, Slovak Conscripts, an organization in some ways akin to the Czech paramilitary militias in their pan-Slavic and pro-Russian outlook, but explicitly rejecting any far-right connotations)[66] stated that he "does not like values which are propagated and defended by the EU. From LGBT to excessive humanism, according to my perception the EU destroys nations and brings up a citizen of the world."[67] Such thoughts, expressed by a former member of an organization whose current members are said to privately consider "refugees, LGBT community, the Roma and [...] Antifa" as "threats,"[68] situate the SB closer to Western European far right, despite bonding with their Russian contacts and comrades, including the biker gang of the Night Wolves, over "anti-fascist" issues and values.[69] This duopoly serves as a repetition of a situation from the Czech Republic where the likes of the "Czechoslovak Soldiers" were coming from a post-communist, pan-Slavic milieu and seemingly had nothing to do with the far right but examining some of their statements, and those of their members, forced anyone studying them to alter their reading of these organizations.

In reality, however, the above-mentioned lofty motivations as to why a given Slovak joined the forces of the "People's Republics" seemed to have, at least partly, cover up for more mundane rationalizations or push factors before trekking eastward. Some were former criminals or had been escaping the latest sentences handed down by the Slovak courts or allegedly could not have found their place back at home.[70] One was a former soldier, he was allegedly joined by at least two anonymous others, who traveled to Donetsk while "on leave."[71] The contacts for such travels were allegedly found, just like in the Czech case, on the social media, as was admitted by Sojka, who later got married while in Donetsk and settled there.[72] He was allegedly joined by two of his countrymen and up to four Czechs who are still in Donetsk.[73]

Hungary

Hungary, just like Poland and Slovakia, is one of Ukraine's western neighbors. The country is seen as Russia's "closest ally"[74] in the EU and has a history of tension with Ukraine related to the situation of the Hungarian minority in the latter country.[75] The country possesses a vibrant far-right scene which, although anti-communist and by default anti-Russian in the 1990s, turned decidedly pro-Moscow in the 2000s. This trend has accelerated especially after the emergence of the Jobbik (The Movement for a Better Hungary) in 2003.[76] What is more, the far right has displayed an overtly paramilitary tinge with Jobbik's

Hungarian Guard and other, smaller outfits, emerging in the 2000s and contributing to, alongside the rightward shift of the post-2010 conservative government of Viktor Orban, the country's image as a "Venezuela for the new right."[77] In these conditions, one could have expected a groundswell of interest in the conflict in Ukraine, and potentially more than a trickle of volunteers into the ranks of especially the pro-Russian "separatists."

Allegedly, the Hungarian far right did not disappoint and its "Legion of St. Istvan" was said to have appeared in the ranks of the "separatists." It styled itself as "a right wing traditionalist organization linking Russians and Hungarians." Thirty of such Hungarians were said to have been wounded in the fighting and one was said to have been killed.[78] Despite such grandiose claims, and French fighters' sightings of individual Hungarians in the "separatist" ranks,[79] neither the author nor the Hungarian experts interviewed found any evidence of the "Legion" being more than just an online creation.[80] Indeed, journalists admitted there were just two Hungarians amongst the foreign fighters in Donbas.[81] These disappointing numbers emerged against the backdrop of the above-mentioned staunch pro-Russianness of the far-right milieu,[82] which, in the words of one well informed observer, suited Russia just fine: "The Kremlin wanted to use the Hungarian [far right] parties and organizations to shore up support for itself in the country by infiltrating the far-right movement, more specifically, Jobbik, the main far-right party of that time. Their members were never intended for combat – they rather divide the far-right movement and the Hungarian society along relations to the West and Russia, while spreading pro-Russian narratives."[83] Only one far rightist, an assistant to a Jobbik MP, and a veteran of the Yugoslav wars of the 1990s, came forward to state he was meant to join the "separatists" but had to stay behind while working in the parliament.[84] This statement indicates the idea of trekking to Ukraine to fight in the war there seemed like an attractive proposition to veterans of previous wars, themselves members of a rather exclusive, former fighters' society.

One Hungarian, however, coming from a post-communist and pro-Russian, and not the far-right milieu, trekked eastward and fought in the ranks of the Sparta Battalion of the "separatist" forces.[85] A former policeman, awarded for his participation in the defense of the Hungarian national broadcaster's building during the 2006 Budapest riots,[86] he found himself shunned after the change of government which, allegedly, saw him as a black sheep in the police force. He eventually traveled to Donetsk via Moscow. It remains unclear if he had accomplices in Hungary but he later spoke of someone who helped him master the Russian language beforehand. He returned to Hungary to claim the inheritance from his deceased father and upon return was arrested. He later received a suspended sentence for serving in a foreign military without the authorities' consent (i.e. a military that was not allied with Hungary and was outside NATO).[87] This was a pretty rare occurrence for any country in Europe which to a large extent chose to ignore the issue of such returnees.

Poland

In 2017, a prominent Polish monthly nationalist publication carried an article on the country's alleged "timid nationalism" as the movement failed to create a "wide social front" to support its goals. This, the author decried, was happening against the backdrop of nationalism "enjoying the best of times in its post-World War II history" with "nationalist organizations flourishing and the nationalists' marches [...] attracting thousands." What is more, the term *narodowiec* (describing a member of the Polish nationalist milieu) "stopped being associated with a subculture and lost its pejorative connotations, and a result of that many young people openly call themselves nationalists [...]."[88] Indeed, the nationalists' successes, associated especially with the celebrations of Poland's independence day on November 11 in Warsaw, which they came to dominate, was widely noted abroad.[89] Consequently, the Polish milieu and other Central-Eastern European nationalist or far-right scenes began to be viewed as rising stars in the broader extreme right wing (XRW) European family.[90] As it turns out, the local nationalists themselves had a different view of the situation.

> "Timidness" of Polish nationalism mostly concerned its ongoing (lack of) political success and the fact that the divided milieu punched above its weight for one event a year – the above-mentioned November 11 – but failed to translate it into a vehicle for closing ranks and achieving a profound and long-lasting political success.[91] What is more, the "timidness" also extends to the issue of militancy and by extension, foreign fighting in the name of causes which, as was demonstrated, were close to the hearts of Europe's far right, i.e. the Ukraine war. Of course, the Polish far-right scene took an interest in the conflict, and sections of the milieu picked sides, but very few, if any, of its members actually trekked eastward to fight. In short, the milieu, which allegedly brought out "60,000 nationalists" onto the streets of downtown Warsaw resembled, to paraphrase the title a famous film, "a mouse that failed to roar and instead squeaked."[92]

The conflict put the Polish far right in an unenviable position. It could not, as many of its Western counterparts did, claim any degree of remoteness as Poland borders Ukraine and, at the end of 2020, 500,000 plus Ukrainian migrant workers were registered in Poland.[93] What is more, during the Euromaidan and the early stages of the war a sizeable contingent of Poland's journalists, experts, humanitarian activists deployed eastward to assist, observe and report from the country.[94] Consequently, the Polish public had been relatively well informed of the situation on the ground and generally sided with Ukraine.[95] The Polish nationalist position went against the grain as the milieu had traditionally been anti-German and had spells of pro-Russian pan-Slavism or even pro-Sovietism post-1945. After 1989, it also displayed a fair degree of anti-Americanism and opposed integration with the EU or NATO, which hardly won it popularity amongst the wider Polish public.[96] At the same time, however, the war in a neighboring country resulted with a "paramilitary boom" in Poland as "the phenomenon was normalized by the media and in the public," and consequently, organizations seen as "patriotic" enjoyed a surge in popularity and/or membership. These, however, had rarely been ideological or outright "nationalist" in nature but the above-mentioned boom was subsequently inaccurately interpreted outside of Poland as a part of a political wave which carried the right-wing conservative Law and Justice party to power in Poland in late 2015.[97] In fact, the paramilitary organizations had existed before the war in Ukraine and the far right had been mobilizing successfully before the arrival of the Law and Justice party in power[98] – e.g. for the purpose of the so-called "patriots' march" in Wrocław, which annually attracted thousands and had been more radical than the November 11 celebrations in Warsaw.[99]

At the same time, however, normalization of paramilitarism and the Law and Justice's failed and then aborted attempts to politically co-opt the Independence Day celebrations[100] allowed the Polish far right literally to punch above its weight while benefiting from the patriotic surge. One of the axis of this surge, apart from the above-mentioned paramilitarism, had been the rehabilitation of the anti-communist post-World War II underground, the so-called cursed/damned/doomed soldiers, ridiculed or criminalized before 1989 and insufficiently, according to their defenders, celebrated in post-communist Poland.[101] Again, this rehabilitation was an irony of history for the Polish far right – it did bring it young recruits and a wave of public interest in studies devoted to underground units of nationalist background. The recruits, however, idealized these fighters who, in the 1940s, fought against the Polish communist government and the Soviet Russia which supported it. Consequently, they saw modern day Russia as a political inheritor of the USRR and its attack on Ukraine, as much as it might to some extent have pleased them,[102] as a development which was not automatically beneficial to Kyiv's other neighbor (Poland).[103]

Such schisms which divided the new recruits, and majority of the Independence Day fanboys and marchers, from the more established nationalist such as the *Obóz Wielkiej Polski* (OWP, Camp of Great Poland), a far-right outfit continuing the tradition of a pre-World War II organization, re-founded in 2003,[104] which took a pro-Russian position. In fact, the scene would veer in different directions depending on

> your position vis-à-vis social issues: so nationalists who were anti-capitalist supported Ukraine. The pro-market types, on the contrary, favoured Russia. If they were more Christian or in Poland's case, Catholic then they would be pro-Russian. If atheist or pagan, more pro-Ukrainian. Outright nazi types? They would go for Ukraine. Reactionary monarchist types? For Russia.[105]

Consequently, some of the most-well known groups, such as Młodzież Wszechpolska (MW, All-Polish Youth) or Ruch Narodowy (RN, the National

Movement) found themselves on pro-Russian positions whereas Obóz Narodowo-Radykalny (ONR, The National Radical Camp) warned of a "Banderite" chaos in Ukraine and the need to support "anti-Banderite" forces in the country, *Autonomiczni Nacjonaliści* (Autonomous Nationalists), who before the war had contacts with anti-Putin nationalists in Russia, Ukraine, Belarus and Lithuania, took a more pro-Ukraine line, so did *Narodowe Odrodzenie Polski* (NOP, National Rebirth of Poland, country's oldest far-right party, functioning without a pause since 1983)[106] and *Szturm* (Storm, the currently inactive outfit but some of its members still publish a magazine under this name).[107]

Technically, the Polish nationalists, political (great)grandchildren of a movement founded in late nineteenth century, which was vehemently anti-German, and pro-Russian and pro-Entente in World War I, seemed like ideal recruits for the "separatists."[108] Additionally, they had predominantly anti-Ukrainian views, fanned by the growing interest in pre-1989 censured episodes of history, including the so-called "Volhynia massacre" of 1943 in which the Ukrainian Insurgent Army murdered 40,000–60,000 Poles.[109] All of this, however, failed to sway potential nationalist Polish recruits to join the pro-Russian side in meaningful numbers. One former member of Polish nationalist organizations, saw the explanation for this in the content of the Russian messaging on the war which was influencing his comrades: "Russia's propaganda actually disheartened the nationalist as Moscow was claiming that the 'separatists' fought against fascism [of Ukraine] which, paradoxically, was also Jewish as it was financed by Ukrainian oligarchs of such descent."[110] Such an approach should partly suit the nationalists, as the fight was against the Ukrainian "fascists," but they had problems seeing themselves as fighters in what was to amount to an anti-fascist struggle for the sake of "People's Republics" beaming with nostalgic pro-Soviet imagery and propaganda.

Some Polish nationalists, however, seemed not to have minded such imagery and allegedly unsuccessfully plotted to travel as a group to join the ranks of the fighters on the "separatist" side.[111] These wannabe foreign fighters, who eventually failed to trek eastward, were said to have been connected with the *Zmiana* (Change). *Zmiana* was a hybrid leftist/rightist, if not Eurasianist political party, known for its unashamed pro-Russian and anti-American positions.[112] The party was led by Mateusz Piskorski, former parliamentarian and a founder of the *Europejskie Centrum Analiz Geopolitycznych* (European Centre of Geopolitical Analysis, ECAG), which provided "independent election monitors" for different elections, such as those held in the "People's Republics" in late 2014.[113] In 2016, Piskorski was charged with spying for Russia and China, was detained by Poland's *Agencja Bezpieczeństwa Wewnętrznego* (ABW, Internal Security Agency), and subsequently spent three years in pre-trial detention.[114] He later remarked that "potentially all [of Poland's] pro-Russian circles gravitated towards organisations which [he] founded."[115]

These circles included Bartosz Bekier, former prominent member of ONR and former vice-chairman of *Zmiana*, who founded his own *Falanga* political party.[116] He was later to travel to Crimea, Chechnya, Donbas and Syria, from which he reported on political developments but has not participated in actual fighting.[117] Bekier admitted his organization was often referred to as "Russian agents or Putin's trolls" but he regarded this as a compliment. He stressed, however, that despite his intellectual fascination with Duginism, *Falanga* was "nationally solidarist" and negated liberalism, Atlanticism, and was vehemently opposed to any American military presence in Poland.[118] In the summer of 2015, Falanga organized "motorised civic patrols," with few of its members, kitted out in paramilitary style outfits, patrolling the Polish-Ukrainian border zone so that "illegal immigrants or [Banderite] militants" would not sneak into Poland.[119] In 2018, the same party's members, allegedly acting without the consent of the party's leadership, fire bombed a Hungarian cultural center in Uzhorod, Western Ukraine. The attack was meant to be attributed to Ukrainian nationalists and was allegedly ordered and sponsored by a parliamentary worker in the German AfD party.[120] If this had indeed been the case, then such an attack constitutes the best proof of not only political but also militant axis between pro-Russian actors on Europe's far or extreme right.

Piskorski and Bekier had not been the only Zmiana alumni who traveled to the "People's Republics." The party actually produced one of the very few Polish foreign fighters – Ludmiła Dobrzyniecka who, on the back of her communist convictions, joined the far-left *InterUnit* of the so-called *Prizrak* (Ghost) Brigade of the "separatist" forces.[121] Her presence was picked up by another Pole who resides in the "People's Republics," Dawid Hudziec, a former member of the nationalist OWP, who has been producing Polish language content for the "separatist" news agency.[122] He also profiled Dariusz Lemański, a Pole who came to Donbas from the UK, and who was called by Hudziec "the only Polish volunteer in the army of Novorossiya."[123] This statement summed up the lack of mobilization of nationalist or in reality, any Poles for the war in Ukraine. Hudziec would not comment on the issue as to whether others joined the war on the "separatist" side, despite profiling the Rusich unit whose members were photographed with a Polish flag. Ironically, Lemański's case was said to have been the "last straw" for the only known Polish foreign fighter on the other side – an individual of Ukrainian ancestry who rushed to join "Donbas" volunteer battalion. For him, "a dude [Lemański] who flew from London to fight fascists in Ukraine is an idiot."[124]

The fact that Hudziec, a nationalist, positively profiled Dobrzyniecka, a self-confessed communist who gave interviews on how North Korea was developing,[125] was a testament to the existence of the Polish flavored brown-red cocktail. Not all, however, ingredients of this cocktail, or even outright brown nationalists, took the side of the separatists. The national-radical *Szturm*, a monthly magazine edited by the members of an organization of the same name, carried a string of publications on the Ukrainian Azov movement.[126] What is more, both Szturm, the organization, and Azov would coordinate their simultaneous commemoration of Polish and Ukrainian victims of the "Volhynia massacre" and the reprisals by the Polish underground.[127] One of *Szturm*'s contributors, who since then has left the far-right milieu, was even to produce books on Azov.[128] Dawid Czerwonko, a Polish extreme nationalist based in the UK, but later deported, was alleged to have been responsible for recruiting British, and Polish – but based in Britain – extremists who wanted to join the war in Ukraine and fight in the ranks of its nationalist "militias."[129]

Conclusion

As demonstrated in this chapter, the CEE far-right milieus (brown) had difficulty mobilizing its members for the war in Ukraine – on either side. This is evident when studying the sheer numbers, or lack of, such fighters either on the Ukrainian or the "separatist" side in the war. Surprisingly, the red part of the brown-red cocktail proved more apt at sending people eastward – into the ranks of the "separatists" (see Czech and Slovak cases and, to some extent, the Polish cases as well). The local radical, be it far-right or post-communist or brown-red milieus, seemed to have been dominated by a pro-Russian/pro-"separatist" sentiment which led only a few dozen – especially Czech and Slovak fighters – to Donetsk. These fighters, sometimes escaping trouble at home (a powerful push factor for any foreign fighter mobilization) had either been by-products of social media mobilizations – they found contacts to "the People's Republics" e.g. via pro-Russia Facebook groups, or traveled from Russia where they had already been working – or were sent "there" by local pan-Slavic paramilitary organizations. These had seemingly nothing to do with the far right but an analysis of their statements, or the views of their members, situate them firmly in the brown-red cocktail.

Notes

1 Kacper Rekawek, *Career Break or a New Career? Extremist Foreign Fighters in Ukraine* (Berlin: Counter Extremism Project, 2020), 16, https://www.counterextremism.com/sites/default/files/CEP%20Report_Career%20Break%20or%20a%20New%20Career_Extremist%20Foreign%20Fighters%20in%20Ukraine_April%202020.pdf.

2 Tomáš Forró, "Naši chlapci v Donbase. Babie leto u československých separatistov," *Dennik N*, December 1, 2016, https://dennikn.sk/622947/nasi-chlapci-v-donbase-babie-leto-u-ceskoslovenskych-separatistov/.

3 As was shown, similar sentiment was to be found amongst members of the far-right scenes of Western European countries.

4 For instance, some of the Latvians were members of "disaster preparedness" groups or "preppers," who had "equipment" stored in their own bunker in the forest. See Girts Vikmanis, "Cīnījos par Latviju. Saruna ar latvieti, kurš karojis Ukrainas brīvprātīgo bataljonā," *LA.LV*, March 3, 2015, https://www.la.lv/latvietis-kurs-karojis-ukrainas-brivpratigo-b-ataljona-cinijos, accessed: April 12, 2021.

5 Professional fighters, especially with special forces' training, usually had little difficulty connecting to the appropriate units and making their way there.

6 Author's interview with Egle Murauskaite, senior researcher and simulation developer at the ICONS Project, University of Maryland.

7 Egle E. Murauskaite, *Foreign fighters in ukraine: assessing potential risks* (Vilnius: Vilnius Institute for Policy Analysis, 2020), https://vilniusinstitute.lt/wp-content/uploads/2020/02/foreign-fighters-in-ukraine-assessing-potential-risks.pdf, accessed: April 12, 2021 for more on the issue.

8 Halya Coynash, "Czech national charged with terrorism after fighting for Russian-backed militants in Ukraine," *Kharkiv Human Rights Protection Group*, February 1, 2019, http://khpg.org/en/index.php?id=1548645601, accessed: April 12, for more details on the issue.

9 *Red Star Over Donbass*, "Benes Ayo Is Free," February 14, 2020, https://redstaroverdonbass.blogspot.com/2020/02/benes-ayo-is-free.html?m=1, accessed: April 12, 2021.

10 For the best available overview of the Czech fighters in the war in Ukraine see Miroslav Mareš, "Čeští zahraniční bojovníci v ukrajinském konfliktu: právní aspekty a využití v propagandě," *vojenské rozhledy*, 2017, https://vojenskerozhledy.cz/kategorie-clanku/ozbrojene-konflikty/cesti-bojovnici#_ftn26, accessed: May 3, 2021.

11 Tomáš Forró, "Naši chlapci v Donbase: Babie leto u československých separatistov," *Dennik N*, December 1, 2016, https://dennikn.sk/622947/nasi-chlapci-v-donbase-babie-leto-u-ceskoslovenskych-separatistov/, accessed: May 4, 2021.

12 Ján Petrovič, "V separatistickej armáde na Ukrajine založili česko-slovenskú jednotku. Hovorili sme s nimi," *Aktuality.sk*, June 8, 2015, https://www.aktuality.sk/clanok/277366/exkluzivne-v-separatistickej-armade-na-ukrajine-zalozili-cesko-slovensku-jednotku-hovorili-sme-s-nimi/, accessed: May 4, 2021.

13 Forró, "Naši chlapci v Donbase."

14 Ján Benčík, "Jaroslav z Nitry, ktorý zrejme bojoval na Ukrajine v oddiele Azov," *Dennik N*, November 20, 2018, accessed: May 5, 2021.

15 Author's interview with Prof. Miroslav Mareš, Masaryk University, Brno, the Czech Republic, April 23, 2021.

16 Roman Máca, "Věří konspiračním teoriím, fandí Zemanovi, odešel bojovat za proruské separatisty," *iDNES.cz/BLOG*, May 11, 2017, https://maca.blog.idnes.cz/blog.aspx?c=603636, accessed: May 3, 2021.

17 Author's interview with Prof. Miroslav Mareš, Masaryk University, Brno, the Czech Republic, April 23, 2021.

18 Vojtěch Jochim and Josef Škrdlík, "Český Velitel Čety V Doněcku: Taky Jsem Křičel Havel Na Hrad!," *Respekt*, April 5, 2019, https://www.respekt.cz/externi-hlasy/cesky-velitel-cety-v-donecku-taky-jsem-kricel-havel-na-hrad, accessed: May 3, 2021.

19 Tomáš Forró, *Donbas. Svadobný apartmán v hoteli Vojna* (Bratislava: N Press, 2019), 2077, Kindle.

20 Author's interview with Prof. Miroslav Mareš, Masaryk University, Brno, the Czech Republic, April 23, 2021.

21 *iDNES.cz*, "Místo podmínky vězení. Čech, který bojoval na Ukrajině, si odsedí tři roky," December 3, 2020, https://www.idnes.cz/ceske-budejovice/zpravy/ukrajina-boje-separatista-ucast-vojak-pomoc-vezeni.A201203_133335_budejovice-zpravy_mrl, accessed: May 4, 2021.

22 *CT24*, "Je mrtvý, potvrdila sestra Čecha bojujícího na Ukrajině," September 3, 2014, https://ct24.ceskatelevize.cz/domaci/1019231-je-mrtvy-potvrdila-sestra-cecha-bojuciciho-na-ukrajine, accessed: May 3, 2021.

23 See https://www.youtube.com/watch?v=Cp_rfM1o5dE, accessed: May 3, 2021 for his interview broadcast by Russian TV's First Channel on June 18, 2014.

24 *CT24*, "Za ukrajinské povstalce bojuje muž z Brna: Nemůžu nečinně přihlížet genocide," June 19, 2014, https://ct24.ceskatelevize.cz/svet/1028946-za-ukrajinske-povstalce-bojuje-muz-z-brna-nemuzu-necinne-prihlizet-genocide, accessed: May 3, 2021.

25 As of May 2021, five have already received their sentences for participation in the war.

26 *Echo24.cz*, "Až dvacet Čechů je podezřelých z bojů na Donbasu, tvrdí ukrajinský velvyslanec," June 2, 2019, https://echo24.cz/a/SJyGR/az-dvacet-cechu-je-podezrelych-z-boju-na-donbasu-tvrdi-ukrajinsky-velvyslanec, accessed: May 4, 2021.

27 The Soufan Center, *White Supremacy Extremism: The Transnational Rise of the Violent White Supremacist Movement* (New York: The Soufan Center, 2019), 29, https://thesoufancenter.org/wp-content/uploads/2019/09/Report-by-The-Soufan-Center-White-Supremacy-Extremism-The-Transnational-Rise-of-The-Violent-White-Supremacist-Movement.pdf, accessed: February 10, 2021, for Arkadiusz Legieć's data on numbers of such fighters. Legieć worked with the author on the first attempt at estimating the phenomenon's scale – see n 1 in Kacper Rekawek, "Neither 'NATO's Foreign Legion' Nor the 'Donbass International Brigades': (Where Are All the) Foreign Fighters in Ukraine?," *PISM Policy Paper* no. 6(108) (March 2015), https://www.pism.pl/files/?id_plik=19434, accessed: February 10, 2021.

28 Author's interview with Prof. Miroslav Mareš, Masaryk University, Brno, the Czech Republic, April 23, 2021.

29 Forró, *Donbas*, 2770.

30 Save Donbas, "Oldřich Grund. Občan ČR ... Vyznamenaný hrdina Novoruska," YouTube, August 6, 2014, https://www.youtube.com/watch?v=b_9dOSmTgZ0, accessed: May 3, 2021 for a short video clip of Grund commiserating about his time on the front line.

31 František Roček, "Muže z Lounska odsoudili za terorismus. Jemu je to však jedno, žije na Ukrajině," *denik.cz*, December 1, 2020, https://www.denik.cz/krimi/soud-teroristicky-utok-donecka-lidova-republika-20201201.html, accessed: May 3, 2021.

32 *Novinky.cz*, "Bojoval za Doněckou lidovou republiku, v Ústí dostal 15 let," December 21, 2021, https://www.novinky.cz/krimi/clanek/bojoval-za-doneckou-lidovou-republiku-v-usti-dostal-15-let-40345866, accessed: May 3, 2021.

33 *iDNES.cz*, "Dělal na Donbasu odstřelovače, zní v žalobě. Čechovi hrozí 20 let," April 27, 2021, https://www.idnes.cz/zpravy/domaci/donbas-cech-ukrajina.A210427_143141_domaci_kzem, accessed: May 3, 2021.

34 *iDNES.cz*, Soud snížil muži trest z 20 let na šest let za činnost u proruských separatist, January 11, 2022, https://www.idnes.cz/plzen/zpravy/lukas-novacek-terorismus-karlovarsko-boje-ukrajina-separatiste.A220111_122558_plzen-zpravy_vb, accessed: April 22, 2022.

35 *iDNES.cz*, "Nebojoval jsem, jen škrábal brambory, hájí se muž obžalovaný z terorismu," January 7, 2021, https://www.idnes.cz/plzen/zpravy/terorismus-utok-krajsky-soud-plzen-muz-mladik-ukrajina-separatiste.A210107_110900_plzen-zpravy_vb, accessed: May 3, 2021.

36 *iDNES.cz*, "Pomáhal jsem proti fašistům, řekl muž obžalovaný kvůli bojům na Ukrajině," July 27, 2020, https://www.idnes.cz/praha/zpravy/belorus-fadejev-terorismus-ukrajina-doneck-praha-soud-separatismus.A200727_115229_domaci_brde, accessed: May 3, 2021.

37 See https://twitter.com/_Roman_Maca/status/1386652941700960259?s=20 for a April 26, 2021 tweet by Roman Maca, accessed: May 3, 2021.

38 For more on them see Forró, *Donbas*, 1641.

39 Tomáš Forró, "Český legionár Kaukaz: Počkám na protézu a znovu sa postavím na front," *Dennik N*, January 24, 2020, https://dennikn.sk/1729760/cesky-legionar-kaukaz-pockam-na-protezu-a-znovu-sa-postavim-na-front/, accessed: May 3, 2021.

40 Roman Máca, "Čeští bojovníci na Donbasu konvertovali k islámu. Ze zákopů se přesunuli do kuchyňského studia," *HlídacíPes.org*, June 9, 2020, https://hlidacipes.org/cesti-bojovnici-na-donbasu-v-chladnouci-valce-ze-zakopu-se-presunuli-do-prodejny-kuchyni/, accessed: May 3, 2021.

41 Tomáš Forró, "Když vlastence vzrušuje válka," *Reportér*, June 27, 2019, https://reportermagazin.cz/a/pnscW/kdyz-vlastence-vzrusuje-valka, accessed: May 3, 2019.

42 *Aktuálně.cz*, "Českoslovenští vojáci v záloze zanikli, nebyli akceschopní, já chtěl domobranu, říká jejich exšéf," December 10,2015, https://video.aktualne.cz/dvtv/ceskoslovensti-vojaci-v-zaloze-zanikli-nebyli-akceschopni-ja/r~b2874f-c29e8d11e5bc8c002590604f2e/, accessed: May 4, 2021 for an interview with the organization's former leader.

43 Roman Máca, "Zákaz ozbrojených skupin: Kdo jsou čeští 'domobranci'?," *Institut pro politiku a společnost*, Policy Paper, (January 2020), https://www.politikaspolecnost.cz/wp-content/uploads/2020/01/Z%C3%A1kaz-ozbrojen%C3%BDch-skupin-Kdo-jsou-%C4%8De%C5%A1t%C3%AD-domobranci-IPPS1.pdf, accessed: April 26, 2021.

44 Lukáš Prchal, Jakub Zelenka, "Podporovali Zemana na Albertově, válčili na Donbasu. Co víme o Československých vojácích v záloze, pro které si přišla policie," *Denik N*, April 26, 2021, https://denikn.cz/611564/podporovali-zemana-na-albertove-valcili-na-donbasu-co-vime-o-ceskoslovenskych-vojacich-v-zaloze-pro-ktere-si-prisla-policie/?cst=25ab23b847ec39601d6ebfdd804ce050e678585f, accessed: April 27, 2021.

45 See BIS' annual report for 2017: https://www.bis.cz/vyrocni-zpravy/vyrocni-zprava-bezpecnostni-informacni-sluzby-za-rok-2017-d85907e6.html, December 3, 2018, accessed: April 26, 2021.

46 Roman Máca, "Bojoval na Donbasu, aby v ČR chystal teroristické útoky. Teď je zpět a s Foldynou vítá Noční vlky," *HlídacíPes.org*, May 25, 2020, https://hlidacipes.org/bojoval-na-donbasu-aby-v-cr-chystal-teroristicke-utoky-ted-je-zpet-a-s-foldynou-vita-nocni-vlky/, accessed: April 26, 2021.

47 Patrik Biskup, "Mladík z Karlovarska válčil na Ukrajině, hrozí mu 20 let," *Novinky.cz*, December 16, 2020, https://www.novinky.cz/krimi/clanek/mladik-valcil-na-ukrajine-hrozi-mu-20-let-40345356, accessed: April 26, 2021.

48 *CT24*, "Čech podmíněně odsouzený za účast v konfliktu na Ukrajině nakonec půjde do vězení," December 3, 2020, https://ct24.ceskatelevize.cz/domaci/3235324-cech-podminene-odsouzeny-za-ucast-v-konfliktu-na-ukrajine-nakonec-pujde-do-vezeni, accessed: May 4, 2021.

49 *ČTK*, "Boj za proruské separatisty nebyl terorismus, řekl soud. Vojákovi dal jen podmínku," September 17, 2019, https://zpravy.aktualne.cz/domaci/soud-zmirnil-vojakovi-trest-za-ucast-v-bojich-na-ukrajine/r~5fe1de66d93211e984260cc47ab5f122/, accessed: May 4, 2021.

50 Bellingcat Investigation Team, "Senior GRU Leader Directly Involved With Czech Arms Depot Explosion," *Bellingcat*, April 20, 2021, https://www.bellingcat.com/news/2021/04/20/senior-gru-leader-directly-involved-with-czech-arms-depot-explosion/, accessed: May 4, 2021.

51 *Aktuálně.cz*, "Policie viní spolek z podpory terorismu. Jeden z členů se cvičil v boji na Donbasu," April 24, 2021, https://zpravy.aktualne.cz/domaci/policie-vini-spolek-z-podpory-terorismu-jeden-z-clenu-se-cvi/r~3841fdb4a4e211eba22aac1f6b220ee8/, accessed: May 4, 2021.

52 Lukáš Valášek, Ondřej Kundra, "NCOZ při rozsáhlém zátahu zatýkala členy polovojenských jednotek napojené na Rusy," *Aktuálně.cz*, April 21, 2021, https://zpravy.aktualne.cz/domaci/ncoz-pri-rozsahlem-zatahu-zatykala-cleny-polovojenskych-jedn/r~544007fca21911ebaedf0cc47ab5f122/, accessed: April 26, 2021.

53 Author's interview with Prof. Miroslav Mareš, University of Brno, the Czech Republic, April 23, 2021.

54 See https://www.zakonyprolidi.cz/print/cs/2021-14/zneni-20210130.htm?sil=1 for the text of the above-mentioned bill, accessed: April 27, 2021.

55 Jiří Hrebenar, "Proruský žoldák pavel botka by asi na pivo nešel s nelou liskovou," *Blog.Respekt.cz*, June 9, 2020, https://gisat.blog.respekt.cz/prorusky-zoldak-pavel-botka-by-asi-na-pivo-nesel-s-nelou-liskovou/, accessed: May 4, 2021.

56 Forró, *Donbas*, 2551.

57 Tomáš Pika, "'Doněcký konzulát' zrušen. Vrchní soud v Olomouci potvrdil rozsudek krajského soudu," *HlídacíPes.org*, January 26, 2018, https://hlidacipes.org/donecky-konzulat-zrusen-vrchni-soud-v-olomouci-potvrdil-rozsudek-krajskeho-soudu/, accessed: May 4, 2021.

58 Martin Fendrych, "Česká domobrana: Proti vládě, proti NATO, proti EU, proti muslimům. Pátá kolona Putina," *Aktuálně.cz*, July 13, 2016, accessed: May 4, 2021.

59 Forró, "Když vlastence vzrušuje válka."

60 Ján Benčík, "Slovenskí žoldnieri na Ukrajine, ich usilovní pomocníci a naše slovenské Kocúrkovo," *Dennik N*, January 23, 2017, https://dennikn.sk/blog/658256/slovenski-zoldnieri-na-ukrajine-ich-usilovni-pomocnici-a-nase-slovenske-kocurkovo/, accessed: May 4, 2021.

61 Radovan Bránik, "O Martinovi, slovenskom bojovníkovi na strane proruských separatistov," SME *blog*, February 20, 2015, https://branik.blog.sme.sk/c/375590/o-martinovi-slovenskom-bojovnikovi-na-strane-proruskych-separatistov.html, accessed: May 4, 2021.

62 *topky.sk*, "Na Ukrajine bojuje ďalší Slovák, preslávil sa pálením vlajky EÚ: Moja vojna proti Západu!," January 30, 2015, https://www.topky.sk/cl/11/1453517/Na-Ukrajine-bojuje-dalsi-Slovak–preslavil-sa-palenim-vlajky-EU–Moja-vojna-proti-Zapadu-, accessed: May 4, 2021.

63 Ján Debnár, "Údajný Žilinčan bojujúci na Ukrajine: Išiel som len pomôcť 'národu Donbasu'," *aktuality.sk*, 5 February 2015, https://www.aktuality.sk/clanok/270013/udajny-zilincan-bojujuci-na-ukrajine-isiel-som-len-pomoct-narodu-donbasu/, accessed: May 4, 2021.

64 Ján Benčík, "Kto zo Slovenska bojuje ako žoldnier na Ukrajine? V prvej časti Sojka a Branický," *Dennik N*, December 14, 2015, https://dennikn.sk/blog/318099/zoldaci/, accessed: May 4, 2021.

65 ČTK, "Žoldnieri, zločinci a idealisti. Z Čechov a Slovákov v Donbase sú vzorní občania diktatúry," *Hospodářské noviny*, December 2, 2016, https://hnonline.sk/svet/869897-zoldnieri-zlocinci-a-idealisti-z-cechov-a-slovakov-v-donbase-su-vzorni-obcania-diktatury, accessed: May 5, 2021.

66 Dušan Mikušovič, "Rozhovor s brancami: Čo je zlé na cvičení so zbraňou v lese?," *Dennik N*, February 25, 2015, https://dennikn.sk/57900/rozhovor-s-brancami-co-je-zle-na-tom-cvicit-v-lese-zbranou/, accessed: May 4, 2021.

67 Ján Benčík, "Kto zo Slovenska bojuje ako žoldnier na Ukrajine? V prvej časti Sojka a Branický," *Dennik N*, December 14, 2015, https://dennikn.sk/blog/318099/zoldaci/, accessed: May 4, 2021.

68 Eva Niňajová, "Slovenskí branci pobehujú ozbrojení po lesoch, šíria nenávisť o Rómoch a LGBTI. Sú bezpečnostné riziko, vravia odborníci," *STARTITUP*, January 13, 2021, https://www.startitup.sk/slovenski-branci-pobehuju-ozbrojeni-po-lesoch-siria-nenavist-o-romoch-a-lgbti-su-bezpecnostne-riziko-vravia-odbornici/, accessed: May 4, 2021.

69 Kacper Rekawek, *Looks Can Be Deceiving: Extremism Meets Paramilitarism in Central and Eastern Europe?* (Berlin: Counter Extremism Project, May 2021).

70 Bránik, "O Martinovi."

71 Author's interview with Radovan Bránik, independent Slovak journalist who focuses on criminality and extremism, March 31, 2021.

72 Radovan Bránik, "Rozhovor s dôstojníkom armády Doneckej ľudovej republiky Martinom Keprtom," SME *blog*, February 24, 2015, https://branik.blog.sme.sk/c/375808/rozhovor-s-dostojnikom-armady-doneckej-ludovej-republiky-martinom-keprtom.html, accessed: May 4, 2021.

73 Author's interview with Radovan Bránik, independent Slovak journalist who focuses on criminality and extremism, March 31, 2021.

74 *RFE/RL*, "Orban Defends Hungary's Good Relations with Russia," October 30, 2019, https://www.rferl.org/a/putin-to-visit-eu-nation-hungary-as-russian-presence-grows/30243531.html, accessed: April 12, 2021.

75 *Reuters*, "Hungary, Ukraine top diplomats aim to defuse dispute over minority rights," January 21, 2021, https://www.reuters.com/article/us-ukraine-hungary-idUSKBN29W0WA, accessed: April 12, 2021.

76 Author's phone interview with Lóránt Győri, geopolitical analyst at Political Capital, a think tank in Budapest, Hungary, April 7, 2021.

77 Nick Cohen, "For the new right, Hungary is now what Venezuela once was for the left," *The Guardian*, February 8, 2020, https://www.theguardian.com/commentisfree/

2020/feb/08/hungary-now-for-the-new-right-what-venezuela-once-was-for-the-left, accessed: April 12, 2021.

78 Alexandr Litoy, "Putin's International Brigades," *openDemocracy*, October 2, 2014, https://www.opendemocracy.net/en/odr/putins-international-brigades/, accessed: April 12, 2021.

79 Author's Facebook Messenger interview with a French foreign fighter who wished to remain anonymous, April 17, 2016.

80 Author's email exchange with dr András Rácz, senior fellow at DGAP, Berlin, April 19, 2015.

81 Tomáš Forró, *Donbas*, 2703–2704.

82 Péter Krekó, Lóránt Győri, and Edit Zgut, *From Russia With Hate. The activity of pro-Russian extremist groups in Central-Eastern Europe* (Budapest: Political Capital, April 2017), 26–32, https://www.politicalcapital.hu/pc-admin/source/documents/PC_NED_summary_analysis_EN_20170428.pdf, accessed: April 12, 2021.

83 Author's phone interview with Lóránt Győri, geopolitical analyst at Political Capital, a think tank in Budapest, Hungary, April 7, 2021.

84 Krekó et al., *From Russia With Hate*, 30.

85 For more on him see *444.hu*'s documentary about the case: "Így lett a tévészékházat védő magyar rendőrtisztből az oroszok háborújának katonája," November 19, 2018, accessed: April 12,.

86 The riots erupted in the aftermath of a recording in which the then Hungarian prime minister confessed to lying so that his party would be elected into government. *BBC News*, "We lied to win, says Hungary PM," September 18, 2006, http://news.bbc.co.uk/2/hi/europe/5354972.stm, accessed: April 12, 2021.

87 Author's phone interview with Peter Erdelyi of 444.hu who directed the above-mentioned documentary on the Hungarian foreign fighter, September 7, 2020.

88 Witold Dobrowolski, "Najonalizm nieśmiały?," *Szturm*, April 26, 2017, https://szturm.com.pl/index.php/miesiecznik/item/523-witold-dobrowolski-nacjonalizm-niesmialy, accessed: April 5, 2021.

89 Matthew Taylor, "'White Europe': 60,000 nationalists march on Poland's independence day," *The Guardian*, November 12, 2017, https://www.theguardian.com/world/2017/nov/12/white-europe-60000-nationalists-march-on-polands-independence-day, accessed: April 5, 2021.

90 Kacper Rekawek, Alexander Ritzmann, and Hans Jakob Schindler, *Violent Right-Wing Extremism and Terrorism – Transnational Connectivity, Definitions, Incidents, Structures and Countermeasures* (Berlin: Counter Extremism Project, November 2020), 7, https://www.counterextremism.com/sites/default/files/CEP%20Study_Violent%20Right-Wing%20Extremism%20and%20Terrorism_Nov%202020.pdf, accessed: February 9, 2021.

91 Przemysław Witkowski, "Co z tym marszem?," *Krytyka Polityczna*, November 11, 2019, https://krytykapolityczna.pl/kraj/witkowski-marsz-niepodleglosci-2019/, accessed: April 5, 2021.

92 Author's phone interview with professor Jarosław Tomasiewicz of the University of Silesia, one of Poland's academic authorities on the issue of radical ideologies, March 25, 2021.

93 Jacek Rosa, Liczba cudzoziemców pracujących w Polsce rekordowo wysoka na koniec 2020, *300Gospodarka*, January 11, 2021, https://300gospodarka.pl/wykres-dnia/cudzoziemcy-pracujacy-polska-statystyki-2020, accessed: April 5, 2021.

94 See the chapter on the war in this monograph where interviews with such individuals are quoted.

95 See https://www.youtube.com/watch?v=hmHlYuAbXLQ for an interview with the author Marci Shore, whose work is cited in the chapter on the war in Ukraine, where she explained that Polish experts, opinion-makers and the public "would get it," i.e. stayed well-informed.

96 Author's phone interview with professor Jarosław Tomasiewicz of the University of Silesia, one of Poland's academic authorities on the issue of radical ideologies, March 25, 2021.

97 *Kultura Liberalna*, "Gdy państwo się zwija, rodzi się paramilitaryzm. Z Weroniką Grzebalską rozmawia Tomasz Sawczuk," No. 542, May 28, 2019, https://kultur-aliberalna.pl/2019/05/28/grzebalska-paramilitarne-spoleczenstwo-obywatelskie-wywiad/, accessed: April 5, 2021.

98 See Rekawek, *Looks Can Be Deceiving*, for more on the (lack of) intersection between the far right and paramilitarism in Poland.

99 Witkowski, "Co z tym marszem?"

100 Przemysław Witkowski, "Wojna domowa w Marszu Niepodległości. Interweniują służby specjalne, PiS wkracza do gry," *oko.press*, November 24, 2019, https://oko.press/wojna-domowa-w-marszu-niepodleglosci/, accessed: April 5, 2021.

101 Rafał Wnuk, Sławomir Poleszak, Agnieszka Jaczyńska, Magdalena Śladecka (eds.), *Atlas polskiego podziemia niepodległościowego 1944–1956* (Warszawa-Lublin: Instytut Pamięci Narodowej, 2007) for the most comprehensive mapping out of the cursed/damned/doomed soldiers in Poland.

102 The Polish far right has historically been predominantly anti-Ukrainian in nature. Attempts to break the logjam of hatred amongst both countries' nationalists are relatively new and are yet to resemble strides made in similar developments amongst their counterparts in Western Europe. See *Szturm*, "Wspólna Pamięć," August 20, 2016, https://szturm.com.pl/index.php/miesiecznik/item/405-wspolna-pamiec, accessed: August 5, 2021.

103 Author's phone interview with professor Jarosław Tomasiewicz of the University of Silesia, one of Poland's academic authorities on the issue of radical ideologies, March 25, 2021.

104 Agnieszka Kazimierczuk, "Polski rzecznik prorosyjskich separatystów," *Rzeczpospolita*, October 17, 2014, https://www.rp.pl/artykul/1149907-Polski-rzecznik-prorosyjskich-separatystow.html, accessed: April 5, 2021.

105 Author's interview with dr Przemysław Witkowski, one of Poland's leading experts on the far right, assistant adjunct profesor at Collegium Civitas in Warsaw, March 25, 2021.

106 Przemysław Witkowski, "Faszyzm? My jesteśmy gorsi!," *Krytyka Polityczna*, December 15, 2018, https://krytykapolityczna.pl/kraj/faszyzm-nop/, accessed: April 5, 2021.

107 Author's phone interview with Jakub Woroncow, an independent analyst and a writer studying the far right in Poland, March 25, 2021.

108 Roman Wapiński, *Roman Dmowski* (Lublin: Wydawnictwo Lubelskie, 1989) for a biography of the movement's founder and leader, Roman Dmowski.

109 Grzegorz Motyka, *Od rzezi wołyńskiej do akcji „Wisła." Konflikt polsko-ukraiński 1943-1947* (Kraków: Wydawnictwo Literackie, 2011) for a comprehensive overview of the issue.

110 Author's phone interview with a member of the Polish far right milieu with wide contacts in Ukraine and who wished to remain anonymous, April 7, 2021.

111 Author's interview with dr Przemysław Witkowski.

112 Ibid. For more on Zmiana see Grzegorz Tokarz, "Polska i Rosja w narracji historycznej Partii Politycznej 'Zmiana'," *Wchodnioznawstwo*, no. 10 (2016), http://cejsh.icm.edu.pl/cejsh/element/bwmeta1.element.desklight-7c571d5e-a0ed-43eb-834d-4859d3a3f9c9, accessed: April 7, 2021.

113 Shehovtsov, *Russia and the Western Far Right*, 189–191.

114 Łukasz Grzegorczyk, "Piskorski wyszedł na wolność: Oskarżony o szpiegostwo już udzielił wywiadu Rosjanom," *natemat*, May 21, 2019, https://natemat.pl/273411,kim-jest-mateusz-piskorski-oskarzany-o-szpiegostwo-wychodzi-z-aresztu, accessed: April 7, 2021.

115 Witold Jurasz, "Mateusz Piskorski: wszystkie środowiska prorosyjskie skupione były w organizacjach, które założyłem," *onet.pl*, July 30, 2019, https://wiadomosci.onet. pl/tylko-w-onecie/agent-rosji-mateusz-piskorski-mam-takie-poglady-ale-nigdy-nie-wspolpracowalem-z/0sn16xv, accessed: April 7, 2021.

116 Przemysław Witkowski, "Polscy faszyści na smyczy Putina," *Krytyka Polityczna*, April 5, 2018, https://krytykapolityczna.pl/kraj/polscy-faszysci-na-smyczy-putina/, accessed: April 7, 2021 for Bekier's critical profile.

117 See e.g. *Xportal.pl*, "Bartosz Bekier o wizycie Falangi na Krymie i w Czeczenii," November 6, 2018, https://xportal.pl/?p=34197, accessed: April 7, 2021.

118 *Xportal.pl*, "Bartosz Bekier: Tworzymy antyglobalistyczną awangardę," February 13, 2019, https://xportal.pl/?p=34340, accessed: April 7, 2021.

119 *Xportal.pl*, Polska: ochotnicze patrole antybanderowskie, August 3, 2015, https://xportal.pl/?p=21938, accessed: April 7, 2021.

120 *Deutsche Welle*, "AfD worker accused of ordering arson attack in Ukraine," January 15, 2019, https://www.dw.com/en/afd-worker-accused-of-ordering-arson-attack-in-ukraine/a-47093618, accessed: April 7, 2021.

121 Dawid Hudziec, "Polish communist youth joins army of Lugansk People's Republic," *Red Star Over Donbass*, October 7, 2016, http://redstaroverdonbass.blogspot.com/2016/10/polish-communist-youth-joins-army-of.html, accessed: April 7, 2021.

122 Anna Pawłowska, "Ja wspieram Noworosję," *Gazeta Wyborcza*, December 30, 2014, https://wyborcza.pl/1,75398,17192534,Ja_wspieram_Noworosje.html, accessed: April 7, 2021.

123 Rekawek, Neither 'NATO's Foreign Legion' Nor the 'Donbass International Brigades'," 4.

124 Agnieszka Lichnerowicz, "Polak walczy w Donbasie po ukraińskiej stronie. 'Nie jestem najemnikiem. Jestem idealistą. Nikt mi nie płaci. To taki wolontariat'," *TOKfm.pl*, March 3, 2015, https://www.tokfm.pl/Tokfm/1,103454,17510645,Polak_walczy_w_Donbasie_po_ukrainskiej_stronie___Nie.html, accessed: April 8, 2021.

125 Konrad Stachnio, "Ludmiła powie ci jak walczyć z burżujami," *Vice*, March 20, 2015, https://www.vice.com/pl/article/kwmedv/ludmia-powie-ci-jak-walczyc-z-burzujami.

126 P., "Pułk Azow i Europejska Rekonkwista," *Szturm*, May 26, 2015, https://szturm.com.pl/index.php/miesiecznik/item/175-pulk-azow-i-europejska-rekonkwista, accessed: April 8, 2021.

127 *Szturm*, "Wspólna Pamięć," August 20, 2016, https://szturm.com.pl/index.php/miesiecznik/item/405-wspolna-pamiec, accessed: August 5, 2021.

128 Witold Dobrowolski, *Ruch Azowski. Ideologia, działalność i walka ukraińskich nacjonalistów* (Warszawa: Capital, 2020).

129 Matthew Collins, "Recruiting for Ukraine," *Hope Not Hate*, March 1, 2018, https://www.hopenothate.org.uk/research/state-of-hate-2018/violence/recruiting-for-ukraine/, accessed: April 8, 2021.

10

THE ELEPHANT IN THE ROOM

Russian Foreign Fighters in the War in Ukraine

Introduction

Discussing the issue of any Western foreign fighter involvement in the war in Ukraine without at least acknowledging the presence of their Russian counterparts is counterproductive as far as developing the story of the former is concerned.[1,2] The latter constituted the largest group of such fighters and fought on both sides of the conflict and their presence in Donbas had been acknowledged as early as August 2014 by the "separatist" leaders.[3] The Westerners in general, and the members of the brown-red cocktail in particular, literally rubbed shoulders with the Russians who often had a pre-war connection to the warring parties and thus, an easier access to the battlefields. This was especially evident in the light of their knowledge of the local reality and the language (also on the Ukrainian side as most of the volunteer battalions were effectively bilingual) which allowed them to more easily blend in with the indigenous population.[4] Consequently, they fought in larger numbers and sustained more casualties but had also been given the chance to contribute to the war effort in a more meaningful manner than their Western, way less numerous, colleagues. The Russian fighters, especially the early arrivals who were instrumental in instigating the conflict in Eastern Ukraine, won admiration from e.g. members of the French foreign fighter contingent who, as was shown earlier, had different opinions on some of their local commanders and regarded these as incompetent. Moreover, the self-sacrifice of the Russian foreign fighters was also appreciated by the more secure and wealthy Westerners who on many occasions successfully funded their war involvement and were later able to recuperate their losses while working in the West.[5] Their Russian counterparts had no such options and were more prone to battlefield injuries than the Western fighters, who were often relegated to public-relations roles for the "separatists."[6]

DOI: 10.4324/9781003192992-10

The Mobilization

The Western literature on the subject of Russian involvement in the war in Ukraine concentrates on the presence of the regular military units on the battlefield or in its proximity.[7] The irregular units, militias or "volunteers," effectively – foreign fighters, get less attention and are often viewed as "mercenaries" (a term deliberately used to denigrate their status)[8] or "raiders,"[9] or, due to their irregular and multi-faceted or "Cossack"[10] character, "a fun-house mirror of contemporary Russia."[11] Some spotlight was shed on individual celebrity fighters, i.e. people such as Igor Girkin, the actual instigator of the conflict in Eastern Ukraine,[12] or Zakhar Prilepin, a famous Russian writer,[13] or the Chechen presence in the "separatist" ranks.[14] Few sources, however, account for the scale and the style of a genuine, yet state supported, foreign fighter mobilization in Russia and their subsequent deployment in Eastern Ukraine.[15]

As Rácz rightly points out, the study of the Russian foreign fighters in the war in Ukraine is hampered by a variety of issues, mainly – the fact that Moscow attempted to "conceal regular armed forces units as volunteer foreign fighters" in order to disinform the outsiders of its actual involvement in the conflict or to account for such individuals as soldiers on leave who decided not to spend their summer holidays in e.g. the resorts along the Black Sea but on the front lines in Eastern Ukraine. Mixing such rebuttals with actual "large-scale criminal schemes operating on both sides of the front line" and a widespread involvement of Russians in humanitarian convoys for Donbas (different fighters would travel to Donbas as the workers of the Russian Red Cross and upon arrival "remained there [and] were given weapons and combat tasks")[16] blurred the picture for the external observers.[17]

Just as Russia was attempting to proverbially spun a web of deception related to its involvement in Ukraine, it did not, however, do "anything to stop the flow of volunteers" and "openly [promoted] the idea of sending them there [to Eastern Ukraine]" for the audiences at home. Adds promoting "anti-Bandera … people's squads" began to circulate early as in February 2014.[18] Calls including comments such as:

> "Kiev [Kyiv] has fallen […] Armed bastards are planning to take over the East of Ukraine. Kharkiv, Donetsk, Sevastopol are under siege. Their inhabitants are ready to stand up to the end. If we defend them, we will defend Russia too, preventing the fire of war on our borders from being ignited, which will inevitably spread to us. Currently, volunteer detachments are being formed, which are to go to the East of Ukraine to contain the forces of the militants. We call on strong young people with at least basic military training to join the ranks of the defenders of Ukraine."

Adverts were to be found on the Russian social networking site *VKontakte* and helpfully included word questionnaires to fill in for the wannabe volunteers.[19] Thus, one should not be completely surprised that the likes of the well-known Russian far-right activists were spotted in Odessa, a future venue of a failed pro-Russian "uprising," just like Kharkiv, in the early stages of the conflict in Ukraine.[20]

At the same time, pro-"volunteer" organizations were said to have "mushroomed" in places like St. Petersburg,[21] and "patriotic organizations"[22] were involved in online recruitment for what was dubbed "armed charity."[23] According to the so-called *Nemtsov Report*, a high-profile report whose author was shot dead in Moscow before it was published,[24] the process of recruitment of such "volunteers" was channeled through "nongovernmental organizations that are loyal to the Kremlin," such as "Regional Fund of Special Forces Veterans," "Combat Veterans," "Afghan Veterans," "Battle Brotherhood," "Internationalist Warriors," which are mostly accepted veteran organizations of the Afghan or the Chechen wars[25] and which utilized the data accumulated by the military recruitment/enlistment office (*voienkomaty*) to sift through CVs or target potential candidates.[26] The Russian security service (FSB) was also said to have been involved in the recruitment process as it had allegedly been their members who interviewed the candidates at offices of the above-mentioned organizations.[27] The transfer of such fighters was said to have been centrally organized and sponsored,[28] with the FSB assuring "secrecy" and the ministry of defense allegedly responsible for the "supply side" of the operation. After their arrival in Rostov, a major urban center close to the Ukrainian eastern border, they would hand in their "papers in return for a receipt," get photographed and fingerprinted, be assigned a call sign, a "nom de guerre," and receive further training while housed in a hotel within Rostov.[29] They would also be assigned equipment ("all are old, even from the Soviet warehouses"), uniforms ("all are dressed in army clothing, without any stripes, markings and even the labels of manufacturers") and combat missions.[30] According to different estimates, as many as 50,000 of such fighters were involved in the hostilities in Ukraine but Rácz, an authority on the subject, "conservatively" put their number at 12,000–15,000.[31] Whatever their final number, it was large enough for the fighters to then form a "Union of Donbass Volunteers," an NGO aimed at safeguarding the rights of the Russian "volunteers" from the war in Ukraine. It was rumored to have acted in concert with "the intelligence agencies, immigration services, and border authorities of the Russian Federation" and also allegedly assisted in the transfer of foreign fighters from outside Russian into the "separatist" republics.[32] Moreover, as was shown in the "Balkans" chapter, it also maintains a robust relationship with Serbian and especially Bosnian-Serb veterans of the wars in Yugoslavia.[33]

There are conflicting account as to how much these fighters were paid – non-Russians in the "separatist" ranks interviewed by the author stressed the salaries of their colleagues were low[34] whereas other sources suggest they would be receiving twice the average Russian salary for a monthly deployment.[35] At the same time, many allegedly refused to accept any pay for their service as technically they could have been later sought by the Russian authorities for acting as "mercenaries," a practice illegal in the country.[36] As was already discussed in the introductory chapter, the fact that these were salaried individuals does not necessarily nor automatically mean that they should not be labelled as foreign fighters. Moreover, in the case of the Russians, these payments, although potentially constituting a seemingly attractive top up of one's salary from a regular job, had not been the primary motivation for many of the Russian fighters. Thus, one would struggle to classify them as "mercenaries" with Rácz noting that "antifascism, the need to step up against the allegedly fascist Ukrainian government, has played a key role among some Russian volunteers, particularly in the early 2014 phase of the conflict."[37] Other fighters stressed more nationalist or imperialist motivations, in line with the classic foreign fighter narratives of assisting or defending one's own people (Russians or Russian land) in the time of need.[38] Interestingly, some were said to have been prodded into deploying to Donbas, e.g. individuals with "serious criminal backgrounds" who might have either been escaping from justice or were "encouraged" or simply blackmailed into doing this by the Russian security authorities.[39] Such was the case with the representatives of the Russian far-right milieu whose Ukrainian exploits will be discussed below.

Russian Far-Right and the War in Ukraine

Historically, Russia has witnessed a high number of terrorist or militant attacks/events associated with/perpetrated by individuals from the far-right milieu.[40] As Johannes Due Enstad noted, "taking into account differences in population size and the number of years [...] Russia has seen five times more violence [by right-wing militants] than the U.S., 750% more than Western Europe as a whole, nearly four times more than Germany, and twice as much as Sweden (Sweden and Germany have the highest counts in Western Europe)."[41] By the second decade of the twenty-first century, however, the Russian far right was becoming aware that their period of "revolutionary terrorism," during which they were involved in more than 400 deadly events, failed to "destabilize the state." Further change was afoot when the milieu effectively split due to the war in Ukraine with some of its members jailed or "forced into emigration" as the Russian state moved to clamp down on the most active and extremist elements of the milieu.[42] This marked a rapid change from the Kremlin's earlier approach toward "radical Russian nationalism [... which] the Putin regime [... wished to] harness in the population [...] for their own purposes, as for instance the establishment of the pro-Putin youth movements." However, as Laryš argues, "around 2009/2010, Kremlin strategists seemed to have second thoughts about the wisdom of this strategy. The disenchantment was mutual: Russia's nationalists felt that Putin has betrayed them by welcoming immigrant laborers and sending billions of dollars in subsidies to the Muslim regions in North Caucasus. When the hard-line nationalists were driven out of the Kremlin's embrace, some of them transferred to the anti-Putin opposition."[43]

Consequently, in the eyes of its leading activists, the now repressed milieu suffered from an "ideological crisis" as it seemed not to have been able to plot a new political path forward. This crisis was only compounded by disagreements over the country's foreign policy, i.e. the intervention in Ukraine. In these conditions, the fact that "hardly more than a couple of hundred" of far-right activists actually did travel to Ukraine to fight in the war was seen as impressive, especially given the lengths to which the Russian state went to "clean up" the milieu (read: arrests its members and dismantle its structures) to dismantle its appetite and capability for further "revolutionary terrorism."[44]

The split saw "the ultra-right milieu [divide] into two opposing groups – the ones who saw the new Kyiv authorities as "Banderites" harassing the ethnic Russians of the South-Eastern regions, and those who saw the events in Kyiv as an example of a nationalist revolution." Thus, the former, majoritarian group, found itself effectively siding with the Kremlin, which in the 2010s worked against them to get the far-right violence in Russia under control. At the same time, the latter echoed some of the positions of the Russian liberal opposition which never perceived the Euromaidan as a "Western plot" against the rulers of Ukraine and Russia.[45]

The respected SOVA Center's estimates from the late summer of 2014 indicated that up to 200 Russian nationalists left to take participate in the war in Ukraine.[46] Most were said to have been "members of relatively organized groups such as the neo-Nazi Russian National Unity, or RNU, headed by Alexander Barkashov; the Eurasian Youth Union inspired by Alexander Dugin; the Russian Imperial Movement, or R.I.M., of Stanislav Vorobyov." These individuals allegedly joined the conflict early – during the attempts to instigate "Russian Spring" in cities such as Kharkiv or Odessa, and then traveled eastward into Donbas.[47] There was also "a Russian [far-right] contingent" on the Ukrainian side in the war – according to some sources, its size (up to 200 men) matched that of the one present in the "separatist" ranks.[48] This latter number might be inflated but it is true that the Russian far-right milieu suffered serious loses as "all pro-Ukrainian activists from the Misanthropic Division and Wotan Jugend" immigrated to Ukraine and that effectively destroyed the movement of autonomous nationalists in Russia.[49] Wotan Jugend later reconstituted itself in Ukraine and its leading light called for supporting the Azov movement. Moreover, its members were also to be found in the so-called "Russian Center," a groupuscule consisting of Russian far-right exiles in Ukraine, "who have been forced to leave their homeland for political reasons," and whose members e.g. made it to the events organized by the far-right *Légió Hungária* in Budapest,[50] and also networked with other Central and Eastern European far-right organizations at different events in e.g. Czech Republic.[51]

In Hungary, the Center's member was interviewed by a Hungarian nationalist portal, who offered a telling take on the events in Russia and the situation of the far-right in the country, which seemed to have surprised his pro-Putin hosts. In his view, "power [in Russia is] neo-Soviet, [...] Stalinist and anti-Russian in nature [...] without freedom of speech nor freedom of thought." He ridiculed Russia's alleged role of standard bearer of "traditional values" which is open to immigration from Central Asia or the Caucasus, "abandoned without a fight [...] much of Siberia" to China, is run by corrupt oligarchs, and represses "patriots from all sides [... with] 2,000 sitting in jail."[52] In these conditions, relocation to a neighborly Ukraine and networking with the Azovians, themselves often former members of the Social National Assembly, Ukraine's primary far-right entity before the 2014 war, seemed like a logical and natural choice.[53] Moreover, the Ukrainian and the Russian activists might have bonded more easily as the latter were accused of professing not "classical nationalism" but "national socialist views" and these would allow for construction of transnational, Russian-Ukrainian coalitions aimed at opposing the common enemy, i.e. the Kremlin.[54] Indeed, one of the Azov's Russians, himself a former activist of *Restrukt!*, "notorious Russian neo-Nazi movement,"[55] openly praised Hitler ("a genius strategist who revived Great Germany after defeat in the world war and the subsequent financial crisis, restored the army and declared war on the entire modern world") and "racial idealism" of the Third Reich, which fought against "multiracial materialism." He also called President Putin a dependent of "the Jewish oligarchs" who jailed hundreds of nationalists in Russia.[56] Interestingly enough, his organization, famous for anti-gay hunts in Russia, sided with the forces behind the Novorossiya project and some of its members indeed ended up in the ranks of the "separatists."[57]

Most prominent, and to some extent bizarre as its twists and turns beggar belief, case of a Russian far-right militant involved in the war had been that of Sergei Korotkikh. He had been prominently involved in the far-right scene in Russia since the early 2000s and became one of the leaders of the he National Socialist Society (NSO, *Национал-социалистическое общество*).[58] In later years, however, he fled Russia for Ukraine, fought in the ranks of Azov and then, in reward for his service, received Ukrainian citizenship.[59] He was later accused of being a mole of the Russian security services within Azov, an allegation seemingly strengthened by the fact that he e.g. served in the Russian military in the 1990s and then attended a KGB academy in Belarus.[60] Regardless of these accusations, his ability to move between the three countries – Belarus, Russia and Ukraine – and maintain robust links on the activist far-right scenes of these, speaks volumes about the transnational connectivity of the wider ideological milieu in the former Soviet Union and the fact that the war had been almost an unwanted disruption of these connections. In such conditions, the fact that some far-right militant Russians, or Belarussians, indeed fought against the Moscow-supported "separatists" seemed just a bit less surprising, and so is their desire to obtain, just like Korotkikh did, Ukrainian passports.[61]

Conclusions

The Russians participated in the war in Ukraine in huge numbers. They started the war and then a Russian intervention saved the "separatists" in the summer of 2014. However, it had not only been the special forces nor the regular army nor the mercenaries who took part in the hostilities. Their involvement had been preceded by a genuine Russian foreign fighter mobilization. It started early in the conflict and the Russian government did nothing to stop it. It actually assisted it while deploying the state's administrative bureaucratic muscle in the process.

In practice, it lent its infrastructure, the military recruitment offices, to make it happen and yet, to the external observer it feigned ignorance. Russia then clothed, armed and trained the recruits, and sent them on their way to Donetsk via Rostov. While there, the Russian military men attempted to keep a close eye on their compatriots. This oversight was also extended to the period after the fighters' return home as an NGO representing them and arguing for their rights within Russia was said to have also been "overseen" by the Russian state.

A peculiar group of these foreign fighters stood out amongst them – the representatives of the Russian far right. This had been a vibrant and violent milieu which found itself on the wrong side of the Kremlin political machinations in the second decade of the twenty-first century, and saw hundreds if not thousands of its members jailed. As a result of the repression, some even left for Ukraine before the outbreak of the war, joining their far-right comrades there – a move testifying to the depth of pre-war relationships of the milieu in the post-Soviet republics. Some of their Russian brethren, often professing equally extreme thoughts, fought for the "separatists," with some allegedly pressurized to do so, in exchange for leniency, by the Russian security services. Their nationalism, however, proved flexible enough so that the members of the very same milieu were able to lend it either to a genuinely "patriotic" Russian cause or a more transnational cause of defending another brotherly country (Ukraine). The latter view regarded Ukraine as involved in a fight with a "neo-Soviet" regime of President Putin which dismantled the far-right's "revolutionary" potential in Russia before 2014. Those responsible for this, brothers in arms then, often later faced each other off in Eastern Ukraine.

Notes

1 András Rácz, "The Elephant in the Room: Russian Foreign Fighters in Ukraine," in K. Rekawek, ed., *Not Only Syria? The Phenomenon of Foreign Fighters in a Comparative Perspective* (The Hague: IOS Press, 2017), 60–73 for a strong attempt at capturing the features of the Russian mobilization for the war.

2 Nader Ibrahim and Ilya Barabanov, "The lost tablet and the secret documents," August 11, *BBC News*, https://www.bbc.co.uk/news/extra/8iaz6xit26/the-lost-tablet-and-the-secret-documents, accessed: September 17, 2021.

3 In August 2014, Prime minister of the Donbass People's Republic (DNI), Alexander Zakharchenko. said: «We have never concealed the fact that there are many Russians among us." See "The Boris Nemtsov Report in English, in full length: 'Putin. The War,' about the Involvement of Russia in the Eastern Ukraine conflict and the Crimea," *European Union Foreign Affairs Journal*, Special Edition (May 2015), https://archive.org/stream/B-001-004-132/EUFAJ-Special-NemtsovReport-150521_djvu.txt, accessed: August 19, 2021.

4 This ability was, however, constrained. As a journalist from Luhansk remembers, the Russian arrivals into the ranks of the "separatists" had some trouble in the process as e.g. they spoke Russian with different accents and initially were heard converting the local prices (in Ukrainian hryvnia) into "their" roubles in the street. Author's interview with Euegeny Spirin over WhatsApp, March 14, 2020.

5 Author's exchange with a French foreign fighter over Facebook Messenger, August 28, 2015.

6 Tatyana Voltskaya and Daisy Sindelar "Volunteer Now! Russia Makes It Easy to Fight in Ukraine," *RadioFreeEurope/RadioLiberty*, February 3, 2015, https://www.rferl.org/a/russia-ukraine-volunteers-kremlin-easy-to-fight-/26828559.html, accessed: August 16, 2021.

7 Igor Sutyagin, "Russian Forces in Ukraine," *RUSI Briefing Paper* (March 2015), https://static.rusi.org/201503_bp_russian_forces_in_ukraine.pdf, accessed: August16, 2021; Shaun Walker, "New evidence emerges of Russian role in Ukraine conflict," *The Guardian*, August 18, 2019, https://www.theguardian.com/world/2019/aug/18/new-video-evidence-of-russian-tanks-in-ukraine-european-court-human-rights, accessed: August 17, 2021.

8 Andrzej Wilk Piotr Żochowski Wojciech Konończuk, "Konflikt w Donbasie – wymuszona deeskalacja?," *ANALIZY OSW*, June 11, 2014, https://www.osw.waw.pl/pl/publikacje/analizy/2014-06-11/konflikt-w-donbasie-wymuszona-deeskalacja, accessed: September 26 2022.

9 Michael Kofman, "Raiding and international brigandry: russia's strategy for great power competition," *War on the Rocks*, June 14, 2018, https://warontherocks.com/2018/06/raiding-and-international-brigandry-russias-strategy-for-great-power-competition/, accessed: August 16, 2021.

10 Thomas Barrabi, "Who Are the Cossack Fighters Who Spearheaded Rebels' Capture of Debaltseve in Eastern Ukraine?" *International Business Times*, February 19, 2015, https://www.ibtimes.com/who-are-cossack-fighters-who-spearheaded-rebels-capture-debaltseve-eastern-ukraine-1821514, accessed: August 16, 2021.

11 Charles Clover, *Black Wind, White Snow. The Rise of Russia's New Nationalism* (London: Yale University Press, 2016), 327, Kindle.

12 Christopher Miller, "The Executioners of Slovyansk," *RadioFreeEurope/RadioLiberty*, July 23, 2020, https://www.rferl.org/a/the-executioners-of-slovyansk/30743132.html, accessed: August 17, 2021.

13 *DFR Lab*, "Following 'Russia's Hemingway' to War," April 28, 2017, https://medium.com/dfrlab/following-russias-hemingway-to-war-8a109ffec435#:~:text=Following%20%E2%80%9CRussia%E2%80%99s%20Hemingway%E2%80%9D%20to%20War, accessed: August 17, 2021; Lucian Kim, "Should Putin fear the man who 'pulled the trigger of war' in Ukraine?" *Reuters*, November 25, 2014, https://www.reuters.com/article/idUS368525725520141125, accessed: September 14, 2021.

14 Emil Souleimanov, "Chechen Units Deployed in Eastern Ukraine," *CACI Analyst*, June 4, 2014, http://www.cacianalyst.org/publications/analytical-articles/item/12990-chechen-units-deployed-in-eastern-ukraine.html, accessed: August 17, 2021; Thomas de Waal, "Chechen Mysteries in Donetsk," *Carnegie Moscow Center*, October 9, 2014, https://carnegie.ru/commentary/56883, accessed: August 17, 2021.

15 For an exception published early in the conflict see Nikolay Mitrokhin, "Infiltration, Instruction, Invasion: Russia's War in the Donbass," 222, https://spps-jspps.autoren-betreuung.de/files/07-mitrokhin.pdf, accessed: February 22, 2021. This publication is a translated, expanded and revised version of an article previously published in Russian: "Grubye liudi," Grani.ru, August 27, 2014; and in German: "Infiltration, Instruktion, Invasion. Russlands Krieg in der Ukraine," *Osteuropano* 64, no. 8 (2014): 3–16, accessed: August 17, 2021. For a later re-appraisal on the phenomenon see Rácz, "The Elephant in the Room," 60–73.

16 *European Union Foreign Affairs Journal*, "The Boris Nemtsov Report," 25.

17 Ibid. 62.

18 See e.g. https://tinyurl.com/2r5vz5rv, accessed: September 14, 2021.

19 VKontakte post of February 23, 2014, https://vk.com/oborona_ua?w=wall-11336883_7582, accessed: September 15, 2021.

20 *Українська правда*, "В Одессе в сепаратистских митингах принимает участие неонацист из Петербурга," March 25, 2014, https://www.pravda.com.ua/rus/news/2014/03/25/7020243/, accessed: September 14, 2021.

21 Voltskaya and Sindelar "Volunteer Now!"

22 *Meduza*, "'You could say we proved ourselves': War stories from Russians returned from fighting in eastern Ukraine," February 19, 2016, https://meduza.io/en/feature/2016/02/19/you-could-say-we-proved-ourselves, accessed: August 17, 2021.

23 *BBC News*, "Ukraine crisis: 'We recruit volunteer fighters from Russia'," June 23, 2014, https://www.bbc.com/news/av/world-europe-27971176, accessed: August 17, 2021.

24 Oleg Bolydrev, "Nemtsov report exposes Russia's human cost in Ukraine," *BBC News*, May 12, 2015, https://www.bbc.co.uk/news/world-europe-32703353, accessed: August 19, 2021.

25 *MKRU*, "«Интербригады» Донбасса," June 25, 2014, https://www.vnovomsvete.com/articles/2014/06/25/interbrigady-donbassa.html, accessed: September 14, 2021.

26 The Russian army is still partly conscripted and the military maintains a web recruitment/enlistement office to assess potential recruits' suitability or preparedness for draft military service.

27 Elena Kostyuchenko, "Russia's recruiting for fighting in Ukraine as told by volunteer: 'It's a total mess'," *Euromaidan Press* (reprinted from *Novaya Gazeta*), September 4, 2014, http://euromaidanpress.com/2014/09/04/russias-recruiting-for-fighting-in-ukraine-as-told-by-volunteer-its-a-total-mess/, accessed: September 14, 2021.

28 *E1.RU*, "Глава фонда свердловских ветеранов спецназа: 'Я помогаю добровольцам отправиться воевать на Украин'," December 24, 2014, https://www.e1.ru/text/gorod/2014/12/24/52928711/, accessed: September 14, 2021

29 Kostyuchenko, "Russia's recruiting for fighting in Ukraine."

30 "The Boris Nemtsov Report," 24–26.

31 Rácz, "The Elephant in the Room," 64.

32 *InformNapalm*, "Russia opens visas for terrorists operating in Ukraine – leaked passport data of mercenaries," April 4, 2016, https://informnapalm.org/en/russia-opens-visas-terrorists-operating-ukraine/, accessed: September 14, 2021.

33 Semir Mujkic, "Ukraine War Veterans Bind Russia and Bosnian Serbs," *Balkan Insight*, May 22, 2019, https://balkaninsight.com/2019/05/22/ukraine-war-veterans-bind-russia-and-bosnian-serbs/, accessed: September 14, 2021.

34 Author's exchange with a French foreign fighter over Facebook Messenger, August 28, 2015.

35 "The Boris Nemtsov Report," 25.

36 *Meduza*, "You could say we proved ourselves."

37 Rácz, "The Elephant in the Room," 68.

38 Ibid.

39 Tatyana Uskova, "Как скинхед из Братеево русским националистом стал, а русский национализм взял и помер," *МБХ медиа*, January 8, 2021, https://mbk-news.appspot.com/suzhet/skinxed-iz-brateevo/, accessed: September 14, 2021.

40 For a succinct summary of the state of play on the Russian far right, its composition, divisions, militancy, see Martin Laryš and Miroslav Mareš, "Right-Wing Extremist Violence in the Russian Federation," *Europe-Asia Studies* 63, no. 1 (2011): 129–154.

41 There were "406 deadly events [perpetrated by the right-wing militants] causing 459 deaths over a period of eighteen years (2000–2017)." See Johannes Due Enstad, "Right-Wing Terrorism and Violence in Putin's Russia," *Perspectives on Terrorism* 12, no. 6: 90 https://www.universiteitleiden.nl/binaries/content/assets/customsites/perspectives-on-terrorism/2018/issue-6/a6-due-enstad.pdf, accessed: September 15, 2021.

42 Ibid. 99.

43 Martin Laryš, "Violent attacks against migrants and minorities in the Russian federation," in Tore Bjørgo and Miroslav Mareš, eds., *Vigilantism against Migrants and Minorities* (Abingdon: Routledge, 2019), 79.

44 Vladimir Vaschenko, "Проявлений русофобии не замечал," *Главные новости - Газета.Ru*, May 25, 2015, https://www.gazeta.ru/social/2015/05/21/6696285.shtml, accessed: September 14, 2021.

45 Natalia Yudina, Vera Alpovich, "Ukraine Upsets the Nationalist Apple-Cart: Xenophobia, Radical Nationalism and Efforts to Counteract It in Russia during the First Half of 2014," *SOVA Center for Information and Analysis*, August 6, 2014, https://www.sova-center.ru/en/xenophobia/reports-analyses/2014/08/d30003/, accessed: August 20, 2021.

46 Again, their arrival on the front lines had been an open secret. See e.g. a photo from September 9, 2014 of the contingent from the National Bolshevik Party in Donbas: https://twitter.com/olliecarroll/status/509316380131221505, accessed: September 14, 2021.

47 Natalia Yudina, "Beware the Rise of the Russian Ultra-Right," *SOVA Center for Information and Analysis*, September 14, 2014, https://www.sova-center.ru/en/xenophobia/reports-analyses/2014/09/d30212/, accessed: August 20, 2021.

48 Leonid Ragozin, "Brothers in Arms. Why Russian ultranationalists confronted their own government on the battlefields of Ukraine," *.coda*, June 29, 2017, https://www.codastory.com/disinformation/armed-conflict/brothers-in-arms/, accessed: August 20, 2021.

49 Vera Alperovich, "Transformation of the Russian Nationalist Movement: 2013-2016," *SOVA Center for Information and Analysis*, 23 August 2016, https://www.sova-center.ru/en/xenophobia/reports-analyses/2016/08/d35252/, accessed: August 20, 2021.

50 *Nacionalista Zóna*, "Kommunizmus elleni harcotok tiszteletreméltó számunkra-interjú az LH felvonulás orosz szónokával," http://nacionalistazona.org/2019/10/21/kommunizmus-elleni-harcotok-tisztetremelto-szamunkra-interju-az-lh-felvonulas-orosz-szonokaval/, accessed: August 20, 2021.

51 Michael Colborne, "The 'Hardcore' Russian Neo-Nazi Group That Calls Ukraine Home," *Bellingcat Anti-Equality Monitoring*, September 4, 2019, https://www.bellingcat.com/news/uk-and-europe/2019/09/04/the-hardcore-russian-neo-nazi-group-that-calls-ukraine-home/, accessed: August 20, 2021.

52 *Nacionalista Zóna*, "Kommunizmus.»

53 Yudina, "Beware the Rise of the Russian Ultra-Right."

54 Amalia Zatari, "Украина расколола русских националистов," *Главные новости - Газета.Ru*, March 26, 2015, https://www.gazeta.ru/social/2015/03/25/6614029.shtml, accessed: September 14, 2021. Some of these individuals, as will be shown in chap. 3 in this volume, also, because of their professed radicalism and explicit neo-nazism, had constituted a public-relations headache for their Ukrainian colleagues. See e.g. https://twitter.com/ColborneMichael/status/1339257174334332929?s=20, a twitter thread of December 16, 2020 documenting the activities of Alexey Levkin, head of the above-mentioned Wotanjugend, accessed: September 14, 2021.

55 Anya Hrytsenko, "Misanthropic Division: A Neo-Nazi Movement from Ukraine and Russia," *REFT < > LIGHT*, September 30, 2016, http://reftlight.euromaidanpress.com/2016/09/30/misanthropic-division-a-neo-nazi-movement-from-ukraine-and-russia/, accessed; September 14, 2021.

56 Типові Чорні Чоловічки, "Интервью Романа Железнова," August 1, 2014, https://vk.com/romanxzhlx?w=wall-49956024_162303, accessed: 8 August 2014 and archived by the author as it is no longer publicly available. For more examples of *Restrukt!* Members on the Ukrainian side of the conflict and their subsequent problems with the Russian law enforcement see *BBC News*, "Проукраїнського блогера затримали на вимогу Росії. Чому ця історія така скандальна," November 26, 2020, https://www.bbc.com/ukrainian/news-55085979, accessed: September 14, 2021.

57 See the archived, from 2014, wall of *VKontakte* of a Restrukt! Member who fought on the "separatist" side in the war, http://vk.com/restrukt78, archived by Johannes Due Enstad on February 17, 2015 and then shared with the author.

58 *SOVA Center for Information and Analysis*, "A High Profile Neo-nazi Leader Currently Under Investigation," October 2, 2007, https://www.sova-center.ru/en/xenophobia/news-releases/2007/10/d11682/, accessed: September 15, 2021.

59 *Українська правда*, "Порошенко вручив паспорт громадянина України іноземцю з батальйону 'Азов'," December 5, 2014, https://www.pravda.com.ua/news/2014/12/5/7046604/, accessed: September 15, 2021.

60 Polina Vernigor, "З'явилося відео, де соратник Авакова погоджується працювати з ФСБ. Розповідаємо, що відбувається," *Zaborona*, August 6, 2021, https://zaborona.com/na-anonimnomu-yutub-kanali-zyavylosya-video-de-sergij-korotkyh-pogodzhuyetsya-praczyuvaty-z-fsb/, accessed: September 15, 2021.

61 Vyacheslav Shramovich, "Чому я хочу український паспорт? Історії росіян з 'Азова'," *BBC News Ukraine*, September 20, 2018, https://www.bbc.com/ukrainian/features-45592393, accessed: September 15, 2021.

11
FOREIGN FIGHTERS IN UKRAINE 2014–2022

Concluding Remarks

This monograph is the first single volume dedicated to the issue of foreign fighters present in the war in Ukraine. However, unlike another forthcoming monograph in the series,[1] it focuses specifically on Western foreign fighters who belonged to the brown-red cocktail, i.e., an odd political mixture of far-rightism and far-leftism, back in their home countries, and arrived at the frontlines between the spring of 2014 and early 2022. The previous chapters not only outlined the ideological background of this phenomenon but also zoomed in on the key Western mobilizations which produced foreign fighter contingents for either side of the war in Ukraine, introduced the conflict there to readers less well versed in Eastern European history and politics, and discussed the so-called hosts – effectively hubs of foreign fighter recruitment for this war. The monograph features opinions and voices from the fighters themselves whom the author interviewed between 2015 and early 2022 as it aims to depict their trails eastward and their travails while out there. It sets their mobilizations, bottom-up, haphazard, often with a huge doses of farce in the preparations, with that of the largest foreign fighter contingent, the Russians, who benefited from considerable state assistance while mobilizing and deploying to Ukraine. In this sense, the monograph contextualizes the often-sensationalized issue of more than 17,000 foreign fighters (predominantly Russians) involved in the war in Ukraine and discusses the real scale of foreign recruitment for this conflict in the West. As was shown, these had been relatively modest contingents, sometimes featuring a handful of individuals from a given country, who often were proverbially lost in translation while the experts, scholars and policy-makers focused their attention on the foreign terrorist fighters in the ranks of the Islamic State of Iraq and Syria (ISIS). These had been more numerous and constituted an immediate threat to the West.

DOI: 10.4324/9781003192992-11

The story of the rag-tag brown-red cocktail has been less straightforward and, perhaps for this reason, less captivating. This monograph, however, has set out to bring to light the ins and outs of another foreign fighter mobilization developing against the backdrop of that for Syria. It has largely told a story of a less public and less successful mobilization which, ironically, was happening for a war being waged closer to the proverbial "West" than the civil war in Syria. Its limited size, at least before February 24, 2022 re-escalation, however, might have put off some of the potential recruits from joining. Moreover, Russia seemed to have successfully muddied the information waters around this war and might have actually convinced some that this was a civil war and not a Russo-Ukrainian war. If one was to add the fact that Ukraine's diasporas in the West were nothing like that of the Sunni Muslim states, then it should not be a surprise that the Ukrainian cause lacked its proponents. Consequently, passions could have hardly been ignited "here" so that the fighters would trickle "there."

The monograph has attempted to plug an obvious research and market gap which exists in studies on foreign fighters, which usually focus on foreign terrorist fighters. What is more, it situated the recruitment for this war, and the subsequent deployment of hundreds of Westerners to the front lines, in the context of the brown-red cocktail present in Europe, i.e., conditions which to some extent pre-ordain the European far-right and far-left's interest in a war such as this in Ukraine. Back in 2014, the author might have been surprised if not shocked with the appearance of the first French fighters in Donetsk but deployment of such militants to this conflict should not have come as a surprise as it offered not only a chance to test oneself or to feel a rush of adrenalin for a given fighter. The war in Ukraine also enabled Thiriart's theory of the "outside lung" to be tested in real life and allowed the fighters to redress this conflict as a titanic Russia versus the U.S. clash of immense international impact.

Unlike in some other conflicts, and contrary to the commonly held wisdom,[2] neither side of the conflict especially and for a prolonged period of time encouraged recruitment of Western, or more broadly – non-Russian, foreign fighters. This was, of course, to change in late February 2022. Yes, (some) Ukrainian volunteer battalions did not mind having military specialists from NATO countries in their ranks before that date but, as shown above, their pull was relatively modest and in reality, only the few hubs managed consistently to attract dozens of fighters into their ranks. At the same time, from 2015 onward the Ukrainian state, while attempting to bring all of the battalions under its control, effectively quashed the chances for further recruitment of such volunteers. From then on, foreigners could join the military on a contractual basis but the bureaucratic obstacles in the process (such as the necessity of a Ukrainian residence permit) proved formidable and successfully deterred many of the wannabe applicants. Simultaneously, on the "separatist" side, moves to curtail the bottom-up character of the militias and their integration into army "corps," while some of their most independent commanders were being purged, effectively ended the early improvisational days of the (para)military effort of the "People's Republics," which welcomed arriving foreigners. These proved useful while the "republics" attempted to present themselves as transnationally oriented "anti-fascists" in a struggle akin to that of the Spanish Civil War of the 1930s. At the same time, however, the radicalism of some of the foreign recruits, and their often brown or brown-red credentials, embarrassed the hosts who were keen on not turning into hotbeds or hosts of Europe's far-left or far-right radicals. They were, however, happy to see Ukraine in such a role and always reminded the global public opinion that theirs was a struggle with "Ukrainian neo-Nazis" or "banderites."

Regardless of the extent to which the sides in the war were willing to attract foreign fighters, their exploits while at war often proved less than remarkable. Fighters on both sides were aghast with what they called the "post-Soviet mentality" of their hosts – lack of initiative, chaos, abuse of alcohol, improvisational chains of command, quarrels between units and their commanders etc. At the same time, however, it seemed that the Ukrainian volunteer battalions were more adept at deploying and then making the most of the foreign fighters in their ranks. They might not have had the best equipment but they were given a chance to contribute to the Ukrainian war effort and some felt appreciated and vindicated.

On the "separatist" side, however, things looked rather more gloomy. Some of the fighters were relegated to the status of "cool little tourists," useful for propaganda purposes but without proper front line assignments. To get into the fight, they had to shop around for more active units but such chances were disappearing as the war was maturing into 2015. Much depended on a given fighter's connections, his route into the war, his standing with the commanding officer, and that very officer's track record with the neighboring "separatist" units or the overarching, but at times, chaotic, command structures.

Nothing symbolizes the haphazard nature of the foreign fighter reality of this war than their actual arrivals on the front lines or attempts at getting there. These often resembled farce and give testimony to the fact that neither side counted on huge mobilization of foreign volunteers for the war. Missed meetings, unanswered calls, Facebook messages without response, arrests of the arriving fighters while on the way to and from the Donetsk People's Republic (DNR)/Luhansk People's Republic (LNR) being turned down for a "nationalist" unit in Ukraine on the basis of one's Middle Eastern looks, etc. constitute the proverbial tip of the iceberg as far as farcical foreign fighter stories from Ukraine are concerned.

Consequently, and regardless of the at times grandiose rhetoric of their hosts, no legions or brigades of these fighters appeared on either side – there simply had not been enough of them. Moreover, this can also be gleaned from the casualty list as very few Western brown-red cocktail members died in the war. Their relatively low numbers and the difficulty with deployments actually enabled them to get through this conflict more easily, often to their chagrin as they sought combat experience. The issue of not fighting, not receiving missions, frustration with the relatively early ceasefires and the inaction on the front, contributed to the disillusionment felt by many of the foreign fighters in the war in Ukraine. If one was to couple that with the above-mentioned chaos, improvisation, disregard for human life, Soviet infantry tactics, command style and language barrier, then a picture of a foreign fighting existence which was far from perfect emerges. In addition to this, the fighters often felt they were not properly compensated for their service in Ukraine – not financially but, for example, by granting of Ukrainian citizenship, or Russian for some of the pro-"separatist" fighters.

Despite all of the above, some Westerners did travel eastward and fought in the war in Ukraine. Their large section was christened as a brown-red cocktail in this monograph. Its key components were fighters who saw themselves as "nationalists." Even if one takes such a self-description at face value, then it is also necessary to contextualize what this term amounts to in the reality of the twenty-first century. These fighters certainly had not been nationalists of the nineteenth or twentieth centuries who advocated or promoted the interests of one particular, usually theirs, nation or state. Their nationalism is "post-national" in nature, as nation no longer acts as the virtue or value they most strongly care about. This has been supplanted by the likes of Europe (as they often see themselves as European patriots and are eager to bond with their like-minded peers from other European countries), traditional style of life (Christian, family centered, often connected to a particular homeland) or, in the most extreme cases, race. For such individuals, a call to arms coming from a seemingly far away and foreign land is less outlandish than commonly perceived. Moreover, it might arrive from different places and this only strengthens the flexibility of the fighters from the brown-red cocktail. There is always another war to look forward to and there will be another chance to make a stand and cover oneself in glory. However, it is to be sought away from home as one "cannot have Donbas here," since these fighters see no option of engaging in anti-state violence at home. In their view, the state, with its repressive apparatus and the almost infinite means at its disposal, would always emerge victorious from such a confrontation.

Some of the brown-red fighters had known each other from before the war as they often originated from the same militant, anti-systemic milieu and literally met at demonstrations, protests, marches or in places inhabited by the members of the brown-red cocktail. They greeted one another in their social media pronouncement from their time on the front lines and allegedly held no grudges against their comrades who ended up on the other side of the war. Some appreciated being "the two sides of the same coin," and openly mused as to what would have made them join their protagonists in the conflict. Sometimes, a striking appreciation of Vladimir Putin was to be found amongst the far-right foreign fighters on the Ukrainian side. Simultaneously, however, other fighters rejected any comparison or alleged linkages with their "brethren" on the other side of the front line and openly mocked their naivete, while joining with Ukrainians/or "separatists." Interestingly, some foreign fighters who arrived in Ukraine functioned outside the brown or the brown-red circles and milieus in Europe. This especially concerned the central and eastern European fighters, who would claim to have come from the left, and to pay homage to different post-communist traditions which were easily to be found in the proto-communist "separatist People's Republics." Their views, however, had more in common with these of their brown comrades or opponents on the other side of the front line (anti-liberal, anti-Western, anti-U.S., anti-NATO, anti-LGBT, anti-migrant, pro-Russian and socially conservative). In these conditions, one would have to 'look left to spot the far-right'[3] from central and eastern European countries, rather than at outright brown-red circles.

As shown above, the war in Ukraine featured representatives of the far-right European milieu on either side of the conflict. This fact, however, has not been the result of a split in the milieu back in the West. It is true that the radical right mostly sided with Russia and followed its narrative on the war in Ukraine and it had been the more extreme elements of the far-right, and those not organizationally, structurally or financially dependent on Moscow, who were more willing to contemplate the arguments of the Ukrainian nationalists, such as the Azov movement. In some organizations, such as the German National Democratic Party (NPD) or the broader Swedish extreme right milieu, these "Russia vs Ukraine" disagreements might have been more pronounced but generally, the issue at hand failed to make a significant mark on the brown European milieu. In this sense, the Ukrainian far-right groups with transnational agendas and strategies, which attempted to sway some of their counterparts in the West away from the Moscow narrative, were largely unsuccessful in this process. However, they, especially via Azov, were able to forge strong connections with selected groups, especially in the countries immediately to the West of Ukraine (central and eastern Europe, "new" EU Member States).

Bizarrely, the most profound, or perhaps – the only – major split, on the far-right outside of Ukraine because of the conflict, happened in Russia. Its far-rightists lined up on different sides of the conflict – some fought against the hated Putin regime in the Ukrainian ranks, others – out of patriotic conviction or because they were pressurized to do so, joined the "separatist" militias. A significant number of Russian extreme right activists effectively decamped to Kyiv where they maintained their pre-war links to their Ukrainian brethren.

As the milieu was splitting in Russia, some of the Western European, and far-right at that, fans of Russia were doubling down on their connections to the country so that they could join the separatist "militias." As was shown, this was the case of the Italians who ventured eastward – these individuals mingled with Russian expats. Simultaneously, the Czech or Slovak fighters were forging connections with Russia via pro-Russian Facebook groups, which would put them in touch with relevant "handlers" on the ground. Last but not least, the pre-2014 Russia-Serbia (and Republica Srpska) ties, including foreign fighting of Russians in the pro-Serbian ranks in the Yugoslav wars of the 1990s, also proved a useful conduit for recruitment of fighters into the "separatist" ranks.

Patterns

This monograph concludes with a set of observations or patterns which could offer an interesting future departure point for scholars studying foreign terrorist fighters or other foreign fighters. These add to our knowledge on foreign fighters in general and offer a rare comparative perspective and context to research endeavors aiming to explain why and how people go to foreign wars. They are as follows:

1. Fresh start

   Foreign fighters treat foreign wars as a chance for a fresh start – the ISIS bound contingents of fighters included many such individuals. Ironically, in the case of Ukraine this meant traveling to a region, a proverbial Ukrainian "wild East," in which one could historically hope for such a start. It had been a magnet for outlaws, misfits, the restless, a place for literally resetting one's existence. Interestingly, the 2014 Russo-Ukraine war, which is still conducted in Donbas, rejuvenated such a status of this particular region of Ukraine. Back in 2014, it attracted not only the likes of the members of the volunteer battalions who later e.g., made careers for themselves in the military, National Guard or even Ukrainian politics, or "separatist" militias who made the most of the collapse of president Yanukovych's *simja* and sometimes almost overnight rose to become the DNR and LNR's warlords, but also the foreign fighters. As was shown, many of these came to Ukraine, or the "separatist" territories, to make a name for themselves as fighters, future military contractors, to receive military experience, to test themselves in battle, etc. Moreover, some were evidently running away from trouble back at home and Ukraine, be it government or "separatist" controlled parts, offered a fresh start. Here was a chance, just like in the past, to reset one's life and to give it a new meaning. The extent to which this process was successful remains debatable but many tried to accomplish this. Some even decided to settle in either Ukraine or the DNR/LNR, get married and have children, giving further meaning to the fresh start theory.

2. A "bigger" war

   As people seek meaning in their lives, the foreign fighters look for "big" issues with which they can explain their decision to go for a foreign war. Such issues allow them to dispel doubts whether it makes sense to deploy to the front lines thousands of miles away from home. The foreign terrorist fighters in Syria fought, at least initially, for the sake of their Sunni Muslim brethren and the foreign fighters in Ukraine were no different. Many of them saw this conflict in grandiose terms: as a fight between (a) the U.S., liberal West, NATO etc., and (b) Russia, the East, illiberalism, etc. Thus, they failed to see it as a Russo-Ukraine conflict or even a civil war (although the more red fighters stressed the local rebellion versus oppressive, "fascist," center aspect of it in their deliberations). Such an approach allowed for a disregard of many of the local nuances and peculiarities as, ultimately, the conflict, its fall out and confusion around it could be brought down to the denominator of Russia versus the U.S. This reading of the war also enabled the fighters to see themselves as actors in something which was bigger than a relatively minor war in Eastern Europe.

   Of course, not all of the fighters, especially on the Ukrainian side of the war, agreed with this reductionist reading of the situation. They hardly ever saw themselves as fans of the U.S. and wished not to be seen as pawns or stooges of the liberal West while fighting for Ukraine. This is not to say, however, that they disagreed with the other part of the grandiose equation – they saw the "separatists," rightly, as this monograph suggests, as tools of the Russian foreign policy. Moreover, they often interpreted the fact that they actually fought aggressive Russia in Eastern Ukraine as a part of a larger, more historically grounded, tradition of having to stop it somewhere so it does not come to/invade their home countries (that approach was especially true for Azov's Swedes). They also equated Russia with Asia – that was especially true for some of the most brown foreign fighters – which was meant to belittle and demean this Euro-Asian country in the eyes of their allies, backers or supporters.

3. A post-modern war

Not all of the world's foreign fighters are able to provide articulate ideological explanations as to why they joined a foreign war in the first place, and why this but not the other side in this very conflict. Sometimes, as was the case with the ISIS bound foreign terrorist fighters, other issues are at play here and a given individual deploys as s/he follows friends, colleagues or acquaintances or, as was shown above, looks for a fresh start. In the case of the war in Ukraine, however, there exists another explanation for these seemingly more accidental and less ideological decisions to go to the front lines: perception of the conflict as a post-modern war.

The fighters' motivations for joining the war were sometimes shallow and not much thought was given as to why one was joining this or that side of the conflict. In some cases, the fighters themselves would even admit that not much divided them from their foreign counterparts on the other side of the front line. It seemed that at times it had not been the politics of this or that side but the symbols, logos, graphics they were using in their fight that attracted the specific fighters. Moreover, personal connections, friendships also played a role in one's recruitment and prevailed over a given political reason for joining a given side. In this sense, the war in Ukraine became almost trivial, irrelevant to the fighters – it literally could have happened anywhere and some, if not most of them, would have also joined in. As a result, certain fighters, especially from the Western brown milieu, ended up literally shooting at one another in Eastern Ukraine. In the end, however, this fact did not amount to much as they agreed to disagree and upon their returns to their home countries often attempted to reconnect and restore their pre-war relationships with their erstwhile enemies from Ukraine.

Another post-modern aspect, as far as the foreign fighters were concerned, was the fact that it attracted individuals from different ideological backgrounds. This might not have been a surprise – the Spanish Civil War featured foreign fighters on the governmental (communist or far-leftist) and the rebel (fascists, monarchists, ultra-conservatives) sides. The fighters there flocked to their colors and fought against their ideological foes while in Spain.

In Ukraine, however, this division was no longer observed as the "separatists" fielded foreign fighters of both brown (far-right) and red (far-left) political persuasions. The fact that they fought for the same side and in the same units effectively destroyed the foreign fighter dichotomy of the Spanish Civil War. Nonetheless, some of the red fighters clung on to it so that they could justify their participation in this very foreign war and simultaneously, to demean the other, "fascist" or "banderite" side of the conflict. Of course, it would not withstand the test of everyday reality on the ground where the same far leftists who preached about rejuvenating the concept of the international brigades, found themselves in the trenches, and in the same unit, as the French far-right fighters who in the 1930s would have most probably joined general Franco's rebels in Spain. This seeming conundrum, however, could have also been explained away without much problem by the supposedly confused fighters. The author's interviewees gladly exclaimed that the left-right division no longer made sense (a twentieth century issue, in their view) as both the far rightists and far leftists knew who their real enemy had been – the U.S. This common ground provided a haven for a "hands across the divide"[4] approach amongst them. Ultimately, such fighters perceived themselves as "political soldiers," capable of seeing the bigger picture and going beyond the above-mentioned artificial left-right divides.

Simultaneously, the other side featured "highly political units," such as the Azov Battalion/Regiment and the RS which also attracted the foreign fighters. Some of their foreign recruits also had plans of turning their outfits into transnationally active political entities which would attract the "nationalists" of Europe and provide them with a platform to forge and tighten cross-border connections within the far-right milieu. Ironically, the far left *InterUnit* of the "separatists" also saw itself as a military-political vehicle for the world's anti-fascists.

4. Reconquest

Historically, the foreign fighters joined insurgencies that aimed to win or reconquer something (territory, state, glory, dignity) for a given oppressed group or minority. In the twenty-first century reality, this reconquest theory was rehashed as a mean of justifying one's involvement in the war as it pointed out to a given fighter's participation in a noble, higher cause and their individual quest for glory. Quite often the glory argument, or its permutations, has been a cover for something much more banal or trivial as the foreign fighters in reality have not been running toward glory but rather, away from something back at home. This was visible especially while looking at the Czech, Slovak, French, Swedish and Dutch contingents of these fighters – debts, impending incarceration, threat of severe legal punishments, difficult family situation, etc. featured largely in some of their stories.

Nonetheless, as shown above, both sets of "political soldiers" saw themselves as participants in a *Reconquista* – a term that harks back to the medieval ages in which the Iberian Peninsula was reconquered for Christianity from the Islamic rule. The original concept saw Christians, Westerners, battle it out with the allegedly Easterner, heathen, barbaric Muslims, etc. and it proved a popular magnet for the current day members of the brown-red cocktail. This was especially the case with the brown pro-Ukraine fighters who had already been anti-Islamic and anti-Muslim immigration to Europe. This particular *Reconquista*, however, would not solely be about the Muslim immigration into Europe but would also be directed at other adversaries of the current day European far-right, namely: the liberals, the feminists, the LGBT, and in some cases – the Jews. It would mean coloring Europe brown and moving it away from the post-Cold War ascendancy of the Washington Consensus, NATO and the European Union.

Ironically, some of the fighters on the "separatist" side also saw their fight in terms of *Reconquista*. They had also been less than favorable, to say the least, toward Muslim migrants in Europe but for them the *Reconquista*'s aim was not only be political, i.e., anti-liberal but also geopolitical in nature. Its aim would be to rid Europe of the American influence and push for the Russian inclusion into the future Eurasia, combining the two continents. The general anti-Americanism of such fighters would be acceptable to the *(Re)conquistadores* fighting on the other side. However, both sides would disagree on its geopolitical aspect as Azov's foreign fighters looked up to NATO in general, and the U.S. military in particular for support in their fight against the pro-Russian, if not Russian, "separatists." In this aspect, the brown foreign fighters, split across the two sides of the war, could not and would not come to an agreement.

5. Trailblazers

As far as wannabe foreign fighters in any war are concerned, some foreigner always gets to a front line first. These individuals act as trailblazers, i.e., those who forged the necessary connections and trekked "there" first. The war in Ukraine had not been any different in this respect. It goes without saying that this had been the easiest for the Russian foreign fighters – these had relatives, friends or colleagues in Donbas or wider Ukraine, spoke the local language(s) and had very little difficulty blending in with the larger group of local fighters. Their advantages in the process of getting there were to a large extent shared by some Serbian fighters who had worked in Russia or Belarus, usually on construction sites, before the onset of the war, and later gravitated to the "separatist" side in Ukraine. On the Ukrainian side, things looked a bit more complicated for the fighters – only individual volunteers had some Ukrainian, e.g., political, pre-war connections to Ukraine. Some, such as Mikael Skillt or Francesco Fontana, found themselves on the Euromaidan and gravitated from observers to fighters in the Ukrainian volunteer battalions. They then opened the door to the next foreign arrivals. Finally, the conflict saw a group of foreign trailblazers who had none of the above contacts or ways into Ukraine. They literally had to trek (just like Viktor Lenta and his group or Denis Šeler Croats) to the conflict zone and present themselves to the authorities on either side of the conflict.

6. Getting there

Logistics, understood here as the art of getting to the front lines, is key to any foreign fighter mobilization. Getting it wrong or complicating it too much nullifies the chances of a successful deployment of foreign volunteers to a given war. ISIS foreign terrorist fighters learned of this while traversing the, at first, relatively open Turkish-Syrian border. The Ukraine bound foreign fighters had diverse experiences related to their logistical arrangements for the war. Foreign fighters arriving to join the Ukrainian volunteer battalions had a much easier route to the conflict zone. Sometimes, all it took was to land in Kyiv and then presenting oneself at the office of a given battalion, e.g., located in the vicinity of the Euromaidan. In other cases, however, the fighters used their predecessors, the trailblazers, such as Mikael Skillt or Gaston Besson, as conduits into the war and reached out to them directly, therefore bypassing the command structure of a given battalion. Most usually, such contacts took place online, via Facebook, where early Euromaidan arrivals/turned foreign fighters openly advertised their units and spoke of a possibility of joining them in Eastern Ukraine.

To some extent, a similar situation developed on the other side of the conflict. Here the wannabe foreign fighters, in most cases with no local contacts or knowledge of Russian, shopped for conduits into the "People's Republics" (or at that time, Novorossiya) online. This time, however, it had not only been the fighters but individuals who had arrived there earlier and were able to establish themselves on the ground, namely: journalists sympathetic to the "separatist" cause or political/humanitarian activists (in some cases the fighters came to the DNR/LNR under the cover of a given "humanitarian convoy"). They might not have always agreed with the wannabe fighters' desire to join a war but often proved instrumental in provision of introductions and connections to the relevant people on the ground, most usually in Russia as the pro-"separatist" had to travel through Russia (with the city of Rostov as a key springboard into DNR/LNR). Again, Facebook profiles of these gatekeepers or pro-Russian, to a lesser extent pro-"separatist," Facebook groups, played a major role in this process as these allowed for the least cumbersome procedure of establishing contact between the two communities.

Interestingly, but perhaps not surprisingly, the pro-"separatist" gatekeeper-facilitator community of non-fighters attracted a group of wannabe business opportunist who wished to enrich themselves while in Donetsk and, to a lesser extent, in Luhansk. These dreamed of export-import businesses moving goods between their host countries and the DNR or established embassies or consulates of the "People's Republics" in Europe. Some of these ventures attracted individual Western members of the brown-red cocktail who, after a more or less intense period at the front, wished to settle in the DNR and looked for an opportunity of a stable income while there. Such chancers also appeared on the Ukrainian side – they were, however, less business oriented but at times wanted to ingratiate themselves with some of the most popular volunteer battalions and e.g., act as their recruiters abroad. Such bottom-up initiatives, rarely, if at all, coordinated with the top brass of the likes of Azov, usually fizzled out relatively quickly but oftentimes added to the embarrassment of their host units.

7. Elephant in the room

Conflicts often feature groups of underappreciated or understudied foreign fighters. Such was the case with the pro-Franco far-right fighters from the Spanish civil war or the Shia militants in the pro-Assad ranks of the war in Syria. The war in Ukraine also featured such a proverbial elephant in the room, the Russian foreign fighters. The non-Russians foreign fighters might have been present in every major military engagement of this war but their low numbers prevented them from making their mark. The Russians of the "separatist" forces, however, played a major role as they contributed to the salvation of the "People's Republics," whether as cannon fodder in the ranks of the "separatist" militias or individuals holding the front line before the arrival of the regular Russian troops in the summer of 2014. They were the by-product of the only state supported mobilization of foreign fighters for this conflict – other states, at best, adopted a "hear no evil, see no evil" policy of not interfering in the fighters' recruitment, departures or deployment. Moreover, the Russian fighters came in their thousands and some of them also, bizarrely, fought on the Ukrainian side. Interestingly, the latter group included some of the most ideologically brown individuals on the front lines whose presence also influenced the wider public's perception of the likes of the Azov Battalion/Regiment (as a proverbial hotbed of extremism) which hosted them.

8. (Lack of) women in the ranks

A prominent track of research on foreign terrorist fighters concerns the role played by women in their ranks. As was shown, this phenomenon is hardly replicated amongst the foreign fighters in Ukraine, brown-red or not, with very few women actually joining the ranks. This is not to stay that they would not play a role as far as reasons for deploying to Eastern Ukraine were concerned – effective honeytraps, allure of winning stunningly beautiful Slavic spouses on the back of one's marital exploits featured in some of the foreign fighters' biographies. Some even decided to remain in the East, either in separatist territories or in Ukraine after marrying local women. Only one, again – a major difference with the ISIS bound foreign terrorist fighters, decided to take his whole family to the "separatist" territories.

9. Money

Foreign fighters are ideally volunteers who join a foreign war without a pecuniary award. As the stories emerging from the ISIS ranks clearly showed, however, this had not been the case with the foreign terrorist fighters in Syria. They were salaried and were paid more than the local fighters. Similarly, the Ukraine bound foreign fighters, be it on the Ukrainian or "separatist" side received (paltry) salaries. Some protested and wished not to receive these but this did not change the fact that this was to ensure their enrolment into standing and professionalizing units which would have such individuals on their payroll and no longer as volunteers for "rag tag" forces.

10. Arguments

Members of any organization at times quarrel with one another. This is especially true in volunteer, bottom-up, rag tag structures which cannot rely on rigid hierarchies which would impose conformity and/or obedience amongst its members. The foreign fighters are not different in this respect and neither are the foreign terrorist fighters – the likes of the 2020 *Caliphate* Netflix series underscored this point in an especially vivid manner.[5] Unsurprisingly, the same can be said about the Ukraine bound brown-red contingents. The war featured much infighting, especially amongst the foreign fighters in the "separatist ranks" – the author even christened some of them as members of "drama contingents." There were plots, counterplots, assassination attempts, public wars on social media and, sometimes, mending of fences after returning home. Some of these quarrels were about money as some fighters accused their colleagues of e.g., misappropriating crowdfunded finances which were supposed to fund a certain unit or a group of foreign fighters.

11. (The threat of) returnees

There is considerable literature on the threat from the ISIS foreign terrorist fighters returnees. Moreover, a debate amongst experts on the issue is still ongoing as countries accept or refuse to repatriate captured fighters and their families from the Middle East. There is less of a debate in relation to the foreign fighters who are returning from "non-jihadi" conflicts and had not been members of terrorist organizations while fighting abroad. In many countries such war tourism is perfectly legal and seemingly, no sanction threatens or deters a wannabe foreign fighter from deploying to a war. Of course, given the fact that some of these individuals had been known to the police or the security services due to their pre-war political activism, they might have constituted a cause for concern or a red flag to security authorities. Consequently, some of the returnees, e.g., former Swedish members of Azov, were "interviewed" by their country's security service upon their return. However, this fact did not result in any further consequences for the fighters. They must have been deemed a relative low security risk and no further actions seemed to have been taken. This does not change, however, what they called "social" consequences as, in their words, the media allegedly targeted them and compared their exploits to those of the Swedish contingent in the ISIS ranks.

Other returnees faced less harassment upon their returns as many countries adopted a "hear no evil, see no evil" approach to the fact that some of their inhabitants effectively went to a foreign war and later returned back home. Bizarrely, some of these countries (usually in central or eastern Europe) seemingly had a case against such fighters as they banned any foreign fighting, not just terrorist fighters. However, they seemed not to take much notice or vigorous action against their citizens who openly moved to e.g., Donetsk. A striking example here is Serbia, which adopted a stringent anti-foreign fighter law on one hand and then "prosecuted" the returnees on the other, who usually received paltry suspended sentences. It was rumored that in the likes of the Baltic states this was a part of a deliberate policy of laying low and minimizing the Russian blowback by not advertising any facts about "their" foreign fighters in the Ukrainian ranks. Others, like Croatia, initially saw no problems with their citizens traveling to Ukraine as the country benefited from the inflow of such fighters into the ranks of its armed forces during the war of the 1990s.

Simultaneously, a group of countries vacillated as far as their policies on foreign fighter returnees were concerned. They clearly were interested in and disliked their sojourns eastward but, just like Sweden, found it hard to move beyond the initial steps of e.g., arrests upon return. Such was the case with Italy, Spain and Austria. Some of these initial actions were also happening against the backdrop of either Ukrainian or Russian pressure to go after a specific set of fighters or to drop charges against others. A most extreme case was the Czech Republic, which at first "saw no evil," then gave light suspended sentences to the fighters and in 2021 moved on to prosecute the pro-"separatist" fighters on the grounds of their involvement in "terrorist attacks" against a legitimate and recognized state – Ukraine.

Some of the fighters who deployed to Ukraine had truly been "career foreign fighters" as they also had fought in other wars (Yugoslav wars) before fighting there or sought other conflicts after Ukraine (mostly in the Middle East). This mostly concerned the Russians who, e.g. deployed in high numbers as members of the private military companies (PMCs) to Africa or the Middle East but there has also been community of allegedly PMC oriented Serbs amongst them. Some observers compared these to "mercenaries" as they were said to have gone to Ukraine not only for ideological reasons but also to earn money. They would, unsurprisingly, mask this involvement by revoking the fact that they were there to "repay a debt" to Russia as it had been the Russian fighters who flocked to the Serb colors in the Yugoslav wars of the 1990s (similar motivation was expressed by some of the Croats fighting on the other side of the war in Ukraine – these wished to repay the debt they owed to their foreign supporters from the 1990s).

It is also true that others, such as some of the French or Swedish fighters, also dreamt of continuing their post-Ukraine careers, preferably as members of the PMCs. They roamed the world looking for next assignments and even wrote recommendations for one another. In this sense, they constituted a true "Western foreign fighter" society or a club, a brotherhood of which one could hear or learn but not necessarily join. The fact that, unlike their ISIS counterparts, they had not been termed foreign terrorist fighters, and could actively plan future deployments to conflict zones after Ukraine.

What is even more striking, some saw their trip eastward as the ultimate test and or preparation for continuation of the fight back at home. This was in line with Thiriart's "outside lung" theory, according to which far-right fighters were to train in what would be called near abroad and then redeploy back home for what would effectively be a European civil war. Organizations such as the Nordic Resistance Movement (NRM) but also the Czechoslovak Soldiers for Peace sent their members into the ranks of the separatists or to organizations in Russia which fought on the side of the separatists so that they would get the necessary training experience. Such activities, obviously, constitute a direct threat to the West as its inhabitants actively sought paramilitary training with illegal actors, including the Russian Imperial Movement in Russia (*Russkoe imperskoe dvizhenie*, RID) – consider a terrorist organization by the U.S. In this sense, the foreign fighters from Ukraine could be a security challenge to their host countries but it must be stressed here that relatively few were directly involved in these activities. Some of these questions will later be addressed in the current author's next research project, to be conducted while at the Center for Research on Extremism, C-Rex, at the University of Oslo, which will focus on the postwar careers of the Western foreign fighters in Ukraine. This project will primarily aim to assess the scale of the threat emanating from such veteran fighters after their return from the front lines in Ukraine. Thus, one could say that the current author's research adventure with the foreign fighters in Ukraine, which started back in 2014, will continue.

Notes

1 See: Daniel Koehler and Miroslav Mares, *Fighting on the Right Side. Exploring the Phenomenon of Extreme Right-Wing Foreign Fighters*, Abingdon: Routledge, forthcoming.
2 Kacper Rekawek, "Neither 'NATO's Foreign Legion' Nor the 'Donbass International Brigades': (Where Are All the) Foreign Fighters in Ukraine?," *PISM Policy Paper* no. 6(108) (March 2015), https://www.pism.pl/files/?id_plik=19434, accessed: February 10, 2021 for a discussion of this issue.
3 See *Counter Extremism Project*, "Episode 8: Extreme Right Foreign Fighters in Ukraine," May 13, 2021, https://www.counterextremism.com/content/cep-podcast-fighting-terror, accessed: December 2, 2021.
4 *Hands across the Divide* is a sculpture in (Londonderry, Northern Ireland, symbolizing reconciliation amongst the two communities divided by the Irish Troubles from 1969 to 1999.
5 See https://www.netflix.com/title/80240005, accessed: December 8, 2021, for a website of this series.

12

"CONCERNED CITIZENS OF THE WORLD?" FOREIGN VOLUNTEERS FOR UKRAINE IN 2022

Introduction

Before the author progresses with this chapter of the current monograph, a disclaimer is in order. The previous chapters demonstrated that the issue of foreign fighting in the Russo-Ukraine war seemed largely over by 2015/2016 when the war in Donbas became a static affair, resembling the trench warfare of the Western front from World War I. Such a dreary and non-glorious conflict failed to attract new fighters, who had no intention of wasting a foreign fighting opportunity while in a trench in Eastern Ukraine. As was also shown, both sides seriously curtailed the opportunity for wannabe foreigners effectively to enlist in their ranks. Ukraine had no volunteer battalions, apart from the rump Right Sector, which was "tolerated" by the military while deployed on the front lines. Moreover, its National Guard, which fell under the ministry of internal affairs, and which featured some of the previous volunteer battalions such as Azov, forbade foreigners from joining. Thus, the only option was enlisting as a contract soldier in the Ukrainian military, but that was only possible after a lengthy bureaucratic procedure. At the same time, the "separatists" also brought their units under the local ministries of internal affairs which also were unwelcoming toward new foreign recruits. Consequently, such a state of affairs would slowly see the numbers of foreigners involved, as some of the last diehard foreigners were allowed to stay in the ranks (as is evident in the Swedish, French, Western and Central-Eastern European chapters of this monograph), dwindle toward zero.

As became evident, this assumption held as long as the war continued in its static manner. There were periods in which the exchanges of fire and casualties on either side of the so-called "contact line" were negligible, to say the least, and one might have seen this as a harbinger of a more profound diplomatic

DOI: 10.4324/9781003192992-12

de-escalation among the belligerents. At the same time, however, Russia dramatically built up its forces along the border with Ukraine at first in the spring of 2021, which suggested that an escalation might also be in the works.[1] If the latter was to be true, the current author reasoned while completing the final chapters of this book, then there was a possibility of an uptick in foreign recruitment by either side of the war. As it was to turn out shortly after February 24, 2022 and the Russian re-invasion of Ukraine, this was precisely what happened.

The author was initially skeptical that, given the full scale character of the reignited conflict, and the potential for a swift Russian victory, which looked likely in the last days of February 2022, that a new, significant mobilization of foreigners would actually take place. His skepticism was heightened by the Ukrainian claims, which will be discussed below, of recruiting tens of thousands of foreigners to their cause in a manner akin to the Spanish international brigades. However, it quickly dawned on him that this skepticism was at least partly misplaced. Numerous individuals expressed an interest in joining the Ukrainian side, with "thousands crossing the border [into Ukraine]."[2] The key question of how many would join the fight remained open. An individual involved in the recruitment process stressed that according to his guess "hundreds" would actually get to the front lines and, by the summer of 2022, it looked as if he had been right in his estimates.[3] What initially looked like a tidal wave of volunteers for Ukraine who would attempt to change the course of the war through their service in the Ukrainian ranks began to resemble groups of "well-networked [foreign] individuals fighting here and there."[4] As it transpired, one needed luck, connections, tenacity and perseverance actually to get to fight for Ukraine as it took months for its "international legion" to take off the ground.[5]

This chapter will attempt to take stock of the post-February 24 developments and account for the initial enthusiasm behind the recruitment of foreigners by Ukraine and the subsequent "reality check" as far as their numbers were concerned. It must be stressed, however, that the story of foreigners fighting in the Russo-Ukrainian war is by no means over and is still a process in the making. For this reason, the following must be seen as preliminary findings of a research process which the author plans to continue during his postdoctoral period at the Center for the Study of Extremism (C-Rex) at the University of Oslo. Moreover, an important distinction must be made among the author's objects of study. The pre-2022 foreigners fighting in Ukraine had mostly been foreign fighters, individuals who joined either the pro-Russian "separatist" popular militias or Ukraine's volunteer battalions before they were integrated into Ukraine's armed forces. The post-February 24, 2022 pro-Ukraine recruits, however, differed from their 2014 predecessors, as they have been joining the forces of a legitimate and recognized state actor – Ukraine. Thus, the author will refer to them as "foreign volunteers." As will become evident, some of the former foreign fighters of 2014 also returned to fight in 2022 and thus naturally evolved into volunteers. Moreover, the pro-Russian separatists featured some of the 2014 veterans who remained as fighters in this status as they fought in the ranks of the non-recognized "People's Republics." All of these individuals will be discussed below and the distinctions between them will be maintained in this postscript chapter to the story which initially seemed to have ended in 2015/2016.

Ideology and Motivations

The 2022 mobilization of foreign volunteers for the Russo-Ukraine war is less ideological than that of 2014. Brown-red elements are still present in the ranks but are most probably per capita less significant and consequently less visible to outside observers. In short, back in 2014 Mikael Skillt, the alleged "'white power' warrior from Sweden,"[6] had been one of the, if not the, face of foreign fighters in Ukraine. Ironically, he was back on the front lines eight years later but kept a low profile and shied away from publicizing his deeds in Ukraine.[7] His place as the most well-known foreigner to deploy in the war was taken by a former U.S. service-man, James Vasquez, whose war exploits outside Kyiv turned him into a celebrity amongst the foreign volunteers in Ukraine.[8] Vasquez had no prior connection to Ukraine, nor was he ideologically motivated along the lines of the members of the brown-red cocktail. He admitted that his grandmother was from Latvia and she shared with him the stories of her family's prosecution under the "Russian" (Soviet) rule. These memories, coupled with the news of the Russian re-invasion of Ukraine convinced Vasquez to "go do this," join the war on Ukraine's side.[9] Thanks to members of the Ukrainian diaspora in the U.S. and a chance encounter with a Ukraine-born UK national, he was able quickly to deploy to the front lines around Kyiv.[10] As was shown in the Chapter 6 of this monograph, Skillt's decision to go to Ukraine might have been taken on the spur of the moment but he none-theless possessed contacts in the Ukrainian nationalist circles which allowed him to navigate the local reality in a less chance-like manner.

When the call for foreign volunteers was first issued by President Zelensky, it was followed by news of allegedly 20,000 individuals from all over the world who were said to have volunteered for Ukraine's "international legion" (or the legion).[11] Ukraine even issued a seven-step "algorithm" on how to join the legion.[12] The process, unlike in 2014, would start with a given individual con-tacting a Ukrainian embassy and it was on this basis that the above-mentioned 20,000 applications/expressions of interests were received by Ukraine. As such, this was a state led and a state organized process which featured submitting one's documents and a vetting of the potential recruit. Thus, no longer was this to be run along the improvised 2014 lines with volunteers showing up on the Maidan in the offices of a given volunteer battalion.

Consequently, this state enterprise, widely advertised and supported by the global popularity of President Zelensky and Ukraine's status of the attacked underdog, attracted the attention of individuals of different backgrounds and coming from all walks of life – "concerned citizens of the world," as was claimed by one of their recruiters.[13] In sum, one could find a Canadian comedian,[14] a "Scottish grandad,"[15] a Latvian parliamentarian,[16] and veterans who fought alongside Kurdish forces against the Islamic State of Iraq and Syria (ISIS)[17] trekking eastward to join "the International Legion of Defence of Ukraine."[18] In the earlier days, it seemed a mobilization which was far larger than that of 2014, more colorful in its contents and harder to break down into neat categories of volunteers. Moreover, it was mostly conducted in the open, with people eagerly sharing their intention to join the conflict.[19] Thus, unlike in 2014, no "ghosts," individuals who deployed to the front lines secretly and later returned home without going public, initially appeared amongst the post-February 24, 2022 foreign volunteers.[20] It is still too early to determine how many of the arriving fighters were "re-setters" who might have wished to "re-set" their lives in Ukraine or start afresh, with the war acting as a demarcation line for a new stage of their lives.[21] Some, just like their counterparts in 2014, might still reach a conclusion on viability of such a re-set after some time in Ukraine; others might still be unsure of what to do next. The above-mentioned Vasquez returned home in late spring 2022 but also announced that he would be coming back and sold his house in the U.S.[22] More of these cases are likely to follow later on in 2022. Apart from the "ghosts" and the "re-setters," the 2014 mobilization also featured numerous "adventurers," the backbone of the Western foreign fighter secret society, individuals ready to deploy from one war to another, while looking for adrenalin and a thrill. This category of foreign volunteers prominently came to the fore shortly after February 24, 2022. They were the people who moved quickly, participated in the fighting and then often returned home. For example, "I could only stay that long. I have a mortgage to pay, you know"[23] or "Kyiv was defended and we had nothing else to do out there."[24]

As the conflict dragged on, however, the reality on the ground began to change for the foreign volunteers. As was confirmed to the author by a journalist embedded in Ukrainian units, these might have featured foreigners but hardly any of them was willing to speak to the media.[25] It seemed that the enthusiasm of the early days, which featured the "concerned citizens of the world" rushing to Ukraine to defend its capital, gave way to a more downbeat reality of the eastern or southern fronts. No longer was enthusiasm and availability of a given wannabe volunteer a commodity sought by the Ukrainian hosts, as warfare in Donbas or around Kherson pitted the Ukrainian military against well-supplied and determined Russian forces. In short, the space of enthusiastic foreign adventurers on short-term deployments, often with no military experience, was shrinking. Moreover, the legion, the alleged umbrella organization for any arriving foreigner, began openly to advertise the fact that, from then on, it was only interested in individuals with combat experience.[26] As will be shown, other units, which seemingly favored recruiting foreigners, also opted only for the experienced ones or effectively cut all avenues available to potential foreign recruits to join them. Consequently, the number of fighting volunteers present in Ukraine in the early summer of 2022 dropped and the above-mentioned 20,000 who allegedly initially applied to join the legion were just a distant memory. As one of the American volunteers remarked on the numbers of his compatriots: "6,000

Americans came over. 3,000 immediately rejected. About 100 are serving in the ZSU [Armed Forces of Ukraine]."[27] Such pronouncement might be slightly incorrect but it was becoming evident that it had become "a war in which the only fighting foreigners are the well networked ones."[28]

One could argue that such developments transformed the "concerned citizens of the world" type of a mobilization of foreign volunteers into a more professional but less headline-friendly phenomenon. At the same time, it dawned on many that the war would be no short-term affair, that the enemy possessed immense material advantage over Ukraine and that one had to negotiate across a series of bureaucratic obstacles which prevented some foreigners from signing up with a given unit or even receiving a gun.[29] This process was happening against the backdrop of the legion's very slow start, as it only announced fielding of its first "battalion" three months after being founded.[30] This outlet, designed to accommodate arriving foreigners, largely failed in its task after the March 13, 2022 bombing of the Yavoriv base in Western Ukraine, an alleged "turning point" as far as deployment of foreigners for the war was concerned.[31] The cruise missile attack on this base resulted in a string of casualties amongst the arriving foreign volunteers who were being processed and trained at this base.[32] This "blowing up" of the legion seriously dampened the morale of its future members and many returned home, unsure of what to do next.[33] Some were said to have literally run away from Ukraine and did not come back.[34]

In the meantime, some volunteers, like Vasquez, who felt unsure of what to do next looked for their own assignments and attached themselves to units of the Ukrainian Territorial Defence Forces (TDF) or the Ukrainian military. This resulted in the fact that large Ukrainian formations would literally host groups or teams of foreign volunteers, mimicking the tactic employed by the Ukrainian volunteer battalions back in 2014. Some of these volunteers would also be directly picked up from the border by recruiters, representing different units. Thus, in this way they by-passed the process which Ukraine established early in the conflict (the above-mentioned "algorithm") and, to some extent, proverbially surfed beneath the radar, while officially not being legionnaires (members of the legion).[35]

In such conditions, it looked as if the legion would not recover from the doldrums of the Yavoriv bombing as it simply might have outlived its purpose. Astonishingly, however, it seemed to have staged a comeback during the heavy fighting for the city of Severdonetsk in Donbas (Luhansk *oblast*, province) when its fighters were deployed to stem the Russian advance in this city.[36] Of course, this development brought news of the first casualties from amongst the legionnaires.[37] Interestingly, some of these fallen legionaries have been eulogized on far-right telegram channels as their "brothers." In a case of a French foreign volunteer and a former member of the French Foreign Legion,[38] it seems that the eulogizing was not out of place as he was rumored to have been a member of different far-right outfits before departing for Ukraine. Presence of such individuals in the ranks of the legion, widely suspected by many external observers,[39] embarrassed Ukraine, which has been battling accusations of morphing into a "laboratory" and "training ground" for the world's far-rightists.[40] The next section of this chapter will address this issue thoroughly to account for the perceived, or invented, brown-red character of the 2022 foreign volunteer mobilization for Ukraine.

Brown-Red 2022?

As was shown throughout the previous chapters of this monograph, the 2014 mobilization of foreign fighters for either side of the Russo-Ukraine war had been brown-red in characters. Far-left and far-right individuals trekked eastward from different Western countries and fought, especially in the early phase of the conflict. Simultaneously, the fact that some of Ukraine's volunteer battalions were ideological in nature and welcomed some right-wing extremists into their ranks helped establish Ukraine's black legend as far as welcoming foreign extremists was concerned.

Fast forward eight years and, in 2022, Ukraine once again had to answer questions on whether it had been fielding foreign right-wing extremists in the ranks of its TDF.[41] This accusation neatly complemented that put forward by Russia, which allegedly re-launched its war on Ukraine in the name of "de-Nazification" of Ukraine in general, and its elite in particular.[42] Couple all that with a viral video in which an Azov TDF fighter was filmed putting bullets allegedly destined for Chechens in the Russian service into pig fat and the scene was set for another episode of Ukraine being seen as a global "laboratory" of the far right.[43] Moreover, Azov, widely seen as a "neo-Nazi" unit,[44] attracted a great deal of attention on itself by its brave stand in Mariupol, where it was besieged by superior Russian and DNR forces in an iconic siege in the steelworks plant of Azovstal.[45] Its bravery and fame sat uneasily with many as e.g. the BBC, which earlier interviewed the current author about the pig fat bullets video, was backtracking on its coverage of "nazis" in Ukraine and showcased Azov as Ukrainian nationalists defending Mariupol.[46] Suddenly, the "neo-Nazis" of Azov became one of the key stories of the spring 2022 phase of the war and the next episodes of their story were played out in the international media.[47] Simultaneously, it seemed as if everyone was keen on "explaining" the Azov Regiment and the Azov movement and the extent to which it could have been truly called "neo-Nazi" or extremist.[48] In short, the brown dimension of the Russo-Ukrainian war, an aspect which was far from key for its development between 2014 and 2022, found itself under the spotlight.

Interestingly, all of this was happening against the backdrop of a "civil war" on the Western far right over the Russian (re-)invasion of Ukraine. As was shown on the pages of the earlier chapters, different organizations or individuals took either the side of Kyiv or Moscow back in 2014 but February 24, 2022 once again pushed this issue to the fore. A meme circulating on pro-Ukraine far-right telegram channels encapsulated the "dilemma" for Western extremists in the most striking of fashions: it depicted President Putin as an ape like figure and listed his "white saviour policies" such as: launching wars in the name of "denazification," imprisoning Russia's "nationalists" (far-rightists), running a "corrupt and multi-ethnic empire," which is full of "Muslims" and sees a "total decline […] of white population," and suffers from "insane abortion numbers" and "African AIDS numbers."[49] In short, in the words of one far-right influencer, the Russian Denis "Nikitin" Kapustin, founder of White Rex, a popular among far-rightists clothing brand, twenty-first-century Russia would not "free" his Western brethren. They might "hate [their] governments because they force feed [them] with LGBT, diversity, migration, gender politics and all that s^&*." At the same time, however, Putin "will *not* bring white Christian freedom to you, but GULAG and death!" He finished his call, issued quickly after February 24, with a call for the Western far-rightists to "pick [their] side."[50]

This picking of sides was being forced upon the West's far right by the likes of Kapustin after a prolonged struggle between the likes of Azov on one hand and Russian or Russia inspired sponsored far-right actors on the other to dominate the milieu.[51] As was shown earlier in the monograph, the battle lines were to an extent clearly demarcated with most of the radical right siding with Russia and the far right's more extreme or identarian elements, not financially beholden to Moscow, more receptive to the Ukrainian far-right message. The post-February 24, 2022 reality hardly saw the above-mentioned actors change their positions, regardless of all the memes circulating on telegram or Kapustin's admonitions.[52] Thus, one could have expected that, just like in 2014, the brown element of the brown-red cocktail would be prominently represented among the foreigners fighting in Ukraine. This, however, has so far not been the case. The relatively low in number cases of individual far-right individuals drowned in the initial proverbial sea of volunteers who flocked to Ukraine.[53] It is true that some Western far-right entities organized collections and donated medical or tactical equipment to their like-minded brethren in Ukraine, such as Azov linked TDF units, or sent "humanitarian missions" to Ukraine but very few of their members actually trekked eastward to join the fighting.[54] This chapter's next section will provide details on the issue and discuss why this has been the case.

Avenues Closed

With the 2022 phase of the Russo-Ukrainian war, it was becoming evident that one thing was literally to pontificate on one's social media platforms about going "there," whereas another was the question of how to find oneself deployed to the front lines. Moreover, the pro-Russia far-rightists who might have wished to have fought on the Russian side had a convenient excuse of simply not being able to fly to Russia as the predominant majority of European countries closed their airspace to jets flying to and from Russia. Consequently, the only representatives of the brown-red cocktail who were to surface on the Russian side had been very few and mostly veterans of the 2014 phase of the conflict, such as "an Italian extreme leftist, a Serbian nationalist" who both died, a further two Serbs, including Bratislav Živković, the leader of the nationalist "chetnik" movement, "a far-right French army veteran, and a Slovak right-wing extremist."[55]

At the same time, recruitment efforts either run by individuals with wide-ranging connections in the West (such as Kapustin) or from Ukraine by the likes of local far-right organizations (such as the Azov Movement), yielded surprisingly paltry results. Kapustin's telegram channel showcased "his" recruits, who were then sent to the likes of Battalion "Revenge" (more on the unit below) but these were individual cases.[56] The Azov Movement, a political entity which grew out of the original Azov Battalion, represented by the likes of the National Corps (Natsionalnyi korpus, NK) political party, seemed best positioned to recruit and field foreign volunteers for Ukraine.[57] "Its" Azov Battalion (then Regiment) featured some foreign fighters back in 2014 and NK developed wide-ranging contacts abroad.[58]

Thus, it could have theoretically hoped to entice a respectable number of individuals to join one of the TDF units dominated by the original Battalion/Regiment's veterans. These were then rebranded as e.g. "Azov Kyiv," "Azov-Dnipro," "Azov-Kharkiv" etc. to indicate their place of origin. They were regular TDF battalions which were, in fact, smaller than regular army battalions, sometimes numbering fewer than 200 men. They, however, developed a distinct identity due to the fact that they were led by former soldiers, veterans of the original Azov. Simultaneously, NK's international department was tasked with helping the recruitment effort for the legion so that it could channel individuals enticed into coming to Ukraine by the Azov Regiment's military exploits into the former structure.[59] Given all of this, the recruitment expectations might have been high, as both the recruiters and entities were seemingly ready to field new volunteers.

Unfortunately for Azov and Ukraine, this proved not to be the case. NK-led recruitment efforts netted 20 to 30 individuals, of whom a minority had been of far-fight backgrounds as the legion was consumed by discussions related to the status, contracts and deployment of the arriving volunteers.[60] The Azov-linked TDF units also effectively signed themselves out of contention as hosts of the arriving foreigners as they came under the command of the "the Ukrainian Special Operations Forces (SOO or Syly spetsial'nykh operatsiy Zbroynykh Syl Ukrayiny). This formal and bureaucratic move is to help ensure their eastward deployment as not all of the [...] TDF units will fight for Donbas. It does not mean, however, that these volunteer formations and their soldiers acquired the status of SOF (Special Operations Forces) operators nearly overnight. [...] this route is not open to foreigners who will not be able to enlist in what formally is a SOF [special forces] formation."[61]

All in all, just like in the case of the pro-Russian foreign volunteers or fighters, the only notable component of the brown-red cocktail in the post-February 24, 2022 ranks of Azov had been the veterans of 2014. Mikael Skillt, the de facto leader of the Azov foreigners and the face of the Swedish contingent in Ukraine,[62] resurfaced and ended up, through his connections in the country, with SOO units fighting in the east of the country.[63] Denis Šeler, a Croat veteran of the Azov Battalion,[64] was rumored to have led a group of Croat volunteers during the battle of Kyiv in March 2022.[65] Additionally, a few other and anonymous foreign veterans of Azov fought in the ranks of the so-called "foreigner group" adjacent to one of the Kyivan TDF units.[66]

The Right Sector, another 2014 volunteer battalion which was ready to receive and deploy foreigners in its ranks on the front lines in the war's first phase, seemed like another perfect fit for the volunteers of 2022. It still had the status of the last Mohicans among the former volunteer battalions – the Right Sector remained outside the command structures of the Ukrainian military and marketed itself as the only truly independent force on the front lines.[67] This story, however, came to a close on April 1, 2022 as the Right Sector opted, just like Azov TDF battalions, to join the SOO and automatically lost the right to enlist new foreigners in its ranks[68] (a fact confirmed to the author by Right Sector recruiters).[69]

These conditions enable smaller and lesser known "challengers" to emerge and attempt to move into pole position on foreign volunteer recruitment and deployment on the Ukrainian side. Battalion "Revenge," a paramilitary arm of Tradition and Order, an Azov linked groupuscule, has already been mentioned but "Bratstvo" and Carpathian Sich also need to be mentioned here. None of these formations developed any sophisticated "enlist foreigners" strategies but ended up including Belarusian, Czech, Danish, Irish, Polish and Canadian members.[70] This might also have been the by-product of the fact that they were rumored to have an open door policy of "get to Kyiv and we will get you to the front" and also deployed their recruiters to the Polish-Ukrainian border to intercept impressionable wannabe volunteers so that they could join their and no other TDF units.[71]

Regardless of the "challenger's" successes in recruitment of foreign volunteers, another unit, already profiled in this monograph, the Georgian National Legion (now also re-Christened as Georgian Foreign Legion or simply Georgian Legion) once again proved the most successful in this field. The Georgian National Legion (GNL) allegedly grew to a multi-national battalion of 500 to 600 combat experienced individuals. Its members were dispersed in squads around different formations both on the southern and eastern fronts of the war. The GNL was not ideological in its recruitment and claimed to have successfully spotted and deterred some extremists from joining its ranks. Predictably, however, not in every case were the recruiters successful in this and cases of individuals known, e.g. from the U.S., were featured in the media.[72] The Belarusian units, mono-national in their make-up and thus not open to Westerners, might have even beaten the GNL in terms of foreigners in their ranks. Initially, the Belarussians formed one battalion, named after Kastus Kalinouski, the 1863 anti-Russian rebel of joint Belarusian, Lithuanian and Polish background, and this later grew into a regiment of the Ukrainian military with other smaller detachments functioning within the Ukrainian SOO or the TDF.[73] The initial was led by a former French foreign legionnaire or former members of the Azov Battalion, which had its share of Belarusians in 2014.[74] It also featured prominent football hooligans of the Belarusian Dynamo Minsk,[75] representatives of a milieu which has a long history of far-right radicalism. The unit, however, steered clear of associations with extremism and was embraced by what is effectively the democratic Belarusian government in exile as "patriotic."[76] Finally, one also has to mention the presence of the reconstituted Sheikh Mansour battalion, staffed by diaspora and anti-Russian Chechens residing in the West,[77] and the so-called "Freedom for Russia" legion consisting of former Russian prisoners of war.[78]

The 20,000?

Throughout the spring of 2022 different estimates attempting to capture the scale of the mobilization of foreign volunteers for Ukraine appeared online. These erred on the side of overestimation, to put it mildly, as they seemed almost randomly to assign high numbers to some nationalities and neglect contributions from others.[79] At the same time, Russia was also keen on flouting figures of "terrorists" or "mercenaries" deployed on the side of Ukraine (i.e. foreign volunteers) and in an attempt to embarrass Western countries. An example of this phenomenon was the current author's alleged "Polish" contributions, with as many as 1,831 in the ranks and 378 dead or alleged hundreds of volunteers from the neighboring Baltic Republics (which all have a population of 6 million).[80] If these figures were true, then we would almost constantly hear of (a) returns back home or (b) funerals of the fallen volunteers taking place in cemeteries in the cities and towns in which they were born. No such thing was happening and, for this reason, it can be assumed that the Russian figures are widely off the mark as the states allegedly "sending" such volunteers could not have all been involved in a conspiracy covering up returns and funerals of the dead volunteers returning from Ukraine.

In short, one has to have a critical eye toward any published statistics, especially as the legion provides sparce information on its numbers. This could, of course, be the result, of operational security but at the same time, it can be assumed that the number of its actual fighters is far lower than initially anticipated. Moreover, remembering the comments from the fighters on the fact that only the "networked" got to the front lines on their own, the current author agrees with one of his interviewees who spoke about "hundreds" of foreign volunteers who will actually fight for Ukraine throughout 2022.[81] It is also becoming obvious that it will take months, if not years, and certainly for this period of the war to finish, to attempt an accurate and objective estimation of the volunteers' numbers. One must remember that this book, which includes "national" estimations of the numbers of foreigners on both sides of the war, mostly focuses on the 2014 to 2016 period and is a by-product of the current author's years of researching the issue. Comparatively, it might take another few years for more information, testimonies, accounts, etc. to resurface, which will allow the likes of the current author to account fully for the story of the 2022 foreign volunteer mobilization for Ukraine.

Apart from the above-mentioned individuals such as Vasquez or the 2014 veterans, and the foreigners recruited by the likes of Azov (a very low number) or the GNL (a more sizeable number), the other "new" Western foreigners who actually got to the front lines featured representatives of the following countries:[82]

1. Belgium: Allegedly, more than 100 individuals did apply to join the legion but only 18 left for Ukraine, with half of them back by the end of March.[83]

2. Canada: Initially, Canadians allegedly constituted the fourth largest group of foreign volunteers wanting to join the nascent legion.[84] However, this has been a notable contingent among foreign volunteers in Ukraine for two other reasons: (a) The presence of a "celebrity" fighter in its ranks, sniper "Wali," and (b) discord in the ranks of a Canadian "brigade" present on the front lines. "Wali," a former Canadian soldier and a veteran of the fight against ISIS in Iraq, attracted an inordinate amount of attention due to his status and fame as an extremely successful sniper who was coming to Ukraine to repeat his Middle Eastern feats. As it later turned out, he found the Russo-Ukraine war a totally different experience from that in the Middle East and returned home relatively early.[85] At the same time, the so-called "Norman Brigade," effectively a team or at best a platoon of Canadian fighters in Ukrainian ranks, suffered from internecine feuding among the fighters who threw accusations of incompetence and nepotism at each other.[86]

3. Czech Republic: By no means a numerically significant contingent, with some fighters in the ranks of the far-right Battalion "Revenge" or allegedly the Carpathian Sich (see above for more on the issue), the Czech contribution deserves a mention for a set of different reasons. Throughout 2021, the Czech authorities prosecuted fighters who in the 2014 phase of the war fought in the "separatist" ranks and had them sentenced to lengthy prison terms for the crime of conducting "terrorist attacks."[87] In short, Prague decided that fighting in the ranks of anti-Ukrainian, sub-state "separatists" could be equated with "terrorism." Any doubts over the status of the pro-Ukraine volunteers in 2022, however, were quickly dispelled as the government announced that none of the individuals who venture to fight in Ukraine on Kyiv's side will face prosecution upon returning home.[88]

4. Denmark: The Danish contingent suffered its first casualty in late April 2022.[89] A Danish sniper in the Ukrainian ranks claimed to have killed 100 Russian soldiers.[90] Another Danish fighter, initially in the ranks of the "Bratstvo" battalion then formed his own "Team Viking" with other Scandinavians fighting in the Ukrainian ranks.[91]

5. Finland: Early reports indicated that volunteers from that country were traveling to Ukraine.[92] Two months into the war (after the end of the battle of Kyiv, which saw some volunteers leave the country as they felt they had given enough for Ukraine in the war's allegedly most iconic battle – for the capital) a Finnish volunteer shared a photo of his "Finnish brothers in arms" with 14 individuals visible.[93] This is not to say that this is the full Finnish contingent in the ranks of the Ukrainian military but it could be treated as a

helpful indicator on what to expect once more information becomes available later in the year or during the next years.

6. France: Allegedly up to 150 Frenchmen went to fight in Ukraine in 2022 – again, an improbable number,[94] with between 20 and 30 of them potentially belonging to a "brown" category.[95] The current author found no evidence of the presence of such a number of Frenchmen, or far-right Frenchmen, on the front lines. At the same time, the conflict galvanized the likes of the French identitarians into action as they sought to support the Ukrainian cause via e.g. collections, donations or sending "humanitarian missions" into the country.[96]

7. Germany: Germany follows a similar pattern to that of many other countries whose citizens are involved in the war with reports of presence of German fighters published in the country,[97] authorities publishing far from impressive numbers of extremists who either went to Ukraine or were returning (27 by late March 2022).[98] One of the Germans present in Ukraine died while fighting in Severodonetsk.[99]

8. Italy: The contingent was rumored by the Russian media to have suffered a highly improbable 11 casualties by late April.[100] Interestingly, its most well-known member had been an individual who fought on the other side – an Italian communist with a long presence in "separatist" ranks, who died early in the conflict.[101]

9. Netherlands: this is a contingent which in the summer of 2022 suffered its first casualty.[102] Notably, it also initially featured a female volunteer who was, however, quick to return home.[103]

10. Norway: Stand-out facts about the Norwegian volunteers in the Ukrainian ranks concern the fact that a female veteran, and a member of the Sámi Parliament, an "indigenous parliament" addressing "matters concerning the Sámi people in Norway,"[104] fought alongside British and American volunteers for Ukraine (the so-called Dirty Dozen team[105]).[106] Moreover, the legion's speaker, although originally of French origin, is a naturalized Norwegian citizen.[107]

11. Poland: One of the few cases in which fighting abroad without the authorization of the country's ministries of defense or interior is considered a crime. However, one could hardly expect the Polish justice system to pursue any volunteer returning from Ukraine who fought in this war against Russia. Perhaps for this reason, some of the wannabe volunteers decided to more or less openly admit their intention of going to Ukraine,[108] which seemed a safe thing to do as the Parliament moved to amend legislation on the issue.[109] As mentioned above, some fighters found themselves in the "challenger" Revenge Battalion and there are also representatives of the Polish football hooligan scene fighting in Ukraine or alongside such prominent far-right influencers like Denis "Nikitin" Kapustin.[110]

12. Sweden: Just like in many other countries, initial news spoke of "hundreds" allegedly signing up for the legion in Sweden.[111] The most prominent news, however, related to the Swedish contingent present in Ukraine concerned one early fighter who returned home after the bombing of Yavoriv base,[112]

and the capture of a single fighter in Azovstal and Russia's subsequent moves to have him prosecuted for alleged war crimes.[113]

13. Spain: Notable participation of Spanish citizens came early in the conflict when a group of Spanish volunteers arrived in Kyiv on March 1, 2022 but, ironically, missed their rendezvous with a nascent Azov TDF unit, and instead linked up with a randomly encountered formation.[114]

14. The UK: Allegedly, 300 British veterans were coming to join either the GNL or the legion.[115] The former did recruit many individuals in the UK but the number mentioned here seems excessive to the current author. Their ranks included such high-profile individuals as a veteran of the UK armed forces and a son of an MP.[116] The most outstanding story emerging related to the British volunteers in Ukrainian ranks concerned two Brits who fought for the Ukrainian army even before February 24, 2022 but were nonetheless captured by the Russian "separatist" forces and then put through a mock trial by the latter.[117]

15. The U.S.: As mentioned above, allegedly thousands of Americans applied to join the legion,[118] including numerous military veterans.[119] As such, their story probably merits a separate chapter or a monograph devoted solely to this contingent. Moreover, a sizeable section of this book would have to address the issue as to why only so few of them, in the low hundreds (see the earlier part of this chapter) actually made it to the front lines. Nonetheless, the fact that they still constituted what has potentially been the largest foreign volunteer contingent in Ukraine means they were bound to suffer casualties or some of them becoming prisoners of war of the Russians.[120] While writing this, however, in the summer of 2022, none of them has gone through a mock trial akin to that of some of the British prisoners of war.[121]

Oddities?

Apart from the legionaries or "networked individuals" fighting for Ukraine, or the veterans returning to the ranks on both sides of the war, the 2022 phase of the conflict saw the emergence of other foreign volunteer/fighter related stories which deserve a mention in this chapter. First, as early as March 2022, the media outlets were full of mentions of alleged Syrian fighters joining their Moscow allies in Ukraine.[122] Four months later, however, the author is yet to see evidence of their arrival on the battlefield. At the same time, other group of 2014 veterans, mainly the well-known "Rusich" group, and other Russian PMCs/mercenaries, was back in Donbas supporting the Russian offensive.[123] Simultaneously, the other side featured 20 to 30 individuals who had earlier fought ISIS in Syria in the ranks of irregular Kurdish formations.[124]

Conclusion

This chapter is the author's first attempt to take stock of the foreign volunteer reality on the front lines in Ukraine after February 24, 2022. Many issues are still unclear and the current author is hoping to learn more about the volunteers as he continues his research into them at C-Rex, UiO. Initially, one might have thought that Ukraine would be able to field battalions, if not brigades, of foreign volunteers who would greatly assist its war effort. However, the enthusiasm around foreign volunteering was quickly dissipated by developments such as the bombing of the Yavoriv base or the difficulty in fielding the legion as a separate military force due to a string of petty bureaucratic obstacles. At the same time, "networked" foreigners got to the front lines and fought on all the war's fronts. In short, it seemed as if determination and perseverance enabled most dedicated of the volunteers to get to the frontlines. Thus, they continued the story of foreigners involved in the Russo-Ukrainian war since 2014. However, no longer are they members of the brown-red cocktail but rather "concerned citizens of the world."

Notes

1 See Mykola Bielieskov, "The Russian and Ukrainian Spring 2021 War Scare," CSIS: Center for Strategic and International Studies, September 21, 2021, https://www.csis.org/analysis/russian-and-ukrainian-spring-2021-war-scare, accessed: July 15, 2022.
2 Author's conversation with a foreigner recruiter of foreign volunteers for Ukraine, March 9, 2022, who wished to remain anonymous.
3 Ibid.
4 Author's conversation with an American foreign volunteer in the Ukrainian ranks, April 15, 2022, who wished to remain anonymous.
5 See below for more on its story, the incident which hampered its development and the legion's first deployment in Eastern Ukraine.
6 Dina Newman, "Ukraine conflict: 'White power' warrior from Sweden," *BBC News*, July 16, 2014, https://www.bbc.co.uk/news/world-europe-28329329, accessed: July 4, 2022.
7 A rare exception to this rule was the Azov Movement's showcasing of his return to fighting in Ukraine. See: https://www.facebook.com/intermarium.today/videos/373162417985165/, post by the Intermarium Support group of March 8, 2022, accessed: July 4, 2022.
8 As of early July 2022 Vasquez garnered 380,000+ followers of his twitter account. See https://mobile.twitter.com/jmvasquez1974, accessed: July 4, 2022.
9 *News 12*, "Interview: Norwalk's James Vasquez shares story of fighting on Ukraine's front lines," June 22, 2022, https://www.youtube.com/watch?v=zXMZj8DzKVk, accessed: July 4, 2022.
10 *Speak the Truth*, "Exclusive Interview With American Volunteer Fighting in Ukraine: Part 1," June 2, 2022, https://www.youtube.com/watch?v=QNXkc07ihiY, accessed: July 4, 2022.
11 *CNN*, "Ukraine says more [than] 20,000 foreign volunteers want to join special unit to combat Russian forces," March 7, 2022, https://edition.cnn.com/europe/live-news/ukraine-russia-putin-news-03-07-22/h_dc1526f075096e276baec8fa7632f300.
12 *Ukrinform*, "How to join International Legion to defend Ukraine – algorithm," February 28, 2022, https://www.ukrinform.net/rubric-ato/3415272-how-to-join-international-legion-to-defend-ukraine-algorithm.html, accessed: July 4, 2022.
13 Kacper Rekawek, "A Trickle, Not a Flood: The Limited 2022 Far-Right Foreign Fighter Mobilization to Ukraine," *CTC Sentinel* 15, no. 6, (June 2022) https://ctc.westpoint.edu/a-trickle-not-a-flood-the-limited-2022-far-right-foreign-fighter-mobilization-to-ukraine/, accessed: July 4, 2022.

14 *CBC*, "Why a Canadian comedian is heading to Ukraine to fight against Russia," February 28, 2022, https://www.cbc.ca/radio/asithappens/as-it-happens-the-monday-edition-1.6367495/why-a-canadian-comedian-is-heading-to-ukraine-to-fight-against-russia-1.6367623.

15 David Cowan, "Scottish grandfather travels to Ukraine to fight Russians," *BBC News*, March 7, 2022, https://www.bbc.com/news/uk-scotland-edinburgh-east-fife-60646428, accessed: July 5, 2022.

16 See: https://twitter.com/uawarinfo/status/1501138291348934657, accessed: July 5, 2022.

17 See: https://twitter.com/guicorneau/status/1516161853700939784?t=-8Hn_i8xhZUx D7G19AyFdg&s=09, a twitt by Guillaume Corneau from April 18, 2022 in which he documents the numbers of anti-ISIS volunteers who then went to fight for Ukraine.

18 See: https://fightforua.org/ for the Legion's website, accessed: July 5, 2022.

19 An example of this practice could be the above-mentioned James Vasquez. He confirmed in an interview that he had told friends and other local acquaintances of his intention to leave. See: *News 12*, "Interview.

20 For more on "ghosts" see: Kacper Rekawek, *Career Break or a New Career? Extremist Foreign Fighters in Ukraine* (Counter Extremism Project, May 2020), https://www.counterextremism.com/sites/default/files/CEP%20Report_Career%20Break%20or%20a%20New%20Career_Extremist%20Foreign%20Fighters%20in%20Ukraine_April%202020.pdf, accessed: July 5, 2022.

21 Ibid.

22 See his twitter message of July 5, 2022: https://twitter.com/jmvasquez1974/status/1544158970935476227?s=20&t=-R7SVXA1AfhPqARi3-tq3Q, accessed: July 5, 2022.

23 Author's conversation with an anoymous British foreign volunteer who fought in Ukraine in the first month of the reignited war and then returned home, 12 April 2022.

24 Author's conversation with an anonymous Croat foreign volunteer who fought outside Kyiv but as the Russian troops retreated from the city in late March 2022 he and his fellow Croat volunteers decided to return home, 10 May 2022.

25 Author's conversation with an anonymous American reporter covering the Southern and Eastern fronts of the war, 9 June 2022.

26 See: https://www.facebook.com/ukr.international.legion/posts/pfbid02GiSXzX ccVgGBYuaffpDsNX2aDZXEj6seWRF2LHv6hQsgyrkzPPKiLFEE7zSeAkYml for a Q and A with the Legion's spokesperson, March 27, 2022, accessed: July 5, 2022.

27 See: https://twitter.com/SpaghettiKozak/status/1538064831487549440?t=_-70 AYYXYw4EEotnY-Bz7w&s=09, accessed: July 5, 2022.

28 Author's conversation with an anonymous American foreign volunteer in Ukraine, 15 May 2022.

29 See: Tom Blackwell, Canadian sniper dodges death in Ukraine: 'It was pretty much close calls every week'," *National Post*, May 17, 2022, https://nationalpost.com/news/canada/how-canadian-sniper-dodged-death-in-ukraine-and-learned-how-to-use-anti-tank-weapon-on-youtube for a story a Canadian sniper in Ukrainian service which highlights all of the aformentioned difficulties for the arriving foreign volunteers in Ukraine.

30 See: https://www.facebook.com/ukr.international.legion/posts/pfbid0cBEmZm-6RPkYGP5ZApS8JZQNVKaxzAsuS9FnnDpYxjVqQMJj5eEYdSs1De7C7THbel, accessed: July 5, 2022.

31 Antifascist Europe, "How Foreign Far-Right Volunteers Are Arriving to Fight in Ukraine," 13 May 2022, https://antifascist-europe.org/ukraine/how-foreign-far-right-volunteers-are-arriving-to-fight-in-ukraine/#Turn, accessed: July 5, 2022.

32 Author's interview with an anonymous Canadian foreign volunteer, March 17, 2022.

33 *News 12*, "Interview.»."

34 Boris Benulic, "Granskning: Jesper Söder, Vår Tids Hjälte? Är han en stridsmaskin – skjutskicklig underrättelseofficer som är expert på närstrid; med ett hjärta som klappar för de svaga – eller är han en person som ständigt överdriver sin egen betydelse?," *Morgonposten*, April 3, 2022, https://morgonposten.se/2022/04/03/granskning-jesper-soder-var-tids-hjalte-ar-han-en-stridsmaskin/, accessed: July 5, 2022 for a discussion of one fighter who allegedly did so. The Azov Movement also shared on its social media platforms a poem dedicated to a volunteer who "only came for posing" and whose "plans to be a hero have swiftly been unravelling" as he ran away to Poland to become a "Polish border guard."

35 Author's interview with an anonymous American foreign volunteer for Ukraine, May 15, 2022.

36 See: https://twitter.com/ukraine_world/status/1532777317340258304?t=683w1 jCwdKnx2ZU52yFmAg&s=09 for the announcement, June 3, 2022, accessed: July 7, 2022.

37 See: https://twitter.com/Int_Legion_UA/status/1533752144821735424?t=S846Hg-pqgcmq4ktAmdShqg&s=09 for the Legion's announcement of one such casualty on its twitter account from June 6, 2022, accessed: July 7, 2022. The legionnaries who died in early June 2022 were not, however, the first casualties among foreign volunteers fighting for Ukraine. Belarus and the Georgian contingent, organized in separate units, took the brunt of the casualties with the former even losing a volunteer who led one of the two Belarus battalions of the Kastus Kalinouski regiment, a unit which was integrated into the Ukrainian military and not the TDF. See author's twitter account at: https://twitter.com/KacperRekawek/status/15445675168481689 60?s=20&t=4trwxmVD96FkLmSrGYGDZA for the news of his death, added and accessed on July 7, 2022.

38 Guillaume Dominguez, "Exclu Europe 1: la mère du combattant français mort en Ukraine témoigne," *Europe 1*, 4 June 2022, https://www.europe1.fr/international/exclu-europe-1-je-respecte-son-choix-la-mere-du-combattant-francais-mort-en-ukraine-temoigne-4115491?fbclid=IwAR3GswlMQ4lYIvvO2BhIZ0TT6Yl lwEV8IuCRxrai1UwSDWF1mCciRmNbnxU, accessed: July 7, 2022.

39 See: Kacper Rekawek et al., *Western Extremists and the Russian Invasion of ukraine in 2022 All Talk, But Not a Lot of Walk* (Counter Extremism Project, May 2022), https://www.counterextremism.com/sites/default/files/2022-05/Western%20 Extremists%20and%20the%20Russian%20Invasion%20of%20Ukraine%20in%20 2022_May%202022.pdf, accessed: July 7, 2022 for a wide ranging discussion of this issue which studied the extremist scenes in 7 large countries and the presence of their representatives on the frontlines in Ukraine. The research found very little evidence of this being the case. This is not to say that individual cases of such volunteers would not be found and some of these will be discussed in the next sections of this chapter.

40 Max Rose and Ali H. Soufan, "We Once Fought Jihadists. Now We Battle White Supremacists," *New York Times*, 11 February 2020, https://www.nytimes. com/2020/02/11/opinion/politics/white-supremacist-terrorism.html, accessed: July 7, 2022.

41 See: Naureen C. Fink and Colin P. Clarke, "Foreign Fighters Are Heading to Ukraine. That's A Moment for Worry," *Politico*, March 10, 2022, https://www.politico.com/ news/magazine/2022/03/10/foreign-fighters-are-heading-to-ukraine-thats-a-moment-for-worry-00016084, accessed: July 7, 2022 for the discussion of the issue.

42 Olivia B. Waxman, "Historians on What Putin Gets Wrong About 'Denazification' in Ukraine," *TIME*, March 3, 2022, https://time.com/6154493/denazification-putin-ukraine-history-context/, accessed: July 7, 2022.

43 Rimal Farrukh, "Ukraine's 'Neo-Nazi' Battalion Is Greasing Bullets in Pig Fat for Russia's Muslim Soldiers," *VICE News*, 1 March 2022, https://www.vice.com/en/ article/xgd73j/ukraine-neo-nazi-battalion-azov-bullets-pig-fat-chechen-russia, accessed: July 7, 2022.

44 *Ibid.*
45 *BBC News*, "Mariupol: Key moments in the siege of the city," May 17, 2022, https://www.bbc.com/news/world-europe-61179093, acccessed: July 7, 2022.
46 *BBC News*, "What untruths is Russia spreading about Nazis in Ukraine?," March 27, 2022, https://www.youtube.com/watch?v=2gNp0PfK0CI, accessed: July 7, 2022.
47 Isobel Koshiv, "Ukrainian soldiers captured at Azovstal plant in 'satisfactory' conditions," *The Guardian*, May 24, 2022, https://www.theguardian.com/world/2022/may/24/ukrainian-soldiers-captured-at-azovstal-plant-in-satisfactory-conditions, accessed: July 7, 2022.
48 The current author was inundated with requests for explainers on Azov during March and April 2022, during the siege of the Azovstal steelworks. Miłada Jędrysik, "The Azov Regiment: Neo-Nazis, Football Hooligans or Defenders of Ukraine," *oko.press*, April 1, 2022, https://oko.press/the-azov-regiment-neo-nazis-football-hooligans-or-defenders-of-ukraine/, accessed: July 7, 2022.
49 The author is in possession of the said meme, circulated on July 4, 2022 but will not be sharing the link to the telegram post as it is his intention not to give away and distribute sources of extremist propaganda.
50 Rekawek, "A Trickle, Not a Flood."
51 Kacper Rekawek, Alexander Ritzmann, and Hans-Jakob Schindler, *Violent Right-Wing Extremism and Terrorism – Transnational Connectivity, Definitions, Incidents, Structures and Countermeasures* (Counter Extremism Project, November 2020), 13–16, https://www.counterextremism.com/sites/default/files/CEP%20Study_Violent%20Right-Wing%20Extremism%20and%20Terrorism_Nov%202020.pdf, accessed: July 7, 2022.
52 See national chapters of Rekawek et al., *Western Extremists*, 28–73 for evidence on this.
53 Ibid. 11–16. and Rekawek, "A Trickle, Not a Flood."
54 See previous note for sources documenting this issue.
55 Rekawek, "A Trickle, Not a Flood."
56 Rekawek et al., *Western Extremists*, 24–25.
57 Ibid. 20–22.
58 See chap. 3 of this monograph for more on Azov's story.
59 Rekawek et al., *Western Extremists*, 19–22.
60 See *PolskieRadio.pl*, Волонтер: Люди со всего мира приехали воевать за Украину, а их не пускают на фронт," April 1, 2022, https://tinyurl.com/2abwu5tc, accessed: July 7, 2022.
61 Rekawek et al., *Western Extremists*, 20.
62 See chap. 6 of this monograph for more information on him.
63 See https://www.facebook.com/watch/?v=373162417985165 March 8, 2022, accessed: July 7, 2022, video announcing his return to the ranks.
64 See chap 7 of this monograph for more information on him.
65 Robert Bajrui, "Da, jedan Hrvat je zarobljen i tocno znam gdje je pao u ruke Rusa. Sigurno nije u Azovstalu," *JutarnjiList*, May 7, 2022.
66 See: https://twitter.com/fri_skytt/status/1512135749247844352?t=z091KEnagTwg-bNsiCS5B2g&s=09, tweet by another Azov veteran from April 7, 2022, accessed: July 7, 2022 announcing the existence of this group.
67 See chap. of this monograph for more on the Right Sector.
68 See https://twitter.com/Militarylandnet/status/1509898184730058752, April 1, 2022, accessed: July 7, 2022.
69 Rekawek, "A Trickle, Not a Flood."
70 Ibid. 25. For alleged presence of Czech fighters in the latter unit see: Jan Wirnitzer, "Z Třebíče přes klášter až na frontu. Michal žil na 200 procent, vzpomínají známí na padlého Čecha," *Deník N*, June 16, 2022, https://denikn.cz/900606/z-trebice-pres-klaster-az-na-frontu-michal-zil-na-200-procent-vzpominaji-znami-na-padleho-cecha/?cst=042c316d59f20f938f36a8f7949d647972261438, accessed: July 7, 2022.

71 Rekawek, "A Trickle, Not a Flood."

72 Rekawek et al., *Western Extremists*, 23–24.

73 Ibid. 25–26.

74 *Белсат Life*, Камандзір палка Каліноўскага пра бой у Бучы | Командир полка Калиновского про бой в Буче, June 19, 2022, https://www.youtube.com/watch?v= LuNBfsSR50o, accessed: July 8, 2022.

75 *Бомбардир*, "Білоруські ультрас за Україну/ Хацкевич розносить лукашенка/ війна в режимі тік-ток," May 7, 2022, https://www.youtube.com/watch?v= LwLaJbNOqYU, accessed: July 8, 2022.

76 See a tweet by Franak Viačorka, a senior advisor to Sviatlana Tsikhanouskaya who has been elected Belarusian president in 2020 but the country's regime annuled the results, in which he eulogizes one of the battalions commanders of the Kostas Kalinouski battalion from July 5, 2022: https://twitter.com/franakviacorka/status/ 1544432430546821124?s=20&t=iIG8dNEzeSiuFDK2hf_y7Q, accessed: July 8, 2022.

77 *The New Voice of Ukraine*, "Commander of Chechen volunteers fighting for Ukraine talks of wars with Russia," April 7, 2022, https://english.nv.ua/en/nation/command-er-of-chechen-volunteers-fighting-for-ukraine-talks-wars-with-russia-50232014. html, accessed: July 8, 2022.

78 See: Rekawek, https://wartranslated.com/day-115-june-18-summary-of-arestovych-and-feygin-daily-broadcast/, Rekawek et al., *Western Extremists and the Russian Invasion of ukraine in 2022 All Talk, But Not a Lot of Walk, op. cit.*, pp. 26-7. This Legion apparently had a "wave" of circa 250 new members in mid-June 2022 but its video materials published up to date show only a handful of members. See: Dmitri, "Day 115, June 18. Summary of Arestovych and Feygin daily broadcast," *wartranslated.com*, https://wartranslated.com/day-115-june-18-summary-of-arestovych-and-feygin-daily-broadcast/June 19, 2022, accessed: July 8, 2022.

79 See: https://twitter.com/Nrg8000/status/1534923485658886146?t=_qBYBDBs97 D2BkHgHKPc_Q&s=09, a twitter post of June 9, 2022 with a reported graphic on the Maidan in Kyiv which featured numbers of foreign volunteers fighting for Ukraine and the numbers of the ones who died fighting.

80 See a tweet which translated the original telegram post by the Russian ministry of defence on these numbers: https://twitter.com/maxfras/status/1537727605897670656?s= 20&t=4M6vGHQJhTXDb4t03_FiTg, June 17, 2022, accessed: July 11, 2022.

81 See the beginning of the current chapter for the relevant comment from the anony-mous recruiter of foreign volunteers.

82 By "new" the current author understands individuals who, unlike the returning veterans, did not fight in in the previous phases of the conflict.

83 Esther de Leebeeck, "Meer dan de helft van de Belgische strijders in Oekraïne is teruggekeerd naar ons land: "Ik verloor mijn gehoor na raketaanval op ons mil-itair kamp," *HLN*, March 22, 2022, https://www.hln.be/nieuws/meer-dan-de-helft-van-de-belgische-strijders-in-oekraine-is-teruggekeerd-naar-ons-land-ik-verloor-mijn-gehoor-na-raketaanval-op-ons-militair-kamp~a096b4e3/?referrer= https%3A%2F%2Ft.co%2F, accessed: July 12, 2022.

84 *CTV News in Lviv*, "International fighters joining Ukrainian foreign legion," March 15, 2022, https://www.youtube.com/watch?v=mLgRTrB6ets, accessed: July 15, 2022. For more on the Canadian foreign volunteers in Ukraine see: Guillaume Corneau-Tremblay, "Country Case Studies: Canada," in Rekawek et al., *Western Extremists and the Russian Invasion of ukraine in 2022 All Talk, But Not a Lot of Walk, op. cit.*, pp. 35-42.

85 Tom Blackwell, "Canadian sniper dodges death in Ukraine: 'It was pretty much close calls every week'," *National Post*, 1 May 7, 2022, https://nationalpost.com/news/ canada/how-canadian-sniper-dodged-death-in-ukraine-and-learned-how-to-use-anti-tank-weapon-on-youtube, accessed: July 15, 2022.

86 Tom Blackwell, "Incompetence or the realities of war? Turmoil for Canadian-led foreign battalion in Ukraine," *National Post*, May 6, 2022, https://nationalpost.com/news/canada/turmoil-for-norman-brigade-canadian-led-foreign-battalion-in-ukraine, accessed: July 15, 2022.

87 Kacper Rekawek, "An effective ban on foreign fighting? Wider implications of the Czech policy towards foreign (terrorist) fighters," *RightNow!*, September 20, 2022, https://www.sv.uio.no/c-rex/english/news-and-events/right-now/, accessed: July 15, 2022.

88 See https://twitter.com/P_Fiala/status/1499459342260744193 for the Czech PM's announcement on the issue, March 3, 2022, July 15, 2022.

89 Thomas Berndt, "Dansker formodes dræbt i krigen i Ukraine," *Politiken*, April 28, 2022, https://politiken.dk/udland/art8745214/Dansker-formodes-dr%C3%A6bt-i-krigen-i-Ukraine, accessed: July 12, 2022.

90 https://nyheder.tv2.dk/udland/2022-04-05-dansk-snigskytte-haevder-at-have-draebt-taet-paa-100-russere-i-ukraine, accessed: July 12, 2022.

91 See: https://www.facebook.com/100010546457614/videos/429565049147820/ for the announcement. accessed: July 12, 2022.

92 Antti Halonen, "Yksisuuntainen tie helvettiin," *Iltalehti*, March 14, 2022, https://www.iltalehti.fi/ulkomaat/a/ef01dbf0-6361-4c79-af85-c7f04059411d, accessed: July 12, 2022.

93 See https://twitter.com/rsiren2/status/1518899395122630662?t=g0IoFsiNBGKvb-rcz2mBQQ&s=09, tweet from April 26, 2022, accessed: July 12, 2022.

94 Sébastien Bourdon, Matthieu Suc, "150 Français participent à la guerre en Ukraine," *Mediapart*, March 26, 2022, https://www.mediapart.fr/journal/international/260322/150-francais-participent-la-guerre-en-ukraine?utm_source=twitter, accessed: July 15, 2022.

95 Jean Yves Camus, "Country Case Studies: France," in Rekawek et al., *Western Extremists*, 54–59.

96 Ibid.

97 *Die Stadredaktion*, "Deutsche Ukraine-Kämpfer – Nach dem Gefecht zittern sie und übergeben sich," March 19, 2022, https://www.die-stadtredaktion.de/2022/03/redaktionsempfehlungen/empfehlungen/deutsche-ukraine-kaempfer-nach-dem-gefecht-zittern-sie-und-uebergeben-sich/, accessed: July 15, 2022.

98 Alexander Ritzmann, "Country Case Studies: Germany," in Rekawek, et al., *Western Extremists*, 59–66.

99 See: https://twitter.com/Int_Legion_UA/status/1533752144821735424?t=S846 Hgpqgcmq4ktAmdShqg&s=09 for the Legion's announcement on the issue, June 6, 2022, accessed: July 15, 2022.

100 Francesco Verderami, "Mosca: in Ucraina morti 11 combattenti italiani. E avverte: 'Ai mercenari non si applica il diritto umanitario internazionale'," *Corriere della Sera*, April 24, 2022, https://www.corriere.it/politica/22_aprile_24/mosca-ucraina-morti-11-combattenti-italiani-avverte-ai-mercenari-non-si-applica-diritto-umanitario-internazionale-512ca0da-c346-11ec-b8f2-6e6ac278e36c.shtml, accessed: July 12, 2022.

101 Rekawek et al., *Western Extremists*, 8.

102 See https://twitter.com/TheDeadDistrict/status/1523706678394318848?t=tlHzi6 dWdypzXrg3eqYoHQ&s=09, May 9, 2022, accessed: July 12, 2022 for the announcement.

103 Amy van den Berg, "Joyce gaat vrijwillig naar Oekraïne om te vechten: 'Mijn kinderen zijn verdrietig en boos' Joyce Koster (40) vertrekt morgen vrij," *AD*, March 22, 2022, https://www.ad.nl/binnenland/joyce-gaat-vrijwillig-naar-oekraine-om-te-vechten-mijn-kinderen-zijn-verdrietig-en-boos~a78edc8f/?referrer= https%3A%2F%2Fwww.diigo.com%2F, accessed: July 12, 2022.

104 See https://sametinget.no/about-the-sami-parliament/ for the Parliament's website, accessed: July 12, 2022.

105 See the team's twitter profile: https://twitter.com/DirtydozenEira, accessed: July 12, 2022.

106 See: https://twitter.com/Gerashchenko_en/status/1527241656054980608?t=fG5O aaZdgMaBYH-GCdda_w&s=09 for her profile by the adviser to the Ukrainian minister of internal affairs, May 19, 2022, accessed: July 12, 2022.

107 See: https://twitter.com/vera_mironov/status/1503858638930251785?t=bX3nBt R7RvIN8jUM_gpX1Q&s=09 for his profile, March 15, 2022, accessed: July 12, 2022.

108 Tomasz Molga, "Polak formuje oddział do walki w Ukrainie. 'Przyłączymy się do obrony Kijowa'," *WP*, March 2, 2022, https://wiadomosci.wp.pl/formuje-sie-polski-oddzial-do-walki-w-ukrainie-przylaczymy-sie-do-obrony-kijowa-6742958396684896a, accessed: July 12, 2022.

109 Wiktor Ferfecki, "Polscy ochotnicy chcą walczyć z Rosją na Ukrainie," *Rzeczpospol-ita*, February 28, 2022, https://www.rp.pl/konflikty-zbrojne/art35776471-polscy-ochotnicy-chca-walczyc-z-rosja-na-ukrainie, accessed: July 12, 2022.

110 Gabriela Jatkowska, "Rosjanie walczą po stronie Ukrainy: Polski ochotnik opowi-ada o wojnie," *Polska Times*, June 6, 2022, https://polskatimes.pl/rosjanie-walcza-po-stronie-ukrainy-polski-ochotnik-opowiada-o-wojnie/ar/c15-16417941, accessed: July 12, 2022.

111 Jan Samuelsson, "Hundratals svenska frivilliga till Ukraina," *Svenska Dagbladet*, March 2, 2022, https://www.svd.se/a/PoBvpJ/hundratals-svenska-frivilliga-till-ukraina, accessed: July 12, 2022.

112 Boris Benulic, "Granskning: Jesper Söder, Vår Tids Hjälte?"

113 Fria Tider, https://www.friatider.se/rysk-media-svensk-legosoldat-atalas-i-ukraina, accessed: July 12, 2022.

114 See https://twitter.com/KacperRekawek/status/1498690344522854692?s=20&t= IgoSKGjXSn_mxxALXi7BdA for the author's tweet of March 1, 2022, accessed: July 12, 2022 in which he was the first to announce the arrival of the Spaniards (on the back of information received from anonymous Azov sources).

115 *Sky News*, "War in Ukraine: 'More than 300 UK fighters heading to Ukraine'," March 10, 2022. https://www.youtube.com/watch?v=_nSZt1m-gdE&feature= youtu.be, accessed: July 12, 2022.

116 Nils Adler and Matthew Weaver, "Tory MP's son among UK ex-servicemen heading to Ukrainian front line," *The Guardian*, March 8, 2022, https://www.theguardian. com/world/2022/mar/08/tory-mps-son-among-uk-ex-servicemen-heading-to-ukrainian-front-line, accessed: July 12, 2022.

117 See https://twitter.com/cossackgundi/status/1514589647476871170?t=PjKFrRt3n-ltL6unED6rvmg&s=09, April 14, 2022, accessed: July 12, 2022 for the announce-ment of their captivity. A Morrocan fighter was also put on trial alongside them and another Croat was also captured by the invading forces in Mariupol. See: https:// www.youtube.com/watch?v=TnAoTEFHXbM for the announcement of the latter by a Serbian fighting in DNR ranks, May 8,2022, accessed: July 12, 2022.

118 Mike Brest, "More than 3,000 in US apply to join Ukrainian forces: Report," *The Washington Examiner*, March 5, 2022, https://www.washingtonexaminer.com/ policy/defense-national-security/more-than-3-000-in-us-apply-to-join-ukrainian-forces-report?utm_campaign=article_rail&utm_source=internal&utm_medium= article_rail&s=09, accessed: July 15, 2022.

119 Dave Philipps, "'I Just Can't Stand By': American Veterans Join the Fight in Ukraine," *The New York Times*, March 5, 2022, https://www.nytimes.com/2022/03/05/us/ american-veterans-volunteer-ukraine-russia.html, accessed: July 15, 2022.

120 See https://twitter.com/TFBaguette/status/1537001641114746880?t=HwVCPdk84s6 Aej00oIMoXQ&s=09 for an announcement of such a fact on behalf of a squad of foreign volunteer fighting in Ukraine, June 15, 2022, accessed: July 15, 2022.

121 For more on the American contingent see Joshua Fisher-Birch, "Country Case Studies: United States of America," in Rekawek et al., *Western Extremists*, 28–35.

122 Suleiman Al-Khalidi and Laila Bassam, "Some Syrian veterans ready for Ukraine fight, commanders say," *Reuters*, March 20, 2022, https://www.reuters.com/world/some-syrian-veterans-ready-ukraine-fight-commanders-say-2022-03-20/, accessed: July 15, 2022.

123 Michael Sheldon, "Meet the Irregular Troops Backing up Russia's Army in the Kharkiv Region," *bellingcat*, June 17, 2022, https://www.bellingcat.com/news/2022/06/17/meet-the-irregular-troops-backing-up-russias-army-in-the-donbas/, accessed: July 15, 2022.

124 See https://twitter.com/guicorneau/status/1516161853700939784/photo/1, tweet from April 18, 2022 in which Guillaume Corneau-Tremblay showcases the data on volunteers in Ukraine who earlier fought ISIS in Iraq (as foreign fighters), accessed: July 15, 2022.

INDEX